Best wishes,

Ken Morley   Margaret Morley
26. 11. 99.

For Prudence Goodwin

(née Rickard),

whose enthusiasm for all things Wingravian
never falters

First published November 1999
by
The Book Castle
12 Church Street
Dunstable
Bedfordshire
LU5 4RU

ISBN 1 871199 99 9 (hardback)

Typeset by the Authors

Printed in Great Britain by Antony Rowe Ltd
Chippenham Wiltshire

CONTENTS

By the Same Authors

Ken Morley

Voluntary Social Organisations in Redditch (with Ken Laugharne)
Communiversity
Social Activity and Social Enterprise
Some Morleys of Southwest Lancashire
One Man's Words 1894-1920: From Mansfield to the Marne
One Man's Words 1920-1946: The Road to Lunghua

Ken and Margaret Morley

Yeomen of the Fens
Echoes 9 and 10
The Great Upheaval

Introduction and Acknowledgments

This book continues the story of the parish of Wingrave with Rowsham, which we began in an earlier publication, 'The Great Upheaval': a description of the enclosure of the parish in 1798. This new volume is mainly concerned with the years from 1800 to 1960, though these boundaries are extended where necessary. In writing it we have tried, where appropriate, to put local events in their regional, national and international contexts, and secondly to achieve authenticity by quoting extensively from contemporary accounts in newspapers, letters, reports and memoirs. Initially, this second aim seemed likely to elude us, for unfortunately in the 19th century Wingrave's Vicars and Vestry rarely responded to government requests for information. Villages all around might submit their views, but not Wingrave. Consequently, although the great Parliamentary enquiries into Agriculture and the Poor Law often provide good accounts of the Vale of Aylesbury, they do not provide quotations from the lips of Wingrave's parishioners. "No problem," we were told, for apparently the late Hilda Roberts (1877-1962) was a villager with a flair for writing, whose Remembrances would solve our problems. There was just one slight snag. No-one had seen her writings for very many years, and no-one knew where they were. It took some time before they were all located, firstly in a Wingrave loft, and later in a Worcestershire attic. We are grateful to Hilda's daughter-in-law, Pat Roberts, both for her persistence in locating them, and for permission to quote from them.

Others who have made major contributions include the following. Ted Griffin, several generations of whose family had farmed in Wingrave, provided farm accounts for wages, butter sales and milk sales in the middle of the 19th century, plus a collection of family anecdotes, and our earliest photographs. The late Daphne Rickard provided a marvellous compilation illustrating the development of the Independent Church in Wingrave, and also a lengthy account of old Wingrave. Gerry Tomlinson generously allowed us to quote extensively from his unique collection of letters from Wingrave emigrants. These letters are reproduced in full in his book, "Bring Plenty of Pickles" (see page 293, Chapter 5, note 5). We are similarly indebted to Baird McClellan, headmaster of Wingrave with Rowsham C. of E. Combined School, for providing access to the school log books, without which our account of Wingrave's schooling would have been pretty threadbare. Reg Darvill's painstaking examination of local newspapers in the 19th century saved us aeons of valuable time by focussing upon just those topics on which we needed information. We particularly thank Frank and Grace King for all the information they have provided during many happy hours spent "chewing over Wingrave's past". We are grateful to the editors of the Bucks Herald, and the Leighton Observer for permission to reproduce photographs, and to Douglas Dunker for information on the early days of Primitive Methodism, and for waiving copyright on some of the late Christine Dunker's poems. We sincerely thank Deryck Bell for entrusting to our care George Griffin's map of the parish in 1876, while we copied it. Julian Hunt, the Bucks County Records and Local Studies Manager, and his staff provided their usual combination of encouragement, advice and practical assistance. Peter Hoare of Cublington miraculously improved some incredibly derelict photographs.

Throughout the preparation of this book we have been supported and encouraged by Prudence Goodwin, and we are especially grateful for the use of her extensive files, which have solved a seemingly endless stream of problems, and for access to her photographic collection from which she has generously allowed as to publish without restriction. Due to the breakdown of our ancient and unrepairable word processor, we had to learn to type-set the book on our new computer. Fortunately, we were introduced to David Hill, without whose unstinting and expert assistance we should have been well and truly stuck. Our debt to our publisher, Paul Bowes, is obvious, and we are truly grateful.

None of the above lessens our debt to the many other people without whose help our research would have been fruitless. Between them they provided over two hundred photographs and postcards, submitted to lengthy interviews and/or provided written recollections.

The following list covers all contributions other than pictorial material appearing in the text.

James A. Beck, Alec Bignell, the late Horace and Connie Bignell, Ron Bignell, Bodleian Library, Vanessa Bonham, Carmel Bourke, Norman and Sylvia Brackley, Buckinghamshire Archaeological Library, Buckinghamshire Records and Local Studies Service, Rose Camp, the late John Camp, Gillian Campbell, Betty Carter, Vic Clay, Susannah Edmunds, Gerald Evered, Alan Frost, Michael Griffin, Diana Gulland, Hertfordshire Record Office, Michael Higgins, Lucy Holloway, Doreen Honor, the late Nancy Horsfield, Charlie Horwood, Rosemary Jenkins, Richard Keighley, the late Pamela Kirby, Fred Kirby, Annie Marsh, Rosemary Masters, Trevor May, Mercers' Company Archives, John Millburn, the late Phyllis Norman, Open University Library, Oxfordshire Record Office, Michael Page, Muriel Page, Don Paine, Ethel Perkins, Public Record Office, the late Donald Rand, Douglas Rickard, the late Fred (Buller) Rickard, the late Minnie Rickard, Rothschild Archives London, the Earl and Countess of Rosebery, Bill Simpson, Dorothy Simpson, Joyce Sinnott, the late Iris Tompkins, Michael Tunnicliffe, Joyce Whipps, the late Joan Whitfield, Lesley Williams.

The following list is of those contributing photographs which appear in the text, and the numbers which identify them.

Allotments & Gardens Society (Wingrave with Rowsham) 132, 133, 146; Mrs Joan Barksfield 12; Margaret Bateman 144; James Beck 21; Deryck Bell 13, 136, 138, 140; Terry Benwell 92; Alec & Sue Bignell 9, 14, 121; Carmel Bourke 24; Terry Bracey-Wright 107; Bucks Archaeological Society 46; Bucks Herald 54, 73-4; Bucks Records and Local Studies Service 1, 2, 11, 33, 39, 45, 91, 93, 99, 100, 122, 149; Betty Carter 129; H.C.Casserley 90; Vic Clay 150; Jean Davis 16; Susannah Edmunds 29, 38, 41-4; English Heritage 6, 65; the late Helen Fleet 79, 80, 97, 101, 104; Alan & Janet Frost 6, 65; Prudence Goodwin 7, 10, 16, 18-19, 27, 30, 35, 47, 49, 51, 56-61, 63, 66-67, 70, 76, 78, 83-84, 89, 106a, 108, 117, 120, 126-127, 130, 134, 137, 139, 142-143, 148, 152-153, back cover; Edward Griffin 23, 50, 82, 104, 110, back cover; Daphne Haynes 26; Rev. John Heffer 48; Ellen Higby 40; Charlie Horwood 87-8, 125; Frank & Grace King 8, 85, 118, 123; Pam & Fred Kirby 15, 53, 68, 102, 115, 119; 124; Leighton Buzzard Observer 72, 154; Luton Museum Service 17; Annie Marsh & Pat Johnson 27, 34, 135, 151, front jacket; Rosemary Masters 94; Mary Mountain 86; Rev. David Newman 3, 4, 20; Muriel Page 69; Don Paine; 37; Ethel Perkins 77, 98; Bim Pullen 106, 145, 156-157; the late Daphne Rickard 52, 55; Douglas Rickard 103; Pat Roberts 13, 28, 64, 111, 141, Earl and Countess of Rosebery 25, 31-2; Dorothy Simpson 62, 128; Peter Smith 5; Gerry Tomlinson 22 a, b, c, d; Joyce Whipps 71, 112-3; Tony White; Wingrave Recreation Ground Committee 114.

With research spread over a number of years it is possible that some names may have been overlooked. If so we apologise most sincerely. Where those pictured are named, this was done only after consultation with others, and usually with several others. If, despite this, there are any errors, these are much regretted.

Ken and Margaret Morley
121 Winslow Road
Wingrave
HP22 4QB

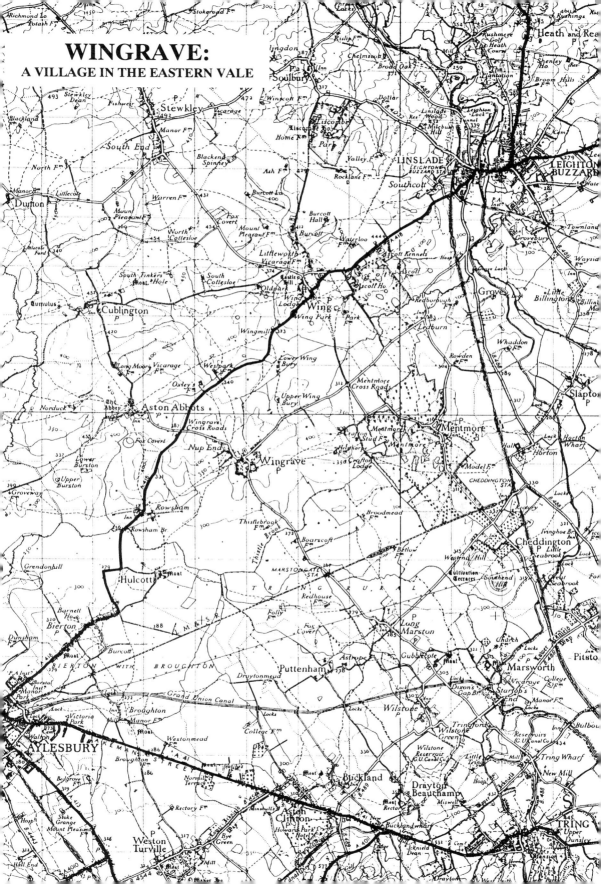

WINGRAVE:
A VILLAGE IN THE EASTERN VALE

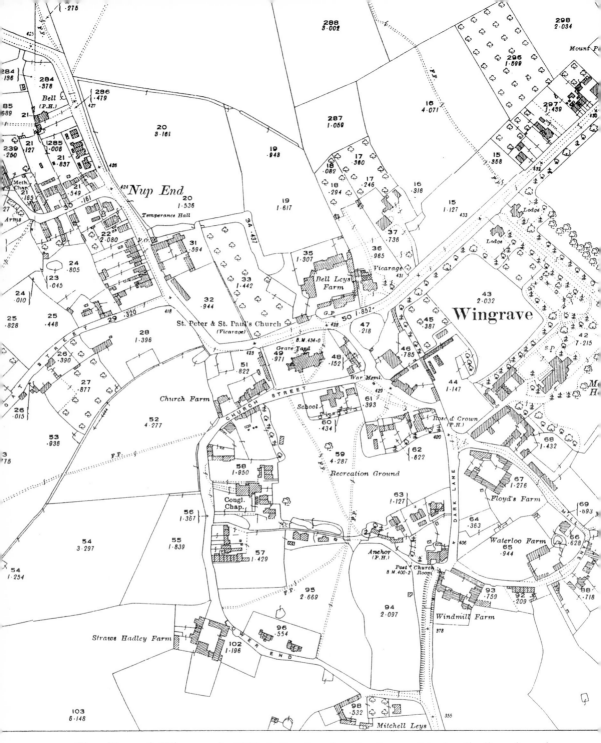

The village of Wingrave in 1923, before housing development had radically enlarged the built-up area. In the centre of the map note the pond (47), the parish church (49), and Windmill House (46). For an elevated view of the area around the Green, see especially pictures 45 (page 102), 64 (page 140), 149 (page 278), and 158 (page 289).

Part One: Hard Times

Chapter One

Fifty Years After Enclosure

In 1848 Victoria had been queen for eleven years, the Penny Post was well-established, Peel had invented the 'Bobby', income tax had been introduced at 7d (3p) in the pound; and the canal mania was over, for these waterways were declining as the railways (the latest wonder of modern transport) snaked across the land. At this time Britain was well into an era of reform: slavery had recently been abolished throughout the British Empire; women and children had been banned from working down the mines; voluntary bodies were starting to build schools for the children of the poor; women's work in factories had been limited to sixty hours per week;[1] Nonconformists had been given the right to marry in their own churches and be buried in their own graveyards; the right to vote had been extended, though it still did not include the working classes; and the fight for Free Trade was advanced when the import duty on corn was abolished.

Very little of this had any effect upon Wingrave. The farmers worried about the repeal of the Corn Laws. The Poor worried as to how they could keep their children at work and earning, rather than at "learning school" and "idle". The Vicar worried about the size of his congregation. In fact, most of Wingrave's population were too busy scratching a living, from whatever source it could be obtained, to give much thought to national economics and politics, about which news reached them late and indirectly, if at all. As for the unemployed, they could not think much further than the next meal. In these circumstances, it is doubtful whether anyone noticed that 1848 was the fiftieth anniversary of Wingrave's enclosure: the greatest upheaval ever to affect life and work in the parish.

Indeed, by 1848, only the older folk remembered the days of the open fields, and would speak of 'before enclosure' as the elderly now say 'before the war'. They would speak nostalgically of their freedom to walk all over the parish, along the winding baulks and headlands, instead of being restricted to a few footpaths. They would remember the commons where they played as children, and Old Daisy, the cow they were able to graze there. They might also recall the long trudge to their scattered strips; their anger when a neighbour's animal got loose and destroyed their crops; the lack of shelter when winter winds blew across the four vast hedgeless fields; and the disputes with neighbours whose plowing had encroached on the baulks and headlands which separated the narrow cultivated strips. For everyone else the hedges, the hedgerow trees and the large rectangular fields that enclosure created were an accepted part of the only landscape they had ever known. By 1848 it was a landscape that had almost reached maturity, for trees planted at the beginning of the century were now forty feet tall, and the hedgerows which had already been plashed[2] at least twice, now supported the rotten fencing which had once protected the newly planted quicks.[3]

1. Before road improvements and Dutch elm disease, mature trees dominated the landscape, even within the village. This is the Winslow Road c. 1930, as it passes the parish church on the left, and begins to turn at Black Gutter Corner.

2. The old turnpike road (the present A418) winds through the trees before improvement c. 1930. Opposite the seat, the road (known to villagers as Handpost Hill) leads up to Wingrave.

THE SETTLEMENT PATTERN OF WINGRAVE VILLAGE

Despite its 650 inhabitants,[4] a stranger passing through Wingrave in 1848 might well have dismissed it as just an oversized hamlet, for most of its buildings were concealed in the byeways amongst the heavily-treed hedges of the fields and closes that reached right into the heart of the village. For over 80% of the population lived off the main road in three clusters: Nup End and Cat Street; Mill End and Moat Lane; and an arc comprising Church Street, Hogs' Hole and Lower End. In these leafy backwaters the farms and cottages nestled comfortably into the south-facing[5] hillsides: warm in summer; well-drained in winter; with water provided by springs, ponds and shallow wells; and often enjoying extensive views across the Vale to the Chilterns.

Today, Winslow Road is the residential face of Wingrave with 119 properties lining it: a long ribbon of development stretching half a mile to the west of the old village and completely distorting its medieval pattern. In 1848 it was just another country road. In the three-quarters of a mile from the Aylesbury-Hockcliffe Turnpike to the centre of Wingrave the only development on the southern side was the overspill from Nup End: the Bell Inn, George Snelling's malthouse, and four properties housing nine families. On the northern side it was all countryside until you reached a group of barns known as Parsonage Farm, by which time you were within a hundred yards of the Parish Church, the Green and the Town Pond.

It was not only its elevation and the dominance of the twelfth century church which made this area the focal point of the village. It also had important social functions. Sunday services at the church brought together families and friends from Wingrave and Rowsham for a weekly exchange of news. The Rose and Crown was a popular alehouse, where the perennial problems of agricultural life could be guaranteed a sympathetic hearing, and perhaps be put into perspective with a sup or two of the local ale.[6] The town pond was also a meeting place: at the end of the day farmers drove their carts and horses through it to wash away the mud from the fields,

while most every winter the pond was covered with ice for weeks on end. How the boys, and the menfolk too, used to slide up and down on it, and the boldest of the girls! Some were too timid of the ice, and so there were usually plenty of lookers-on.[7]

The smithy was another place where the village lads and men could gather, especially the unemployed, the elderly and the infirm. Here, sheltered from summer heat by the spreading chestnut tree [8] and from winter cold by the warmth from the forge, they could put the world to rights, or just admire the ease and precision with which the blacksmith swung his sledge, and the nonchalance of the farrier as he lifted the heavy feet of the shire horses to pare their hooves.

Domestic properties in this area included substantial buildings like the Vicarage, Baldway House,[9] Windmill House and three farmhouses, as well as more modest houses, humble cottages and tenements. Between them these properties housed the Vicar, the blacksmith, a carpenter, a wheelwright, a dealer, several tailors, a dress-maker, two ladies of independent means and seven farm labourers with their thirty-one dependants. This mixture of buildings, occupations and social classes was (and to some extent still is) typical of Wingrave. For instance, there were no less than thirteen farmhouses and farmyards within the village, and as the farmers were the principal employers, so 'masters' and 'men' lived in close proximity and encountered one another on non-work occasions such as church and chapel.

THE SOCIAL STRUCTURE OF WINGRAVE

There was a definite recognition of socio-economic class in 19th century Wingrave. This was not a question of titles: no members of the aristocracy were resident. Certainly, the Earl of Chesterfield and Lady Salisbury had owned land in the parish, but they were rarely, if ever, seen. Like many landowners they simply rented their holdings to local farmers. There was not even a lord of the manor. Despite this, some inhabitants were definitely more equal than others. The conduct of the 1841 census made this quite clear. There was no question of interviewing people street by street. The enumerator started with the elite and worked his way downwards.

The Vicar

With no hereditary or even courtesy titles to grace the parish, the Vicar came first in the parochial hierarchy, though this was not necessarily a role which he sought, as the Reverend John Butt explained in 1854.[10]

The absence of gentry is very prejudicial. Much more might be effected if persons of independent means resided here, who felt the paramount importance of aiding the minister in his arduous duties.

The Vicar's eminence was not surprising, for his duties were certainly extensive. From the pulpit he sought to exercise over the parish a social control based on the religious teaching of the church, but much influenced by the still prevalent notion that one should accept the social level into which one was born. In addition, as the senior member of the church Vestry, the vicar was responsible for the civil administration of the parish. This included the determination and collection of local taxes, and the appointment of, and responsibility for, parochial officials: a surveyor to organise the maintenance of the roads; the Guardians of the Poor; and two constables to maintain law and order.

The minutes of the Vestry[11] illustrate the extent of its powers, which must have seemed awesome to the poorer parishioners:

It is agreed by the Vestry that Joseph Bates, Joseph Kempster and Wm Bateman to Shift for themselves for their bad behaviour. (Vestry: February 1834. This meant that their poor relief dole would be terminated.)

It was agreed by the Vestry that every pauper having four children under ten years to receive one shilling per week for fuel. (Vestry: December 1834)

Richard Bonham was ordered in Vestry on account of his having an illitamate (sic) child by Thomas Hedge's daughter, and he, in Vestry, agreed to pay one shilling per week and authorised his Master, Mr Cox, should stop the money weekly and also to pay five shillings for the midwife. (Vestry: April 1835. If Richard Bonham had refused to pay, he might well have lost his job and been blacklisted by the rest of the farmers.)

It was proposed by Mr Griffin and seconded by Mr Orchard that William Bateman should pay his rent now due up to Ladyday last, the sum of two pounds, in the space of five weeks, or have his goods taken away. The above proposition was unanimously agreed to. (Vestry: April 1835)

Hannah King applied in Vestry respecting burying her daughter, asking the favour of the Vestry to allow the price of a coffin. It was unanimously agreed. (Vestry: May 1835)

In the 19th century vicars tended to remain in the same parish for many years. Thus, in 1850, after thirty-four years as vicar, the Reverend Denton was replaced by the

Reverend Butt who stayed for a further thirty-five years. Residence in the village for such long periods enabled the Vicar to become a mine of information on village life. In particular, he knew a great deal about the families in his congregation, often over several generations. This greatly reinforced his authority. A farmer or craftsman seeking additional labour, or a servant to live in, might well seek advice from the Vicar as to the character of the persons under consideration. Similarly the Vestry, the Guardians of the Poor and the trustees of the village charities might consult him to ensure that their funds went to the most needy.

The Landowners and the Farmers

Next in the village hierarchy came the landowners and the farmers. There were several reasons for this. They clearly had a much higher standard of living than the labourers: better accommodation and thus less overcrowding; ample meals and a more varied diet; more furniture; better clothing; and even servants to lessen the daily grind. They dominated the powerful Vestry, the decisions of which could be so important to their poorer neighbours. But what counted above all else was their demand for labour: they were the only significant employers in the parish. In total they needed about one hundred men, mainly for field work, but also as servants.[12] In addition they employed about a dozen female servants, and an unspecified number of farm boys. Of course, some farmers had more influence than others. The views of William Griffin, who farmed the largest area in the parish (580 acres) and employed 28 men, were likely to carry more weight that those of old Thomas Keen of Cat Street Farm, who kept only 14 acres in hand and let out the rest.[13]

Two factors reinforced the farmers' influence on the job market. Firstly, the competition for jobs was fierce. Between 1801 and 1851 the population of the parish had risen from 602 to 813. The demand for jobs had risen accordingly, and about one third of the agricultural labourers could find no regular employment.[14] Secondly, the man who was unemployed faced an awful dilemma. In 1834 a draconian revision of the Poor Law denied the able-bodied unemployed any support from public funds unless the whole family was prepared to endure the harsh discipline, sparse diet, regimentation and segregation of the Aylesbury Union's workhouse, a fate which most families did their utmost to avoid. So the labourer with regular, or even occasional, work thought himself fortunate indeed. His diet might be monotonous and inadequate, but at least his family did not have to choose between starvation and incarceration. No wonder that both the employed and the jobless called the farmer 'Master', tipped their hats or pulled their forelocks when greeting him, and ran to open gates when he rode by. It was not usually respect that made subservience and obsequiousness the hallmarks of the agricultural labourer, but the rumblings from the empty bellies of himself and his family.

The Craftsmen and the Tradesmen

Until the beginning of the 20th century, Wingrave was isolated by distance from the surrounding towns. Even using the footpaths across the fields, a visit to Aylesbury market meant a round trip of nine miles, while Leighton Buzzard and Tring markets were even further away. Only the few who owned a horse, or a pony and trap, could conveniently visit the towns and bring back their purchases.[15] Consequently, the village was to a large extent self-sufficient. By 1798 there were twenty-nine craftsmen and tradesmen in Wingrave: bakers, blacksmiths, brewers, butchers, carpenters, dealers, cordwainers, higlers, shopkeepers, tailors, victuallers and wheelwrights.[16] They ranked next after the farmers, who provided the largest part of their business. However, they did not create so many job opportunities as the farmers, their total need being less than twenty labourers (usually with specific skills) and perhaps six women, mainly as servants. Sooner or later most villagers, at all levels of society, needed to employ a tradesman's specialised knowledge, skills and judgements based on long experience. In medieval times a craft was called a mystery, and to most villagers it still was.

The blacksmith's thought pierced the molten deeps of the fire and he knew the transformation that was taking place there. He judged the heat required for the mere shaping (of metal) or for the more subtle process of welding two pieces of iron together, and knew the precise moment when they must be withdrawn from the fire, and held on the anvil, ready for the blows of his hammer.[17]

The ability to make such judgements reinforced his status, ensured him of work, and made competition from interlopers unlikely, for self-employment in a trade was usually impossible unless one had had a lengthy prior training, substantial experience, and could afford the appropriate tools and premises. Traditionally, this experience had been obtained by apprenticeship to a master craftsman, followed by employment as a journeyman. However, by the 19th century the law relating to apprenticeship[18] was a dead letter. In Wingrave in 1798 only one apprentice was recorded; in 1848 there were none. For many years families had trained their own children, or relatives, to carry on the family business. For example, in both 1798 and 1848 the Fleets were carpenters, the Griffins were bakers, the Mortimers were publicans and butchers, there were several Dimmocks amongst the cordwainers, and the tailors still included a Keen. The will of Thomas Fleet underlines this hereditary factor:[19]

I also give and bequeath all my carpenter tools which are accustomed to be used in that branch of my business to my two sons, Samuel and Caleb Fleet, to enable them to procure a living.

Usually there was plenty of work for the craftsmen. In 1798, quite apart from any new business, there were fifty-seven carts and sixteen waggons in the parish to keep Thomas Payne, the wheelwright, busy. No less than nine cordwainers (including three Dimmocks) made and repaired the boots and shoes of the eight hundred parishioners, over one hundred of whom worked on the land, thus giving their boots some very rough treatment. Similarly, the carpenters (John, William, Samuel and Caleb Fleet) were in great demand: by farmers to repair buildings, renew barn floors and construct such things as new gates, troughs and bins; and by householders for items like new doors, ladders and window frames.

At a time when horsepower always came on four legs, the village blacksmith was indispensable if only as a farrier. However, most villagers valued his skills. He produced tools such as hoes, rakes, forks, scythes and spades, and these were often tailored to the needs and physical characteristics of the particular labourer and the local countryside. So he would make left-handed scythes, billhooks of specified weights and shapes, and spades and ditching tools adapted to the characteristics of the local soil. He also ground old tools to a new edge. He made plowshares and gates for the farmer, hooks for the shepherds' crooks, iron tyres for the wheelwright, and catches, hinges, nails and handles for the carpenters. For local households he made spits and pans, repaired pots and leaky kettles, and forged the rings which he inserted in the noses of the cottagers' pigs to limit the damage done by their grouting.

By 1851 the number of craftsmen and tradesmen had risen to eighty-three, partly

3.   To the left is the white-painted door of Mary Ann Gibbs' shop, "between the churchyard and the pond".

4.   The village green pre-1914. Behind the white fence stands the parish house, long since demolished, but then let at a low rent to poor families. Mary Ann Fleet's shop occupied the single storey building on the right. On the far side of it, set well back from the road, and sheltered by the spreading chestnut tree, was the village forge, now a private garage.

due to the addition of new occupations such as sawyers,[21] bricklayers, carriers, maltsters, coopers, and a nurse, but also due to the increased population. For example, there were now four tailors, two dressmakers, five butchers, and six dealers. Many artisans had more than one string to their bow. Carpenters doubled as undertakers because they made the coffins, and the wooden posts, rails and headboards used to identify graves by those unable to afford a headstone. As the wheelwright and black-smith used pliers and had strong arms, they were obviously the people to extract teeth. When George and Robert Griffin had removed the loaves from their bread oven, they would happily bake a cake, or roast a joint of meat for a small consideration: a service which was very popular with those unable to afford fuel or who lacked a suitable oven or fireplace. The Mortimers at the Rose and Crown, and the Fleets at the Bell both combined butchery with the retailing of beer. James Kirby was a grocer, but also a plait dealer, while Matthew Simmons was a tailor and village postmaster.

The Agricultural Labourers
Still further down the social order came the agricultural labourers who, with their families, constituted 'the Poor'. At this time it was thought that poverty was the inevitable 'lot' of the agricultural labourer. Indeed, the new Poor Law of 1834 was not intended to help 'the Poor', but only the paupers i.e. those who were physically unable to earn a living. People who were poor simply because they couldn't get a job were not classed as paupers. Also, though without much justification, work on the soil was considered inferior to work at a craft. This was probably because with over a hundred men employed in agriculture and thirty-two families occupying closes and smallholdings, most villagers regarded themselves as experts on agricultural matters, whereas the craftsman's expertise involved less common skills, and more specialised knowledge. At this time there are no statistics for the poverty-stricken able-bodied unemployed. Neither can we be sure how many were forced by hunger or sickness to accept indoor relief in Aylesbury Workhouse.

The social classification used in this chapter is based entirely upon the occupations of the adult males. However, there was another large occupational group which consisted almost entirely of the wives and children of agricultural labourers and artisans. These were the strawplaiters, whose earnings often protected an agricultural labourer's family from poverty. Even though the rate for plait went down due to competition from abroad, the sheer weight of numbers in some families made the plaiters' earnings significant.

The Paupers
At the very bottom of the pile came 'the paupers', this term being reserved for persons totally dependent on doles from the poor rates. In 1851 there were twenty-five: a mere three per cent of the population. However, due to the changes in the Poor Law this figure represented mainly the aged and infirm poor: in 1851 twenty-three of the twenty-five were aged sixty years or over.

THE CHANGING FACE OF WINGRAVE

Between 1800 and 1850 the appearance of Wingrave did not alter fundamentally, but there certainly were changes. The most dramatic was the addition of Wingrave's windmill. In 1809 John Griffin, the village baker, bought from a Mr Goodson of Whitchurch a recently built smock mill, then driving one pair of millstones. It was dismantled, carted to Wingrave, and re-erected a short distance behind his cottage. It not only added a distinctive feature to the view of Wingrave from the south, but also conferred the name Mill End on the western end of what has since become Mill Lane. By 1851 the site contained the baker's cottage, his bakehouse, a grocer's shop, and the windmill, which by then was driving three pairs of stones.

Perhaps the most controversial change concerned Wingrave's poorhouse. Before the Poor Law changes of 1834 the workhouse had sheltered, fed and cared for those villagers who were unable to support, or look after, themselves, and it had done this in a place where they were close to friends and relatives. Now Wingrave's paupers had to go to the Union Workhouse in Aylesbury. This made the village refuge redundant. In 1841 the Vestry decided to demolish it, and its site was "laid into the church yard".

In a few cases old buildings were extended or replaced so as to provide better homes for the more affluent Wingravians. Windmill House, which was originally built in 1742, was significantly enlarged in 1819 when single storey outhouses at the back were built over to provide two more bedrooms. In 1827 and 1848, two further extensions were built, which are now used as a living room and a kitchen. Sometime between 1820 and 1840, a new vicarage was built by the Church of England. Presumably as an economy, it incorporated at the rear, part of the previous vicarage.[22] Also at this time, a one-bay extension was added to Mollards Cottage in Nup End.[23] Rather more ambitious was the building of the Georgian extension to Mercers' Farmhouse at Rowsham, which completely dominated the original building.

The first half of the 19th century also saw the erection of the first public buildings in the parish since the foundation of the parish church seven centuries earlier. Two of them were to house the village's increasing congregations of Nonconformists: a chapel and Sunday school in Church Street for the Congregationalists, and a chapel and Sunday school on the corner of Nup End and Pages Lane for the Primitive Methodists. Then, in 1847, an Anglican schoolroom was built on the south side of the parish church, possibly to compete with the attractions of the Nonconformist Sunday schools.

Between 1798 and 1848 the increase of 210 in Wingrave's population resulted in the creation of more homes.[24] At least three of these new houses were not typical in that they were purpose-built detached houses. In 1817 William Mortimer senior converted a barn at Nup End Yard into a cottage. When William Mortimer junior inherited it, he ran it as a beer house. Despite competition from the Rose and Crown, the Bell and the Anchor, it seems to have been successful for in 1841 it was bought by Messrs Lucas and Lovett, the Rowsham brewers.[25] The conversion must have been soundly built for it survives to this day. It is no longer licensed, and is now called The Old Dairy![26] Thistlebrook Farm, just off the Tring Road, was built before 1841. It was the first farmhouse in the parish to be built right outside the village, and its location enabled land near the parish boundary to be worked more easily. The Manse in Church Street was built in 1842 by the Congregationalists to house their minister.

Such accommodation was much too expensive for farm labourers, for whom low rents were the first consideration. Landlords tried to oblige them. For example, adding to an existing property considerably reduced building costs. Thus the thatched cottage at 4, Nup End was extended on both sides to create a terrace of three cottages, while in Church Street the terraces known as Church Row and Chapel Row had additional cottages built onto one end. Even more economical than adding to buildings was to divide the existing property into a greater number of tenements. The cramped and insanitary conditions which could result from such 'conversions' did not seem to embarrass the originators of such schemes. Thomas Fleet, the landlord of the Bell Inn, who died in 1846, even proposed one in his will.[27]

I give and bequeath and devise to my son Samuel Fleet the north end of my freehold cottage in Nup End and the building adjoining with the pigsty nearest the same, together with the west side of the garden from the east edge of the middle walk. And I give, bequeath and devise unto my other son, Caleb Fleet, the south end of the aforesaid cottage together with the building called the stable and the eastern side of the garden. And each of my said sons with their heirs and assigns to have a mutual right to the Privy, Pump and other necessaries for their mutual accommodation.

Many of Wingrave's older houses and cottages had steeply-sloping thatched rooves over timber-framed walls with an infill of wattle and daub, lath and plaster, or brick, usually resting on shallow foundations. By the middle of the 19th century many of these buildings were considerably dilapidated. Even so, at this time the increased population ensured that the demand for rented property was high, thus forcing up rents. So, if its rent was low, tenants could still be found for property in a poor state of repair. This situation appealed to landlords who simply could not afford to carry out repairs, or where the cost of repairs was greater than the likely return from rents. It also appealed to the irregularly employed agricultural labourer, who could not afford anything better. A surprising number of Wingrave's properties seem to have been in this derelict category. The problem is considered in more detail in chapter 2.

For the visitor to Wingrave, such property probably improved the appearance of the village! It was surely not by chance that in 1828 the artist William Page ignored the better maintained buildings of Wingrave in preference to its dilapidated cottages. To the artist, and other visitors from the towns, such cottages were 'quaint' and 'romantic', whereas to the occupants their principal merit was their low rents.

5. Ancient cottages at Wingrave, drawn by William Page, R.A., in 1828. The line of the distant Chilterns suggests a location at the southern end of the village, possibly Hogs' Hole.

Chapter Two

Death and Life in Nineteenth Century Wingrave

DEATH WAS NO STRANGER

Today, in Wingrave, death in the first ten years of life is very unusual. Less than 1% of children die before the age of one year, and only 2% fail to reach ten years of age. Of the survivors, less than a quarter die before their 65th year, and half live beyond 75. Things were very different in the 19th century when (as Fig.1 shows) Death was a regular visitor to most of Wingrave's homes. Between 1841 and 1875 death in the first ten years of life was commonplace. One out of every five infants died in their first twelve months, and by the age of ten years two out of every five children had been buried. Only half the population survived to 25 years of age. Two-thirds had expired by the age of 55 years, and nearly nine out of ten were buried by their 75th year.[1]

Fig 1: Parish of Wingrave with Rowsham
Percentage of Population Dead by the Age Stated [2]

Age in Years	1	10	25	35	45	55	65	75	Total
	%	%	%	%	%	%	%	%	Burials
1841-1875	22	40	50	55	60	66	75	88	627
1876-1910	15	28	37	41	44	52	65	84	512
1921-1955	3	5	8	10	15	21	35	61	324
1956-1990	1	2	4	5	7	11	23	51	306

Sources: Burial Registers of Wingrave Parish Church and Wingrave United Reformed Church

In 19th century Wingrave the major causes of this 'carnage' included poor quality and overcrowded housing, contaminated food and water, inadequate diet and medical ignorance. Unfortunately, the economic policy of 'laissez-faire', which dominated the 19th century, was accompanied by a lack of government action (or even concern) which has been dubbed 'laissez-mourir'.[3] It was the high death rates of the cholera epidemic of 1830-32 which shook the nation out of its complacency, and a series of major investigations followed, which made clear the connection between insanitary conditions and public health. Even then, there was little effective action until - prompted by out-breaks of cholera in 1854 and 1865/6 - the Sanitary Act of 1866 compelled local authorities to appoint sanitary inspectors, to identify problems and to enforce solutions. Their work was made easier in 1875 when the first Housing Act enabled them to close, without compensation, houses "unfit for habitation".

HOUSING

Thus, until 1866, the people's housing needs were still at the mercy of the speculative builder and rapacious landlord, who could provide whatever type of house gave him the greatest profit. At this time Wingrave still contained ancient cottages in a state of tottering dilapidation. They provided unacceptably poor living conditions, due to basic design faults; the ravages of damp, vermin and woodworm; and years of neglect. Even after Hannah Rothschild's model cottages of 1876 replaced some of Wingrave's worst hovels, much remained to be done. The cottages behind Mill House, which had been built with but a single exit, were still occupied well into the 20th century. The cottages known as Church Row (in Church Street) did have doors at the back and front of each house, but the only route to the back was through the house. One couple, who tethered their donkey in the back garden, had to lead it through the living room twice each day. Coal was delivered by the same route. Like most terraced cottages, these were two-up/two-down (a kitchen and living room, with two bedrooms above), though cottages with a single upstairs room were not unknown. Typically, the cottages of the poor had rooves of decaying thatch, shallow foundations, no damp course, and sometimes walls of single brick.

Even a well-made roof of wheat straw only had an effective life of about thirty years, after which its deterioration would allow water to work down into the timbers of the building. In time tile rooves also deteriorated, especially where tiles were swept round valleys created by dormer windows. Poor foundations produced settlement, which might look picturesque but could crack the brickwork, and distort window and door frames, allowing wind and water to penetrate. Without damp-proof courses, the ascent of water from the ground, plus rainwater descending from faulty rooves and chimneys, ensured damp patches and mouldy growths on walls. At worst, wet and dry rot developed, which would eventually destroy the building's structural timbers. In the meantime such cottages were cold, damp and draughty. Of course, not all cottages were refrigerated wind tunnels. The single storey cottage at the end of Church Row (nearest the Manse: see p.13) had just one living room, one bedroom and a little kitchen. With a well-stoked fire and solid brick floors which retained the heat, everywhere got warm.

In the search for greater profit, terraced and semi-detached cottages often had a common yard, privy and well. The common yard ensured that families shared their infectious diseases with their neighbours. The common privy, with its open bucket, did the same by courtesy of the local flies, but also because when a number of families shared a privy there was "almost always neglect of proper cleaning of the seat and the floor". Earth closets were even more neglected, for the receptacle was merely a shallow hole in the ground, which (especially if it served several families) might not be emptied until the increase in excrement made the privy inaccessible. So mere use of the privy, especially by children, could mean contact with faeces, and that could mean infection with disease. In January 1887, Aylesbury's Medical Officer, Dr Hilliard, wrote:[4]

The case of typhoid at Wingrave has terminated fatally. Two other cases have occurred: one in the same row of cottages (as the dead girl) and with the same water supply; the other (which also proved fatal) is a few yards away in a separate row of cottages, with a different well of water. However, the closets and cesspits of all these cottages are close together. I suspect that the contagion has been conveyed through the medium of the closets. The first case was a girl who came home ill from Leighton, and the second girl took the disease from her in some way. When this second girl was taken ill, she used the closet, and probably thus disseminated the germs (to the third girl). Acting on this suspicion I have forbidden people to go near the closets, until they have been thoroughly emptied and lime-washed.

Due to their lower rents, small properties were in great demand. Some landlords catered for this by dividing up larger properties. The original Chapel Row, situated behind the Congregational Church, was once just two tenements. These were converted in-into four tenements and then into eight. When Hannah Rothschild acquired the property

6: *Old cottages in Mill Lane, the earliest of which date back at least to the 17th century. The cottage on the left, with the twisted chimney, has been demolished.*

7: *This was Church Row in Church Street. The cottages survived until the late 1930's, but the site is now occupied by council-built bungalows.*

in 1875 for £360, it had reverted to six tenements. She had it demolished, and the present terrace of three cottages was built on the site.[5] Later, Windmill Hill Farm was for a time divided into three or four cottages. Too often such small cottages were occupied by large families, who either could not afford the larger rents of roomier cottages, or preferred to spend their money in other directions. This resulted in gross overcrowding, which was made worse by poor ventilation. Windows were tiny, and often unopenable, and there were no fireplaces in the bedrooms to help create a draught. One investigator reported, "While standing on the stairs outside the bedroom, the air was so foul that a speedy retreat was imperative". Such conditions were ideal for the spread of infectious diseases by airborne droplets or direct contact. The censuses confirm that overcrowding happened in Wingrave. In 1841 over one-third of the population of the parish endured such conditions, and in 1851 about one-quarter. (Fig. 2)

Fig. 2: Parish of Wingrave with Rowsham: The Overcrowding of Cottages

Size of Family	1841 Census		1851 Census	
	Number of Cottages	Total Occupants	Number of Cottages	Total Occupants
11	2	22	-	-
10	1	10	3	30
9	5	45	5	45
8	16	128	7	56
7	14	98	12	84
Totals	38	303	27	215
Population	814		813	

Overcrowding eventually became a national concern due to its association with epidemic disease on the one hand, and immorality on the other. To the Victorian middle classes, immorality was guaranteed when unmarried people of different sexes slept in the same room, let alone the same bed! In May 1868 the Burnham Magazine's reporter was appropriately but discreetly scandalised:

To talk modestly about 'overcrowding' is simply to use a decent word to keep out of sight a shameless indecency: the details are wholly unfit for publication. There is so little accommodation in many of these cottages that the families who live in them must be huddled together irrespective not only of kindred but of sex. Church-going won't cure this: all the sermons in the world won't give a cottage another room.

The most specific local examples were recorded two miles from Wingrave in the village of Wing, the first by a doctor from St. George's Hospital, London:[6]

A young woman of 19, having fever, lay in a room occupied at night by her father and mother, her bastard child, two young men (her brothers) and her two sisters each with a bastard child, ten persons in all.

The results of this overcrowding are not recorded, but another doctor reported:

A young man from Wingrave came to Wing despite having fever. He slept in a room with nine other persons. Within a few weeks five out of the nine had fever, and one died. From this point fever spread all over the village.

It was the Sanitary Inspectors and the Inspectors of Nuisances who had the job of rectifying the causes of such problems. They would inspect the property and issue a formal notice requiring 'the nuisance' to be ended. They might insist that overcrowding was reduced. They might order disinfection of the cottage, and this could include destroying the bedding and bedclothes, disinfecting and limewashing the bedrooms and stairs, scrubbing the floors (four times in one case), and then washing them in chloride of lime. If necessary, there would be a final notice warning that, unless action was taken, the landlord would be prosecuted. Remarkably few concessions seem to have been made to social status. The following are examples of action taken in Wingrave.[7]

February 1885: *Three cottages in Nup End belonging to William Hart and occupied by J. Carter and others were ordered to be pulled down as unfit for human habitation.*
March 1886: *The condition of six of Mr Leopold de Rothschild's Wingrave cottages was unsatisfactory, and notices were served. Two of these were final notices indicating that his lordship had failed to respond to earlier requests for action.*
May 1896: *Proceedings were taken against Henry Paxter to compel him to abate the overcrowding of a cottage occupied by him.*
October 1896: *Proceedings were taken against John Rickard to compel him to abate the nuisance of two cottages in dilapidated condition and unfit for habitation. The houses were condemned and closed.*

THE CONTAMINATION OF FOOD AND WATER

The contamination of food and water was a common cause of gastroenteritis, varying in severity from mild to fatal. The milder conditions were generally accepted as an unavoidable part of everyday life, but they could be terminal in the case of babies and the elderly. In the Aylesbury Union, in 1884, half the deaths from infectious diseases were from 'infantile summer diarrhoea'. The severe conditions included cholera and typhoid. Even a population accustomed to 19th century death rates went in fear of cholera, which killed quickly and nastily, and for which there was then no cure. In June 1832 an observer reported:

A cholera funeral took place in Aylesbury last night. It was a dismal sight. It was late and quite dark. The coffin was preceded by a lantern and the procession walked fast. There were no mourners to follow. The person buried had been in good health that morning.[8]

Gastroenteritis is most commonly spread when food and water are contaminated by sewage, but also when people and flies carry the bacteria from infected faeces to food and drink. It follows that pure drinking water, washing the hands after visiting the toilet, and control of flies are vital. In villages like Wingrave such goals were not easily attained in the 19th century. Until 1940, every drop of drinking water had to be drawn by pump or bucket from the wells which still exist in many parts of the village. Wingrave's wells are generally shallow and in a hot summer could easily run dry. It was a recurring problem, and even at the end of the 19th century the authorities could offer no remedy. Thus in 1885, the Medical Officer of the Aylesbury Union simply reported: "In consequence of the dryness of the (1884) season, those places which depend on wells have been very badly off, the water being scanty and of bad quality". Bearing this in mind he regarded the mortality figures as being "not heavy"![9]

To obtain sufficient water at such times, many Wingrave villagers bucketed it from wells, butts, ponds and moats, from distances of up to two hundred yards. It was hard work, and very time-consuming. And it did nothing to promote thoughts of personal hygiene. On a dark winter's night, when it was pouring with rain and one had just returned from the cold and soggy journey to the privy at the bottom of the garden, one's first thought was to get warm and dry, not to plunge one's hands into a bowl of icy water.

In the 19th century the protection of food from contamination by flies was a perennial problem, compounded by the subsequent spoilage as bacteria and maggots developed rapidly in hot weather. Before the invention of chemical sprays the housewife had to rely on fly-swatters, sticky fly-papers and a variety of fly traps to destroy the pests; and until domestic refrigerators came into general use (post-1945), foodsafes with perforated metal sides, dome-shaped metal covers, muslin covers (beaded round the edges to keep them in place), and patented coolers were used to protect and preserve the food. In a heatwave, each day's menu was determined by the perishability of the food. In Wingrave some houses had a private well, in which case the perishables could be put in a large bucket, covered with a cloth, and lowered down to benefit from the cooler, fly-free conditions near the water level. Of course, it complicated the drawing of water from the well, and added yet another chore to the housewife's day. Moreover, it was a losing battle, because ideal conditions for the feeding and breeding of flies were spread throughout the village, in the form of animal manure and human excrement.

Thirteen farmsteads were situated within Wingrave village, and a further five at Rowsham, each with its pig-sties, cow-sheds, stables, large dunghills and slurried yards. In October 1849 there were complaints to the Vestry regarding manure heaps in Wingrave village, and it was agreed that the manure hole near Mr Eustace's farm must be filled up. However, it was a recurrent problem. In July 1860, due to the reappearance of a fever which had visited the village in 1859, a village meeting decided that the local Inspector of Nuisances should "survey the village and order the instant emptying of all overfull privies and the removal of all offensive heaps".

Problems of this sort continued well into the 20th century. In 1915 the Parish Council received a report on the dirty state of the footpath by the Primitive Methodist Chapel, "caused by cows belonging to Mr Thomas Payne being driven along the path". So long as transport was horse-drawn, and cattle and sheep were regularly driven through the village, animal dung littered the roads, as it always had. The flies bred on it, and fed on it!

The village ditches were often seriously polluted and some stank to high heaven. Many cottages did not even have a slop drain, and noxious liquids were usually dumped into the nearest ditch. Even when sewage was piped away it usually leaked en route, and inevitably ended up in a local ditch. At Cuddington the Medical Officer recommended that the existing sewer be extended, but only so that it emptied into the ditch at the bottom of the village. However, it was the run-off from the farmyards that caused some of the worst problems, as Hilda Roberts remembered:[10]

Black Gutter Hill was the sharp little rise on top of which the parish church stands. At the bottom was a horrible deep ditch through which flowed a thick black liquid, no doubt the drainage from one of the farms.

It was 1888 before the Vestry considering piping the Black Gutter, only to find that it was not really a parish matter. And that (it appears) was that. After all, it was only one of Wingrave's many stinking ditches, and it was probably not the worst! For instance, Mill Lane also had an open ditch which received drainage from Waterloo Farm. It was stagnant and foul, and very offensive. It ran close to a cottage called the Old Mill occupied by George and Jane Badrick and their five children. There had been several

8, 9, 10: How the other half lived! The cramped conditions of Chapel Row cottages (Church St., Wingrave) contrast strongly with the farmer's spacious accommodation (Hale Farm, Rowsham).

ROWSHAM

cases of 'low' fever at this cottage, and there was currently a case of typhoid. The Sanitary Inspector decided that the ditch was responsible, and in May 1890 served a final notice on Mr Leopold de Rothschild, the owner.[11]

Even closer to people's kitchens were a variety of fly nurseries: the domestic pig-sties, chicken houses and runs; the privies with their open buckets; the earth closets and dungle holes; overflowing cesspits; and the ashpits into which kitchen waste, privy buckets and chamber pots were often emptied in the search for quicker disposal and cheap manure.

The same sources, helped by the rainfall, provided putrid liquids, which soaked into the ground. If a well was nearby, the liquid could enter it before being filtered through an adequate depth of soil. In Wingrave, this contamination of wells was made easier because many wells were built of uncemented brick. In the period 1885 to 1890 no less than thirty of Wingrave's cottages were found to suffer from "bad drainage" as the Rural Sanitary Authority blandly described it. For example:[12]

December 1885: *Bad drainage at three of Leopold de Rothschild's Wingrave cottages, occupied by Bignell and others. He was notified of this.*

January 1887: *A notice was served on Miss Gibbs regarding bad drainage affecting five cottages in Wingrave occupied by Jane Goldney and others.*

December 1890: *Bad drainage was found at four cottages owned by Joseph Rickard of Wingrave and occupied by W. Rickard and others. Joseph ignored the order, and the Inspector instituted legal proceedings against him.*

Fortunately, in some cases we have the reports of doctors to provide the missing detail:

Dr Ord, 1864: *Within six feet of this well, which is shallow and unprotected by puddling, (i.e. the brickwork is not watertight) is a large refuse pit, about four feet in diameter and two in depth, made for the reception of ashes, slops, kitchen refuse and excrements, which accumulate to form manure. There were diarrhoeal excrements on the heap when I visited the place. The soakage from this hole after heavy rains can hardly fail to reach the the well.*[13]

Dr Hilliard, 1887: *I have discovered that a private closet in an outhouse belonging to the first house in Fleet's Row, Wingrave, is within ten feet of the well supplying the Row. This closet is emptied by a drain pipe which runs close alongside the well, and which is flushed by a pail of water from time to time. Leakage is most likely to occur and thus foul the well. The closet and pipe should be removed or an earth closet substituted. In the meantime, the well has been closed by my order.*[14]

Dr Hilliard, 1887: *I have tested some water from a well with 15 feet of water at one of Lord Rosebery's properties at Nup End, Wingrave. It is intended to be the water supply for three cottages occupied by William Horwood and others. I never examined worse water. The well, which is sunk close to a drain in a gravel soil, should be condemned. The water is quite unfit for any domestic purpose.*[15]

On the above evidence it is not surprising that, where they existed, the state of drains was often so bad that it devalued the very idea of drains. "Thank God, we have none of them foul stinking things here!" commented one woman.[16]

The contamination of food might occur before it reached the consumer, some-times quite innocently. For example, in Wingrave, milk was delivered direct from the udder to the doorstep. It was certainly fresh, but might be contaminated by bacteria from the cow that produced it. These could cause diseases such as tuberculosis.[17]

However, some retailers deliberately adulterated food. For instance, the profit on milk (and beer!) could be increased by diluting it with water. This was not harmful if the water was pure. Unfortunately, the water often came from the water butt or the farmyard pump, 'the cow with the iron tail'. If so, it might well be contaminated.[18]

Vic Chapman of Maltby Farm is the only Wingrave milkman on record as having diluted his milk. Apparently, he had sent too much milk to Nestles, could not bring himself to reduce the amount fed to his calves, and only added water so that there was enough 'milk' for his customers. People still remember Vic as 'a lovely old man', but his slip cost him dear, for many customers deserted him. Far more serious was selling meat from diseased animals. In the 19th century disease was widespread amongst cattle, sheep and pigs, and if detected many farmers immediately slaughtered the animal for consumption as human food. If he acted quickly, the deception was almost certain to succeed, but any delay was fatal. In 1896, George H. Griffin, one of Wingrave's bakers, but also dealing as a pork butcher, received from Mr Elliott, a local farmer, a cow with its throat already cut. Perhaps he knew or suspected why it had been slaughtered, and decided not to risk selling it to his own customers. Perhaps being a pork butcher, he just didn't have much call for beef. Whatever the reason, he butchered it and sent the four quarters to the Central Meat Market in the City of London. In court the beef was described as without fat, dark, congested, partly decomposed and emitting a foul odour. The prosecution claimed that the eating of it would be attended with great danger. Mr Griffin was fined £50 and costs, and narrowly missed being sent to prison. There is no record of what he said to Mr Elliott when next they met![19]

POVERTY AND DIET

Especially after 1834, the reduced doles provided by the new poor relief system ensured that the Paupers still had insufficient clothing, housing, heating and food, while the labouring poor were worse off than before. The food of both groups was insufficient, and important foodstuffs were missing from their diet. Not that people died directly from starvation, but they did suffer considerably (especially the very young and the very old), from illness, malaise and even death, due to nutritional deficiencies. Thus diseases such as measles had a mortality as high as 20% in malnourished children. Tuberculosis was more prevalent where resistance had been lowered by malnutrition. A shortage of certain foods, now known to contain particular vitamins, caused medical problems. For example, a deficiency of Vitamin A reduced resistance to infection, while insufficient vitamin C caused scurvy, and lack of vitamin D caused rickets.

The Diet of the Poor circa 1840

In 1838 Dr Ceely of Aylesbury, a surgeon at the Royal Bucks Hospital, was convinced of the link between poverty and disease.

The condition of the poor is greatly increased by the inefficient diet. Their diet is bread and a little animal food, and what they have of that is bacon. The poor are compelled to be frugal: their means are very limited. In consequence they have more ills than the wealthy and need more medical care. Better diets would lead to quicker recovery.[20]

What Dr Ceeley did not mention was that their means were so limited that to obtain medical attention, or even to bury their dead, the Paupers and even the Poor often had to apply to the Overseers of the Poor for an extra dole.

We have only one statement on diet from a Wingrave villager. Harriet Gibbs was the eldest of the six children of Henry Alcock a farm labourer who, in 1841, lived in Chapel Row South.[21] She claimed to have had a happy childhood, but her diet was typical of a poor family.

We only saw meat once a week: a toad in a hole; or sometimes a bit of fat bacon and a few potatoes. We ate the pudding on Sunday and left the meat for Father to take to work all the week. Buttermilk, coarse home-made bread and black treacle was good to us in them days. We never tasted cake, and as for all they new sorts of fruit as there is now, well we'd never heard of sich things.[22]

Her statement agrees substantially with information from other sources.[23] So, the thirty-two paupers of Bledlow, whose average weekly income of 7s-9d included five weeks' harvest work, were "very much pinched". Their income did not cover such essentials as fuel and clothing, except shoes for the father of the family. Indeed, even with the utmost scrimping, their income did not cover their expenditure.

Fig. 3: The Bledlow Labourers' Weekly Budget 1834

8 quarten (4 lbs) loaves	4s – 0d	
Bacon	1s – 9d	
Soap,candles,thread,tea,etc.	1s – 3d	
Towards one pair of shoes	4d	
Rent	1s – 2d	8s – 6d

Like the Bledlow labourers, many farm workers were permanently in debt and relied on their pig (if they could afford to feed one), gleanings, family earnings at the hay and corn harvests, and any charity that was available to 'balance the books'. This is why a death in the family was not only a personal tragedy, but also a financial disaster.

Of course, if the husband, wife and two children were all working, the family's budget was transformed. In 1840, with father's wage of 7s-0d from the farm, mother and daughter working twelve hours a day plaiting to earn 3s-0d each, and a son 'crow-starving' for 2s-0d a week, the weekly budget would have looked much better:

Fig. 4: The Budget of a Family with Working Dependants 1840 [24]

5 quarten (4 lb) loaves	3s –9d	
5 lbs meat	2s –1d	
7 pints small beer	1s –2d	
½ cwt coal	10d	
40 lbs potatoes	2s – 0d	
3 ozs tea and 1 lb sugar	1s – 6d	
1 lb butter	7d	
1 lb soap and 1lb candles	5d	
Rent	1s – 3d	
Schooling	2d	
Sundries	1s – 3d	15s – 0d

In fact, this budget would be appropriate for the family of an artisan. Unfortunately, as a budget for a farm labourer, some of its attractions are illusory. Thus, the income of 15/-assumes regular employment and stable prices and, in practice, neither could be relied upon. The father and son could be laid off due to bad weather, seasonal variations in labour demand, or simply a drop in farm income. Similarly, the income of the wife and daughter was at the mercy of the volatile plait market, in which the season of the year, the fashion of the moment, and competition from imports caused considerable variations in the price of straw plait. Also, the price of the two main items of food varied considerably: in a scarce year potatoes could be six times as expensive as in a plentiful year, while the price of wheat could double in a poor year. And if income fell or prices rose, the first things to be cut were the star attractions of the budget: meat, butter and beer.

However, the budget does include potatoes, now known to be rich in calories and starch, and a valuable source of iron and vitamin C, the antidote for scurvy. Indeed, when the potato crop failed in 1846/7, there was a prompt outbreak of scurvy. Otherwise minerals and vitamins are conspicuous by their absence: there is no mention of milk, eggs, green vegetables, fruit or oily fish. Also absent are salt, clothes, footwear, medicine, and savings to cope with rainy days.

The Diet of the Poor in 1867

In 1867, the parliamentary commission enquiring into agriculture,[25] decided to talk to the families of the labourers as well as the farmers and the clergy. Wingrave (as usual!) did not respond to the Enquiry, but the evidence from other mid-Bucks villages was consistent. Thirty years after Dr Ceeley linked diet and disease, the diet of most agricultural labourers' families was unchanged. The exceptions were those (about one in every five) whose masters provided them with allotments.

Thomas Clever, an Oving labourer, had a wife and seven children to support on his wages of 11s-0d per week plus 5s-9d from the rest of the family. The only food items in their budget were bread, flour and tea, which absorbed 13s-7d. Fortunately, Thomas had a half-acre allotment where he grew potatoes and other vegetables. Even so, by the end of the winter his wife reported, "We have no potatoes just now, and I don't know when I did have any butter or meat. It has been awful bad for us lately." It certainly had, for the family was living on bread alone. It was the basic element in the agricultural labourer's diet: bread and cheese, bread and bacon, bread and milk, bread and broth, and bread and dripping. This was not so bad if you had plenty of cheese, bacon, milk, etc.. Otherwise the family just ate bread. This was why striking labourers in East Anglia carried banners reading 'Bread or Blood'. Of course, even when Mrs Clever gave the family meat, it would be pluck (the heart, liver and lungs of a beast), or perhaps half a pig's head, from which every bit of meat would be scraped. If the brains remained in the head, they would be carefully removed, gently simmered in a cloth, and served on toast. For no part of an animal was wasted. It was said of Wingrave's housewives that they could use every part of a pig except the grunt.

Unfortunately, in Wingrave the availability of vegetables, fruit and eggs was reduced by the number of small gardens and the lack of allotments. Given a larger plot, even poultry and pigs could be kept and grain grown to feed them. Some villagers overcame the shortage of land by cultivating the gardens of the elderly and infirm.

As in 1841, a family with several incomes had a better standard of living. However, the reservations of 1841 still applied: short-time working and unemployment still threatened income, while poor weather still raised prices. The comments of Mrs Betts' of Cuddington have a familiar ring about them. "When the boys can't get work we can't buy pork or as much tea and sugar". It was apparently some comfort that "there's plenty of families of four and five with only the man's money coming in."

21

Food Preparation

Affording the ingredients for a meal was one problem: cooking them was another. Wingrave lacked woodlands, and so lacked free fuel. Coal was expensive for it had to be brought from the Midlands by barge or train. When, in 1864, an investigator found that most farm labourers enjoyed one hot meal a week, this was regarded as a real improvement.[26] However, labourers' cottages rarely had bread ovens let alone kitchen ranges or cookers. So roasting was out of the question. Of course, when his bread was finished, the local baker's oven was still hot and he would roast a joint for a penny or two. People who couldn't afford that boiled the meat in a pot swinging on a swivel over the fire. The vegetables went into the same pot, kept separate in string nets. A by-product of this process was the 'water' which made a savoury and nourishing broth, for it retained the vitamins and minerals from the vegetables which when cooked separately in more recent times are often discarded. But cooking over the fire made it difficult to control the temperature, and in summer, when the broth needed to be brought to the boil to destroy any bacteria, this didn't always happen. Illness from this cause was probably quite common, but its extent was concealed by the great variety of gastric disorders prevalent in the 19th century.

MEDICAL IGNORANCE

In the 19th century, when medical knowledge was depressingly slight, disease was often attributed to the Almighty. Thus the Cholera Act of 1832 included the words, "Whereas it has pleased Almighty God to visit the United Kingdom with the plague called Cholera . . . ." In similar vein, in 1845, a coroner's jury recorded death from a stroke as 'a visitation of God', though the enemies of the deceased might claim that he had been "stroked by the wings of the Devil". Many felt that plague, pestilence and disease were a divine retribution for the sins of mankind. One churchman described cholera "as a judgement on the country for favouring Popery". So, in July 1860, when a fever, which had visited Wingrave in 1859, reappeared, the Vestry resolved that the Vicar should see the Medical Officer and ascertain whether he could suggest anything which – *under Divine Providence* – might check the spread of the fever, or prevent its return. [27]

Small wonder then that ordinary people regarded much of the illness and premature death that affected them as inevitable. This attitude surfaces repeatedly. Thus in May 1885 Dr Hilliard, the Medical Officer of Health for Aylesbury, reporting deaths from whooping cough commented, "People take no precautions against whooping cough. The prevailing idea is that it is a distemper of childhood, which must be passed through by all." The same view was taken when there was an outbreak of scarletina at Rowsham. Dr Hilliard urged that cases should be isolated at a Hulcott cottage. The mother promised that it would be carried out, but instead allowed contact with other inhabitants of Rowsham during the period of infection. A prosecution under the Sanitary Act 1866 was possible, but no action is reported. Similarly, the Health Authority believed that "Universal vaccination would eliminate smallpox completely but for obstinate scepticism from a great portion of the public". This public scepticism continued despite the fact that contact with the medical profession was slowly increasing. As early as 1835 the Vestry had agreed [28] that "Mr Heyward should undertake the surgical and medical attendance of the poor of Wingrave and Rowsham from Lady-day 1835 to Ladyday 1836 for the sum of £24 with no extras excepting midwifery which would be 15s-6d each". Then in 1860 the Bucks Herald [29] reported that a grant of £10 would be made to the Medical Officer of Wingrave District "for the purpose of establishing a surgery in a convenient part of the parish which is six miles from Aylesbury. There is a parish room at liberty which will obviate the need to pay rent for a room." Perhaps Mr Heyward didn't inspire confidence! Anyhow, the records make no further mention of local doctors. In the late 1870's, if you wanted the doctor to call, you first had to find someone going to Aylesbury to take a message. Fortunately, John Goodwin the postman was always ready to take messages to Aylesbury to the doctor and elsewhere. Looking back to her childhood, Hilda Roberts remembered,[30]

The only doctor near to us
Lived just six miles away.
No telegraphs nor telephones
To tell him what you say.

No motor car to bring him quick,
He rode his old roan nag,
And so sometimes he got behind,
Or come without his bag.

No nurses coming round each day
To take yer tempers measure
You had to chance yer luck most ways
An' get well at yer leisure.

A horse, or horse and trap, had been the standard means of travel for as long as there had been country practices, and was to continue for some time yet. Indeed, if a country practice was up for sale, it would be described as a one-horse practice, two-horse practice, etc.. Medicine was just beginning to emerge from the Dark Ages, and when the doctor arrived there was often little that he could do besides offer cordials, stimulants and tonics. Poultices were the usual recommendation for chest conditions including pneumonia. When she was a child and visiting friends in Surrey, Sybil Fleet was taken to see their local doctor. She reported his diagnosis to her parents in Wingrave:

The pain in my stomach is because I am anaemic, and my body sometimes swells and something in my stomach touches my heart. So I am to take a tonic beginning today for three weeks out of every month for three months. The doctor thinks the only thing for my finger is to have the nail extracted. He says the tonic may help it, but he doesn't think so.

In 1831, when there was an outbreak of puerperal fever in the Aylesbury area, Dr Ceeley recommended explosive and repeated doses of a mercury-based compound as the only treatment likely to save life.[31] A modern doctor commented, "It is surprising that the poor women survived the treatment, let alone the disease". Until almost the middle of the 19th century, pain relief during surgery relied upon such things as alcohol, opium and cannabis. Surgeons at the Bucks Infirmary first used a modern anaesthetic in 1847.

A patient had his leg taken off whilst under the influence of ether. He felt no pain whatsoever. Mr Ceeley performed the operation very skilfully.

Skilful surgery was helpful, but the patient's survival was always in considerable doubt until antiseptics revolutionised surgery forty years later. So much for The Good Old Days!

Chapter Three

Poverty

In the first half of the 19th century a large proportion of Wingrave's population was poor to a degree which we find difficult to understand. Only 40% of Wingrave's families "felt no want". The remaining 60% included the Poor "that fare hard", and the Paupers "that really pinch and suffer".[1] The Poor were principally agricultural labourers, of whom the supply exceeded the demand, so that some could find no regular employment, and even those who found it received very low wages. Moreover, for the agricultural labourer in the South of England the custom was, "No work, no pay", so sickness, injury, or just a spell of bad weather could quickly turn poverty into privation. This had long been the labourer's lot, but the 19th century brought a further problem. Wingrave's population rose from 602 in 1801 to 814 in 1841. This further increased the demand for jobs, just when the greater use of farm machinery was reducing the number of jobs available. As early as 1809, it was said that in Buckinghamshire, "Thrashing machines are becoming more common every day". Even when regular work was available, the agricultural labourers' wages were so low that they had insufficient food, fuel and clothing, and could only afford inadequate and dilapidated accommodation.

The Paupers comprised the unemployables, including the old, the infirm, cripples, harmless lunatics, the handicapped, the senile, widows (especially those with young children) and the abandoned. Their plight was desperate. With little or no income, they faced at best deficiency diseases due to insufficient food and an un-balanced diet, and at worst hypothermia and starvation.

OVERSEEING THE POOR

The Landed Interest dominated Parliament, and was well aware of the excesses that starving peasants had inflicted upon their lords and masters in the course of the French Revolution. Parliament feared a repetition of those events in England, and used the product of a compulsory poor rate[2] to relieve the worst sufferings of 'the inferior multitude'. The Poor Rate was levied upon the owners or occupiers of property within each parish, and collected by three members of the parish Vestry, known as the Overseers of the Poor. They also distributed the proceeds to the impoverished in cash or kind. These doles were called 'outdoor relief' to distinguish them from 'indoor relief', which required the recipient to leave home and go into the parish workhouse, a step which was only contemplated by the really desperate. In general, the doles were based on the least amount thought necessary to avoid starvation. In Wingrave the benchmark seems to have been the minimum wage paid to agricultural labourers in the Vale of Aylesbury: about seven shillings per week in the early 19th century.[3] In practice this became the maximum payment to any individual. Anything greater was exceptional, as when the doctor prescribed two bottles of wine for the ailing Ann Gugen, at a cost to the poor rate of ten shillings. That must have raised some eyebrows!

THE ADMINISTRATION OF POOR RELIEF

Before 1834 the administration of Poor Relief varied from parish to parish. The Vestry of Wingrave with Rowsham appears to have experimented with different ways of distributing relief, but to have relied mainly on the methods described below. As a general rule, doles were only paid to the unemployables (i.e. the paupers) and to those unemployed who proved their willingness to work by accepting jobs under the Roundsman System. The agricultural labourer with a regular job, but wages too low to support his family, was expected to accept the resultant poverty as appropriate to his station in life.

The Roundsman System

Unemployment amongst men who were able and willing to work was a major problem, for the majority had families and nobody liked to think of women and children actually starving. The number varied from week to week and from year to year. In 1811 the parish had about a dozen unemployed. By 1816 it had risen to twenty. They were employable, but simply unable to obtain a regular job. They became known as roundsmen because the Overseers provided them with tickets, and they trudged round from farm to farm, until they found a farmer who could provide at least a day's work. Whatever the farmer paid them per day, the Overseers guaranteed to raise it to the level of the minimum wage: seven shillings for a 6-day week, or ls-2d per day. Figure 5 illustrates the result. Notice that the farmer always paid less than ls-2d per day, for he knew that any deficiency would be made up by the Parish, from the rates paid by the local farmers and property owners. The records indicate that one shilling per day was the standard rate actually paid by Wingrave's farmers, who clearly knew the local labourers' worth, for a quarter of the roundsmen received a still lower rate of 10d per day. Francis Bates is an example. The reduction probably reflected the farmers' belief that Francis was not a very productive worker. One man, who was lame, was paid only 8d per day. Such reductions made no difference to the labourers' take-home pay: they simply received a larger subsidy from the Poor Rate.[4]

Fig. 5: Parish of Wingrave with Rowsham
Examples of Doles Paid to Roundsmen in December 1811

Labourer	Week	Farmer	Days Worked	Farmer Paid	Parish Paid
Jonas Humphrey	1	Mr Cox	6	6s--0d	1s--0d
	2	Mr Cox	6	6s--0d	1s--0d
	3	Wm. Cox	4	4s--0d	8d
	4	Mr Bates	5	5s--0d	10d
		Thos. Keen	1	1s--0d	2d
		Jos. Keen	1	1s--0d	2d
Francis Bates	1	Mr Paine	1	10d	4d
		H. Cook	4	3s--4d	1s--4d
	2	Mr Paine	4	3s--4d	1s--4d
	3	Mr Paine	5	4s--2d	1s--8d
	4	Mr Paine	5	4s--2d	1s--8d

Relieving The Paupers

The paupers received regular doles, known locally as the 'Constant Collection'. For example, in September/October 1811, weekly doles were paid to twelve males.

However, only one received the full 7s-0d, and the average payment was just 5s-5d, perhaps because most had children to help them, or wives who could still earn by straw-plaiting. Probably for similar reasons, the twenty-three women (including seventeen widows) averaged just 2s-10d per week. Only six received more than that. Without this regular assistance, the recipients would have starved or seriously hungered. The little Wingrave workhouse was the last resort for up to ten parishioners who were totally destitute, usually mainly the elderly. There were also four 'parish houses', which were particularly useful for accommodating elderly married paupers, or destitute families.

Bending the Rules

In a small agricultural community like Wingrave with Rowsham, where everyone's life was, very largely, an open book, there were times when a sound case could be made for bending the rules. Even in the early 19th century there was some sympathy for the man who was suddenly laid off for a few days due to illness, the weather or his master's need to economise. Such problems were recorded in an account known as the Extra Collection:

Daniel Keen: at home three days	2s-6d
Thomas Bonham: Dr. – ill	2s-6d
Richard Turner: at home one day	10d

In addition, over a year as many as eighteen parishioners might receive payments from this account to provide for occasional necessities and emergencies. Payments for such things as boots, shirts, breeches and stays, schooling, nursing, and fuel are mixed in with a lot of unidentified payments. Typical entries include:

Oct 14	Hat 2/-, Stockings 4/-, Breeches 3/9, etc. for King	10s-0d
Oct 24	Schooling, bobbins, pins, etc. for E. Brown	5s-0d
Oct 28	Pr Stays for Ann Brown	7s-6d
Oct 29	Pd Wm Smith for going with Ann Pryor to her place	1s-0d

Undoubtedly the Extra Collection introduced a little humanity into Wingrave's system of poor relief.

THE NEW POOR LAW

Between 1785 and 1832 expenditure on poor relief more than quadrupled both in Wingrave and nationally. During the early part of this period, the receipt of poor relief became the norm: approximately two-thirds of the families in the parish received it in some form each year. Fortunately, due to the Napoleonic Wars, farming was prosperous, and farmers and property owners could bear the cost of the rising poor rate. However, from 1818, the high poor rates coincided with an agricultural depression during which wheat prices collapsed. Many farmers and landowners complained that the poor rate was removing what little profit was left in farming.

Fig.6: Poor Rate Expenditure

Year	Wingrave/Rowsham[5]	England and Wales
1785	£331	£1,530,800
1803	£858	£4,077,891
1817	£836	£7,870,801
1832	£1403	£7,036,969

11. *Knocker Barlow, a stone-picker and knapper at Frieth, epitomises the poverty at the lowest level of farm labouring circa 1900. He would go on working as long as possible, in order to avoid the dreaded Union.*

12. *Below, the new Aylesbury Union Workhouse, erected in 1844/5. The buildings are still in use as part of Tindal Hospital.*

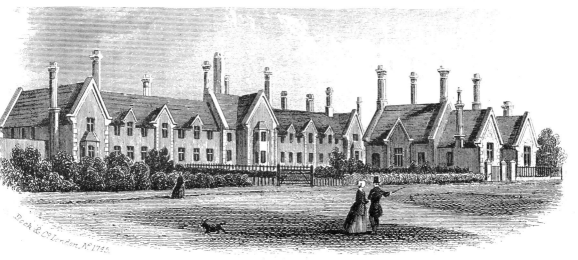

Robert Gibbs in his History of Aylesbury noted:

Many parishes were reduced to such a state of pauperism that the Poor Rate on the whole of their property was insufficient for the maintenance of their poor. Landlords could not obtain their rents, farmers were impoverished, and the agricultural labourer received just enough to enable him to procure for his family and himself the barest necessities of life.

Consequently, even the labourers who benefited from the poor rate were dissatisfied, and at the end of 1830 Buckinghamshire suffered from the 'Swing' riots.[6] In many parishes a great deal of farm machinery was wrecked. There is no evidence of any violence in Wingrave, but it must have been an anxious time for the farmers of the parish. Wingrave's location on a ridge above the Vale provides views for many miles around, and the fires often started by machine breakers would be clearly visible. Fortunately for the farmers, the riots were quickly subdued, and any likelihood of repetition was discouraged by hanging, imprisonment or transportation to the colonies.

Encouraged by the ease with which the 'Swing' riots had been controlled, Parliament determined at long last to tackle the problem of soaring poor rates. The result was the Poor Law Amendment Act of 1834. Its aim was to force the unemployed labourer to support himself and his family, while preventing the pauper from starving.

The Act removed the administration of poor relief from the individual parish, and gave it to unions of parishes. Thus Wingrave became part of the Aylesbury Union, an amalgam of forty parishes, with a population of 22,000, the whole being administered by a Board of Guardians, to which Wingrave contributed just one member. The Act also established that symbol of Victorian pauperism, the large centralised workhouse, known in Wingrave as the 'Union' or 'the workus'. This replaced the small parish workhouses, and for the next century cast a dreadful shadow over the lives of the destitute. As in the past, those villagers completely unable to maintain themselves had to go into the workhouse. But the massive new 'Union' at Aylesbury was very different to the cosy little Wingrave workhouse.[7] It was six miles from the inmates' friends and relatives in Wingrave; husbands and wives were segregated into different wards; their lives were run by strangers who knew nothing of them; and their relatives were compelled to contribute to their support on threat of prosecution:[8]

George Badrick of Wingrave was charged by the relieving officer to Aylesbury Union with neglecting to contribute towards the support of his aged mother, Sarah Badrick, who is chargeable to the common fund of the Union. He was ordered to pay 1/- per week and costs.

Fortunately the authorities soon realised that it was considerably more expensive to maintain a person in the workhouse than to provide outdoor relief. So outdoor relief for the destitute continued, though it was granted less readily than in the past, as a minute of Wingrave Vestry in 1834 confirmed in almost impenetrable English.[9]

The list of paupers taking constant collection have gone under an examination by the Vestry respecting their weekly wages and (the Vestry) have agreeably and unanimously altered and levied on them due to (their) ages and needfull necessarys for their support.

Still harsher was the assumption that able-bodied agricultural labourers could get work if only they tried hard enough. On this assumption the Act abolished relief for the able-bodied unless they too entered a workhouse. If they did, then the workhouse regime was of a severity designed to discourage any future reliance on public funds. For instance, the able-bodied were given less food than the elderly and infirm. Inmates had to seek "leave of absence" just to go in search of work for a couple of days. The work provided was often hard and humiliating: breaking stones for the roads, and crushing bones to make bone meal for sale to the farmers, for example. The inmate who failed to do the work expected of him in (or outside) the workhouse was prosecuted and could expect a sentence of 21 days' or a month's hard labour. If the pauper took his children into the workhouse with him, then they too were subjected to severe restrictions. Thus it was 1839 before the Board of Guardians of Aylesbury Union made provision for them to have just two hours superintended recreation (out of the House) per week. The Union's first priority was to find work for the children. In practice this meant farming them out to some local employer. Eventually, Robert Nixon of Kayes Silk Mill at Tring came to an arrangement with the overseers of the Aylesbury Union Workhouse, who donated £200 and land adjoining the workhouse towards a new mill. In the 1830's there were thirty handlooms. In 1844 the mill changed hands, and by 1859 there were two hundred employed, and the looms were steam powered.

THE ATTITUDE OF THE MASTERS

In 1836 a Select Committee of the House of Commons enquired into Agricultural Distress.[10] William Cox, a Buckinghamshire farmer of 1800 acres, gave evidence to it. By 1836 he lived at Scotsgrove House near Thame, but he and his family had long lived in Wingrave. They still owned Windmill Hill Farm and a large acreage in the parish. As a member of the Wingrave Vestry, he had been an overseer of the poor. He was a Nonconformist and had given the workshop and orchard on which Wingrave's first chapel was built. Before the Manse was built, the Nonconformist pastor and his family lived at Windmill Hill Farm, doubtless courtesy of William Cox. In other words Cox knew Wingrave and the condition of its people well. Or he should have done!

In his evidence (page 31) Cox acknowledged the poverty of the agricultural labourer, but appeared to have no idea of the difficulty of maintaining a family on seven shillings per week. All that was needed from employers was a little sympathy! Later he explained what he meant by this:

I know many parishes where indiscriminately the farmers pay the man without a family and the man with a family the same wages; and I do the same, but I give all the men that have large families the best taskwork, so that by working more hours in the day they can earn a little more money.

While extremely poor men doubtless clutched gratefully at any straw, it is certain that 'a little more money' would not have provided them and their families with a fraction of the food and clothing that Cox thought was essential for himself and his family.

Although William Cox was well aware of the agricultural labourer's prejudice against the workhouse, he offered the committee no explanation for it, and simply said blandly that "they are well-clothed and well-fed in the workhouse", as though man lived by bread alone. Would Cox really have felt "well-fed" on workhouse fare: a punitive diet in which 62% of the meals consisted of bread and gruel, or bread and broth, or just soup? (Fig.7) It is more likely that, like most nineteenth century masters, he put the labourer into a very low social class, where poverty was the norm and the poor were expected to be grateful for the crumbs that fell under the table. Ironically, many labourers had long existed on an inferior diet to that provided by the workhouse.

William Cox shared with William Gilbert (another prominent Bucks master) the

Fig. 7: Aylesbury Union Workhouse: Weekly Diet, June 1837 [11]

Breakfast	Bread and gruel
Dinner	Cooked meat and potatoes (4 days per week)
	Soup (2 days per week)
	Suet or rice pudding (1 day per week)
Supper	Bread and broth (4 days per week)
	Bread and cheese (3 days per week)
	Small beer daily (men: one pint; women: half pint) if aged 60 years upwards.

view that (due to migration into manufacturing districts, emigration, the construction of railroads, and other public works) there were very few out of employment in Buckinghamshire. So far as Wingrave and Rowsham were concerned, this view was simply incorrect.[12] Neither does it seem to apply to the rest of the Vale. Despite migration, emigration and the horrendous infant and child mortality, Wingrave's population increased by 9% between 1831 and 1851.[13] Meanwhile, farmers continued to mechanise so reducing the number of jobs available. By 1851 agricultural wages had fallen nationally by 14%: a sure sign of a labour surplus. In Bucks both emigration and arson continued throughout the 1840's and 1850's: a clear indication of dissatisfaction amongst the workers. Indeed, the very slight evidence that has survived suggests that unemployment amongst Wingrave's agricultural workers continued at about 10% at least to the end of the century. There is no evidence that public works (including the building of the railways) absorbed Wingrave's unemployed. Construction of the Cheddington to Aylesbury branch railway did not start until May 1838. Although it used some local labour, it required few earthworks, and so was not particularly labour intensive. On completion, the operational jobs were few and confined to the Aylesbury terminus. The construction of the London and Birmingham Railway started in June 1834, and certainly involved major engineering works such as the Tring Cutting and the Watford Tunnel. However, railway construction was very dangerous work, and the accommodation for the 'navvies', who followed the line as it advanced across the country, was often shocking "with scarcely any provision for comfort or decency of living".[14] There is no evidence that Wingrave's unemployed were attracted by it.

The only public works within the parish were the digging of gravel, its use for resurfacing the roads, and the cleaning out of roadside ditches. However the roads in the parish were in good condition, for the Vestry had long used them to provide work for the unemployed. They were certainly no answer to Wingrave's unemployment problems, as William Griffin, another local farmer and Overseer of the Poor, explained to the Poor Law Commissioners:[15]

We have a great deal of surplus labour which I am at a loss to know what to do with for the best under the new law. I have no public work to send them to, which places me in an awkward position.

Three weeks later the Commissioners replied:

The Board wish to point out a plan which has been beneficially tried in other parts of the county viz. digging and forking the land for the farmers at rather less than the usual rate paid for ploughing in your district to labourers not dependent on the parish. There

EXTRACTS FROM THE EVIDENCE OF WILLIAM COX TO THE SELECT COMMITTEE ON AGRICULTURAL DISTRESS: 6TH MAY 1836

What is the condition of the labourers in your neighbourhood? *The labourers are not well off in Buckinghamshire.*

Are there many out of employment? *There are very few out of employment now, in consequence of the railroads and other public works.*

Has the new poor law come into operation in your neighbourhood? *Yes.* Has that had an advantageous effect upon the conduct of the labourers? *To a certain extent it has benefited the ratepayers. It has also worked well with the idle and the profligate.*

The farmer now expects to get, and does get, a fair day's work from the labourer for the wages he gives him? *Yes.*

Which he did not do before the new poor law came into operation? *No.* Are any workhouses in contemplation under the new poor law? *Yes, throughout the county.* Should you say that the regulation contemplated under the new Poor Law Act, with respect to the separation of the sexes, could be carried into effect without difficulty? *I think it cannot. Anything that does violence to human nature would be attended with difficulty.*

In your part of the country you were not very favourably disposed to the poor law? *I was not.*

You are now of the opinion that it is likely to lower the rates, and to have a good moral effect upon the lazy and indolent? *It will work well where a little sympathy is shown.*

What should you say has been the case with respect to the treatment of the old people; have their allowances been diminished under the new system? *Yes, they have.*

Is that not considered a matter of regret? *It is by the ratepayers themselves.*

Supposing a rise (in the price) of provisions to take place from unfavourable seasons, ought there not to be a greatly increased attention paid to that circumstance, to prevent the new poor law becoming a measure of great severity? *Yes, but they have their remedy. They can go into the workhouse if they like. (The Justices) will always give them an order, if they are dissatisfied with the pay, to go to the workhouse.*

Are they not well clothed and well fed in the workhouse? *Yes, but they have a prejudice against it.*

Do you know any persons that have been removed from a cottage of their own to a workhouse? *I know several that have petitioned their neighbours and friends to assist them to keep out of the workhouse.*

Is there a great inclination in your neighbourhood to emigrate to America or to other countries? *I think that has a little subsided.* Sooner than go to the workhouse they will use every exertion to remain in their cottage? *Yes. The least allowance now is 4s-0d (per week) for a man and his wife out of the workhouse, for old persons.*

Source: Parliamentary Papers, 3rd Report from the Select Committee appointed to Enquire into the State of Agriculture, 1836

is no more about this in the records, but the wage per worker from such an inefficient scheme would be so small, the rate of cultivation so slow, and the reaction of the redundant ploughmen so savage that one wonders whether Mr Griffin's views were printable.

William Gilbert also believed that abolishing outdoor relief [16] would ensure for the labourer more permanent employment than before.[17]

Previously, the farmers in many instances engaged labourers by the day. This evil has begun to diminish, for the farmers already talk of the possibility of being short of labourers, and of the necessity that they will be under to keep them as permanent men.

This was mere speculation! In Wingrave the shortage of labourers did not materialise until the end of the century, and short-term hiring continued. Indeed, in the 1860's the Rothschilds caused quite a stir in the Vale by providing more regular employment.

THE RESPONSE OF THE LABOURERS

So how did the unemployed avoid both the workhouse and starvation? It is difficult to be specific, because statistics were not recorded, and many records have been destroyed. The following were some of the avenues explored.

An Appeal to the Authorities

Unfortunately, there was little that the Poor could do to challenge the situation created by the 1834 Act. Agricultural labourers had no vote until 1884. Even so, under the Act, Wingrave, like the other parishes in the Union, appointed one of the Guardians of the Poor (the new name for the Overseers). In theory the labourers could appeal to Wingrave's representative. Surely that would ensure that Relief was provided more adequately and humanely? In practice it did not happen. As the Bledlow labourers put it:

The Justices tell us they can do nothing. The Guardians tell us they can do nothing. We have looked for work in vain. We have gone here and there and can find none. And when we leave our parish in the fruitless search, we are deprived of the little allowance which the parish gives us. Ready as we are to work, the parish can give us no work.

Of course, the Guardians and the Justices were both drawn almost exclusively from the property owners and farmers: those who paid the poor rate. They were unlikely to sympathise with anything which might increase it. Even if they sympathised and carried their fellow guardians with them, changes were most unlikely. In theory the Overseers managed the Union, but in practice they could do very little without the approval of the Commissioners in London. Even the provision of a limited quantity of small beer at Aylesbury Workhouse had to be referred to London, and was the subject of an extended correspondence.[18] In particular, only the Commissioners could dismiss the paid officials who administered each Union, and who (recognising where the real power lay) implemented the Commissioners' policies to the letter.

Publicity for the Problem

In Wingrave's ale houses the poor might grumble bitterly over their pots, but they rarely went public with their complaints, being too illiterate and too brain-washed into believing that poverty was their lot. There was an exception in 1834 when thirty-two paupers of Bledlow asked a neighbour to put their case in a letter to the Bucks Herald,[19] hoping to arouse public opinion.

The married men among us are paid (a dole of) 7 shillings a week. In harvest we may earn, for four or five weeks, as much as 15 shillings a week, but this is the extent of our earnings during the year. The 7 shillings is spent on bread, bacon, soap, candles, sugar, tea, thread, worsted and such necessaries. We have nothing left. We have no money remaining to buy clothing or fuel, or to pay our rent, which may be taken on average at 60s-0d a year. We must depend on accident for these supplies, and of course, therefore, usually go without them. If we can manage to save a guinea of our earnings in harvest, it is nearly all expended in paying for our shoes, which cost us 15s-0d or 16s-0d a pair. We have no rich neighbours to help out our scanty means by their benevolence. Gentlemen, the distress which we sometimes suffer cannot be conceived by you. Today at 2 o'clock some of us had been without food since yesterday evening. When (the day's) work is at an end we are very much pinched. On Fridays and Saturdays we have scarcely any bread remaining in the house, and no money to buy more. There are about sixty more labourers in our parish who are at present employed by the farmers, but who receive no better pay than we do. Their case is just the same as ours, and their sufferings as great.

It seems that the appeal fell on deaf ears. Certainly, there was no great public outcry. It was 1867 before it occurred to the government to question the rural poor directly about their plight.

Intimidation of the Employers

It was in 1834, when the Poor Law Amendment Act first became law, that arson began to take its toll of farmers' barns and hay-stacks. Although it was 1842 before a Wingrave farmer (Thomas Cook of Floyds Farm) suffered, it certainly gave the farmers a great deal to worry about, for _ as with the 'Swing' riots _ Wingrave's excellent views of the Vale would have left them in no doubt as to the extent of the threat. Arson probably gave some satisfaction to the hot-heads amongst the labourers, but it did absolutely nothing for the income of the poor. Indeed, since the barns and haystacks that were destroyed had to be replaced, it may have made the farmers more careful with their money. Arson continued into the 1850's, and could be exceedingly expensive to the victims. A fire at Brickhill in 1847 was said to have caused £3000 of damage. Farmers close to Aylesbury were so alarmed by the large number of fires that it was proposed to establish a fire brigade in the town.

Maximisation of the Family Income

In 1834 the typical Wingrave household was very different to that of today. Despite the high infant and child mortality, the average family was much larger. With no compulsory education, and no restrictions on employment, children were expected to contribute to the family income as early as was physically possible: typically from five years of age. Usually this contribution continued until they married, for most children remained at home until then. The resultant overcrowding was an accepted part of life, but even in those days small cottages had their limits, and it was quite common for older 'children' to take live-in jobs as domestics, or to lodge with relatives. They were usually welcomed by grandparents, aunts and uncles and young married brothers and sisters, for privacy was much less important than the best use of family resources.

As detailed in chapter 4, Wingrave was one of many villages producing straw plait for the hat industry of Luton and Dunstable. At four or five years of age most children started straw plaiting in one of the village plaiting 'schools'. From the age of seven or eight the lads would look for work with a local farmer, but for girls plaiting usually became a life-long occupation.

All this meant that with good health, with agricultural work available, and with plait in reasonable demand, most of Wingrave's agricultural labourers could expect an income from more than one source. Thus a newly married couple could expect two incomes: the husband's and the wife's. With a grown-up family up to six or seven incomes were possible, though this was the most optimistic scenario. For at the best of times both farming and the price of plait were seasonal, and suffered from European competition. Thus during the Napoleonic Wars when the import of plait was forbidden, some women could earn 30s-0d per week at plaiting, whereas 25 years later "young women worked 12 to 14 hours a day plaiting to earn 3s-0d or 4s-0d a week". Of course, some of a family's incomes were those of children or teenagers, earning less than an adult wage, while a marriage or death could put everyone onto short rations. However, two types of household were especially vulnerable to severe poverty: the elderly, and the married couples with a young family.

The Problem Households: the Elderly and the Infirm

The elderly (defined as those over 60) were either at, or rapidly approaching, the time when agricultural labour was just too strenuous for them. Of sixty-one cases recorded in Wingrave and Rowsham in 1851, thirteen had moved in with a married child. A further eighteen were still living in their own homes supported by unmarried sons and daughters, two-thirds of whom were over thirty years of age, which suggests that some had postponed or foregone marriage in order to assist their parents. Eight elderly couples had found lodgers, leaving just thirteen households struggling along without any visible assistance. If they had no families able or willing to support them, their remaining options were either to accept the inadequate outdoor relief, or to go into the dreaded workhouse.

The Problem Households: the Young Farm Labourer's Family

It was starting a family which caused problems for the young farm labourer. The arrival of the first child considerably reduced the wife's income for several years. A mother could rock the cradle with her foot while continuing to plait, but plaiting was obviously incompatible with breast feeding, nappy changing and baby washing. The second and third children eroded the wife's income still further. However, from the age of four or five the children would have to contribute to their keep by plaiting, and by sharing in the household chores. This 'all-hands-on-deck' policy certainly maximised the family's income, but with wages being so low, even two or three incomes did little more than pay the rent, fend off starvation, and provide for such unavoidables as repairing the fieldworker's boots. If the husband's unemployment coincided with a serious slump in the price of plait, their main options were the workhouse or emigration.

THE PRINCIPAL CANDIDATES FOR EMIGRATION

Despite the uncertainties and dangers, many preferred the opportunities of emigration to the confinement and harsh regime of the workhouse. Young married couples (and their prospective descendants) were very much in evidence, for every voyage saw a number of births, while the deaths at sea always included several young children. Ironically, the people who could respond most readily to the challenge of emigration were the strong, healthy young men without family ties. Some of them could see the problems that the future held for them if they remained in England, and so they featured prominently on the passenger lists of emigrant ships. Families with older children also made the break, but there was no room for the elderly. Unless they could pay for their passages, the elderly had to be left behind. Fortunately, whatever their marital status, every departure helped those who stayed behind by reducing the competition for jobs.

POVERTY PERSISTS!

Over the forty years from 1834 to 1871, life in rural counties such as Buckinghamshire did not improve. The parish of Wingrave with Rowsham was no exception. In 1860 the Bucks Herald referred to it as having "a scattered population of 800 persons, a great portion of whom are paupers and poor people". The persistence of poverty is not surprising, for the fundamental problem remained. Despite migration and emigration, Wingrave's population had increased by 16% between 1831 and 1871, and the demand for jobs still exceeded the supply. And unlike the North and the Midlands there was no new industry to siphon off the surplus labour. It was not until 1870 that Aylesbury acquired its first large employer: the Condensed Milk Factory (now Nestles). It appears to have made no impact on employment in villages as distant as Wingrave. In consequence, the 1870's saw the development of large-scale Trade Unionism, and a strong revival in emigration. We take a closer look at these subjects in chapter 5.

13: Old habits die hard! Like their forefathers, Wingrave's lads were still fascinated by the blacksmith's skills, even in the 1930's.

Chapter Four

Straw-Plaiting In Wingrave

Straw-plaiting in the Vale may well date back to the 17th century or even earlier, for we know that in 1689 and 1719 plaiters were petitioning Parliament. The 1719 petition, from villages in the area between Aylesbury, Leighton Buzzard and Tring, was addressed to Parliament by 'the Poor of the Counties of Hertford, Bedford and Buckingham', protesting against the import of straw plait and hats from Italy. It stated that the making of straw hats and bonnets had been:

an employment time out of mind for the poor people both men, women and children from four to four score years of age, by which many thousands have gained a comfortable sustenance and kept themselves and their families from being chargeable to their parishes whereas imports would prove the total destruction of so useful a manufacture.

The government agreed but did nothing, and imports soared. Fortunately, despite the fears of the local plaiters, imports did not destroy the industry. Although imports dominated the luxury market, the coarser English plait was still in substantial demand for the cheaper mass market. In those days it was unthinkable for a woman to be seen at church, or even just around the village, without her head covered, and straw hats were extremely popular. Not only did the industry survive, but from 1793 it expanded because the war with Revolutionary France cut off Italian imports. Even so, the real breakthrough for the local industry came some time between 1795 and 1801 when a splitting machine (or "sheen" in local parlance) was invented, which enabled a single straw to be divided evenly into a number of narrow splints. The Austin splitter, made off Akeman Street, Tring, even offered a choice of splint sizes. At long last British plaiters had a raw material sufficiently thin to compete with the fine Italian straw. When competition resumed at the end of the wars in 1815, the British government had long since imposed a tax on imported plait and in 1819 it was increased. With this protection the plaiting workforce expanded, with women, children and even men being involved in the trade.

STRAW PLAITING IN WINGRAVE

Until the census of 1851 we know little of straw plaiting in Wingrave. The Poor-house accounts of 1811 simply inform us that plait was made and sold there:[1]

> *8th Oct 1811 Receaval of 4s-9d for plat*
> *31st Oct 1811 Receaval of 8d for plat*
> *8th Nov 1811 Receaval of Badrick 13s-6d for plat*

These paupers were local people and mainly elderly. They used skills which (it was generally agreed) had been learned as children, in the first half of the 18th century. The Vestry minutes of 1835 also refer to straw plaiting, [2]

Nathaniel Arnold applies for loan to pay baker ten shillings. Money to be repaid by son's money from plaiting school.

The 1851 census is the first to reveal that straw plaiting was a widespread and thriving cottage industry in Wingrave, employing between a quarter and a third of the total population of the village. Doreen Honor, who lived in Wingrave as a child, remembers her Grandma Emma Alcock. Friends would meet in her Rothschild cottage on the Recreation Ground to plait, to enjoy the warmth, and to share the local gossip. In the summer, if the weather was fine and warm, they might put on their hats, and plait in the garden. Provided that the finished braid was coiled around one arm to keep it off the ground, one could plait while standing at the doorstep chatting to neighbours, walking along the village street, or 'sweethearting' down a country lane. Women learned it as girls, carried on during their child-bearing years, and then on and on, well into old age, until

14: Emma Alcock

declining eyesight and stiffening fingers forced them to give up. The males usually learned it as children, but later forsook it for fieldwork, or a trade. It had not always been so. In the 1880's, Jemima Mead of Nup End would speak of "earlier days, when men also plaited (full-time) and earned more by that than on the farms, which were very poorly paid jobs at that time." [3] Adult male plaiters were probably always few in number, and by 1851 no male over 19 admitted to being involved in the industry. Despite this some returned to it on winter evenings, or in periods of unemployment, or when bad weather caused lay-offs. This flexibility made straw plaiting a very convenient way to earn money, and until the last quarter of the 19th century it was a valuable supplement to an agricultural labourer's meagre wages, often avoiding the need for poor relief.

Fig. 8: Wingrave Village: Sex, Numbers and Ages of Straw Plaiters in 1851

Sex	Total Popul'n	Total Plaiters	Number of Straw Plaiters by Age				
			>5	5-9	10-14	15-19	20-64
Male	328	46	3	21	20	2	---
Female	331	110 (+55)*	3	35	33	17	22 (+55)*
Total	659	156 (+55)*	6	56	53	19	22 (+55)*

* The 1851 Census for Wingrave with Rowsham shows no occupations for wives. If they all plaited, the number of plaiters would rise by the numbers in brackets. Our figures exclude wives with a child under one, those who could participate in their husband's trade (e.g. grocer, tailor, baker, publican, butcher), and those whose immediate family were paupers, farmers, or of independent means.

John and Sarah Harriss, who lived in Nup End, illustrate how deeply whole families could be involved in the industry. In 1851 John and his three eldest sons were agricultural labourers. However, the younger children, Eliza, Charles, Mary, Ann and even three-year-old Robert were full-time plaiters. Only Job, at one year old, was excused. Although one reads of mothers continuing to plait while rocking the cradle with their feet, there is no indication that Sarah did anything but bear and raise children. The final total reached thirteen, so perhaps she felt that was contribution enough. Eventually the eldest three sons left home, and Charles, Robert and Job 'progressed' from straw-plaiting to farm labouring. This left only Eliza and Mary to continue plaiting. Fortunately, the last four arrows in John Senior's quiver found their target, and eventually this restored the Harriss' strawplait workforce to full strength!

THE PRODUCTION OF PLAIT

The chalky soils of the Chilterns produced the most suitable straw for plaiting: long, even and straight. Wingrave was fortunate in its proximity to supplies. Fields of wheat intended for plaiting were cut by hand and the ears removed from each stem, which was then combed to remove loose fibres before being cut into suitable lengths. Hilda Roberts, a life-long resident of Wingrave, never had to earn her living as a straw plaiter but she lived amongst people who did, and wrote down much of what she learned. She tells us[4] how straws in proper lengths (about six inches) were sold in bundles which were always called 'bunches'. The straws were whole and had to be split lengthwise on a straw splitter, which was a small gadget with various sized cutters. Each straw was pushed into the chosen cutter, and then pulled through, when it would be evenly split into anything from three to nine finer

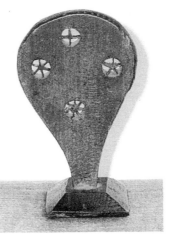

15: The straw splitter used
by Sophia King

straws called splints. These splints enabled the worker to produce a finer plait more suitable for making quality products. "The finer the plait, the more the money," was a common saying.

Then the splints had to be damped, and passed through a mill like a miniature mangle with wooden rollers, worked by a stout wooden handle. How I loved to watch these processes, for almost every household had a splitter and a mill, and most of our villagers, big and small, learned to plait.

Learning to plait usually began in the home. Straw-plaiting 'schools' were just workshops for the production of plait. It was the mothers who taught their children how to plait, and this began at a very early age, almost as soon as the child could walk. The mother would sit plaiting with the toddler beside her clutching a bunch of dampened splints, ready to hand them to her, one at a time, as required. Soon the child would be ready to learn simple plaiting with whole straws, the easiest pattern being Rustic, other-wise known as Pearl.

Criss cross patch and then a twirl,
Twist it back for English Pearl.

was the rhyme that children chanted as they struggled with their work. First attempts were usually 'widdle waddle', but it was not long before they were producing rough plait that could be sold cheaply. Next they would learn Plain, using the rhyme:

Under one and over two
Pull it tight and that will do.

Hilda Roberts even acquired some plaiting skills:

A neighbour had a fancy for earning a bit by running what she called a plaiting school. Six or seven of us children went every morning in the school holidays, and thought it great fun. We paid her 2d per week. Mother used to speak of the many kinds of plait which were produced in our district, including One Pearl, Two Pearl, Whipcord, Feather Edge, Three Notch, Rustic Improved, Twist and Railroad. It was a wider, loosely woven plait called Brilliant which I learned to make when I was seven years old.

Brilliant was introduced in the 1850's. If the finished braid was perfectly regular and free from faults it produced a glittering effect, which was much admired and sought after, and so fetched a very good price. However, it was a very difficult technique and only the best plaiters could master it.

Because payment for plait was by the yard, speed was essential, and so the plaiter performed several operations simultaneously. If a child was not on hand to supply the dampened splints, they would be held under the plaiter's left arm. When a new splint had to be 'set in', the plaiter lowered her head, pulled one out with her mouth, and worked it round with her tongue until it was sticking out at the right-hand side of her mouth. This moistened the splint again and kept it pliable, otherwise it might break. Meanwhile, both hands would be plaiting busily, interrupted briefly but regularly by the swift plucking of a new splint from her mouth for insertion into the braid. Due to this action the right hand corner of her mouth developed unsightly cracks and eventually became permanently scarred. After 'sweethearting' with a plaiter, one lad remarked, "It was like kissing a cow's backside"! Even after they had been incorporated into the braid, the ends of the splints stuck out on both sides, making the unfinished braid look like some bizarre millipede. Finally, these ends were clipped off. Clipping was another task for the youngest children at plaiting school as one mistress explained:[5]

Children can clip the loose straws off when about 3 years old. Lizzie Cook, who was 3 last month, can clip her 'ten' (yards) in the day. In clipping, the scissors sometimes hurt their fingers, and some have to put two in to be able to hold them. They are very troublesome, and I have to use the stick a great deal more then I like.

Then the plait was damped yet again, and passed through a plait mill. Finally, it was rolled into lengths of ten yards (a half score), or twenty yards (a score).

PLAITING SCHOOLS

We saw earlier that, in the 19th century, if the agricultural labourer became unemployed or ill, stark choices loomed: starvation, emigration or the hated workhouse. Extra income from straw-plaiting was one way of avoiding those choices. Consequently, many children were sent to plaiting school at a very early age, in fact as soon as they had mastered the rudiments of plaiting from their mothers. In 1864 a government enquiry into children's employment[6] was told: 'people reckon to set children down to plait at four years old, or even at three and a half, or three". In practice, parents justified their action by the comment, "A child will never make a good plaiter unless it is started young". The underlying truth was not always added, "The sooner the child learns to plait, the sooner it will bring in some money".

Wingravians appear to have been a little more considerate to their infants. Even as early as 1851, only one child of 3 years and five of 4 years were recorded as plaiters: most started at the age of five or six years or even later. (Fig. 9) Of course, the children for whom no employment was stated may well have been employed at home by their parents;[7] and parents could be extremely harsh masters.

Fig. 9: Wingrave Village 1851: Age of Children Engaged in Straw-Plaiting

Age in Years	Number of Children in Straw-plaiting			Total in Age Group	% of Age Group Engaged in Straw-plaiting
	Male	Female	Total		%
3	1	--	1	18	5.5
4	2	3	5	12	41.6
5	6	3	9	16	56.2
6	4	8	12	16	75.0
7	2	10	12	15	80.0
8	5	8	13	15	86.6
9	4	6	10	13	76.9
Total	24	38	62	105	59.0

Source: Census 1851

Plaiting was a cottage industry. This meant that production usually took place in the room of a cottage. Although such rooms were nothing more than workshops, they were dignified by the name Plaiting School. In 1867 Wingrave was one of thirty Buckinghamshire villages in which a total of 103 plaiting schools were located. Of these, three-quarters were in cottage or similarly unsuitable rooms. No detailed information has survived for particular villages, but from the few records available[8] we know at least some of the Wingrave homes used as schools. Probably in the 1850's Harriet Alcock (later Gibbs) ran a plaiting school in Nup End, "where young folks congregated in the big old kitchen, to vie with each other in the lengths of plait they could do in certain times." In 1861 Elizabeth Bateman ran a school in her home, which was one of the Pound End cottages. In 1871 Charlotte Bateman held a 'school' in one of the Chapel Street cottages. Later in the 1870's, Thomas Smith ran one from his home in Floyds Cottage in Mill Lane. The last three venues certainly suffered from the shortcomings common to most cottage rooms. They were usually less than twelve feet square, with a low ceiling little more than six feet high and, when crowded, they generally suffered from inadequate ventilation.

At plaiting school the children worked sitting in rows on stools or little benches, "packed tight as herrings in a barrel". Rooms less than twelve feet square would often have forty or more children in them. They could not plait successfully if their fingers were cold so, in winter, windows and doors were kept firmly closed to keep out all cold (and so all fresh) air. If the plait mistress regularly tried to eke out 'the smallest quantity of fire', or if the fire could not be lit because the children had to sit so close into the fireplace, then the children brought red earthenware 'dicky' pots. These were filled with hot ashes from the local baker's oven, and set on the floor, and under the girls' skirts. The air would then become extremely hot, stuffy and smelly due to the combination of fumes, overcrowding and inadequate ventilation. No wonder that pupils were often absent with coughs, colds and bronchial problems. No wonder a visitor was saddened by "the sallow little badly-fed faces resulting from the cruel necessity of child labour".

The plaiting mistress was just another villager, and quite probably illiterate. She did not provide any schooling, though a verse or two of the Bible might be chanted during the day. She did not even profess to teach plaiting. That was done by the mothers, who also supplied the straw, decided how many yards of plait the child had to complete each day, and finally sold it to the dealer. The plaiting mistress's sole job was to obtain from the children the quota of work set by their mothers, and she presided over them, often with cane in hand to remind the idler of its duty. "In several plaiting schools," an inspector reported, "I noticed formidable walking sticks which the mistresses say they are obliged to keep and sometimes to use. And I have been told that one reason why parents send their children to the plaiting school instead of allowing them to plait at home is because the mistress 'gets more work out of them' than they would do at home." [9] Of course, the greater the amount of work which the school obtained from the children, the more popular it would be with the parents, and the more crowded and unhealthy became the conditions under which the children laboured.

Fig. 10: Daily Hours at 103 Buckinghamshire Plaiting Schools [10]

Hours worked per day	Number of schools
3.5 to 5.5	6
6 to 7	73
7.5 to 9	9
9.5 to 12	6
No information	9

The children not only laboured hard; they laboured long. The younger children worked from breakfast to dinner and from dinner to tea: perhaps a total of six or seven hours. "The children just get a run to stir their legs and are at it again." However, "the big ones, those from seven years old upwards",[11] might attend night school for two or three hours more. For this the 'candle-lighters' (as they were called) paid 3d a week instead of the usual 2d. Moreover, in 1851, there was no effective national regulation and many children were said to work even longer hours. Some plaiting schools openly admitted this, as Figure 10 indicates.[12] In any case, children who did only two sessions per day at school might well find themselves working as late or later at home if they had not finished their quota of yards at school.

Some children are kept at work very late: 10, 11, or 12 p.m. You can hear them out in the street halloing and playing on a cold winter's night at nine or ten o'clock, so no doubt they have been at work all the time before. Some mothers are very brutish. Eight hours is enough for a child and they hadn't ought to do more, poor things.[13]

Harriet Alcock, who attended a Wingrave plaiting school in the 1830's, used to say:[14]

Bless me, we never used to have such easy times; I should think we didn't. Folks don't know what work is these days. We had to be up and splitting straws before daylight, ready to go to plaiting school. Yes, and old Betsy Price was a hard old missus. Didn't she make us work! 2d a week we had to pay her too. There was twenty of us boys and girls in her old kitchen every day of the week except Sundays. She was a 'tight un' she was, and when she measured up yer plait, if it were short, didn't she paste ye! The plait buyer, Old Becky, come every Friday and we sold her our plait in bundles of 10 yards. Then mother give us a ha'penny to spend, and we did think somethin' of that.

Boys left plait school as soon as more suitable employment could be found. Girls left plait school when they could 'sit tight', which meant 'work steadily without constant supervision'. This was usually at the age of thirteen or fourteen, and from then on they worked at home, sometimes for even longer hours. The lady quoted above who criticised 'brutish mothers' also volunteered, "My daughter, Mary, now 14, plaits from 9 a.m. till 10 p.m. That is about the regular thing in this place for girls of her age".[15]

THE PLAIT DEALERS

The production of straw plait took place mainly in the cottages of the 40,000 plaiters in rural Bedfordshire, Essex, Hertfordshire and mid-eastern Buckinghamshire. The production of straw hats took place mainly in the factories and workshops of Luton and Dunstable. The plait dealer was the principal means by which the plait from the rural areas reached these centres of hat production. Not that the local plait dealers all went to Luton and Dunstable. To save a long journey, they might take their loads to subsidiary markets at places like Tring, where plait was collected, but not made up. Whichever route it took, the plait was bought by plait wholesalers who combined the small loads from the villages, and sorted them into large but homogeneous 'lots', which could be 'sold on' to the hat manufacturers.

In 1846 straw plaiters in and around Aylesbury felt that the plait dealer's margin (said to be 50% to 60% on the price paid to the plaiter) was too great. Consequently, a market for plait was established in Bourbon Street, Aylesbury.[16] This enabled the local plaiters to try and sell their produce direct to the merchants. The first market was very well attended by sellers, but the merchants did not purchase so largely as expected, nor did they pay prices as high as had been expected. Eventually, the market closed.

Until her death in 1828, Rebecca Rodwell, known to everyone as 'Old Becky', called at the Wingrave straw plaiting cottages once a week, for she was a plait buyer.[17] She was a weatherbeaten old lady, with a will of iron when bargaining over prices. Plaiters cut notches a yard, and half a yard, apart in the wooden mantlepieces of their fireplaces, so that they (and Becky) could be certain that they were selling her a full score or half-score. Becky also sold bunches of prepared straws ready for splitting and plaiting during the following week. She trudged to market at Tring every Friday, taking all the plait she had collected. It would be bulky, but light in weight, and wrapped in a sheet. She would join the plaiters and dealers lining the street in front of the church. At nine o'clock a bell was rung to officially open the trading, which lasted for two hours. Hat dealers from Dunstable and Luton would haggle with her over quality and price, when taking delivery of plait that they had ordered in advance. An inspector patrolled the market, measuring sample scores with his yardstick. If a sample proved short in length, it was assumed that the rest of the bundle was short, and a reduction was made in the sale price.

In 1851 James Kirby was Wingrave's plait dealer. He lived on the corner of Nup End, opposite George Snelling's old malting. His home, which still exists, was known as The Laurels. At this time he and his wife Ann had three daughters, of whom Mary

16.　*The Fleet family in their Sunday best. Their apparent affluence was hard-earned: see, for example, Will Fleet page 269. From left to right they are (standing) Rosa Fleet, Mary Coleman (nee Fleet), 'Jack' Coleman, Joe Fleet, Will Fleet, Jim Fleet, Sarah Ann Fleet (see page 45), (seated) George Fleet, Sarah Fleet (nee Jarrott), Emily Fleet.*

17.　*James Kirby, the Wingrave plait buyer, dealt with Gray and Horn for many years.*

Ann, the eldest, was a strawplaiter. Ten years later he was also running a small shop from his home and his family had increased to seven children, of whom six were girls. Mary Ann was now a bonnet sewer, while all five sisters were straw plaiters. James was still dealing in straw plait in 1881, by which time he was a "venerable old man with a white beard, and a snowy fringe surrounding a very bald pate".[18] Mary Ann looked after the shop, which sold drapery, sweetstuff and groceries. In fact, "James and his daughter combined the various branches of the business, and many a plaiter worked out her liabilities to Mary Ann for dress materials, shirts and so on by selling tens of plait to James",[19] which was not a strong bargaining position for the customer. By 1891 James had retired, and was living comfortably on his savings, and the rents from his properties.

18: Thomas and Phoebe Mead

In the 1880's, besides James Kirby, three other plait dealers called at houses in the village: one from Aston Abbotts; an old lady from Long Marston; and Thomas Mead of Wingrave. Thomas was recorded in the census as a plait dealer, although his main occupation had been listed as 'baker' for the previous twenty years. He lived in Nup End in a pretty thatched cottage now known as Mollards. After visiting the strawplaiting cottages in their own and the neighbouring villages, the dealers would pile their horse-drawn traps high with bundles of plait, and jog off to the Monday market at Luton. We know that James Kirby regularly dealt with the wholesalers Gray and Horn for his name appears in Henry Horn's[20] account book. The wide variety of plait on offer is clear from the picture of their stand at Luton market. Luton was the mecca of all plait buyers, and the centre of the hat-making trade. The busiest season was the summer, and it was the ambition of many a plaiter to travel to Luton and learn to make hats. In her youth Hilda Roberts' mother attained this ambition, and worked there for two successive seasons as a 'finisher'. That explained why, every summer, she was able to make out of 'one-pearl', a straw hat for her husband to wear in the hot weather, and sometimes one for her daughter. As a child, Hilda often played with the chalky-looking 'blocks' upon which her mother shaped the hats.[21]

THE DECLINE OF STRAW-PLAITING

The Factory and Workshops Act of 1867 prohibited the employment of children under eight years, and restricted the employment of those between 8 and 13. This made life difficult for the plaiting schools, while the Education Act of 1880, by establishing compulsory education to the age of ten, made it impossible. Another equally important threat to this cottage industry occurred during the 1870's, when cheap imports of strawplait from China (and later Japan) flooded the English market, forcing down prices dramatically and making it impossible to earn a living wage. In 1894 it was estimated that English plait cost six times as much as Chinese. Moreover, Chinese plait was sixty yards long, and so far more suitable for the sewing machines, recently used in hat and bonnet manufacture. Women continued to plait, but when they gave up or died, there were few trained workers to replace them. By 1891 women would plait endlessly all week, and then receive but a shilling or two. Many turned to domestic service, and strawplaiting became the occupation of the elderly. In 1891 there were only 59 strawplaiters left in Wingrave. By 1901 there were only 176 in the whole of Buckinghamshire. Rebecca Bignell (nee Humphrey) of Wingrave was one of them. In her later years, she lived in one of the cottages in Leighton Road. Her granddaughter, the late Connie Bignell, remembers her busily plaiting with straws protruding from her mouth. Rebecca was also a hat and bonnet sewer, which many considered a step up in the trade. Connie's mother, Sarah Ann Fleet, helped, "for she was ever so good at sewing." Haberdashery needed for the hats, such as ribbons, cottons and tape, was bought from Mrs Gurney on Winslow Road, where she kept a little shop in her front room. Every year Rebecca would buy a new hat block at Luton, for it was important to keep up with the latest fashions. Connie's mother was always the first to model the latest style that Rebecca produced, wearing it everywhere for villagers to view. Soon orders would pour in. There would be a knock at the back door, and the caller would place her order, specifying variations, such as the colour of ribbons.

In 1926 Hilda Roberts wrote a play called Becky Roddell's Business and produced it with, and for, members of Wingrave Women's Institute. It was based on her own recollections and those of elderly villagers, who at eighty years and above could remember distinctly 'the good old days'. By this date strawplaiting had so declined that it was quite a novelty to see a person doing it.

19. The cast of Becky Roddell's Business after its first performance. From left to right: Kath Alcock, Kate Rickard, Doris Hows, Hilda Roberts, Mrs Johansson and Polly Fleet.

Becky Roddell's Business

by Hilda Roberts

This sketch, depicting life in Wingrave in 1850, was
first performed in The Temperance Hall, Wingrave in July 1926 by the
members of the Wingrave Women's Institute named below.

The Characters
Becky Roddell (a straw plait buyer): Mrs P. Rickard
Jemima Burnham (a straw plaiting schoolmistress): Mrs H. Roberts
Lizzie Smith (another straw plaiting schoolmistress): Mrs W. Fleet
Rachel Burnham (a young lady with ideas above her station): Miss D. Hows
Charles Arnold (a village lad in love with Rachel): Miss K. Rickard
Mrs Scott (the squire's wife): Mrs N. Johannson

The action of the play takes place in a cottage living-room furnished with an old gate-leg table and wheel-back chairs. On the walls hang a warming-pan and some old-fashioned prints.

SCENE ONE: Jemima sits plaiting, when Lizzie (her friend and neighbour) calls.

Lizzie: I've jest popped in to see if you've got a pinch of straws to lend us till Becky comes tomorrow. I've got run out and I do want to finish that score of two pearl she set us to do, else she'll be that awkward. Besides, I wants the money bad. Our young Jim must have a new smock this week and Druces wunt let ye have nothing now without ye pay down two shillin's.

Jemima: I ain't got no straws to lend ye. Them dratted candlelighters takes all mine up, they wastes 'em so. I've got a baker's dozen on 'em coming here every day and it takes all me blessed wits to keep upsides with 'em. I'd never be bothered with 'em if I could afford to do without the 'apence, but tuppence a week's a good bit to lose, 'specially when there's a dozen on 'em. And I can't find my yardstick nowhere. I expects them tiresome lads 'as 'id it agin. I found my last one in bits up the copper hole. Sit down Betsy, and take a pinch of snuff.

Lizzie: Well, I dunno as I won't. I've got me plait under me arm, and me plaiters wunt be back for an hour. They comes back at 2 o'clock. I <u>must</u> have a few minutes to me-self. Goodness knows, I don't get many.

Jemima: Well, what do ye think to the news then? Don't say as ye ain't heard? Becky told us last week. She heard up at Tring market a Friday as there's a new sort of plait out at Luton. I dunno if I got the name right. 'Brilliant' I think she called it. She showed me a pattern. Them as learn it'll soon get rich for it's four shillin' a score.

Lizzie: That's too good to be true, my gel. Don't you get that into your head. Give us another sniff, will ye? When's Becky going to bring us a sample? Course, you and me'll soon learn it if anybody can. Bin a plaiting every day for nigh on fifty year bar Sundays. If anybody knows what a bit o' plait is, we do, Jemima.

Jemima: That's true. You see as I don't learn my candle-lighters to do it. Ye know, Betsy, that there gel o' mines a reg'lar worrit to me. She won't settle her mind to plaiting. I've hammered her, and kep her short and coaxed her, but 'taint no good. She gets her high notions from her father's side. All on 'em is a bit ikey. Never would let folks see them a'plaiting. She says she'll go out in service in a town and wants to learn reading and writing if you please, as if she was the squire's daughter! I told her she'll be struck or somat if she flies in the face o' Providence like that. Why, she can do a couple of yards of whipcord in an hour if she sits tight. A score a day comes to nigh on five shillin' a week, an' I keep her for four shillin', so she'd have heaps to spend. And young Charlie Arnold as comes 'ere for plaitin' is awful sweet on her. He'd take her to the Michelmas Fair if she'd go. He brought her a whole ounce of acid drops last week. He's well off. He earns nearly fourteen shillin' a week. I knows, cos I measures his plait. And I guess he's saved up a bit. But she won't look at him.

Lizzie: Good gracious woman, you're too easy wi' the young hussey. I'd put her through it if she was mine. Fancy her turning up her nose at a clever young chap like Charlie Arnold. Why, he's well off! Earns near double what his father earns, for he only gets seven shillin' a week, and works Sundays, every fortnight. Course, he gets a pitcher of buttermilk twice a week and a bason o' milk for breakfast every day, but he's got eight children besides Charlie. Course, I knows they all plaits, poor things!

Enter Rachel

Rachel: Oh Ma! Can I go out for a walk a little while? I've washed up the dishes and put on the kettle. I do want a little fresh air.

Lizzie: Fresh air be bothered! If you was my gel I'd put you through it me lady, with yer airs and graces princing about. Why can't you sit down and earn yer livin' like other gels, 'stead of gallivanting about the lanes? It's lucky for you as you ain't my gel.

Rachel: Yes, it is lucky I ain't yourn. I wouldn't own such a disagreeable old frump for a mother, and I'm not going to twiddle straws for ever and ever and gossip all day long, and pick decent folks to pieces to earn my living. I've got ideas, I have, and I shan't be content till I've got up in the world, above the ways of this village, anyway.

Jemima: Now, Rachel, my child, for goodness sake don't begin argyfying wi' Mrs Smith. You can go out for ten minutes, but mind you don't go talkin' to any boys. And just you be back to the minute.

Exit Rachel

Lizzie: Well, of all the soft loonies, you're the worst as ever I see. Do you think as I'd ever be messed up like that with a gel her age? Why she ain't but sixteen is she? And she's a fair missus o' you. My word I'd show her the way.

Jemima: It's all very well for you to talk, Lizzie, but you ain't got an extra-sperior girl like our Rachel to deal with. My man says she takes after his father's eldest sister's husband. He was a real gentleman. He kept a toll-gate. He must a bin a wonderful scholar to do that else he couldn't a done it.

Lizzie: Stuff and rubbish. She's too proud to work. That's all as ails her. Laws-a-massey, it's two o'clock. My house ull be full and no plait done. Yesterday I couldn't find a stick all day long so I had to hit 'em with me 'ands. I got two ready for today and blow me if they ain't gone again. Becky ull be coming in the morning so we shall be hearing all about that new plait.

SCENE TWO: Enter Becky, an elderly woman with a black bag over her shoulder.

Becky: Laws, ain't it hot! My old legs nearly said, "No". They just wouldn't go this morning. How many straws do you want? The plait's sunk this week: only 8d a score. And you must do it better. The buyers grumbled somat dreadful about it last week. And the measure were short. You stretches it so, then it goes back again. Five score, that's 40 pence. Three bunches of straw at 4d is twelve pence off. That's 28d. Laws, some folks does earn money easy!

Jemima: I reckons it's you as earn the money easy. 'T ain't us poor plaiters. You gets so much profit.

Lizzie looks in at the door.

Lizzie: 'As Becky got here?

Jemima: Yes. Come in.

Lizzie: I've brought me little bit of two pearl. Only six score. Ain't much, but it's beautiful work.

Becky: Somat's afresh if yourn's beautiful work. Plait's sunk to eight pence. Yourn ain't worth but seven pence anytime. Coarse stuff it is to make the best on it. I don't care whether I has it or not.

Lizzie: Well, of all the cheek. You needn't have it. Stranks of Aston ull buy it and be glad to pay me the right price, so give it me back.

Becky: Come now, don't get huffy. You knows it ain't good stuff, but I'll give eight pence. Trade's very bad though. It's all through them free traders. Now they're sending tons and tons of foreign plait and even hats over from foreign parts and folks are wearing 'em. It makes me blood run cold to think about it. Here I've tramped from Marston to Tring and all round this forty year, and earnt an honest living and now it gets worse every week.

Jemima: What about that new stuff you told us about?

Lizzie: Oh! That's called Brilliant. I don't think you could learn to do it, but I heard tell as Stranks of Aston had somebody down from Luton to learn folks. It's good pay. Four shillin' a score, but it takes an awful lot o' straw and time when you've learnt it. Here's the pattern.

Lizzie: If other folks can do it, I'm sure me and Jemima can. We've plaited miles and miles this twenty years. We'll go and see Mr Stranks.

Becky: Well, I shan't buy it, so ye needn't think I shall. I've got enough to try my temper now. If ye larnt to do yer work well, it would be more to yer credit. I'll bid ye good-day till next week.

Exit Becky. Re-enter Rachel.

Rachel: Oh, ma! I have got some news for you. I've got meself a place. I just met the squire's lady. She said, "Rachel, I hear you want to go into service. I've always thought you a superior girl (that's what she said, ma), and I have a friend who will take you. She lives in Luton, so you'll see a town at last. There's only her husband and herself, and a son away at boarding school. You will have your board and five shillings a month." Now ma, isn't that grand? I said, "Yes" at once, and I'm going the day after tomorrow.

Betsy: Good riddance to bad rubbish, I say. Your high notions ull land you somewhere, me lady, afore you've done. You'll be struck wi' the palsy or somat for yer wickedness.

Rachel: You'll see, I shall come back a lady one day, Lizzie.

Lizzie: Lady! Fiddle-de-dee! I ain't got no patience wi' you.

Jemima: Its a good thing I've got four other children as is good comfortin' children. One bad un is quite enough in a family. But you've made yer bed, so you must lie on it. I suppose I must be getting yer things together and start washing. I shall have to leave me school to themselves today and won't there be some scrummages. I'd better get me long stick ready.

SCENE THREE: Several years later. There is a knock on the door.

Jemima: Come in.

Squire's Lady: Is Mrs Burnham in?

Jemima: Yes, come in.

Enter Squire's lady

Jemima: Oh! I'm ever so sorry, me lady! I really thought it was Lizzie Smith a knocking abut on the door jest to hinder me. (Wipes the seat of a chair with her apron) Won't you take a seat, ma'am?

Lady: Thank you. I have come to tell you some very grave news, Mrs Burnham.

Jemima: Grave news! Laws! I hope nobody ain't bin buried alive. What grave news is it, ma'am?

Lady: Well, it's very serious. You know your daughter Rachel has been living for a long time now with my friends, the Georges, at Luton. It was entirely through my recommendation that she was taken on, so I feel it very bitterly.

Jemima: Good Laws, ma 'am, whatever is the matter? I had a letter from my Rachel only last week. Wrote ever so grand, all her ownself too. She always wanted to learn and it seems she's quite clever at it. She said the young master was very kind to her, and he had learnt her to read and write. I got the man up at the post office to read me the letter.

Lady: Yes, that's the worst part of it. She has abused the kindness of my friends. I have had a letter today to say that young master Tom has gone away and married your daughter Rachel and then had the sauce to bring her home as his wife. His mother and father are furious. They liked Rachel, and tried to improve her, but Tom is their only son. They are having to make the best of it, and are thinking of fixing them up in a business and a home of their own. Luckily the Georges are very well off.

Jemima: There! I always said our Rachel was cut out for a lady, and now her dreams 'as come true. I've never seen her since she went away. Luton is such a long journey, and I couldn't afford to go, but no doubt she'll write and tell me all about it. The postman as is writing the music about Samuel said as he read her letter that she were a good singer, and he always thought she'd make her way in the world.

Lady: That's all very well, but she had no business to 'make her way' through the kindness of my friends. Fancy the daughter of a farm labourer married to the son of my friends. Its preposterous! He'll eventually come into a large inheritance.

Jemima: Call it what you like. 'T won't alter it now the knot's tied. I do hope as he's alright. I did hear once as he was a bit wild.

Lady: Tom George is a gentleman and he must have been led away by your designing daughter, and I shall never forgive myself for ever recommending her to them. I am terribly upset about it.

Jemima: Bless yer soul, don't you worrit yerself about that. They'll be alright. If he's got plenty of money, Rachel will help him to spend it. Now I'd be much obliged if you'd go, ma'am, as me plaiting scholars will be in jest now. And don't you be worriting. I'm sure I shan't. Good day.

SCENE FOUR: 35 years have elapsed, and the room has been slightly modernised. Enter Charlie Arnold.

Charlie: Good day, Mrs Burnham.

Jemima: Good day, sir. And who might you be?

Charlie: Don't you remember Charlie Arnold, who used to come to your plaiting school, and crack up all your sticks, and hide them up the copper hole? Didn't you make us work! And didn't you paste us. I never forgot you, or your daughter Rachel. Where is she now?

Jemima: Well, well! To think as a fine gentleman like you 'as growed out of Charlie Arnold. And where have you been all these years? You'll find the old place looks different now. Yes, times is altered. I expect you be married, and got a growed-up family now.

Charlie: No, I've never married. I've been out in Australia for thirty years and struck lucky. I'm only middle-aged now and I needn't worry about work any more. You didn't answer my question about Rachel.

Jemima: Oh, Rachel's alright. Course, she always did want to be different from other village gels, so she went into service in Luton. She married a man who was well-off, she learnt to do the hat work, and they done ever so well. But she's a widow now, and has come back to Wingrave to live. I expect her to see me today. An' here she is. Coming up the path now, bless her. (Enter Rachel) Here's a big surprise waiting for you, my girl. Do you know who this is?

Exit Jemima to fetch Lizzie

Charlie: How are you, Rachel? Surely you haven't forgotten your old admirer.

Rachel: Why, of all the wonders in the world, it's Charlie Arnold. I thought you were farming out there in Australia and getting rich and famous.

Charlie: I've only just returned home and came here to find out what had happened to you. I'm rich, but there are no riches that I value so much as a smile from you, Rachel. There never has been anyone else that mattered. Don't you think I deserve a reward for all these years of waiting. I've enough money for the two of us, and if you're willing, my dear, don't let's wait any longer.

Rachel: You nearly take my breath away. Have you really waited all this time? Yes, you certainly deserve your reward, Charlie. I've never forgotten you. It shall be as soon as you wish, Charlie.

Charlie embraces Rachel, just as Jemima and Lizzie enter the room.

Lizzie: Well, if these two ain't a sweethearting!

Charlie: Yes. Wish us well. We are going to be married by special licence tomorrow.

Lizzie: Good laws a massey, that's quick work.

Charlie: Perhaps, but it's taken thirty years to do it.

Lizzie: Well, good luck to ye both. I'm 82 tomorrow, and ain't I seen some changes. I remembers the first bicycle in the village, what Joey Bonham had: a penny ha'penny they called it. And now-a-days lots of folks don't even know how to plait. And much good it does them if they do, wi' prices for plait as down as they are. Poor old Becky's passed on, and old James Kirby's talkin' o' givin' up. Soon there won't be such a thing as a plait buyer. Some folks even say that straw'll go out of fashion.

Jemima: Well, here's me snuff box, Lizzie. That'll never be out of fashion.

Lizzie: Well then, let's have a pinch afore I goes ...

Curtain

20. The Town Pond in 1906 showing (foreground and far left) its two entrances, which enabled carts to be driven through to clean their wheels, or draw water. On the far side of the pond are (left) part of Manor Farm and (right) the old Vicarage.

Chapter Five

Looking For A Better Life

Chapter 3 described attempts to solve the problems of poverty and pauperism. This chapter looks at two other potential solutions: emigration and trade unionism.

MIGRATION AND EMIGRATION

The small market towns surrounding Wingrave (such as Aylesbury, Buckingham, Leighton Buzzard and Tring) were typical of the South of England, in their lack of substantial industries, like textiles or steel, which could absorb the surplus labour of the villages. So migration within Britain meant moving to London, or the industrial areas of the Midlands and the North. Wingrave Vestry could (and occasionally did) support this internal migration, as in 1835, when:[1]

Thomas Gurney and John Humphrey applied for assistance to go out of the parish to work and it was agreed to lend them a loan of twelve shillings, and if they don't return to the parish of Wingrave again for the space of twelve months they are to have it as a present, but if they return before the expiration of the said twelve months the money to be refunded back again to the overseers.

No records of other cases have been discovered, but William Cox, a long-term resident of Wingrave, assured a parliamentary enquiry that many labourers from Aylesury Vale had migrated to the manufacturing districts.[2]

The alternative was to emigrate to the U.S.A. or the colonies. Between 1815 and 1914 nearly seventeen million people left the United Kingdom. In just twenty months (March 1873 to October 1874) 7,831 people are said to have left the Aylesbury area, including many from the Vale villages. Moreover, large-scale emigration had been proceeding for at least forty years. Robert Gibbs, a local historian, noted that large numbers of people began to leave Buckinghamshire in the 1830's:[3]

In May 1830 a hundred paupers, including men, women and children, left Bicester for North America. They were preceded by a band of music, which played them out of town. The Aylesbury folk ring the church bells when they build a bigger workhouse, and the Bicester folk blow trumpets when a hundred of their neighbours emigrate to avoid starvation at home.

In April 1832 eighty emigrants embarked at Aylesbury Wharf Yard intending to go to the U.S.. These folks were stowed away in Mrs England's boats and dragged up the canal at the rate of two miles an hour, and in this or some other as miserable a style have to make their way to Liverpool. There is hardly a district in the county of Bucks in which families are not packing up, their intention being to emigrate this Spring to the U.S. or one of the colonies.

It is impossible to obtain precise figures for emigration from particular villages. So far only seventy-five Wingrave emigrants have been identified, but the true figure is undoubtedly much larger. On some emigrant ships the passenger list did not mention the place of origin. Even if it did, the lists are often scattered among the numerous ports of arrival, if indeed they have survived at all.

The earliest record of emigration from Wingrave in the 19th century was in the 1830's, when Edward Needham Paine went to Cincinnati in the U.S.A. The problem was that few could afford the cost of emigration. Although, as early as 1834, the Wingrave Vestry had had the power to increase the poor rate so as to assist emigrants, there is no evidence in the minutes of any action until twelve years later. This omission is understandable. The members of the Vestry were mostly farmers, and farmers paid the largest poor rates. If they subsidised emigration, their rates would be even higher. And their wages bill would also rise, for emigration would reduce the number of men competing for jobs on farms. So it is 1846 before we read in the Vestry minutes:[4]

Agree to pay £19-15s-0d from the poor rate for the emigration of Ephraim Bonham and Elizabeth his wife, and £11-0s-0d for William Bateman, his wife and family.

Then, perhaps realising the financial implications if such generosity became the norm, the Vestry had second thoughts. In December 1847 it called a meeting in Wingrave Church, which imposed an overall annual limit of £30 for the assistance of poor persons wishing to emigrate. In January 1849, on further reflection, it reduced assistance to £1 per adult and ten shillings per child under 14 years. Fortunately, by this time the government was also encouraging emigration by offering free passages. Between 1845 and 1857 this more realistic support saw at least forty-two people leave Wingrave: ten to the U.S.A., and the rest to Australia.

EMIGRATION TO AUSTRALIA AND THE CAPE OF GOOD HOPE

Free passages to New South Wales, South Australia, and the Cape of Good Hope are granted by Her Majesty's Colonial Land and Emigration Commissioners, in First Class Ships sailing at short intervals in succession during the year, to a limited number of Persons, strictly of the Working Classes. The emigrants most in request are Agricultural Labourers, Shepherds, and Female Domestic Servants, and Dairymaids. A few country mechanics, such as Blacksmiths, Wheelwrights, Carpenters are taken for each Ship. At the date of the last advices, the demand for labour was urgent, and the wages considerably higher than in England. On the other hand, Provisions were at a much lower rate. Clothing was about the same price as in this Country.

Such advertisements appeared regularly in the local press, as did articles about emigration, and letters from successful emigrants. Letters arrived in Wingrave from relatives who had emigrated, asking to be remembered to friends and neighbours. Prospective emigrants announced their plans. All this must have generated endless discussion in the homes and inns of Wingrave. The young and healthy, unemployed but ambitious, determined and eager to work would point to local poverty, and the emigrant's opportunity for a better life. Their feelings were summed up by an emigrant from Wingrave, who tried unsuccessfully to persuade a friend to join him in Australia.[5]

My Ever Dear Frend
I now write these few line to let you know that we are safe Arrived at sydney And a most beutful contery that ever was seen. my Dear Isebela never stop in that Lousey cuntery and se yourself starve. com to sydney my Dear were we can save a litel money to keep

us when we get in years with out beolding to aney body and this is the place ware we could Do it. If you can com Do com for it is a place ware you could hurn more money then I could. A good cutter out in the Dres making can have aney money thay like to ask for in thear work. I am satesfide that you will never Repent coming to sydney.
I remain your Ever Dear frend and well wisher,
Charles Paine

Other villagers would put the contrary viewpoint quoting such things as the Bucks Herald's 'Hints for the Voyage', which included the following:

Let nothing be loose; in a short time all will be subjected to pitching, rolling, going first on one side then on another. Expect to be sea sick, and to wonder what could have induced you to leave the shore, and all its comforts.

They would also point out what the emigrants themselves reported in their letters back home: that emigration meant tearing up one's roots and very probably saying farewell for ever to one's family and friends, and to the village which had been one's home; that it meant a long and perilous sea voyage; and that there was only a small chance of return. Doubtless, it would also occur to those remaining behind that the greater the number of emigrants, the smaller would be the competition for each vacant job in Wingrave!

SOME WINGRAVE EMIGRANTS TO AUSTRALIA

Joseph and Frances Humphrey [6]

Joseph Humphrey was described as a labourer, which almost certainly meant an agricultural labourer, though later he claimed to be a carpenter. In 1842 he married Frances Radwell at Wingrave Parish Church. He was 19 and she was 18. Five years later, with their two young children, they left London in the sailing-ship 'Cressey' bound for Australia. Only four years earlier, on its maiden voyage, the ship had transported convicts to Tasmania, so it certainly offered no luxuries for the 278 emigrants on a free passage to Adelaide. The journey lasted 97 days nonstop. Elizabeth, their daughter, died on the voyage, and was buried at sea.

Joseph and Frances settled on land at Gawler River near Adelaide, where they were joined by his brothers George and Henry and their families. They kept cattle and grew wheat, but their crops suffered from a series of droughts. Consequently when gold was discovered at Ballarat about five hundred miles away in the state of Victoria, the brothers decided to try their

21: Joseph and Frances Humphrey

luck in the goldfields. They left their families behind, to look after the cows, the milk from which provided their only income. The gold-digging must have been reasonably successful, for two years later the brothers returned to Adelaide, sold their holdings and packed a horse-drawn waggon with their possessions and supplies for the long journey back to Ballarat. En route they lived off the land whenever possible, thanks to an old muzzle-loading shotgun. They were within fifty miles of Ballarat when Joseph's eight-year-old son William died, and had to be buried by the wayside in a bark coffin.

During the late 1850's the three families prospected for gold at Ballarat, and later at such places as Maryborough, Avoca and Amhurst. It was a very difficult life: living in tents, cooking in camp ovens and washing in creeks. Granny Humphrey (as Frances was known to the family) claimed that she let her daughter Rhoda marry at the age of fifteen years, because her prospective husband, Luke, "was a good honest man, and there weren't many good men around, as there were all sorts of people around the diggings." Throughout this time, Frances was giving birth on average every 26 months, the final total being nine boys and five girls, of whom at least ten survived.

By the early 1860's Joseph and his family had reached the small settlement of Barkly in Victoria, where Joseph bought twenty acres of land and named it 'Aylesbury'. Apparently he turned to carpentry as well as returning to farming, for legend has it that in 1865/6 he helped to build Barkly's first school. Joseph died in 1895 aged 73. Frances lived for another thirty years. She died in 1926 aged 103. By that time she had over three hundred descendants!

The Paine Family: Letters from Australia[7]

In 1984 fifty letters were found at the bottom of an old trunk, which had once belonged to William Stevens Paine and his wife Sarah. William was parish clerk of Wingrave for over forty years. He, his wife and six children were all literate, and the letters, dating mostly from 1849 to 1862, were written by four of their children who had emigrated to Sydney in 1849, 1854 and 1857. Pink ribbon neatly secured them, and a cigar box protected them, clear indications that the letters were treasured mementoes of their long-departed children.

Their youngest daughter, Lucy, together with John Marks, her husband of three weeks, and her brother Charles, sailed from Gravesend in January 1849. When Lucy wrote from Plymouth, the last stop before leaving England, her thoughts were clearly still back in Wingrave. Having covered 350 miles to Plymouth she was already tired of the ship. Charles had been assured by the sailors that "the dainger is All hover now we are got to Plimith", so Lucy was probably unaware that New South Wales was over three months and thirteen thousand miles of open sea ahead.

Dear Mother and Father,   *Plimith: February 1849*
*   we Arrived At Plimeth this Morning Thursday . . . I shall be very glad when we leave the ship for I am tired of it All reddy. I don't know how I shall be before I get their . . . Our Birth is Six foot long and four wide so we are not Scrunged up very much . . . . Dear Mother I am very sorry I am come Away without My Dol but I shall be Much Abliged to you to take care of it till I come Back Again, give my love to All inquiren Frends and Except the same your self. From your Effectinate son and Daughter J and L Marks*

Dear Mother   *Sydney   July 1849*
We have arived At Sydney quite safe and we had A very plesent Passage over. I

wethered it out as well as any of them on board. I was sick two or three times But never kept my bed at all . . . . their was some of the People never went on Deck from one Weeks end to Another and some of them was sick All the voige out. We had Seven Births and seven Deaths on Board the Agenoria. We got in to the Sydney Arbour the 25 of May and went A sure on the 7 of June. Dear Mother I often wish I could see your poor hold face once Again But Never mind I shall live in hope yet. please to send me word wether Mr and Mrs Lucas is Inquired After Me since I have left home and tell me wether Harriot as left their or not and give My love to her. I often wish I was with her. Dear Mother I must Now conclude With Hour Kind Loves to You All.
from your Loving and Effectionate Daughter   Lucy Ann Marks

Life in Australia was very different to life in Wingrave, and things did not work out quite as the publicity had promised. It took John five weeks to find a job, which clearly upset him, for Lucy observed, "I have often wished his sister was hear to see him when he was out of Work for I always tell him it was his friends as persuaded him to come out hear. I shall not persuade anybody to come here at present". The job was in a bakery, and at twelve shillings per week plus board the wages were rather better than in Wingrave. However, he had to live on the premises, while Lucy lodged with friends: "our messmates as we messed with on the ship". For employers certainly wanted their pound of flesh, "It is killing work. John begins at ten at night and has not done till five the next afternoon." Eighteen months later Lucy writes, "John has his health so bad that he is leaving and we are going to the Cuntrey."

No-one had warned them that the Australian countryside was totally different to that around Wingrave. "Tell father we cannot say how high the trees grow for we have not seen any yet for it is all bushes and rocks", wrote a surprised Lucy. Eventually, at a place called Pollocks Flat, John got a job shepherding for £27 per year and rations. Convinced that "we will be able to save more money here than in Sydney", John extended his contract for two more years, by which time he was getting £42 per year and rations: a fortune in Wingrave! There were certainly plenty of sheep – his master had 30 to 40 thousand – but very little else. In Wingrave, just to venture out-of-doors was to encounter people (relations, friends, and lots of well-known neighbours), most of them delighted to exchange the latest gossip, whereas personal encounters were rare at Pollacks Flat, as Lucy explained.

Me and my Lisey (her first daughter) are at home all day by ourselves. We are living about 14 miles from the head (sheep) station, and so there are few comers and goers. The Master or one of the Overseers may pay us a visit about once in five or six months, and about once a month a Man may come with a Pack Horse and bring our rations. And perhaps that Man may be a Black Fellow and I can not understand half of what he says, so that I can pick up no news or Idle gossip of the day to Amuse you with. Nor do I think you would be mutch amused if I did. But between the Children and my little household affairs I can keep myself busy from morn till night.

However, isolation had definite snags. Whereas Wingrave's expectant mothers could rely upon the availability of local midwives, with the back-up of a doctor only six miles away, care was much more limited in the Australian bush, as Lucy discovered during her second confinement.

The pain in my back kept getting worse all night and John got up to fetch the Woman (midwife). It was moonlight, or he would not have been able to travel the Bush in the

22. From top left clockwise: William Stevens Paine, Mark Paine, Lucy Marks (nee Paine), John Marks.

dark. He had not been (gone) An houre before it was all over. But I could not help laughing when the baby was comming on. The girl (keeping her company) was frightoned and ran Away and sent in the Man and so I had A man Midwife. But, thank God it was soon over. I have got her Name Mary Ann but their is no Church or Chapple up in the Bush to get them Crissened.

Solitude also gave Lucy time to think about Wingrave. It all floods out when she writes, and it does not diminish as the years roll by. She is always asking for things to be sent out: newspapers; recipes for catsup and ginger beer; and even a pair of Aylesbury ducks. Four years after reaching Australia she is still pining for the doll which she forgot to take with her. She is especially delighted with a letter from her sister, Eliza Stevens Smith.

I can assure you I am not A little proud of the kepesake my little Nephews and Nieces sent me. I mean the little lock of Hair from each of them. If I cannot see them, I have at least something to remind me of them, and in return my little ones have each sent A lock of theirs.

Above all Lucy wants news, and long letters get a particularly warm welcome.

Dear Mother   *1856*
You said Susanna Roberts was going to be Married, I should like to know how her Sister charlote is getting on and whether she is Married yet or not. Please send me word how my Uncle Gurney and family are getting on, in fact I love to hear how all my old friends and acquaintances, playmates, schoolmates, etc., are getting on and give my love to them all . . . .You sent me a reciept for making Ginger Beer, and told me the exact quantities of everything except the Ginger. But perhaps you have learnt how to make Ginger Beer without any Ginger. If so, you deserve somthing handsome for the invention . . . .

Her brother, Mark, when he emigrated in 1857, was similarly anxious for news.

Dear Father and Mother,   *1860*
I sit down to write you a few More lines which I hope will find you both in good health and all My Relations and friends as thank god it Leaves us at Presant. Tell them that I was Often thinking of them when they was in bed and asleep. I was sorry to hear of so much sickness and so many deaths in your little village. I take it verry unkind of my young Friends and Companions as I never receive one line from none of them. I would love to hear news from friends, if one Cannot find Enough to fill a sheet of paper, then let all have a hand in it. then I should have a meddley. one may say something about a cricket Match, others about some Feast, another about some sweethearting which would suit me as well as anything. I am getting out of Practice now as it is not a common thing to see a thoroughbred English girl.

Fortunately for the emigrant Paines, their parents were literate and did their best to satisfy the demand for news, as Lucy acknowledged in an earlier letter.

My Dear Father,
I was not A little Proud of your Letter. Why it was quite A Little News Paper. I think it should be called the Wingrave Herrald . . . . Pray inform me in your next, who the Mrs Joseph Lucas is, whom you say you consigned the flower seeds I sent you to the care of And there is another name or too you mention in your letter that are strangers to me Mrs Butt and Mrs Catt of Brighton. I am glad to hear you are Able to get A days work

58

now and then at cooking, every little helps. am glad you had such good luck cooking the Dinner at the Ploughing match. I should like to have had a few of the ods and ends, in the shape of A few Pies and tarts. wee are quite out of the way of fruit were wee are living . . .I cannot do as I used to do, go and pluck the fruit from the trees in the garden when I feel inclined. That is one bad thing in this collonoy. People are not sure of remaining long in one place. So they seldom think of putting A Garden in proper trim.

As the years pass, Lucy and Mark show increasing concern for their parents, who are having financial as well as health problems.

I am afraid, dear Mother, that you are hard set to get along comfortably, if my father has nothing but his clerkship to depend on. for I know that is not much. If £5 or £10 will be of any service to you I will try and persuade John to send to you in the course of a few months. (Lucy: 1855)

Dear Father, I don't blame you for selling the garden, nor shall I if you sell Winshill if you make a good price. Sell anything else rather than be destitute, but I am glad you have paid the lease on Twelve Leys. That is the only thing I shall care about if I come home again which won't be long if I am spared and have good luck. I hope I shall be with you in your last days. (Mark: 1859)

For the agricultural labourer in Wingrave there was still no rainbow at the end of a yellow-brick road. The church offered the only ray of hope for the future, but that was not available until you were six feet under. Whereas, in Australia there always seemed to be an infinity of opportunity provided you were prepared to work and to move around. As Lucy put it, in 1855:

one good thing in this Colony there is no fear of going with a hungry belly. any man with ever so large A Family, if he likes to work, may all ways get a belly ful for him self and them and plenty of clothing and save a few Pounds in the bargain

Eventually, all the Marks and Paines joined in the gold rush, trying their luck at Maitland Bar, one of several diggings in the district around the settlement of Mudgee, about 200 miles inland from Sydney. By 1857, after an interval of nine years, all the Paine emigrants were together: Lucy (nee Paine), her husband John Marks and their five children; Charles Paine and his wife Ann; Edward Paine, his wife Sarah and their two children; and Mark Paine, the last to reach Australia (in 1857). They all arrived at different times, and for some it was a journey they would never forget. Thus Lucy had hired a dray to take her family of five, including a month-old baby, to Maitland Bar. Torrential rains made it a hazardous and miserable journey.

Saturday night we Slept under the dray and watter was running over and under us. My bed close and clothing was all wet through. I had the Children to wash and dress out in the cold, and even Baby.

Mark took the train and a coach part of the way, but then completed the journey on foot, walking over a hundred miles in five days.

I had a heavy swag. I was shoulder and foot sore. If I sat down for a few minuits I could scarcely walk . . . . When I arrived, I was not able to do anything for the first three weeks, for I could not put my shoes on through so much walking. I was oblidged to have the doctor and he lanced my foot.

After twenty unsuccessful months, Edward left to rent 35 acres of land two miles from Mudgee, a town serving the local gold fields. Edward's land was woodland and had to be cleared before it could be cultivated. Mark moved to Mudgee and joined up with Edward, who persuaded him to stick to farming rather than join the latest abortive gold rush at Port Curtis. Charles' business supplying meat, milk and stores for the gold diggers did well at first, but he over-extended himself by taking over a similar business in Mudgee. The expenses were too great. "That business has ruined him," wrote Mark, "and I am doubtful if he gets over it very soon". Lucy and John had also moved to Mudgee, where John worked for Charles until his business failed. Eventually they returned to the lonely life of shepherding in the bush, about 60 miles north of Mudgee, though John still saw his relatives when he drove the sheep to Mudgee for shearing.

In their old age Lucy and John returned to the Mudgee district and both were buried there. So was Edward. In 1902 it was said that their numerous descendants still in the area "form a small colony themselves". Charles' final resting place is not known. Only Mark ever saw Wingrave again. He returned to England in 1875, too late to help his parents in their old age, or to see his sister Charlotte, for they had all died in the 1860's. So William and Sarah Paine never saw any of their four emigrant children again, and never met, spoke to, or saw any of their thirteen Australian grandchildren. Photography was still in its infancy, and the telephone did not yet exist. The only personal contact was locks of their hair.

Mark married Sarah Fleet of Wingrave, and died there in 1893. His wealth, acquired from investment in railways, gave him a place amongst the gentry in the local directory. His wife, who died in Wingrave in 1937, is still remembered by some of its senior citizens.

Edmund and Mary Jarrott[8]

More villagers left later. In 1875 Edmund and Mary Jarrott of Wingrave with their five children decided to take assisted passages to Brisbane in Queensland. It was nearly thirty years since the Paines had emigrated to Australia, but it was still an arduous journey of nearly four months. After 1869 steamers travelled via the Suez Canal, but the sailing ships used for emigrants still took the longer route round the Cape of Good Hope. To passengers unused to sailing the oceans in ships of under a thousand tons, it must have seemed very dangerous. It is noticeable that whereas the captain of one vessel described a journey out as "uneventful", an emigrant on the same voyage wrote home that from the Cape to Queensland,[9]

the sea was tremendous. One night was especially terrible. A tremendous wave dashed over amidship, and the jib, the top-sails and part of the bulwark were taken away. The water came down the hatches into the lower deck, swamping some in their beds.

There is no mention of heavy seas on the Jarrotts' journey, but there were six deaths mainly from bronchitis and diarrhoea, and also a mysterious fever which affected many passengers and resulted in them being quarantined in very poor conditions on arrival at Brisbane.

The Jarrotts' first task was to repay their share of the cost of the assisted passages. So for the first eighteen months Edmund worked on a sugar-cane farm or in a sugar mill in the Brisbane area. It was 1877 before the family set off on their thousand mile journey to Whitfield, near Wangaratta in the state of Victoria.[10] As a bone fide 'selector', Edmund was allowed to select and occupy 20 acres of land at an annual rental of two shillings an acre. Provided that he lived on the holding for three years and made improvements to the value of at least one pound an acre, he was entitled to buy the freehold at that price. Edmund selected land at Whitfield, to the north of which were a number of gold diggings, which created a demand for farm produce and timber.

So far the process of emigration had been difficult, and life as a settler was certainly no easier. The land was heavily timbered with trees and shrubs, and it was extremely hard work to clear even a small area. This was the first priority. Timber was needed to build a house, which meant constructing a single storey timber frame and covering it in sheets of bark. Timber was needed as fuel. Hopefully, some timber could be sold, to obtain food and seed, so that crops could be grown or pastures seeded on the land that had been cleared. All this was made extremely difficult by the lack of local facilities, and the distances to 'towns'. For example, the return journey to 'nearby' Wangaratta was made in a horse or bullock-drawn wagon, and for the first few years it took up to two weeks, including twice fording an unbridged river, which often flooded dangerously in winter. Even when the land was ready for crops, most of those best suited to the local climate (maize, millet, hops and tobacco, for instance) were quite different to the typical crops of Wingrave.

Edmund and his family overcame all these difficulties and made a success of their holding. Yet these were the very people whom the Rev. Butt had patronised as needing help "to make them more moral, and to fit them better for the discharge of their duties". One wonders whether he would have been surprised by Edmund's obituary in the Wangaratta Chronicle, which described him as:

a fine type of English farmer, a man who commanded respect throughout the district. The late Mr Jarrott was a quiet, unassuming man who devoted his principal interests to his home affairs. He bore an enviable reputation for honour in all his dealings and straightforward conduct generally. The respect in which he was held was testified by the large attendance at the funeral, there being thirty vehicles and ten horsemen in the cortege. Four grandsons bore the coffin to the grave.[11]

UNION ACTIVITY IN THE VALE [12]

In 1872 Edward Richardson, a young schoolmaster at Dinton, resigned his post in order to establish the Aylesbury District branch of the National Agricultural Labourers' Union. Eventually, due to his efforts, there were at least eighty villages in the Vale with NALU branches. They included Wingrave, where Joey Bonham was the local representative. Richardson's aim was to ensure that agricultural labourers received sufficient wages to house, feed and clothe their families, and to pay for their schooling. He proclaimed this message at village meetings, in letters to local newspapers, and by editing and publishing a weekly newspaper, 'The Spade and the Whip'. He also composed and published a booklet of union hymns and songs to be performed at meetings. One favourite was sung to the tune of God Save The Queen:

Lord of the earth and sky,
Hear now the poor man's cry,
Stand by our cause.
Content shall then abound,
Where want may now be found,
Send up a mighty sound,
And God will hear.

At the end of 1873 Richardson became the official agent for Queensland with an office at Aylesbury. This led him to emphasise emigration as the most realistic solution to the labourers' problems. Fortunately, just at this time, the new state of Queensland urgently needed labour and was offering farm workers free passages, providing they paid £1 for their 'ship kit'. In addition twenty-five million acres had been set aside, which emigrants could purchase at 9d per acre. Despite these inducements, the labourers were slow to take up the offer. Richardson understood their reluctance and apathy. Over the years they had come to accept their lowly place in society. If they spoke their minds, they might well be considered 'too uppity' and lose their jobs. On Richardson's first voyage there were many men whose livelihood of five, six or seven shillings per week had been taken from them simply because they had dared to join 'the obnoxious association', as farmers called the Union. And if you lived in a tied cottage, losing your job meant losing your home. In 1874 a number of Wingrave labourers were sacked for refusing to give up Union membership.[13] Besides, emigration was not a universal panacea, as the local press was quick to relate. Thus, in May 1874, the Bucks Herald reported the suicide of an English emigrant to Canada due to "fruitless endeavours to get employment", while a correspondent to the Toronto Advertiser wrote:[14]

While some English employers seem to be at their wits end for men, and talk of importing Chinese, I would undertake to supply whole shiploads of disappointed or unemployed emigrants now unable to return, but who would jump at the chance to get back.

Despite this, Richardson was convinced that emigration would benefit the vast majority of farm workers, act as a safety valve for those whose patience with conditions in England was exhausted, and provide more chance of employment for those who remained behind. He decided that the best way to encourage emigration was actively to recruit emigrants, and personally to escort parties to Queensland. So he walked the Vale, visiting the towns and villages, to talk, explain, and encourage the labourers to seek a better life on the other side of the world. On the 24th March 1873, a train collected 369 emigrants from Thame, Aylesbury and Tring. At Aylesbury a great crowd gathered to say goodbye to friends and relatives, and listen to Richardson's farewell speech. Finally, as the train pulled out, the crowd waved and cheered until it was out of sight. The departure of the emigrant ship, the Ramsey, was even reported at length in the national press.

Not everyone viewed the occasion positively. Three inmates of Aylesbury Workhouse were eager to join Richardson, one being Henry Newen of Wingrave. Unfortunately, he had no means of raising the £1 for his ship kit. The Board of Guardians refused to help, dismissing his request with laughter. The Bucks Advertiser even printed a letter congratulating the Board for refusing to spend £1 on each of "such choice specimens of the agricultural class". Fortunately, a Queensland farmer offered to pay, and Henry was able to emigrate a month later. The following January the Advertiser printed a letter from him saying, "I am very well, nothing troubles me".[15]

After a successful visit to Queensland, Richardson returned to England, and resumed his campaign, both for the Union and for emigration. In June 1874 he visited Wingrave twice: once to address an evening meeting, and once on a Sunday morning when "a large and orderly gathering of Union men marched in procession to the parish church and listened to a good homely sermon preached by the Vicar". We have no record of this sermon, but when addressing the Wingrave and District Agricultural

Association, the Rev. Butt is on record as saying (in effect) that locally the level of wages posed no problem, while adding that the object of farmers' associations should be (amongst other things) to see that the working class received a better education. Unfortunately, the next speaker (also a clergyman) capped this by defining a better education as "not merely to read and write and sum, but to acquire habits of punctuality and obedience, to be taught to keep their hands from picking and stealing, and their tongues from evil speaking, lying and slandering, and to respect their superiors and betters".[16] With this sort of indiscreet condescension being aired in public, it is not surprising that there was soon a dispute between Wingrave farmers and their men. About twenty-five men from the village demanded a rise of 1/- a week. This was refused, so with Richardson at their head, and sympathisers from elsewhere, they organised a five-day march in the hope of gaining support. Carrying banners, and singing their union songs, they passed through Aston Abbotts, Weedon, Whitchurch, Quainton, Waddesden, Brill, Long Crendon, etc., where they "generally met with a hearty reception from the country folk". They returned to Aylesbury on the Saturday afternoon. When they marched into the Market Square, the men wore the blue rosettes of the Union, and each had a card stuck in his hat, bearing the message 'Locked Out'.

Richardson addressed a crowd said to number three thousand, and a collection was made for union funds. At the meeting George Griffin of Manor Farm, Wingrave, defended the farmers' position. The 'Locked Out' notices should read 'On Strike'. He was quite willing to pay his best men fourteen shillings per week, but not everyone, regardless of their ability.[17]

The Wingrave labourers 'stand' soon collapsed, because the farmers 'locked the men out', and the Union was unable to provide them with financial support. Later, as soon as the harvest was over, some farmers retaliated by laying off men for the winter. The consequent hardship made emigration more attractive. Soon Richard-

23: George Griffin of Manor Farm

son realised that the Great Eastern Counties Lock-out, as the struggle between the farmers and their workforce in Cambridgeshire was known, would also fail due to the Union's lack of funds. He decided to organise and accompany another trip to Queensland. William Honor from Wingrave, with his wife and seven children, joined him on the voyage in September 1874. Others who left Wingrave at this time were Ann Badrick, Thomas Hedges and his wife, and Ann and John Richardson.

DID EMIGRATION BENEFIT THE AGRICULTURAL LABOURER ?

Note: the following comments relate to emigration to Australia, simply because:
(a) this was the principal destination of Wingrave emigrants in the 19th century.
(b) in consequence almost all the available feedback has come from Australia.

Most Wingravians appear to have improved their lives by moving to Australia. Unlike England, Australia had too few labourers for the available land or, from another viewpoint, had too much land for the available workforce. The resulting competition for labour pushed up wages. Moreover, the market for agricultural goods was also very competitive and so farmers could not recover the cost of higher wages simply by raising prices. Sometimes high wages made it uneconomical even to market the crop, as Mark Paine discovered in 1859:[18]

We have 2 acres of green peas Just ready for picking. They are very scarce in Mudgee, but the price won't pay for picking, shelling and takeing into Mudgee. It is not here as it is at home where we could have 2 or 3 boys. They would do as well for that as men. But boys are scarcer here than men are.

Indeed, before refrigeration became commonplace, Australia's warmer climate meant that, if sales were slow, even foodstuffs which had been sent to market might have to be sold at a loss before they perished in the heat.

However, these were problems for the farmer and the shopkeeper, who could usually survive minor calamities. For the labourer, higher wages and stable (or even lower) prices reduced the poverty which plagued the Wingrave labourer. This situation was compounded by the very different social ethos in Australia, where there was no parochial parson to boost the morale of 'the masters' and to warn 'the lower classes' of divine displeasure if they stepped out of line.

Those who remained in Wingrave were also affected by emigration. In itself it did not significantly improve the labourers' bargaining position. However, emigration plus the demand for labour by the railways, the building trades, and the growing rural industry gave farmers much cause for thought. The farmer could opt for the increasing range of farm machinery, though this was expensive and required a surprising amount of labour. Alternatively, he could offer permanent rather than temporary employment, though this was also expensive. Ironically, it was the surplus of foodstuffs produced in Australia (and New Zealand, and the Americas) which, by reducing the price of food, were a major source of poor relief in England.

By the end of the 19th century it was easier to put Australian food on English tables in perfect preservation than it had been to put French or Irish produce there when Queen Victoria came to the throne.[19]

Of course, the gains and losses of emigration cannot be measured in economic terms alone. For most families, the permanent separation which emigration then implied must have generated regret, heartache and even trauma. It would have crossed many an elderly mind that the protection against old age and the workhouse, which children normally supplied, was either reduced or ended. William Stevens Paine and his wife must have sorely missed their emigrant children in 1855, when he sent a note to his daughter in Aylesbury:[20]

Your Mother and self have been very Poorly. I am very weak in my Limbs at present but hope I shall soon get Better. Am sorry to say we are suffering much oweing to the severeness of the weather. I can't get out to earn a Shilling. Never suffered so much in my life.

Life must have been similarly hard for Elizabeth Bonham, whose husband, John, died in 1834, leaving her with nine children to bring up singlehanded, the youngest only 18 months old. Although seven of the children were old enough to contribute something to the family's income, or at least to help in the home, Elizabeth had to struggle to maintain the family. The records of the Congregational Church describe her as "a very excellent character. She hath done what she could". Despite this, by 1848, all but one of her children had emigrated, one to Australia and seven to the U.S.A.. Only her son, James, remained in Wingrave, and was there when she died in 1849.

For some of the emigrant families the wheel has turned full circle. Now their descendants return to Wingrave to find their roots. They search Wingrave's graveyards, inspect the church and the chapels, enquire whether their surnames are still represented in the village, and visit particular streets or homes. Some bring their family trees, or even a history of their family. Their ancestors did make good in the colonies, their descendants are numerous, many holding responsible positions in a wide range of occupations. They seek those who were once the key to their future, and who are now the key to their past.

24. Authors Lucy Holloway (left) and Carmel Bourke (right), both descendants of the Jarrott family of Wingrave, discuss their family history with Brenda Leitch of the Wangaratta Historical Society, Australia.

Part Two: The Tide Begins To Turn

Chapter Six

The Rothschilds to the Rescue

In 1798 young Nathan Mayer Rothschild was sent from Frankfurt to London to establish a branch of the family business. He was highly successful, accumulating and manipulating vast sums of money. Eventually, his four sons joined the business.

In 1833, the family rented Tring Park in the Vale of Aylesbury for the summer. The Vale, with its extensive pastures and lack of woodland, was perfect hunting country. With easy access from London by rail it was the ideal place for Nathan's sons to indulge their passion for riding, which provided the exercise to compensate for their busy but sedentary lives in the City of London. In 1843 Mayer Amschel Rothschild, the youngest son, purchased a small estate of farms in the parish of Mentmore. He converted a farm-house into a 'hunting box', and built extensive stables and kennels.[1] At nearby Ledburn he built a hostel for the stable boys, which is now the Hare and Hounds public house. Mayer made Mentmore his home and lived the life of an English country gentleman. He founded the Mentmore Stud, which was enormously successful in racing circles. His astute solicitor and agent, James James of Horwood and James, Aylesbury, advised him to concentrate his land acquisitions, as the best way for one of Jewish faith to acquire political influence and social acceptance. It was good advice. In 1847 he was even made High Sheriff of the county. At his death in 1874, Mayer owned 4,016 acres in the Vale,[2] almost all the land between the villages of Wingrave, Cheddington and Wing. Two of his brothers followed his example. In 1851 Anthony bought an estate at Aston Clinton while, by 1876, Lionel owned 10,000 acres in the Vale, and was able to create substantial estates for his sons at Tring (for Nathan), Halton (for Alfred) and Ascott (for Leopold). Ferdinand (Lionel's son-in-law) also moved to the Vale, and built a mansion at Waddesdon, while Ferdinand's sister Alice settled on the adjoining Eythorpe estate. Thus by 1890, seven Rothschild estates had been established, all within a radius of seven miles.

The Rothschilds' immense wealth and their religion tended to set them apart, but they settled into their roles as country squires, and were highly regarded as model landlords, improving living conditions for their workers, and even transforming villages. They were known, too, for their generosity in supporting every charitable concern. Gradually, they were accepted into county society, and entered public life.

HANNAH de ROTHSCHILD

Hannah was born in 1851, the only child of Mayer Amschel Rothschild. She was four years old when the family moved into their magnificent new country home, later to be

25. *Facing page: Hannah beside the Rubens chimney-piece in the Great Hall at Mentmore. Artist unknown.*

known as Mentmore Towers, the first Rothschild mansion to be built in Buckingham-shire. Her formal education was badly neglected by a series of governesses. In 1867 her Aunt Charlotte remarked,[3]

Hannah, though naturally gifted, is painfully shy, and in reality has nothing to say for herself. What a pity that her education should be so desultory and, in fact, that she should do nothing and say nothing.

This was rather harsh, though it does seem that her learning benefited more by good fortune than training. She was lucky to be a voracious reader, which taught her much. Her home provided an education in the fine arts, and surrounded by the fabulous furniture, paintings, sculptures and tapestries collected by her father from all over Europe, Hannah became quite a connoisseur. Although adored and admired by her parents, she was both spoiled and over-protected. For instance, she was never allowed "to enter a cottage where sickness and sorrow dwelt", or to visit the village school. Fortunately, this gap in her education was filled by her cousins Constance and Annie (Anthony's daughters at Aston Clinton), whom she saw frequently. They were enthusiastic about helping the needy, for they were given almost unlimited freedom to visit the cottages and strawplait schools in the district. They established and ran a Saturday school for the strawplait children and excitedly watched the building of a girls' school provided by their father. As Connie's sixteenth birthday approached, her father gave her the choice of a present. She asked for an infants' school! Needless to say, her request was granted, and this event was almost certainly the inspiration for Hannah's gift, many years later, of an infant school to Wingrave. Although, as an only child, Hannah is said to have been extremely lonely, it was the loneliness of a child for the company of children. Apart from this she had an enviable social education. Like her father and uncles, Hannah enjoyed riding and hunting, an important social skill at that time. She had access to the family's stables and kennels, and is said to have known the names of all the hounds. Her social education was further enhanced by admission to her mother's drawing room, for many well-known personalities from the literary, political, financial and musical worlds were entertained at Mentmore. Consequently, she became used to moving in society at an early age. Thus, in 1868, when H.R.H. the Prince of Wales visited Mentmore for a day's stag hunting, he was met at Cheddington station by Mayer, his brothers, and the 17 year-old Hannah, deputising for her mother. Cousin Ferdinand (of Waddesdon) noted that she was the only one to keep her composure in all the confusion.

The hunt, which the Prince attended, assembled at Wingrave: 400 huntsmen, all wearing red hunting jackets, were mounted on high-spirited thoroughbreds. The waiting carriages extended for almost half a mile. News of the

26: Releasing the Stag from the Deer Van

Prince's visit had leaked to the newspapers and, when the Royal party arrived, a crowd of villagers was there to greet them, and were able to see the Prince "to their hearts' content". The event was a stag-hunt using a semi-tame deer, a form of hunting favoured by the Rothschilds, for the stag was not harmed, and the huntsmen were virtually guaranteed a good gallop over open countryside. Mayer had already sent the deer van on to Aston Abbotts, and the stag was released on Lines Hill. From there it went across the heart of the Vale, providing a chase of over two hours at a terrific pace. Some of the best riders fell, but the Prince completed the hunt without any accident at all. He returned to London on the Scotch Express, which was specially flagged down at Cheddington.[4]

HANNAH AS ADMINISTRATOR AND BENEFACTRESS

Six years later, Hannah's beloved father died, and she inherited two million pounds, Mentmore Towers with its very valuable contents, and an estate of 4,500 acres. Apart from the Queen, she was almost certainly the wealthiest woman in the country. Fortunately, as soon became clear, she was both a shrewd judge of character, and had an excellent head for business.

She also had a social conscience and, even before adding to her estate, had obviously determined to improve the accommodation, schooling and recreation of the villages within it. That Wingrave was the greatest beneficiary was probably due to a coincidence. Firstly, Wingrave was a greatly neglected village with many of its dwellings in a state of chronic disrepair, and offered considerable scope for improvement. Secondly, a significant amount of Wingrave's property became available for purchase at just the right moment due to the ill-health of Edward Munday Major Lucas, who, in 1875, decided to retire and move away. At a stroke Hannah acquired over two hundred acres of farmland and seventeen cottages, of which she promptly demolished eleven. And if anyone had any doubt as to whether the derelict property had been purchased by intent or error, it was surely dispelled when, in a later purchase, she bought a further group of six tenements near the Congregational Chapel and immediately had them demolished.

Within two years, Hannah had dedicated a field of pasture opposite the church to the use of the parish for sport and general recreation, and as a playground for the children. However, Hannah with typical thoroughness did not just make a field available. The Rev. Butt was so impressed by what he saw that he implored the editor of the Bucks Herald to give publicity to "this Act of Grace":[5]

Only last week Miss Hannah de Rothschild came into full possession of land she had lately purchased in this parish. This week a dozen labourers are busy in a field of about six acres situated in the very centre of the village, on the crown of the hill on which it stands, from whence is obtained a glorious view of the Vale. These labourers are now mowing down the rough grass, taking up the turf, and under-draining preparatory to levelling the field, in which a shrubbery is to be planted and seats placed, so that it may be made a suitable place of recreation for the inhabitants of Wingrave. Miss Rothschild's generous act has created in all hearts feelings of deep gratitude.

This new recreation ground was then surrounded with twenty newly-built cottages: one detached; ten semi-detached; and nine in terraces of three. They were substantially built of brick with tiled rooves, and were finished in the usual 'Rothschild Tudor': white rendered walls, black timbers, tall 'Elizabethan' chimney pots, and memorial plaques bearing Hannah's monogram and the date (H. de R. 1876) on each building. For workers' cottages at this date, they were very commodious and comfortable. Nearly all had three bedrooms, two living rooms and a larder, while outside each had its own barn (outhouse) and earth closet. At least some had cavity walls,[6] a feature not usually found in domestic buildings until seventy-five years later. They were beautifully situated with views southwards to the distant Chilterns. A further fifteen were built at Nup End. This was 1876, so there was no water supply within the cottages. That had to be obtained from a pump or well, of which some had sole use, though others had to share with up to four other cottages.

All were let at very low rents, mostly between 1s-6d and 2s-6d per week. Despite the inclusion of a shop (14'x 11'3"), the rental of a cottage on the corner of Nup End and Main Street was a mere 3s-9d per week. Even a house with four bedrooms, two living rooms, scullery, larder, barn, bakehouse, earth closet, a garden in excess of one-third of an acre, and a further acre of field (with pond) and orchard was only 4s-7d per week.[7] The seventeen families whose homes had been demolished were the first to be re-housed in the new cottages. It is said that some of the dwellings were occupied by estate workers, but we have not yet been able to confirm this.

Hannah was also interested in the cultural and educational development of the village. In 1876 she sponsored a series of lectures by visiting speakers. The first was held on a Friday evening in the Parochial Church School.[8]

The subject was 'The Good Old Times'. In an eloquent and humorous address the lecturer compared and contrasted the various characteristics of bygone ages with the corresponding features of the present time, pointing out the superior advantages of the nineteenth century as regards our educational facilities, travelling arrangements, postal and telegraphic communications, social habits, etc.. There was a large attendance, the schoolroom not only being crowded, but several persons having to stand all the time, and others being unable to obtain admission. The lecture was in every respect satisfactory, and the experiment so highly successful that Miss Rothschild has engaged the services of Mr Simpson for a second lecture, when the subject will be 'Popular Superstitions'.

Hannah was clearly satisfying a very real need. Most villagers had little contact with the outside world, many never having ventured far from the parish. Other interesting evenings followed, one very popular lecture being 'Our Drinking Water'.

By January 1877 Hannah had provided the village with a much-needed and purpose-built Infants' School combined with a Reading Room for adults, and generous accommodation for a resident schoolmistress. It was situated at the corner of Moat Lane and Dark Lane. All this was provided and maintained entirely by Hannah: the teachers' salaries, furniture, equipment, books, newspapers, etc..

Hannah's improvements and initiatives gave the village a feeling of pride and hope as the Bucks Herald noted in September 1878:

Wingrave is continuing its course of improvement. The Countess of Rosebery has done so very much for it, that it has awakened to a sense of its own importance, as regards beauty of situation and of its cottages. Many begin to regard it as a model village. Once more, on the 19th September, parishioners met to thank God for harvest mercies. The parish church was prettily decorated with vegetables and fruit from the cottagers' neat gardens, as well as the Lucas' greenhouses. We have only to add that the afternoon was

The Recreation Ground, Wingrave.

27. *Some of the thirty-five new cottages built by Hannah de Rothschild in the village of Wingrave. These overlook the Recreation Ground, which she also provided. It was leased out for grazing, which not only yielded a useful rental, but kept the grass 'mown' as well.*

28. *'Ivy Bank' is a terrace of three Rothschild cottages in Nup End. On the extreme left is the shop which was part of a pair of cottages on the corner of Nup End and Winslow Road. It began life as a pork butchers run by Harriett and John Gibbs, and is now just extra living space for the owner of the house.*

in fact a holiday and many persons spent many happy hours in Lady Rosebery's Recreation Ground, some playing at cricket, some at football, some at other games, some simply looking on, but all evidently enjoying themselves and glad to see all around them happy.

The Rev. Butt saw other advantages. In an after-dinner speech to the local Agricultural Association he told his audience of landowners and farmers:[9]

For a very long time Wingrave has been left somewhat in the cold in comparison with some other parishes, which have the advantage of a wealthy property owner, but now we have Miss Hannah de Rothschild. In providing a place of recreation I believe she is doing a great moral work, because it will enable myself and farmers and employers generally to walk about and talk freely with the labourers and their wives and children, and in that way do a great deal of good in binding all classes, rich and poor, together. Another thing she is undertaking is a sewing school for girls in the parish. Every Thursday there is a class at which the unmarried women can learn to sew, and that must be good, because if a woman can make a good shirt, she will also probably make a good husband. Wingrave, after being a long time in darkness, is at last coming into the light of the sun.

Hannah's generosity continued over the years. At the age of 81, William Fleet (formerly of Fleet and Roberts, the builders) looked back with appreciation, for his father was killed in 1875, when he was 4 months old, and he was the youngest of six.[10]

And the Countess was so kind. She had little jackets made for the boys and hats with red bands, and they looked so pretty. And the girls all had red cloaks and they looked splendid. And the same colour cloaks were made for the teachers. And the Lady had dinner provided two days a week (rabbit stew, milk, etc.) on Tuesdays and Thursdays, and the children had to pay a penny each. The Countess was very kind to the poor people of Wingrave, and gave them coal and other gifts for Xmas. And the rents of the cottages were very low.

THE ROTHSCHILDS ASCENDANT: THE MENTMORE ESTATE

Over the next four years Hannah continued to enlarge her estate. In 1877, after riding over to view a new acquisition, she wrote to her uncle Lionel:[11]

I am sure you will be pleased to hear that I am extremely satisfied with it, as it far exceeds my expectations, being in remarkably good order, scarcely any alterations will be requisite. I cannot understand what induced Lord Stanhope to part with a property upon which his father spent so much in numerous improvements! I must thank you again, my dear Uncle, for all the trouble you have so kindly taken. My new tenants seemed delighted at their land belonging to me, which was very pleasant to hear. Some of them had evidently been hoping for a Rothschild to be a purchaser of it.

Clearly, Hannah, like the rest of her family, was aware of the Rothschilds' high reputation as landlords and employers. For example, they employed estate hands throughout the year, not only when expedient, as was the general practice; they made substantial improvements and repairs to their tenants' farm buildings, which was by no means the general practice; and they showed a concern for the condition of housing and the provision of amenities on their estates, which distinguished them as unusually enlightened landowners. Wingrave has been claimed as Hannah's greatest memorial, and rightly so. Yet by Rothschild standards, her conduct was by no means exceptional.

From the beginning, Mayer Amschel had set the example of the hospitable squire and caring landlord. For instance, in January 1874,[12]

Baron Mayer de Rothschild gave a substantial supper at the Anchor to all the labouring men who hold houses or cottages belonging to him. Hitherto, they have been entertained at Mentmore, but this year they have been spared a long walk, and spent a most pleasant evening in their own village. Mr E. Hart presided at the supper table, which was well furnished with good old English fare: a noble round of beef, plum pudding, etc.. All the men appreciated the Baron's kindness in remembering them. Several cottages have lately become the Baron's property . . . and the poor may fully expect an improvement to their dwellings.

In various ways, depending upon local circumstances and their personal inclinations, Mayer's brothers followed his lead. For example, at Aston Clinton, Sir Anthony's estate workforce included three bricklayers, three carpenters and eight labourers, who were constantly employed on the estate's cottages. So it is not surprising that the next generation, which included Hannah, demonstrated similar traits. And, quite apart from housing, the Rothschilds built schools, inns, a hospital, village halls; restored alms-houses; and from its formation in 1864 financed the Chiltern Hills Spring Water Company.[13] They also contributed generously to a wide variety of charitable appeals.

THE ROTHSCHILDS ASCENDANT: THE ASCOTT ESTATE

Wingrave and Rowsham were fortunate to have the patronage of two Rothschilds, for Lionel de Rothschild owned very much more of the parish than his niece: 1061 acres or nearly half of it. His estate included six farms: Manor, Floyds, Windmill, Straws Hadley, Hale and Thistlebrook. Although this was only 10% of his total holding in the Vale of Aylesbury, it still received the detailed attention that the Rothschilds gave to all their investments. For example, at Hale Farm, Rowsham, from 1859 to 1869 a total of £555 was spent on such things as new stables, gates and shedding; repairing the farm house and workers' cottages; and improving the drainage.[14] During the 1870's work continued on drainage, repairs and the provision of new ashpits and earth closets for his tenants. In the case of Manor Farm, repairs to buildings and improvements to drainage tend to monopolise the accounts for each of the years between 1867 to 1870. In addition to expenditure on his own properties, Lionel supported many village charities. For example, he gave £15 annually to the Vicar towards the church charities; £2 to

29. *Leopold de Rothschild*

the Wingrave Ploughing Association; donations to the Band of Hope, the Methodist Sunday School, and the Rowsham chapel; and gave financial help to several families who wanted to emigrate.

When Lionel died in 1879, he left all his property in the Vale to his youngest son Leopold, who had already acquired an old, half-timbered farmhouse near Wing, and converted it into the attractive country mansion, which we now know as Ascott House. With the addition of stabling and kennels, he was able to pursue his interest in hunting, and his passion for breeding and racing horses. However, these interests did not reduce his concern for his estate, which he continued to enlarge, steadily purchasing farmland as it came onto the market, until by 1885 he owned farms not only in Aylesbury, Bierton, Hulcott and Wingrave, but also in Weedon, Stewkley, Soulbury, Hardwick, Westcott, Waddesdon, Stoke Hammond, Wing, Pitchcott, Grove, Billington, Linslade, Stanbridge and Long Marston![15]

Despite the extent of his estate, Leopold somehow managed to maintain a personal relationship with at least some of his tenants. For example, at Christmas 1880 he gave the family of tenant farmer George Griffin, of Manor Farm, a magnificent present. It was a beautifully constructed Noah's Ark, complete with Noah and his three sons, and five hundred animals and birds, in pairs, male and female, all carved in wood. Needless to say, it is now a very valuable and treasured family heirloom. This sort of thing helps to explain Leopold's reputation for "generous kindness".

In the 1890's, at very little cost to himself, Leopold made two major contributions to Wingrave's health and facilities. Firstly, he provided Wingrave with land at the western end of the village, to increase the number of allotments available. Consequently, by the end of the century, ninety of the 159 households in Wingrave and Nup End had an allotment, and forty of these households had more than one plot. One family had six! Secondly, in 1894 Leopold offered nine building plots for sale between

30: Late Victorian houses in Winslow Road: see facing page. The horse tethered outside the Post Office belonged to Stewart-Freeman. Ern Bignell, one of his staff, rode down each day to collect the mail for the Old Manor House. The horses and carts of Joe Rickard and William Rickard wait to be loaded up. Meanwhile Bert Bonham does a bit of weeding.

Nup End and Cat Street. Keenly priced, they were quickly snapped up, mainly by local bricklayers and carpenters.[16] Local recollection is that most of the houses were 'self-built', thanks to cooperation between the two building trades. This was quite feasible, since between them brickies and chippies could muster all the skills required: there was no plumbing or electrical work to be done. This development re-housed at least thirty-seven people, and eventually accommodated four businesses: Joe Rickard built his carpenter's shop, storage shed and stable at the bottom of his double plot; William Rickard established his builder's yard in a huge shed at the side of his house, and used the front garden for the overflow. Thomas Jones added a small extension to his house specifically to accommodate the village post office, which moved to it after George Griffin's retirement; and a further house was later converted into the village shop.

THE MARRIAGE OF HANNAH DE ROTHSCHILD

In March 1878, at the age of twenty-seven, Hannah married Archibald Primrose, the 5th Earl of Rosebery. A politician of great promise (though it was never fully realised), Rosebery had long been a close friend of the Rothschilds, and had often stayed at Mentmore. It is said that both were shy and lonely, but were brought together by a shared sense of duty and public spirit, which they exercised by managing their estates efficiently and humanely. They were also deeply in love. A few days after their engagement, he wrote to a friend, "She is very simple, very unspoilt, very clever, very warm-hearted and very shy. I never knew such a beautiful character",[17] whilst Hannah wrote to her future sister-in-law, "I am indeed thankful for my intense happiness. . . . I want very ardently to make him happy". Their marriage was the wedding of the year. The Prime Minister, Benjamin Disraeli, gave the bride away, while Edward, Prince of Wales, signed the register, and proposed the couple's health at the wedding breakfast.

In Wingrave, throughout the day, the church bells proclaimed that Miss Hannah had become the Countess of Rosebery. The school children wore, for the first time, her gifts of clothing. The girls wore white straw hats, trimmed with black velvet, scarlet imitation seal cloaks, and scarlet and white scarves, whilst the boys wore caps with scarlet bands, 'blouses', belts and scarlet cravats.[18] At Rowsham, in honour of the event, Mr and Mrs Roads gave the children of the Day and Sunday Schools 'a capital tea', followed by games. In Wingrave a public tea was held in the church school. This was followed by a concert in the new Infant School when, in honour of the happy couple, George Griffin's oratorio 'Samuel' had its first performance. A few days earlier, the Vicar, the Minister of the Congregational Chapel and George Griffin had presented Hannah with "an album containing views of the improvements effected by Miss Hannah in the village". They also gave her a framed, illuminated address bearing twenty-four signatures "representing fully all ranks in the village".[19]

On the eve of your marriage, we are anxious to assure you, as a great benefactress of our parish, how deeply we feel interested in this event. You have done much to make others happy; we in return wish all happiness may be your portion. Young as you were when left your own mistress, your thoughts were bent on providing for the bodily, intellectual, and moral improvement of our labourers. You have beautified the village while carrying out this design, studding it with cottages, each one a thing of beauty, each one a home of which a poor man may be proud. You have provided for us a recreation ground in the very centre of the village, where our young people may engage in manly and healthful sports after the toils of the day. You have built a noble

31: Hannah when Countess of Rosebery   *32: The Earl of Rosebery*

schoolroom for our infants, and by your liberality it is entirely supported. You have given us a reading-room, well lighted, well warmed, well supplied with the daily and local papers, and amusing and instructive works. These are benefits for which we must feel grateful, and we gladly take the opportunity of assuring you how thoroughly we appreciate and value your actions, and we all wish you may enjoy as large a measure as possible of that happiness which you have been instrumental in securing for others.

After their honeymoon, the Roseberys invited all the workers on the Mentmore estate, and the cottage tenants from Wingrave and other neighbouring villages (470 guests in all) to an entertainment and 'substantial repast' in a large marquee erected close to the mansion.[20]

The Earl and Countess of Rosebery waited upon their guests, and did their best to make all happy and comfortable. His Lordship, genially acting as tapster, waited upon those who were thirsty, who must have been numerous, a large cask being speedily emptied. After tea a variety of rustic sports was enjoyed, each winner receiving the coveted award from her ladyship's own hands. The Berkhamsted Band performed some lively airs to which a number of those present tripped merrily on the grass. As daylight disappeared there was a display of fireworks prepared by Mr Brock from the Crystal Palace. Mr Mackrill of Aylesbury then exhibited his limelight from the top of the mansion, which brilliantly illuminated every object for a considerable distance, and was greatly admired. On the light being turned round, the spectators caught sight of her Ladyship looking over the battlements, which drew forth an enthusiastic outburst of cheering, and brought the festivities to a conclusion.

THE EARL OF ROSEBERY

After their marriage, Rosebery took over the administration of the Mentmore estate, while Hannah devoted all her energies to her husband's welfare. "She made an admirable, unselfish, loving wife", [21] supporting, encouraging and inspiring him in his political career, and entertaining both at Mentmore and at official functions in London. Rosebery felt great respect for his wife's opinions, her tact and commonsense, aware that much of his popularity was due to her. Hannah lived to see him appointed Foreign Secretary, but in 1890, four years before he became Prime Minister, she died of typhoid fever at the early age of 39, after only twelve years of marriage. For Rosebery it was a shattering blow and, in Winston Churchill's opinion, one from which he never quite recovered. To his cousin Ferdinand at Waddesdon, Rosebery wrote, [22]

Our happy home is a wreck, her children are motherless, and I have lost the best wife ever man had. I do not see the elements of consolation, except in the memory of her beautiful unselfish life, and in the feeling of her still encompassing love.

Quite probably Rosebery's many commitments helped him to cope with this very difficult period. Indeed, with another estate at Dalmeny near Edinburgh, and high-level involvement in politics, Rosebery could not even afford time for the details of estate management. As is usual with large landowners he left the day-to-day management to the estates' agents. Over the years, their names (Hart, Edmunds, Bruce, Harrison, Gilmour, etc.) crop up repeatedly in the Mentmore estate papers, while Doretta Moerck, Hannah's one-time companion, seems to have dealt with the infants' school. Even so, it was clearly Rosebery who established the policy, for the management of the Mentmore estate continued to reflect the spirit in which Hannah had conducted it: the tenants still received Christmas gifts of coal; cottage rents continued to be low; the infant school pupils still received new clothing and an annual treat; and the tenants (both farmers and labourers) were treated with sympathy, courtesy and consideration. For instance, in November 1879, with agriculture again in Depression, it was reported that "the Earl of Rosebery has been making remittances in his rents, in some cases of 20%". Similarly, in March 1888, when the provision of allotments at Wingrave was requested, Rosebery conveyed through his agent that he would be "very glad to meet a deputation of Wingrave's labourers" when he next resided at Mentmore.

So, for the villagers of Wingrave, Hannah's death made very little change in their everyday lives. From the time of Baron Mayer they had been used to dealing with the estate's agents, while recognising the real source of power. It will have been noted earlier that even when the genial Baron provided supper at the Anchor for the tenants of his cottages, it was Mr Hart (his agent) who presided at the supper table, and passed on the tenants' thanks.

The estate papers have survived for 1883 to 1913, [23] and vividly convey the everyday concerns of Wingrave's villagers, and the extent to which the details of their lives were influenced by the patronage of whichever 'Noble Lord' they happened to be dealing with. For example, pleas for financial help poured in. The parish church, the parochial church school, and the two chapels all appealed to Rosebery for financial help and the provision of land. He usually responded generously. For example, the Primitive Methodist chapel was granted a 99 year lease on a piece of ground 30 feet by 24 feet at a yearly rent of one shilling (ten pence). [24] All manner of other requests were received from a variety of sources and for a variety of purposes, most of which had one thing in common: a shortage of funds.

My Lord, may it please your Lordship, we have established here a Society called the Wingrave Labourers Friendly Society. Its object is the relief and maintenance of its members in sickness by voluntary contributions and donations. We have had a lot of

sickness this year (1892), and a very trying time, and our funds are getting low . . . . We humbly appeal to you to help us by a contribution which will be most thankfully received.
Samuel Hedges, Secretary [25]

Most Noble Lord, we are desirous of seeing a few influential gentlemen as Honorary Members which we think would assist the management fund. . . .We should be delighted to have the pleasure of including your name. . . . Trusting you will be in sympathy with this appeal,
        I am, My Lord, yours obediently,
        W.E.Griffin, Secretary [26]

My Lord, it is proposed to form a brass band at Rowsham. Our young people meet there in the Schoolroom twice a week for practice at the present time. £20 is required for the purchase of instruments. Would you help us with a subscription?
Thos. G. Lockhart, Vicar [27]

A committee has been formed to carry out a local festival in honour of our Queen, towards the cost of which we beg to ask if you will subscribe.
Thomas Gurney, Hon. Sec. (Rowsham) [28]

If a direct appeal for funds was unsuccessful (or had already been tried successfully), other avenues could be explored. Thus his lordship was in great demand as the patron, vice-president or even just the guest of parochial and village organisations. The reasoning was, presumably, that closer contact might harness his lordship's benevolence to their particular cause. "Please honour us with your company at Tea in the parochial schoolroom," begged the allotment holders in 1889. "May we have permission to rent the Infants' Room for a concert in aid of the Integrity Lodge funds?" enquired Mr W.E. Griffin in 1892, adding hopefully, "I should also be glad if your Lordship would preside on the occasion."

Many letters came from cottage tenants, the main problems being disputes between neighbours, problems with sanitation and water supply, permission to take in lodgers, and inability to pay rent. Fairly typical of the latter were letters from 75-year-old William Mead (Hilda Roberts' father), who lived with his wife Jemima in a rather derelict cottage next to the Rothschild cottages known as Ivy Bank in Nup End Lane. [29]

Dear Sir   February 13th 1893
I ham sorry that i canot do what you say but as soon as i can i will i had but rather short harvest and the winter has been bad to earn much and my breath is so bad that i canot work this cold wether and my club pay is 6 shillings per week as there is not much to spare Sir please bare with me a wile longer and that will much oblige your humble servant   William Mead

Dear sir   May 19th 1893
I ham verrey sorry to tier your paitans but i have been hill so long and my club is Brocken up but i will try and pay that come of a month . . . pleas sir be faverbel with me as you can as i ham a cripel From youre humbel servent
William Mead,   Wingrave

William was not evicted, and when he died two years later, his widow continued to live there until her death in 1910, when the cottage and its outbuildings ceased to be lived in but were retained to provide storage space.

Some pleas were more complex than William Mead's. For instance, Walter Fleet obviously wanted to take over the tenancy of his mother's Rothschild cottage.

21ˢᵗ April 1896

My mother, Mrs Caleb Fleet, is ill and uneasy to know if you will let the cottage go in my name if she should be taken from us. Please sir an answer to me will ease her but no offence I hope Sir by sending this. If so, Sir, I will kindly beg your pardon.
From your humble servant   Walter Fleet

However, did Walter know that six months earlier his mother had written to the estate asking if her married son and his children could live with her? Besides, to which married son was she referring, for Walter had a widowed brother, William? And was brother William also anxious to take over the tenancy when old Mrs Fleet died, as she did in June 1897? Certainly, he might have been interested, for he and his two 'mother-less' children had been living with his mother in 1891, the latest date for which we have information. It was a nice little problem for the agent to tackle. We know that he began to make enquiries, for Walter had to supply information about his employers. The final decision is unknown. The estate files contain only letters received, but not the replies.[30]

Even the Reading Room generated correspondence. It was opened each winter, but was not used much by the parishioners. Consequently, in 1885, when Lady Rosebery offered it for use by the parish on three days per week, she received the following reply:

We, the undersigned, are fully sensible of your ladyship's kindness in offering to re-open the Reading Room, but beg to say we fear it will be appreciated no more than it was before. However, in order to ascertain the opinion of all, we convened a meeting and regret to say only two attended which convinced us that there would be no interest taken in the movement. We beg personally to thank your Ladyship for the generous offer which might result in lasting advantage if they would only avail themselves of the same.
George Griffin, T.E. Biggs, J. Fleet

Eventually, Lord Rosebery gave permission for the room to be used as a second classroom for 'the babies'.

As explained elsewhere, the supply of water, especially drinking water, had periodically been a problem for Wingrave, probably throughout its existence. In the 19th century the problem worsened due to a 50% increase in population. The anony-mous letter on page 80 was sent to Lord Rosebery in 1906.[31]

RETRENCHMENT AND RETIREMENT: THE ROSEBERYS

In 1910 Lord Rosebery decided to auction off all of his "attractive, half-timbered cottages, and small plots of land, in Wingrave, Wing and Cheddington." In Wingrave alone thirty-five freehold cottages, three enclosures, three building plots and several garden plots would go under the hammer. Rumours of this had been circulating for about a year,[32] and had created much anxiety. Would rents increase? (Tenants were well aware that these were very low.) Would tenants be given notice to quit? (The existing tenancies were terminable at a month's notice.) Could the existing tenancies be continued, providing more rent was paid? Could properties be bought privately before the auction? The letters flowed in but, obviously, the estate could give no guarantee about the policies of future landlords, while all requests for special treatment were rejected by Lord Rosebery, "If I do it for one person I should have to do it for another."

Wingrave

My lord

Abreham dug wells before he built his house. We have got the house but no well

Its a verry bad thing to be without any water. You pump harf a hour and you get a spoonful. If my lord you could do somethin for your

tennents they be verry gratful, us cant get it ousselfs everry yer it be wors and this yer wors an all. My little gal wanted some water at schole and they could only have rain water it aint fit to drink. the missis cant wash our close sometime

If you would try and help us it would be a blessing your humble servant yous tennent

33: Anonymous letter to Lord Rosebery (see page 79)

According to the Bucks Herald, there was "great local excitement" on the day of the sale. Many locals attended, while others had come from considerable distances. The auctioneer stated that no reserves had been placed on any of the lots, in order to give tenants an opportunity of buying their own homes and gardens. If this brought smiles to local faces, they were soon wiped off, for the first three lots (a total of seven dwellings) went to Josiah Fleet, a local farmer and property owner. Indeed, by the end of the auction Josiah had acquired ten cottages at an average price of just under £90 each, plus a building site. It was not until lot 9 that a tenant became an owner-occupier. This was George Payne, and when the property was knocked down to him a loud cheer went up from the villagers in the crowd. For £320 he got stabling for two horses, a coach-house, $^3/_4$ acre of meadow and a six-roomed house, now known as The Old Dairy. Shortly afterwards, for £76, William Roberts bought the plot of land, stables, and storage space, which his mother-in-law (Jemima Mead) had until recently occupied, and which he had since rented. On it he built a house for his family. He called it Fernleigh, by which name it is still known. For £300, William Fleet managed to buy the cottage he had rented and the adjoining one with its shop. George Bignell bought a substantial detached house (formerly a pair of Rothschild cottages) near the Methodist Chapel, for £200. Horace

Bignell, his son, remembers his father making regular visits to the solicitor's office in Aylesbury, presumably to pay the mortgage. These last three purchasers were all Sunday School teachers at the Methodist Chapel: see chapter 12. For them home owner-ship was a significant step upwards on the long ladder to greater financial security. Sadly, of the thirty-five cottages sold only three were bought by the tenants. We have not been able to discover how the other tenants fared. (See also Appendix V for sale particulars.)

However, we do know that Lord Rosebery continued to remember the poor of the parish right up to his retirement in 1922. Joyce Sinnott recalls that the Rothschilds and the Roseberys were always well thought of. Everyone spoke of their kindness. She remembered especially the 'Rosebery capes', dark grey and fairly heavy, given to the poor and elderly women, and the Christmas gifts of coal.

During World War One, Rosebery's second son, Neil, and Leopold de Rothschild's second son, Evelyn, both served with the Royal Bucks Yeomanry in the Palestine campaign. Tragedy struck in November 1917, when both cousins were killed on the same day, although on different operations. Rosebery was heart-broken, and a year later suffered a disabling stroke. In 1922 he invited his tenant farmers for a farewell dinner, and explained that he had decided to retire, and that his son and heir, Harry, Lord Dalmeny, would be taking over the entire estate.

On the face of it, the fifth Earl's gift to his son was very generous. However, according to the family, the reality was rather different. Apparently, Rosebery had thrown the keys of Mentmore to his son saying, "You can have this place. It costs far too much to keep up!" Moreover, in financial terms, the Mentmore estate was not a high-yielding property. English agriculture was in depression, and farm rentals were having to be cut by 30% or 40% just to stop the tenants abandoning their farms in financial despair. Then, in 1929, when his father died and Lord Dalmeny became the 6th Earl, he inherited his father's estate at Dalmeny in Scotland. Scottish agriculture was also in depression, but at least he was on home ground, for his family had lived there since 1660, and he did much to improve the estate's stone-built farmhouses and workers' cottagers. It was probably with some relief that, in 1944, he sold off most of the Mentmore estate's 3,900 acres. His passion was for sport, and he devoted much energy to it. He loved fox-hunting, and was a fearless rider. He became Master of Fox-hounds of the Whaddon Chase, and for many years was president of the Jockey Club. Although he loved Mentmore, he made no provision for death duties and when he died in 1974, the mansion and its contents were sold, thus ending the Rosebery connection with the Vale of Aylesbury. Nevertheless, Wingrave has the 6th Earl to thank for its Recreation Ground. His mother had allowed Wingrave to use it, but in 1924 he made an outright gift of it to the parish: to be owned and managed by the Parish Council.

RETRENCHMENT AND RETURN: THE ROTHSCHILDS

Leopold de Rothschild died in 1917, and in 1918 most of the Ascott Estate's Wingrave farms and properties were sold. Since his grandson, Evelyn, became responsible for the estate, several of Wingrave's farms have been acquired: Glebe Farm was purchased in 1969, then Bell Leys and in 1995 Helsthorpe. The estate now occupies a broad swathe of land on the northern edge of the parish, contiguous with the estate's holdings in adjoining parishes, and all characterised by large arable fields. The estate's presence in Wingrave is now purely commercial.

Chapter Seven

The Tide Begins To Turn

Earlier chapters have considered the poverty, poor diet and poor housing of Wingrave's agricultural labourers over the first seventy years of the 19th century. Happily, from 1875, the labourers' situation slowly improved. By 1893 the Royal Commission on Labour felt able to comment:

The old smock frock is very nearly extinct and there is no real difference in the style of dress adopted by the labourer and his wife and that of the class above them. On the clothes line, instead of rags, good linen is to be seen, and in the cottage there is more furniture, and lights are burning late into the night. There is an increasing demand for tinned meat of all kinds.

Those who particularly benefited included 'the best type of labourer': skilled men, who could rely upon regular employment, and who pledged or exercised temperance. Such a man was old John Goldney, whose death aged 86, was recorded in the local press.

Mr John Goldney, noted for his prowess as a ploughman in competitions, has died aged 86 years. He had served as chief ploughman to three generations of the Paine family. Each had employed him on the same farms, and his long experience with cattle and farm work had made him a valued servant whose advice was acted upon. He was deeply affected by the recent death of his master, Mr Charles James Paine of Baldways.

However, by the end of the 19th century, the labourers' standard of living was still very low, and for the majority of people life was far from rosy. Many changes had still to be made if standards were to be raised.

BETTER HOUSING

The thirty-five Rothschild cottages erected in 1875 replaced some of Wingrave's most derelict housing, and by the end of the century the work of the sanitary inspectors ensured that the worst of the remaining hovels were either improved, demolished, converted to storage, stables, barns, etc., or just abandoned to the weather. Widow Mead's cottage in Nup End, an old cottage between Chapel Row and Fleet's Row, and the original Waterloo farmhouse were amongst those abandoned. By 1939 Waterloo Farmhouse was a ruin used to store such items as corn and cows. During World War 2 it was used by the Home Guard for training exercises.

From about 1875 the demolition and abandonment of properties, together with the expanding population, created a market for new houses. Fernleigh in Nup End and some of the late Victorian houses on Winslow Road (between Nup End and Cat Street) were self-built, while others, like the rows of cottages in Leighton Road and Mill Lane, Fleet's Row in Church Street, Hart's Row and Horn's Yard (an earlier enterprise, built in 1852) were speculative building. Retired craftsmen and tradesmen regarded houses as a low risk investment yielding a steady income that would continue to support them in their old age. The new houses still relied upon wells or pumps, and privies or earth

30: Nup End in the 1920's. On the far right is Fernleigh, the house built by William Roberts on the site of his wife's (Hilda's) childhood home. Notice the absence of housing along the Winslow Road at the top of the picture.

closets, but all had at least two bedrooms, were brick-built and slate-rooved, and thus were windproof, waterproof and less attractive to rats and mice. Unlike the timber framing, lath and plaster, and thatch of the old cottages, maintenance of the new structures was minimal. Their sound construction is no real surprise, for the builders usually lived in the village, and the occupiers sometimes included the owner, for whom a slightly larger cottage would be built at the end of the row: John Fincher Hart's cottage in Hart's Row; and Josiah Fleet's in Fleet's Row are examples. As a widow, Mary Ann Butt was content to occupy one of the smaller properties in Horn's Yard.

This activity improved living conditions in Wingrave considerably. Nevertheless, well into the 20th century there were families which grew far too large for their dwellings. They resolved the problem in various ways, as Connie Bignell explained:

There was one family which had ten children, and on the face of it they just hadn't got enough beds for all of them. So what they had to do was get the first lot to bed in all the beds they had got, and get them to sleep. And then they stood them up, and put the second lot in and got them to sleep, and then put them all head to tail on the beds. With all the movement the children woke up a bit, but they were all soon asleep, with up to five or six on one bed if it was a big double bed.

My brothers and sisters were born at one of the little cottages on the village green. How they managed with four children and two adults in that house I don't know. By the time I was born, we had moved to a slightly larger house down Castle Street. It had got a rather big bedroom, and my parents used to part it with curtains right down the middle

83

so that it was made into two 'bedrooms', one for the girls and one for the boys.

'Toddy' Clay, who lived in Leighton Road, had eleven children and used to say that he'd got a cricket team! Two of his children had to sleep at the house of Mrs Walker, their grandmother.

It took the council house programme of the inter-war and post-1945 years, plus a marked reduction in the birthrate, to finally overcome these problems. Eventually 90 houses and 34 old people's bungalows were built by the Council in Wingrave with further provision in Rowsham. Looking back, Muriel Page recalled:

Eventually, in 1955, I was given a council house. This was sheer heaven to have running water, not only cold but also hot, plus a bathroom, electric copper and electric lighting, not to mention a flush toilet.

PURER WATER

The condemning of foul wells did much to reduce illness, especially infantile diarrhoea, which was a potential killer. Not that it made everything perfect. The 'hollow' on the hill (see diagram), which was waterproofed by the underlying clay, supplied all the water for Wingrave's wells and pumps. Unfortunately, it was still fed by both the rains and all the contents of the parish privies, earth closets, cesspits, farmyard middens, and

Fig. 11 Section: The Hollow on the Hill

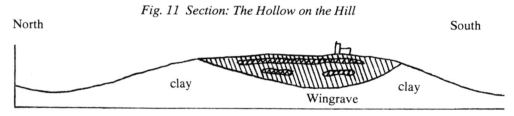

North   South

clay   clay

Wingrave

//// Light brown boulder clay with water-bearing sands and gravels

XXX Mainly water-bearing sands and gravels

foul ditches. Even so, provided there was sufficient distance between the extraction of water and the source of pollution, the passage of foul water through the sands and gravels in the hollow would act as a natural filter and clean it up. Of course, it was not always so simple as that. The sands, gravels and clays are so randomly distributed in the hollow on the Wingrave plateau that one privy might be separated from a nearby well by a barrier of clay, which would block the transmission of pollution, while another well at some distance from the privy might be seriously contaminated by it. It meant that the only sure way to identify foul wells was to test the water. As there could be dozens of wells in a large village, and scores in a town, they were normally tested only when there was a complaint, an epidemic or several deaths. Consequently, some foul wells were not identified until well into the 20th century. Some of the cottages around the Recreation Ground obtained their water from a nearby pump. Not until 1936, sixty years after the construction of the cottages, was the well or borehole condemned. Looking back to the 1920's Doreen Honor told us, "My aunt almost always seemed to be ill when she visited Wingrave. This was probably due to the well water. We were immune to it, because we were used to it." But were they immune? It is quite possible that all sorts of minor gastric problems stemmed from this source. Even so, the overall situation greatly improved as the years passed. For example, in the Aylesbury Union in the five years 1882 to 1891, at least thirty-eight people died from diseases due to consuming water or food contaminated by sewerage. In the five years 1907 to 1911 only two died.[1] Gradually, villages such as Wingrave were becoming healthier.

THE STANDARD OF LIVING OF THE EMPLOYABLES

In the 19th century the standard of living of those who were employable depended almost entirely upon market forces: the availability of employment; the income obtainable from it; and the price of food and goods. As we have seen, if they could not survive in these conditions, then emigration or the dreaded workhouse were their last resort. Fortunately, towards the end of the 19th century, market forces moved in their favour. At the same time, social investigation and the poor physical condition of recruits to the army alarmed the authorities, and encouraged (in some quarters) a more humane attitude to the problems of the poor. Infinitely slowly, official initiatives began to reach the statute book. In the meantime private initiatives tried to bridge the gaps.

The Availability of Employment

By the early 20th century agricultural labour had become relatively scarce. This was a general feature of the countryside. As early as 1893 the Royal Commission on Agricultural Labour reported:

The diminution of the supply (of labour) has made the chances of permanent employment greater and it is a comparatively rare thing for an agricultural labourer to be out of work for any length of time.

This was a bit premature for Wingrave, which still had about twenty unemployed labourers at that time. However, by 1905 it seems that Wingrave also had full employment. In 1905, Mr George Elliott, a tenant farmer renting 316 acres in neighbouring Hulcott, gave evidence to the Tariff Commission, in the course of which he summed up the availability of labour in Hulcott and the surrounding area:[2]

The supply of labour in my district does not exceed the demand. We have no-one out of work in the neighbourhood I live in, that I know of. The young men have been (going) away for some years. They prefer the clean work and the town work so much . . . . and are receiving 4/- or 5/- per week more ready cash. If they can get into the building trade they seem to prefer to stop there.

Emigration had certainly reduced the supply of labour. Farmers might have coped with this but for the fact that it coincided with an increased demand for labour elsewhere. The building trades had certainly expanded as yesterday's children demanded homes, while in Aylesbury there were now major employers like the Aylesbury Condensed Milk Company (from 1880), Hazell's Printing Works (1867), Webster and Cannon's building and brickmaking business (1880's), the Aylesbury Brewery Company (from the 1890's), the Bifurcated and Tubular Rivet Company (1910), two railway companies, and the County Council's burgeoning bureaucracy as it expanded into such areas as health and education. There were also the many minor employers in the retail trade, trying to service the growing population in and around the town. The problem of getting to Aylesbury was solved in two ways. Domestic workers in particular could live in, and the bicycle was an increasingly popular means of transport, especially when freewheeling was adopted after 1894. If the premium for working in Aylesbury was 4/- or 5/- per week (see above), then six months of walking to work would finance a bicycle, even for someone with no savings.

The Income from Labouring
With the supply of jobs greater than the demand for jobs, agricultural wages rose. Nationally, between 1871 and 1891 they rose only slightly, but from 1891 to 1901 they rose by 10%. We know that George Griffin of Manor Farm, paid his best men 14/- per week in 1874. If one applies the rates of inflation mentioned earlier, the job would be paying about 16/- per week in 1905. This was exactly what Mr Elliott paid his labourers two miles away in Hulcott. "It is about 16/- a week now", he told the Tariff Commission, "and the 'perquisites' come to about £3 a year",[3] i.e. about 17s-2d per week.

The Price of Food
Meanwhile prices fell substantially, as cheap food flooded in from both the New World and Britain's colonies after about 1875. In 1893, a Hitchin grocer found an invoice of 1812 and published it alongside his current prices:

Fig. 12: Comparative Food Prices

	1812	1893
Tea	10s -0d lb	1s-10d lb
Candles	1s -0d lb	4d lb
Moist sugar	10d lb	2d lb
Loaf sugar	2s -0d lb	3d lb
Raisins	10d lb	5d lb
Yellow soap	9d lb	3d lb
Coffee	4s -0d lb	1s- 0d lb

A Board of Trade survey in 1904 showed what could be bought with 17s-2d per week.[4]

Fig. 13: Board of Trade Survey 1904 – Household Expenditure

	Approx. Quantity	Cost s. d.		Approx. Quantity	Cost s. d.
(1)Bread	25 lbs	2s- 8d		B/fd	12s-5d
and flour			Sugar	4 lbs	8d
Rice etc.	2 lbs 8ozs	5d	Jam, etc.		5d
(2)Meat	5 lbs 5ozs	3s- 4d	Pickles		2d
Bacon		9d	Rent		1s- 6d
Eggs		9d	Coal	56 lbs	6d
(3)Milk	8 pints	11d	Soap, etc.		4d
Cheese	11ozs	6d	Beverages		1s- 2d
Butter	1 lb 8ozs	1s- 7d			
(4)Potatoes	16 lbs	9d			
Vegs/fruit		7d			
Dried fruit	8ozs	2d			
Carried forward		12s-5d		Total	17s- 2d

The four food groups, which the British Medical Association now regards as essential for a good diet, are all represented in boxes one to four of Figure 13. Thus, compared with the 1840 budget (page 20), this latest diet is much more healthy. With the possibility of a greater variety of main courses and puddings, it could also be more enjoyable.

While a major reason for the labourers' improved fortune was the cheap food flooding in from overseas, it was this same flood that created the Great Depression in English farming, which considerably reduced farm incomes. In past times, farmers might have cut wages, but with labour already in short supply, they simply had to bear the brunt of the reduction. For once, the labourers' gains in one direction were not offset by losses elsewhere.

Of course, all this begs a number of questions. Would the housewife spend her housekeeping money so wisely? Would her culinary skills enable her to create a greater variety of dishes? Would the "greater permanent employment" (forecast by the Royal Commission) mean a regular weekly wage even in slack times? Was the labourer normally in good health? Could he save enough to cope with the occasional illness, or to provide the rest required when he was kicked on the knee by a fractious plough-horse? Would his wages allow for the infrequent but essential expenditures on clothing, medicines and the inevitable 'rainy days'? Was he a regular at any of the seven inns to be found at Wingrave, Rowsham and Aston Abbotts? Over the first fifty years of the 20th century such questions were addressed partly by public and partly by private initiatives.

Public Initiatives: The Local Government Act 1894

The Act required the replacement of the long-established Vestry of the Parish Church by a Parish Council, and gave everyone who paid even the smallest of rates in the parish, a vote in its election. At the first election only two of the eight farmers who had been nominated were elected, with the remaining seats going to four tradesmen and two labourers. It was a victory for democracy which infuriated the Vicar, the Rev. Lockhart, who for some years unsuccessfully tried to obstruct the work of the new Council.[5] The battle was still rumbling on in 1901 and was finally resolved by the Vicar's retirement in 1905 after a long illness.

Throughout these years, the Council also pursued its more conventional business of appointing constables, trustees of the charities, and guardians of the poor; cleaning out the moat and the pond; maintaining the roads; and leading the village celebrations of such special occasions as Queen Victoria's Diamond Jubilee in 1897.

From the 1920's the need to update Wingrave's utilities began to dominate the Council's agenda, but no direct action was possible on a shoe-string budget. Eventually, electricity (1927), mains water (1940), street lighting (1949), mains sewerage (1952), and gas (1988) became available with major implications for the health and welfare of the parishioners. It was the Rev. Lockhart who, in 1891, had advised the villagers that they must make known their need for better services. Ironically, it was mainly through the agency of the Parish Council, that he had opposed so resolutely, that this was done.

Public Initiatives: The National Insurance Act 1911

Part I of Lloyd George's National Insurance Act came into operation in 1912. For a weekly payment of 4d per employee, 3d per employer, and 2d from the state, all workers earning less than £160 per year received free medical treatment, medicine, sickness benefit, etc.. However, this did not apply to their families, who still had to make their own arrangements. So the Nursing Club remained an important part of Wingrave's provision. Nationally, all sorts of 'approved societies', such as insurance companies and friendly societies were involved. We have not been able to discover exactly how the services and payment of doctors were arranged in Wingrave, but it is likely that the friendly societies (of which Wingrave had several) played an important part.[6] One villager thought that patients paid their doctor a small fee every quarter. In fact, the 1911 Act was noted for its anomalies and complexities, some of which were not resolved until the National Insurance Act of 1946 came into operation in 1948.

Public Initiatives: The Fight Against Infection

The fight against infectious diseases did not begin in earnest until 1872, when Parliament made it compulsory for urban and rural authorities[7] to appoint a Medical Officer of Health (usually part-time) with a sanitary inspector working under him. In 1883 when there was an outbreak of cholera,[8] the Local Government Board warned the population of Wingrave (and the other 38 parishes in the Aylesbury Union) of the principal dangers by displaying notices. It also instructed the surveyor of each parish to see at once that the ditches at the side of the roads were cleaned. In 1885 the Vale had two separate outbreaks of smallpox, which had originated in London, but thanks to extensive vaccination, and the strict enforcement of disinfection and isolation, the disease was contained.[9] By 1887 the Aylesbury Union had appointed a Vaccination Officer, and in that year alone 367 children were vaccinated.[10]

By the 20th century the appointment of district nurses and school nurses, and the collaboration of school teachers (chapter 13), all helped to identify potential cases. In addition, the creation of isolation units and the attenuation of some of the diseases greatly reduced the number of cases, as the following figures show.[11] Eventually, immunisation and antibiotics virtually eliminated them.

Fig. 14 Aylesbury Union: Mortality from Infectious Diseases

	1882-1891	1902-1911
Measles	51	24
Whooping Cough	51	22
Scarlet Fever	38	1
Croup	11	3
Total	151	50

Private Initiatives: The Allotments

In 1882 local authorities were empowered to purchase land for the purpose of letting it as allotments; in 1887 they were compelled to do so. Unfortunately, the Aylesbury Sanitary Board provided only "evasive and unsatisfactory answers" to requests for allotments. Eventually, in a hard-hitting letter to the Bucks Herald,[12] the Rev. Lockhart complained at length about this, adding:

Does it not seem hard that the toilers in the pretty hamlet of Rowsham should be surrounded by many acres of beautiful land (land everywhere!) yet the tillers should be debarred from having so small a share as one rood for their own use, when the legislature of our land makes provision for them to have an acre?

Eventually, at Rowsham, the Mercers' Company made provision, while in Wingrave, spurred on by appeals from the Vicar and villagers, the Earl and Countess of Rosebery, and Leopold de Rothschild provided land. In Leighton Road, the Rosebery's allocated five acres, which became known as Kew Gardens. In Winslow Road Leopold de Rothschild provided a further thirty acres, which was dubbed Van Diemens Land after one of the fields which it occupied. An allotment enabled an industrious labourer (with an industrious wife!) to provide his family with a year-round supply of vegetables. With his allotment providing a run for some hens, and corn to feed them, his family could also have eggs (fresh or preserved in isinglas), and extra meat when he culled his layers, while the surplus from the allotment helped him to fatten a pig. The consequent savings on the household budget would help to provide for the missing items in the 1904 budget: clothing, footwear, oil for lamps, medicines, a fund for 'rainy days', etc..

In 1890 the Vicar capped all his previous efforts with a gift to the allotment

Recollections: Van Diemen's Land – Christine Dunker

I see the men go tramping down to dig Van Diemen's Land
In heavy shoes, with spades and forks, and buckets in their hand.
They hail us with a cheery shout and beam a happy smile.
They know the job they mean to do is really well worth-while.

In February they start to dig, but the ground perhaps is dry.
If March is not much better, they heave a weary sigh
And sit to tell each other all the garden news they know,
Of how to grow their things in pots, and then in May to sow.

There's Reg and Frank, and Doug and Mark, Peter and Lionel too,
With Len and Norman – all the gang – too many to go through.
They chat and spin a good few tales – they're quite a happy band,
Who find a joy in toil and sweat on their allotment land.

When June comes in 'tis salad days; they have to cope with bugs,
They all go home so hot and dry, they wash it down with jugs;
For home-made wine is then uncorked, and goes down very well
With lettuce and tomatoes: they say it all tastes 'swell'.

In hot July, with blight about they have to start to spray.
The farmers then are cutting corn, or maybe making hay.
And some perhaps have left their plots to lend a helping hand.
And should they moan about the drought, we all can understand.

For they have toiled for half a year to get their things to grow;
To – maybe – wash and brush them up, to enter in a show.
For humble village gardeners are really very skilled,
And should, perchance, they win a prize, they naturally are thrilled.

September brings the harvest home, and onions hang in ropes,
Together twined with wheat and corn, fulfilling all the hopes
Of those who work with toil-worn hands to gather in the grain
Be what it may: in cold or heat, or drought or falling rain.

holders, as the Bucks Herald reported:[13]

The Vicar, who has always taken much interest in the allotments, has presented the holders with a new iron plough. On September 4th the Vicar took off his coat and set to work to make a ridge on number 5 allotment. With a little help at the end, he accomplished this with fair success. He handed over the implement to the holders wishing them much success with it and with their crops also. He then inspected the allotments and returned home much satisfied with his experiment.

The Vicar's efforts on behalf of allotment holders drew praise from unexpected quarters, when he attended a gathering of allotment holders in the schoolroom in 1891. Firstly, the Vicar's arrival was the signal for great applause from the 250 people present. Then Mr Hart, Lord Rosebery's agent, told the villagers that their Vicar had worked hard to get them the ground; he had given them excellent advice; and had identified himself closely with their welfare. He stood as their greatest friend.[14]

Private Initiatives: The Provident Clubs

In 1892 Britain was still twenty years away from the first tentative attempt (the 1911 Act) at a comprehensive system of social services. In the meantime, each town and village was a hostage to fortune. Wingrave was lucky, though much of its good fortune came from a rather unexpected direction: two successive Anglican vicars. Although his origins were middle class, the Rev. Lockhart realised that it was difficult for the working class to make regular savings to finance occasional large purchases like clothing and fuel, and that it was even more difficult to protect carefully accumulated savings from ill-judged bouts of boozing or betting by a wayward spouse. By 1892 he had established a clothing club, of which the Bucks Herald reported:[15]

The club supplies a great need, and is highly appreciated by the many depositors, church and chapel being all treated alike by the Vicar, who takes the whole of the burden of collecting and distributing on his own shoulders!

No wonder it was appreciated! When depositors withdrew their money a substantial bonus was added.

When he retired in 1905, his successor, the Rev. Francis, continued the club as an adult clothing club, and added two more: a children's clothing club; and a coal club. In the parish magazine, he explained their purpose:[16]

The idea is that, from time to time, members should put by a little, so as to have the money to pay - for example- for their winter's coal when the winter is coming. That is what providence means, "looking ahead". Our provident clubs are not to help parishioners to pay their debts, but to save them from running into debt. The bonus is an encouragement to regular saving. In the case of the Coal Club, the bonus is paid upon deposits up to 52 shillings in the year, six shillings being the maximum bonus. In the children's club, in 52 weeks depositors should have paid in 26 shillings to which 6s-6d is added by way of bonus. So the clubs are intended not only to encourage thrift, but to help those who try to help themselves, and especially the needier among them.

By 1918 the total cost of the bonuses for the three clubs was £53, a substantial sum in those days. As the Vicar pointed out, even the coal club bonus was about fifty times as much as would be paid in interest on a savings' bank account. It appears to have been funded from several sources: donations from such people as Leopold de Rothschild and Mrs Stewart Freeman; a contribution from a General Purposes Account derived from the church collections; and the balance from the Vicar, who fortunately had a private income and a generous nature.

There is little information about the provident clubs after the Rev. Francis retired in 1919. Hopefully, by that time the saving habit had become ingrained, and temperance ensured that income was used more effectively.

Private Initiatives: The Temperance Hall

The temperance movement flourished in Wingrave, for drunkenness had been a major problem in the 19th century. It was a great temptation to drown one's sorrows when life was wretched, but money spent on excessive drinking only increased the wretchedness and deprivation of families. The Nonconformist chapels were especially concerned about the consequences of intemperance, and on several occasions in the 1830's and 1850's the Independent Chapel excluded members for drunkenness. For example, Jonas Humphrey was excommunicated in 1839 "for intemperance after being suspended several months and admonished in vain". Of course, the inebriates included many who had no particular religious affiliation. Thus, at Linslade Petty Sessions in August 1877, Ezra Smith, labourer of Wingrave, was charged with drunkenness. P.C. Kimble had found him lying by the roadside intoxicated, and he had to be taken home in a wheelbarrow. The court fined him ten shillings with 12/6d costs, but there is no record of any subsequent religious penalty.

Wingrave's Total Abstinence Society was formed in 1861, its object being to encourage total abstinence through lectures and public meetings. Although it was strictly non-sectarian, the Society was mainly supported by the Nonconformists. To join, one signed 'the pledge' never to let alcohol pass one's lips. One wore a blue ribbon, so that all who saw it were aware of one's commitment. Children were encouraged to join the Band of Hope, so as to catch them young, before they had acquired the taste for drink. Visitors from the National Temperance League regularly visited the parochial school. One lecturer illustrated his talk with several chemical experiments, which greatly interested the children. Afterwards, an essay competition was set. Even as late as 1920, an essay was set on "the need for temperance in eating, drinking and smoking". Every summer Band of Hope teas, picnics, fetes and outings were arranged, each event occasioning an extra half or full day holiday for the parochial school. An entry in the logbook for July 1891 notes: "This has been quite a broken week with Temperance outings."

Members of the Society became more and more aware that they badly needed somewhere of their own for regular meetings and social occasions. Public houses were obviously 'taboo'. What they needed was a Temperance Hall. Fundraising started in 1887, and by 1890 they had arranged with Leopold de Rothschild for the lease of a small plot of land next to George Griffin's post office in Winslow Road. By then £170 had already been raised towards the £208 needed. Soon an ironclad building to seat 250 was erected, and the opening ceremony took place on Easter Monday 1891. Two years later Baron Rothschild, M.P. attended a temperance meeting. He was astonished to hear that there were over one hundred adults and a further one hundred children in membership out of a total population of less than a thousand. He was overwhelmed to think that one in every five inhabitants must be total abstainers, and concluded that it reflected the greatest credit not only on those at the head of the Society, but also on the consciences and the general morals of the inhabitants of the neighbourhood.[17]

Nonagenarian Horace Bignell explained:

Ninety years ago the village was divided into those who went to pubs, and those who didn't. If you've got a limited income, you can't drink and smoke and have the same sort of life as you could have otherwise. Something's got to go. It was recognised that teetotallers were the first ones to have pushbikes, motor bikes and even cars. You couldn't escape that fact. I could have a pushbike at ten years of age, and there weren't many could say that.

In the early twentieth century twice weekly games' evenings were held in the Hall, where young (and not so young) abstainers could meet and socialise. Billiards, table tennis and darts were played. Later on it was also used for Scouts and Brownies, Women's Institute Meetings, a Youth Club, Bingo, concerts of all sorts and even for cinema shows and "proper dances, not like ones nowadays" as one resident put it. In other words it provided another social centre for the village. It was even more important

35: *The Temperance Hall 1891-1974*

throughout World War Two when the Church Room was used for other purposes.

Eventually, cars, television and a generation with a more relaxed view of alcohol reduced attendances. In addition, nobody wanted to run it. Horace Bignell, who was one of the trustees, even wrote to the Charity Commissioners for advice, but they only said that it was nothing to do with them. So the Temperance Hall was closed and demolished. The site was generously given to the newly-formed Community Association. They sold it for £5000 for a building plot. It was a good start for the Association, which was converting the old parochial school into a community centre.

36: *Some 1906 entries from the Register of Pledges for 1893 to 1911*

PLEDGE :—By Divine assistance, I will abstain from all Intoxicating Drinks as Beve... and discountenance all the causes and practices of Intemperance.

Date.	Number.	NAME.	Age.	ADDRESS.	REMARKS.
1906		Joe Major.	14	Wingrave	
		E. Holwood	11	Wingrave	
Nov 25th		John Pargeter	9	" "	
		Harry Peto	9		
		Bertie Bonham	9	"	
		Tom Major	9	"	
		Ronald Gurney.	13		Life long abstainer
		Wilfred Mead	10		Life long abstainer
		Philip Mead.			Life Long abstainer
		Annie Kempster	15		
		Charlie Alcock	11		
		Hilda Gibbs	9		
		Edith Levick	11		

Private Initiatives: Medical Services

A Nursing Association to serve Wingrave, Rowsham, Aston Abbotts and Cublington was established in 1910 by the Rev. Francis. An advertisement in the Bucks Herald brought Miss Louisa Foulkes to Wingrave. By 1913 the Vicar could write, "There is no doubt but that the services of the Nurse are increasingly appreciated. We have, continually, new subscribers, many of whom pay willingly the fine demanded for the Nurse's immediate attention." In 1912 she made 2,443 visits to patients. This included attending seventeen mothers in their confinements. In that year the Association also arranged a course of ten hours in sick nursing for mothers and young women.

By 1919 the Local Government Board was making a grant of £11 to £13 per year. Due to this it was discovered that Wingrave's fees were the lowest in the county. The charge for the services of a midwife was 17/6d in many parishes as against 6/- in Wingrave. The problem was that Wingrave had always thought of the Association as, in great part, a charity, while the general feeling in the country was that it should be run on business lines. "Those who appreciate having a trained nurse in the parish must bestir themselves to make it possible", warned the Vicar.

They obviously did bestir themselves, for the Nursing Club - as villagers called it - continued to flourish. In the 1920's it was still paid for by a subscription, which (for a time) Hilda Roberts collected. Louisa Foulkes was succeeded by Ada Candy, Florence Kidd and Miss K.M.Oliver. These nurses lived in Ivy Cottage in Nup End, and went round the village on their bicycles. This changed in the late 1930's when Nurse Bell took over. She lived at Bierton, and visited Wingrave in a small Austin car. She wore the typical uniform of the district nurse at that time: a tight-fitting navy blue hat with a turned-up brim, and a navy blue raincoat, under which was a white apron with a bib. Her sleeves were always rolled up, and held in place by elasticated white cuffs. She was still making the rounds in 1941.

Doctors were now far easier, and cheaper, to see. In the 1880's you went to Aylesbury, or he came to Wingrave "on his old roan nag". We don't know just when things changed, but by the 1920's Wingrave had two visiting doctors. Dr Coventon was from Aylesbury and held his surgery in the front room of Lawndale, the home of Phil Rickard, the butcher. The doctor's surgery was on Tuesday afternoons, and there were no appointments. You just turned up and queued in the hall. Dr Chignell and later Dr Langley from Wing held their surgeries twice weekly in Nellie Green's tiny front room in her cottage on the Green. Again there were no appointments. You simply turned up and waited your turn in Nellie's passage, or on the front path, if the practice was busy. There were no seats but, if you were a close friend of Nellie, you might be invited into her living room. However, waiting in the passage had its rewards. Since everyone knew everyone else, you got a quick briefing on the health of the village. Besides which the door to Nellie's front room had a small panel of glass in it, and the bit of net curtain which Nellie had hung over it did little to block the view of the consultation. Neither was the door very soundproof!

If your 'complaint' was specific – heartburn or a cough, for instance – a suitable cure would be dispensed from one of the large bottles of concentrated medication which lined the shelves in the room. Otherwise the consultation might well conclude with, "Mind you, you are looking a bit under the weather. I think you need a tonic. Have you brought your bottle?" Into it would be poured an inch or so of liquid from one of the large bottles, and you would be despatched homewards with instructions to fill up your bottle with water, and to shake it well.

THE STANDARD OF LIVING OF THE PAUPERS

The living standard of the paupers, as the unemployables without means were generally known, depended upon the doles available from public funds, the charity available privately and the extent of family support. Some indication of the latter appears on page 34. In 1891 thirteen of Wingrave's parishioners, with an average age of 76 years admitted to pauperism, while twelve more declared proudly that they were 'living on their means'.

Public Initiatives: The Workhouse

Wingrave's paupers included the long-term sick, the physically and mentally handicapped, the aged and infirm, and widows with young children. They were all dependant upon the not too tender mercies of the Aylesbury Union. Its rules (as published in 1878) for determining outdoor relief (i.e. relief paid to those living outside the workhouse) must have delighted every flint-hearted Scrooge:[18]

Henceforth no new applications for outdoor relief will be accepted.
Ordinary relief for married couples will be 3s-6d and two loaves weekly per couple.
*If **after strict enquiry** relief is granted to a single man, it will be 2s-6d to 3s-0d and one loaf weekly, while a single woman will get 2s-0d to 2s-6d and one loaf weekly.*
No relief will be granted if relatives can maintain the applicant.
A woman who keeps a son's house, and is able to wash for him, is to receive no relief.
Women deserted by their husbands will receive relief only if they enter the workhouse.

By 1879 almost all Wingrave and Rowsham's paupers were over sixty years old. The oldest was 87. Their annual income from outdoor relief varied from £7-9s to 16s-10d. The total for the twenty-seven was £225-18-9d compared with over £300 fifty years earlier. Even so, all the old and infirm had to be visited by the Relieving Officer at least once a quarter. By 1899 the decision of the Union not to consider further applications for outdoor relief, combined with the death of existing claimants, reduced the number of claimants to eight, while the total annual bill for outdoor relief was a mere £75. Even when they could obtain relief, its extremely low level meant that the paupers had to spend it all just to avoid starvation, and so couldn't take advantage of benefits like the fuel and clothing clubs. It also meant that most of the reductions in food prices did not benefit them, as all their income had to be spent on a very few basic items. Astonishingly, the Royal Commission on the Aged Poor which reported in 1895 recommended no major change. "It is essential that the Guardians have power to deal on its merits with each individual case."

Of course, as William Cox had pointed out nearly fifty years earlier (page 31), if they were dissatisfied with outdoor relief the Justices would always give them a ticket to 'the Workus', though it was common knowledge that the majority still regarded this as a fate worse than death.

Public Initiatives: The Old Age Pension

Fortunately, in 1908, Lloyd George and the Liberal Party passed The Old Age Pensions Act, which provided a non-contributory pension of 5 shillings per week to all persons over 70 years, whose income was under £21 per year. In 'Lark Rise', Flora Thompson describes the impact on the aged cottagers of an Oxfordshire village:[19]

They were relieved of anxiety. They were suddenly rich. Independent for life! At first, when they went to the Post Office to draw it, tears of gratitude would run down the cheeks of some, and they would say as they picked up their money, "God bless that Lord

George!" For they could not believe that one so powerful and munificent could be a plain 'Mr.'.

Amongst the aged such feelings must have been almost universal. As they saw it, the tide had certainly turned. By introducing an element of compassion into the treatment of the poor, state pensions marked the beginning of the end for the 1834 Poor Law, and pointed the way to the Welfare State.

Private Initiatives: Charity

The state of the poor had long attracted the attention of the better-off, some of whom left money, land and property to help them. The income from these endowments was distributed annually by the Vicar, the churchwardens and other trustees. In 1875:

the several charities belonging to the parish were given away on the Thursday before Xmas, some having been distributed according to ancient custom in the parish church the previous week. Each poor widow received 7/-, each family 6/-, with the exception of those taking relief. They received 5/6d and the smaller tradesmen 4/6d. Two of the oldest men received a smockfrock each.[20]

At Xmas 1892 the Bucks Herald pointed out that "nearly every inhabitant was a recipient, Wingrave parish being exceedingly well-off for charities". However, welcome as they were, such gifts were distributed but once a year.

Fortunately, Wingrave's villagers did not leave charity solely in the hands of past benefactors. Those of lesser estate would join together to provide baskets of food, while those with more substantial means might make a distribution on their own account, or organise a group meal, or even a regular meal. Mary Ann Butt loaned out a layette to the expectant mothers of poor families. Charity of this order was usually reported in the Bucks Herald, sometimes in considerable detail. See also page 96.

On Tuesday last, through the liberality of the Rev. J.M.Butt, the aged poor of this parish were invited to an excellent supper served in good style by Mr Thomas Gibbs of the Anchor Inn. There was an abundant supply of ham, beef, cake, and bread and butter. About thirty of the above were present, together with several of the leading inhabitants, including the churchwardens. After tea, the Vicar, in a sympathising speech, assured them that it gave him much pleasure to meet them on such an occasion, and he hoped to be spared to do so another year. Several pieces were sung by the church choir, and songs were also given by Messrs. C. and M. Paine, Roads, Wyatt, etc.. The singing of the doxology terminated the proceedings.[21]

Conclusion

In the years after 1875, improvements in housing, sanitation, diet and medical facilities not only improved the quality of life in Wingrave, they saved lives as well. The death rates of Wingrave's children began to improve: see fig.1, page 11. Between 1876 and 1910 only (only!!) 15% of babies died, and only 28% of children had been buried by the age of ten years. Older people were also living longer. Even so, by modern standards the figures were still deplorable. Much that we now take for granted was still in the distant future.

Recollections: Seasonal Liberality in 1874 _ Anon [21]

It gives us much pleasure to record an act of kindness on the part of Mr Charles Paine, of Wing Bury.[22] Having lately erected a building at which his business as a corn dealer can be carried on more conveniently, the happy thought struck him that the best thing he could do would be to celebrate its completion by giving a dinner to all the aged poor of Wingrave and Rowsham receiving relief. Accordingly, on Friday, all except the very infirm were present. The latter either had a dinner sent them, or its equivalent in money. Two good fires blazed on the hearth, the room looked cheerful, with festoons of evergreens, and on the table was placed a huge round of beef, and vegetables smoking hot, of various sorts. Plate after plate was served, but still the joint remained a large one. The first course being removed, plum pudding, fit for any party, was set before the guests, soon to disappear, for they were hungry and happy. A dessert of fruit followed. Then, to help digestion, the old women dipped their fingers into the snuffbox, while the old men smoked their pipes. Of course, such a party must have a few speeches, so Mr Paine spoke feelingly to his aged friends, telling them how glad he was to give them this dinner. W. Allen, an aged shepherd, a man much respected, stood up and made a really good speech, expressing, with evident emotion, the deep thankfulnesss which they all felt. The Vicar, who with Mr Seamons, the guardian of the poor, and Mr. Wyatt, the schoolmaster, had been specially invited to meet this interesting party, all said a few words. The Vicar expressed his great delight at seeing such a gathering, which was one of the many instances of kindly feeling on the part of the farmers towards those who had spent their strength in labouring for them. The Guardian spoke in high terms of Mr. Paine, and said that while an officer he would always do all in his power, both at the Board and in the parish to promote the comfort of the worn-out poor. The schoolmaster alluded to his responsibilities as a teacher of the rising generation, and expressed an earnest hope that the poor would regard him as one of their real friends. Mr Mark Paine then sang 'The Old Oak'. By this time the afternoon had far advanced, and before the party broke up the Vicar gave out, verse by verse, Bishop Kent's fine old Evening Hymn, 'Glory to Thee my God this night'. Then, with hearts full of gratitude to God and man, these aged pilgrims retraced their steps to their own humble homes, and we do not doubt but that they felt that after all there was no land like old England, and no class of persons more kindly disposed towards the poor than the farmers. Mr Paine must be congratulated on having done an act which will linger long in the memory of the old men and old women of Wingrave and Rowsham.

37. *Charles Paine 1835-1898*

Chapter Eight

Wingrave Acquires Its Gentry

Between 1876 and 1878 Hannah de Rothschild built a large country house on the site of the ancient farmhouse, which she had recently acquired with Baldways Farm at Wingrave. She probably intended the property to be used as a hunting box, for the new buildings included a six-stall stable, eight loose boxes, a harness room, a cleaning room and two coach houses with living accommodation above.

The Old Manor House, as it was soon named, provided four spacious living rooms, but only three principal bedrooms, though two of these had dressing rooms adjoining. On the same floor were two bathrooms, supplied with hot and cold running water. The extensive servants' wing was built over the ancient cellars, and included kitchens, pantries, servants' hall, and bedrooms for nine staff. Two large and handsome lodges guarded the main entrance.

It was not long before Mr William Russell Stewart Freeman, the newly-married and wealthy proprietor of Aldridge's Horse Repository of St. Martins Lane, London, leased the property. Then in 1885 he wrote to Lord Rosebery,[1]

The house at present is not equal to the stable accommodation. A billiard room on the ground floor with five extra bedrooms above would greatly improve the property, and make it always sure of a tenant.

The extension was provided and in 1898 the Freemans purchased the property for £11,000, the farm buildings for £1500, and 32 acres of land for £4,800.[2] Freeman then added glasshouses, a palm house, a forge, and an engine house equipped with a 12.5 H.P. oil engine, a 140 volt dynamo and fifty-five accumulators. This made it possible to electrify the bells (for calling the servants) and the lighting.[3] There is no record as to what the villagers thought of this final touch of luxury.

By 1891 Freeman, his wife and three daughters were being cared for by thirty staff. Eleven of these lived in the main house: a butler, footman, cook, kitchen-maid, three housemaids, three stablemen, and a nurse for the Freemans' two youngest daughters. In addition two grooms lived above the coach-houses,

38: William Russell Stewart Freeman

whilst the coachman and a gardener occupied one of the lodges. These resident staff did little to relieve Wingrave's unemployment problem. One stableman came from the village, and the two grooms were local people, but the rest appear to have been recruited on a national basis: the nurse came from Switzerland! Presumably the fifteen non-residents were village people.[4]

After the family moved to Wingrave, Freeman continued to run his London business. At Wingrave, he bred both hounds and horses, and was an expert in handling his own four-in-hand, which he drove frequently from Wingrave to Brighton and back. As a keen huntsman he both hunted and socialised with the 'county set', which included the Rothschilds from Ascott and the Roseberys from Mentmore. In the village, he clearly enjoyed playing the role of squire, which he (and his wife) did with considerable generosity in both time and money. As a churchwarden, and school manager, he donated prizes, arranged and paid for treats and outings for choir boys and Sunday school pupils, and gave considerable sums to the funds for the church restoration, and school building extensions. He also participated socially in the village. He sometimes played in village cricket matches, and he would lend the grounds of the Old Manor House for fundraising events. He was the resident figurehead which Wingrave had long lacked, with the bonus of a generous spirit backed by a deep pocket. The examples which follow, taken from reports in the Bucks Herald, are typical of his generosity.

Many a home was made happy and bright by the bountiful gifts distributed by Mr Freeman of the Manor House. Nearly six hundredweight of excellent beef was dispensed by that gentleman besides other things. Soup is distributed here each week. The wish was expressed that there were more of Mr Freeman's disposition dwelling in our midst, for he possesses not only the means, but an open heart to do good with it.

Tea and entertainment made a red letter day in the lives of the children of Wingrave. Mrs Freeman and Mrs Easton provided tea for about two hundred children besides the church choir and Sunday school teachers. All joined in the singing. Part of the evening was spent witnessing marvellous sleight of hand tricks by a professional entertainer engaged by Mr Freeman. The continuous roars of laughter proved that he was thoroughly enjoyed by the children. The tricks occupied more than an hour and a half, yet not once did the youngsters' earnest attention seem to flag. Next came the presents consisting of nice writing cases, work-boxes, toys, etc., distributed by the Misses Freeman. The beaming smiles upon the faces of the children showed how delighted they were. Mr Baker, on behalf of the children, gave thanks. Many were the hearty wishes for a happy New Year to the residents of the Manor House. (3.1.1891)

Freeman had an extremely volatile temper, but it was very shortlived and left no grudge. We were told of one occasion when a groom displeased him. Freeman picked up a log and threw it at the groom, who promptly threw it back, knocking Freeman down. After telling his master what he thought of him, the groom went home. That evening Freeman called on the groom, apologised, gave him a pound and offered him his job back. We told this story to his great grandaughter, who said, "Absolutely typical of the man!" and gave us some more examples.

In 1905 there was a great scandal in the county when Eveline, the oldest of the Freeman girls, eloped one moonlit night with the dashing twenty-one year old Algernon de Vere, the 8th Earl of Essex, whom she had met at a hunt ball. It was a classic elopement complete with a ladder up to the bedroom window. The lovers soon returned, and were duly married. In 1906 Eveline gave birth to a boy whom they named Reginald. The following year Freeman died and was buried in Wingrave churchyard beneath an

39. *The Hunt in the grounds of the Freemans' home: the Old Manor House. Clearly a considerable income was needed to maintain a stable of suitable horses and hounds, and staff to look after and exercise them.*

40. *The funeral of William Russell Stewart Freeman passing the Green on its way to the parish church in 1907. Mourners came from far and wide. The hand-drawn bier is just off the left-hand side of the picture.*

41. *Eveline, Countess of Essex (and daughter of W.R.S.Freeman) riding with her son Reginald (Reggie), then Lord Malden, and later to become the 9th Earl of Essex.*

42. *"Reggie" clears a fence at the Kimble Point to Point in 1938.*

43. *A later view of the Old Manor House, its beams repainted in traditional black. The extent of the buildings, and the well-manicured lawns and topiary are another indication of the Freemans' substantial income.*

44. *Floyds Farmhouse in the 1930's. The farm was bought in 1918 by Mrs Freeman, and eventually became the home of her grandson "Reggie".*

enormous block of granite.

Although the 8th Earl had eloped with Eveline in 1905, their marriage was dissolved in 1926. He married another three times before he died in 1966. Young Reginald, the result of the 8th Earl's first marriage, became Lord Malden and, when his father died, succeeded him as 9th Earl of Essex. He and his wife lived for some years at Floyds Farm in Mill Lane. Although they might support village organisations it was very much as president of this and patron of that. Most of their socialising was done in very different company. He was very keen on horse-racing, hunting, shooting and steeple-chasing, and was a fine cross-country rider. He rode in the Stock Exchange Point to Point at Kimble, played golf at the Royal Blackheath Golf Club, played cricket for the Druids or Leighton Town, dined at regimental dinners, judged cattle at the Royal Easter Show and galloped with the Whaddon Hunt. He died in 1981.

After the divorce (from the 8th Earl) Eveline remained at the Manor House for many years, breeding and showing dogs with considerable success. On the outbreak of World War 2 she leased the house to the Czech Government exiled in England under their leader Dr Eduard Benes. The Czechs remained at the house until 1945, and a tangible reminder of their stay in the parish is provided by the bus shelter which they had built at Wingrave crossroads in thanks for the kindness shown them by the villagers of Wingrave and Aston Abbotts.

Eveline did not return to the house after the war but leased it to the Sisters of the Cross, a community of Anglican nuns from Edgware, who looked after retarded children. They gave the house the biblical name of Mount Tabor and added a chapel at the southern end of the property. The nuns finally returned to Edgware in 1972, when the MacIntyre Schools of Westoning acquired the property.

45: Floyds Farmhouse is to the right with a large haystack in the yard. To the left is Old Manor Farmyard, flanked by a long barn (ending in a turret) where, at Queen Victoria's Diamond Jubilee, "200 men sat down to a festival dinner with Mr Freeman and the Rev. Lockhart each carving a round of beef." All the farm buildings have now been converted to residential use.

Part Three: Some Fundamentals

Chapter Nine

Worshipping in Wingrave

THE HISTORICAL BACKGROUND TO THE NINETEENTH CENTURY

English Nonconformism dates back to the 16th century, when many Nonconformists hoped that their differences with the Church of England could be reconciled so that a National Church could emerge. This hope evaporated in 1662, when the Act of Uniformity compelled every clergyman to be ordained by a bishop, and to accept the Book of Common Prayer in its entirety. About two thousand clergy rebelled and were ejected from their livings. Small congregations gathered round many of these clergy and continued to meet despite fines, imprisonment and even transportation. After the ejection of the Stuart monarchy in 1689, a Toleration Act was passed. In practice this provided freedom of worship to all religious dissenters except Roman Catholics. By the beginning of the 19th century the principal Nonconformists were the Baptists, Congregationalists, Presbyterians, Quakers, Unitarians and Methodists. Roman Catholicism was still practised, but had declined.

CHURCH AND CHAPEL IN 19th AND 20th CENTURY WINGRAVE

In 1800, the Church of Saints Peter and Paul, standing on the highest point in the parish, was visible and audible to most of its inhabitants: a powerful reminder of the religious and civil functions of the Established Church.[1] Its congregation was united in acceptance of the doctrines and beliefs detailed in the Book of Common Prayer. By contrast the Wingrave Nonconformists were a mixture of Baptists, Quakers, and Congregationalists between whom there was a fair amount of agreement on matters of doctrine and faith, but also sufficient differences to threaten future harmony. They had no purpose-built accommodation in which to hold their services, and until 1813, met in the homes of some of Wingrave's poorest people, though even these humble venues had to be approved by the Archbishop of Buckingham. In 1800 the home of Rebecca Radwell [2] was used, she being the pauper widow of a farm labourer, with three young children to support. In 1801 they met in the cottage of John Edwards, a farm labourer of 21 years, whose widowed mother had recently died, leaving him to care for a younger sister and brother. Clearly, if accommodation is any indication, the Nonconformist congregation was small.

So, fifty years later, the Religious Census of 1851 (Fig.15) provided two surprises. Firstly, at least 72% of Wingrave's population attended a service on Sunday, whereas the national average was only 60%. Secondly, at least two-thirds of Wingrave's attenders preferred the Nonconformist services at the two chapels to those of the Parish Church. This remarkable increase in the popularity of Nonconformism was due to several factors. Firstly, many people were attracted by Nonconformist beliefs. For instance, that the individual could have a personal relationship with God without the intercession of priests and bishops; that the Bible was the only true guide to Christianity; and that some of the doctrines in the Anglican Prayer Book were not acceptable. Many also preferred a simpler and less standardised form of service to that of the Church of England.

Fig 15: U.K. Religious Census, 30th March 1851
Parish of Wingrave with Rowsham

	Sunday Services			Sunday School	
	Morning	Afternoon	Evening	Morning	Evening
Parish Church	58	139	--	43	41
Independent Chapel	35	175	--	82	82
Methodist Chapel	30	--	120	--	--

Secondly, unlike the Anglican Church (chapter 9), Nonconformism was not interested in maintaining social differences due to birth, wealth or occupation. To Nonconformists all Christians were equal in the sight of God. Consequently, all members of the chapels were encouraged to contribute to their life and work, and many positions of responsibility were occupied by people of quite humble social status. For example, in the late 19th century the trustees of the Methodist Chapel included two labourers, nine bricklayers, three dealers and two bakers.[3] In particular, the Nonconformists' ability to choose their own ministers created a strong rapport between preacher and congregation, especially as some of the lay preachers were themselves labourers, and had even retained a Bucks accent. A villager would feel able to welcome a Nonconformist minister into her cottage, and even to take 'pot-luck' at her table, an invitation she would not dare to have extended to such an elevated personage as the vicar.

Thirdly, Nonconformists lightened religion by introducing a strong social element in the form of choral performances, outings, sports' days, teas, concerts and socials. In addition, all sorts of fundraising activities were organised to pay for the extension and improvement of their premises, and to support religious and humanitarian causes. Consequently, for most Nonconformist families, their chapel was the centre of a very active social life.

Finally, in the second half of the 19th century, greater literacy and the development of newspapers began to enlighten the poor on social issues, especially where local newspapers like the Bucks Herald and the Bucks Advertiser tended to back, respectively, the Establishment and the labourers. Some of the poor began to wonder whether their plight really was inevitable, and what they could do about poverty. One possibility was Temperance which, by diverting income from drink to family, not only reduced poverty, but increased self-respect, social acceptability and ambition. In Wingrave, Nonconformists led the Temperance movement, and this boosted attendances at their chapels.

After 1884 two vicars (the Rev. Lockhart followed by the Rev. Francis) radically changed the attitude of the parish church towards the poor, with self-help replacing charity as the main means of relieving poverty. By introducing saving clubs for clothing and coal, the Rev. Lockhart made the financial benefits of temperance much more secure. He also persuaded the principal landlords to provide land for allotments, which not only yielded cheap fresh food, but left the labourer with far less drinking time! Later, the Rev. Francis established a Nursing Association to which all parishioners could subscribe, and this reduced the poverty created by illness and injury. He also acquired, and gave to the church, Hannah de Rothschild's redundant infants' school. Known as the Church Rooms, it provided the parish with a very successful working men's club.

All this put the parish church back into the mainstream of parish life. "The people come to the vicarage for almost every conceivable thing," wrote the Rev. Lockhart in 1892, adding "and sometimes it seems nothing but one continual fret". It would be nice to think that all this effort resulted in much bigger congregations at the parish church, but few statistics are available to confirm or deny this. We do know that in 1909 there were only eighteen regular communicants, though there would be sixty to eighty when it was a church festival. The main morning and evening services also attracted far more support on special occasions. And it must be remembered that there were ten weekday services on offer as well.[4] However, only the children's attendances really pleased the Rev. Francis:

The Children's Service at 2 p.m. has an excellent and increasing attendance. The children attend long after they have left Sunday School, and many mothers attend too. I hope they learn a great deal. We get most of them sooner or later for confirmation. But I cannot pretend to be satisfied. Many have come over from the chapel Sunday Schools and have much to learn. Very few of the lads become regular communicants; more of the girls. They are all fairly regular with the other church services and seem disinclined to revert to chapel." [5]

Much of the above confirms the recollections of the oldest inhabitants that Sunday was a busy day in Wingrave village in the early 20th century. Indeed, Sunday started on Saturday, for Sunday was a dress-up day, and in many homes Saturday night was bath night, which also meant hair washing, and for the girls "the torture of a nest of curlers". Early on Sunday morning the agricultural labourers with Sunday duties went to their farms, and at varying intervals returned. Many of those who were not required for Sunday work would spend Sunday morning on their allotments. No more than the morning, of course, unless they were prepared for tongues to wag, for in practice the Day of Rest began as Sunday lunch ended. The earliest of these allotment holders, in their workaday clothes, would encounter the Primitive Methodists in their Sunday best heading for the 7 a.m. prayer meeting, or the communicants, hurrying to meet the 8 a.m. deadline at the Parish Church. As 10 a.m. approached little knots of children straggled towards the church and chapels, for Sunday school. Less than an hour later the congregation of the Parish Church would begin to respond to the call of the church bells. By 12.30 the roads would be clear as families settled down to their Sunday lunch. Not for long though, for all the Sunday schools met in the afternoon, when both the Prims and the Congs (as they were known) also had adult services in which the Sunday school children joined. Then home they all went, only to reappear after tea for the evening services. As the church and the two chapels met at about the same time and in different locations, up to four hundred people could be moving around the village in different directions, and there was much crossing of paths and hurried greetings. When the dark winter evenings came, little groups would pick their way along the roads (there were no pavements and no street lights) by the flickering light of their lanterns. You could recognise the people you met if you held your lantern high, but few bothered. Recognition was by the sound of voices and the sound of feet. On summer evenings whole families went for a stroll after the service, still dressed in their Sunday best.

Chapter Ten

The Parish Church

EARLIER TIMES

Wingrave's parish church dates back at least to 1190 A.D., when it consisted of just a chancel and nave. In the next three centuries it was greatly extended and improved. A squat 'massy' tower was added, and a ring of four bells was installed. It was considerably widened by constructing aisles on either side of the nave. The roof of the nave was raised, clerestory windows were installed to admit more light, and a rood screen was erected between the chancel and the nave. Later, the tower arch was blocked with a wall of lath and plaster, and a gallery was built in front of it, while box pews were installed in the nave. No more appears to have been done until the Rev. Butt arrived, 400 years later. By this time the church was very dilapidated. Even the churchyard, with its decaying graveboards, leaning gravestones and mossy mounds, was full.[1]

RELIGION IN CONFLICT

However, when the Rev. Butt replaced the Rev. Denton as Vicar in 1850, the physical condition of the church was by no means his only concern. "When I first commenced my ministry here", he wrote, "the church was almost deserted." To the parishioners of Wingrave, and even to Samuel Wilberforce, the Bishop of the Diocese, this was not surprising. As the Bishop noted in 1850, "The Rev. Isaac Denton has been a drunkard".[2] According to William Griffin, who farmed in Wingrave from 1826 to 1864, the Rev. Denton was often late arriving to conduct the service, or was drunk when he did so. One Sunday, the congregation, including William, waited a very long time for the service to begin, but there was still no sign of the Vicar. Apparently this was not unusual. According to the Bishop, "The dissenters proposed to poor Denton to give them the Chancel for their meetings, as he never used it"! On this occasion the congregation began to express its disapproval. William told them that the only solution was to build another place of worship. He and his wife joined the Congregationalists and remained with them for the rest of their lives.[3] One wonders whether many other Wingrave Anglicans followed their example. The Rev. Butt seemed to think so, for on one occasion he reminded the Bishop, "Neglect on the church's part in past times is in part the cause (of poor attendance)".

The Rev. Butt worked hard to repair the damage done by his predecessor, but by 1857 he was clearly dissatisfied with the results of his efforts. "The congregation is, I fear, below one hundred. It is a very varying one: many in the evening, who are absent in the morning". This was a strange remark to come from a parson with seven years' experience of a rural parish. It probably illustrates the gulf between him and his poorer parishioners, for Sunday morning was a busy time for most agricultural labourers. For some it was their only chance to tend their vegetable plot, while others had to go to work watering and foddering the animals, and milking the cows. In most 19th century farmyards these were pretty dirty jobs, so the labourer arrived home in no condition to attend a church service. With only the most primitive washing and drying facilities available, no wonder the evening service was preferred.

In reality, the Rev. Butt's ministry greatly revived the Anglican cause in the parish, even though it never attracted the overwhelming support for which he longed. He consoled himself with the hope that the Church was "regarded with veneration and love". Doubtless it was, by those who attended it, but the Nonconformist was equally committed to his chapel, and it was the intense competition from Nonconformists which was the principal factor limiting the size of the Anglican congregation. The Vicar confided to his Bishop:[4]

Dissent was very strong and popular before I came to the parish. Some farmers and many tradesmen take a great interest in their chapels and Sunday schools. Their example influences the labourers, and the church's work is greatly impeded. The two dissenting chapels have succeeded in beguiling many from the church. In some instances elder girls have been drawn away to become teachers in the Primitive Methodist Sunday School just re-established. The minister of the Independent Chapel has laboured for thirty years in the parish and gained considerable influence. The Primitive Methodists have just erected a new, much larger, chapel. This gives me much uneasiness, but it takes much with the poor, who are led away by the noise and excitement, and have very little regard for the services of our church.

Even if he had wished to, the Vicar could do little about the form and content of the services in his church, for the Church of England was much more prescriptive than the chapels in such matters. And there were other differences.

The parish church had been built in an age when it was thought proper to separate the sacred from the secular by locating the former in the chancel where distance and a wooden screen substantially reduced the congregation's view of the altar, the choir and the priest. In sharp contrast the relatively modern chapels had simple rectangular plans which brought the altar, preacher, choir and accompanist into close proximity with the congregation, creating a feeling of unity and personal involvement, which sometimes became a little too personal. "Can't you get down? Be thy knees sore?" one Methodist preacher would enquire if some of the congregation were slow in settling down for prayer.[5]

Those of independent means, plus some of the landowners and local farmers, together with their families and servants, were the backbone of the Anglican congregation. Their donations and pew fees shored up the church finances, and their business acumen managed the parochial school and dominated the Vestry. They were the principal employers in the parish, and were convinced of their station in life. They believed that the rich man was in his castle and the poor man at his gate by order of the Almighty, and that anyone who challenged the existing social order was wicked. And, through its catechism, the Church of England endorsed this. Thus, anyone seeking full membership of the parish church had to promise:[6]

To submit myself to all my governors, teachers, spiritual pastors and masters; to order myself lowly and reverently to all my betters . . . . and to do my duty in that state of life, unto which it shall please God to call me.

It followed that, "If the labourers did enter the parish church, much that they heard therein they would find uncongenial".[7] Even so, there was no way in which the Rev. Butt could disassociate himself from the catechism, nor is there any indication that he wished to. Indeed, the children in Wingrave's parochial church school, to which he devoted so much time and effort, were very thoroughly catechised. Nevertheless, "as a kind and broad-minded Christian with a strong interest in the people's welfare,"[8] he emphasised not the rigidity of class distinctions, but rather, "the establishment of a kindly feeling between farmer and labourer, that men should do unto others as they wished that others should do unto them." For their part, employers should labour "to elevate the lower classes, to give them a better education, to make them more moral and to fit them better for the discharge of their duties".[9]

This was all very well intended, but many poor labouring families did not feel the need to be converted to respectability by their middle-class 'masters'. They already believed that family life was important, that labouring was better than loafing, and that sluttish and immoral behaviour were unacceptable.[10] To the poor, the best contribution that a 'master' could make to their well-being was a wage packet large enough to provide adequate food and clothing, decent housing, and a basic education for the labourer and his family. Not surprisingly, some poor families found the vicar's aspirations for them at best irrelevant and at worst condescending, and therefore worshipped where social distinction was given less prominence, namely the chapels. [11]

The parish church was built of Totternhoe 'clunch', a chalky, porous, local stone through which damp penetrated to stain and flake the white-washed interior. So the church was not only permanently cold but also very damp. Even the parish chest had to be kept at the vicarage to prevent mildew attacking the church records. The Vicar was determined to make the church more welcoming, and by 1854 could report, "Two good stoves have been erected so that instead of an ice-box the church is comfortably warm". Only a year later, the Vicar's Churchwarden and close friend, Joseph Lucas of Rowsham, gave the church its first organ.[12] "Large and handsome," it must have given the Vicar much joy and encouragement. Unfortunately, it had to be placed at the back of the church, behind the congregation. Eventually, in 1872, the Vicar decided that the church needed a complete restoration, and began the fundraising with an anonymous donation of a year's income. Sadly, in 1875, his wife died and his own health declined. When ill-health forced him to retire in 1884, there had been no further progress. However, in 1877 he had made one further contribution to the village scene.

The old church clock was "dumb and useless". On the Vicar's initiative it was replaced, the Vicar heading the subscription list with £50 from his own pocket. The new clock had two faces, one visible from the Recreation Ground and one from the Winslow Road. As the Bucks Herald noted,[13] "The clock would thus prove a great boon, not only to parishioners, but also to the many that may be on their way to catch the trains at Marston Gate."

The Rev. Butt died in 1887, and was buried beside his wife in the churchyard of the parish he loved so much, only a stone's throw from the school which he had established,[14] extended and managed with such devotion. He was remembered as "a faithful priest and a thorough gentleman of courteous manner".[15]

PROGRESS!

The Rev. Thomas Gostelow Lockhart commenced his duties in November 1884, and by the summer of 1885 his congregation had very noticeably increased. That August the churchwardens provided a tea so that the parishioners could give their new vicar a public welcome. Afterwards the Vicar put his intentions clearly before his congregation. If they would help themselves, he would try to help them too, in the complete restoration of their church. They agreed to the bargain and the Church Restoration Fund was re-launched. The Bucks Herald noted, "There is indeed a decided alteration in the parish already through the instrumentality of the Rev. Lockhart whose motto seems to be PROGRESS". And the Vicar later recalled, "They did help me wonderfully, for, of course, I could not have succeeded without their help".[16] Over the next two years all manner of fundraising activities took place: another 'Tea' based on trays of food prepared and donated by villagers; a two-day Bazaar held in the grounds of the Stewart Freemans' home (the Old Manor House) with the Aylesbury Town Band in attendance; a Harvest Thanksgiving Service; a lecture on Angels; church boxes and collecting cards; and countless social functions. A notable and very satisfactory feature of all this was the contribution by poor people and by dissenters.

Finally, in September 1887, the target of £4,600 was reached, sufficient for a complete restoration of everything except the church tower. The work took twenty months, and included: a new transept to house the organ; new vestries; a new chancel screen; a new stained glass east window; new flooring; new pews; new heating system; reconstruction of all rooves; restoration of the exterior stonework; removal of the gallery; and the unblocking of several windows. The church was re-opened in May 1889 by the Bishop of Oxford. Everyone was "much impressed with the wonderful alteration which had been effected". After a formal luncheon for 130 in the schoolroom, the Bishop expressed the hope that the parishioners "would not let the grass grow under their feet" until they had rebuilt the tower.[17]

In January 1890 the churchwardens, choir, Sunday School teachers and bell-ringers, about seventy in all, were invited by the Vicar to a tea and supper, when he presented his usual gift to each of the choir boys. Mr Charles Paine, the people's warden, thanked him for his unostentatious yet unstinting liberality and his untiring courage in church matters generally. After three hearty cheers the company rose to sing 'For he's a jolly good fellow'. The Vicar thanked them and said that it was one of the happiest moments of his life to see round him his co-workers and friends. He firmly believed no vicar had a more sympathetic and kinder band of workers than he had.

Fund-raising restarted, but first of all existing debts had to be cleared. It was 1895 before the Vicar could launch the Tower Restoration Fund and reveal his ambitious plans. The existing tower would be "pulled down and rebuilt in harmony with the rest of the church". Inside the church, the wall blocking the tower arch was now "dilapidated and an eyesore". The parish "must not rest" till it had been removed, revealing the arch and - at the foot of the tower - space for a baptistry. This would be lit by a large new window in the wall of the new tower. £1100 was required, and the Freemans immediately promised £500. A number of events were arranged including a garden party and a concert. Then in 1898 a committee of forty-two planned a grand two-day bazaar for the following year. During the next winter, many of the village women met for two or three hours, twice a week, to produce articles for sale. When the great day came, the bazaar was opened by The Hon. Walter Rothschild, the new member of parliament for the Aylesbury constituency. Visitors found that Indian scenery had been erected in the school to produce an oriental effect, while one classroom had been fitted up as a tea-room, and another as a 'bijou theatre' where members of the committee entertained the visitors. This event alone raised £230 and the committee decided that the work should start immediately. After five hundred years of neglect the interior part of the tower was said to be in a dangerous condition, and to require immediate attention. In addition, the tower would be raised by fifteen feet to provide a ringing chamber. The six bells would be re-hung in a new wooden frame designed to hold eight bells eventually. An entirely new turret stairway would be built for the whole height of the tower.

The work was completed, and a tower dedication service took place in September 1901, when the Bishop of Oxford returned to congratulate everyone on uniting rich and poor, church and dissent, to provide Aylesbury Vale with a prominent and beautiful landmark. Meanwhile, the reality was not so satisfactory. The Vicar and his supporters felt that the contractors had rushed to complete the work and had used inferior materials. For instance, slate had been used to roof the tower instead of lead, and rainwater was seeping into the tower, where it had already got into the mechanism of the tower clock, which had stopped. Eventually it was all sorted out. Protracted negotiation reduced the payment to the contractors by £80. Joe Rickard, a Wingrave builder and carpenter, boarded up the works of the clock and lowered the timbers of the roof, so that Tofield of Aylesbury could replace the tiles on the tower roof with lead. Still the clock just would not go. Then Charles Paine, who was churchwarden, recommended 'old Kempster' of Cublington. He spent four or five hours a day for several days up in the tower, removing the spindles, and cleaning off the rust with emery paper. When he had finished, the clock was going again. He charged £5 for the work, and said that if God Almighty would spare him he would make it go for a thousand years, with a new bearing now and again. It was not worn out: it just needed casing to protect it from the weather. "If it don't go, I must come again," he said. "A doctor can't always cure you at one visit".[18]

The Rev. Lockhart's sixteen-year sojourn had made a considerable and favourable impression upon the parish: congregations at the parish church had increased; relationships between Dissenters and Anglicans had improved; the parish church restoration was complete; and by championing the cause of allotments, (pages 88-90) a bond had at last been created between parson and poor. So it was unfortunate when the Vicar refused to give Joseph Bonham access to the parish chest, and involved himself in a long-standing conflict with a very persistent parishioner. It was even more unfortunate that the conflict with Bonham coincided with the creation of Wingrave's first elected Parish Council, of which Bonham was a member, and which he managed to involve in his dispute with the Vicar (Recollections: page 112). Even worse, the Vicar decided to challenge (usually incorrectly) some of the rights which the P.C. claimed.[19] The battle was still rumbling on in 1901, and was finally resolved by the retirement of the Rev. Lockhart in 1905 after a long illness. He died in 1906. At his memorial service the congregation were reminded how very unwilling he had been to give up his work in the parish when stricken down with illness, hoping against hope that he would recover. Their beautiful House of God would be a lasting memorial to the energy and zeal of their old friend and minister.[20]

THE REVEREND WILLIAM FRANCIS

Soon after commencing his ministry in Wingrave, the new vicar found himself in an embarrassing position, as he explained to Lord Rosebery:[21]

I know you have been a generous helper already, but . . . after I had accepted charge of this parish, I heard to my surprise that there was £130 due to Barclays upon the Parish School account. Another £142 was due upon the church Tower Restoration Fund. . . .I am extremely anxious that these debts should be paid as soon as possible. Mr Freeman has most generously offered a hundred guineas, and I am very willing to contribute fifty guineas, exactly half a year's income from the living. I know how very much my predecessor has done for the parish, and I by no means complain that he has left me with some slight share of the work. But it prevents other work which I should have been glad to have attempted, such as a club room for our working men. The parish is a poor one. I can see no other way to raise the necessary funds except by an appeal.

Generous help was given by Lord Rosebery and others and the debt was cleared, much to the Vicar's relief.

Now he could concentrate on the project close to his heart, namely the acquisition of a room, for all manner of church purposes: mothers' meetings, for example,

46. *The parish church before restoration. This, the earliest known photograph of the church, appeared in Photographic Views of the Churches, Mansions and Country Seats in the Diocese of Oxford by Charles May assisted by E.Rolls, 1862. (Bucks Archaeological Society Library).*

47. *The parish church after restoration, and the re-building of the tower, which was completed in 1901. Note the new south porch, and the new south transept accommodating the organ and vestries for the vicar and the choir.*

Recollections: Joey Versus The Vicar --Hilda Roberts [22]

Joseph Bonham, who was always known as 'Joey', lived at the Carpenters' Arms. He was quite a character and something of a pioneer. He was the first villager to buy a penny farthing bike, and rode it in the village, and to work. Later he introduced the tricycle to the village. He was always inventing some new gadget, so that anyone who introduced an hitherto unknown article would be asked if it was "one of Joey's new come-outs". He made several agricultural tools including a seed drill, and could do plumbing and drains like an expert. Joey was also the local chimney sweep, while his wife performed the last offices for many of Wingrave's inhabitants. [23]

Joey was of an enquiring mind and looked into all the old parish rules and customs, including the village charities left in earlier times by local benefactors. He was rather dissatisfied with their administration, which was vested mainly with the Vicar and his churchwardens. The old documents were deposited in a chest in the parish church, and eventually Joey demanded leave to see them. The Vicar did not understand Joey's mentality and promptly refused. Undaunted, Joey went to Somerset House in London, a wonderful adventure in those days, which made him the hero of the village, but did not at all please the Vicar. When Joey returned he had all the information he needed about the charities, and let it be known that he held the trump cards.

In 1894 Joey was elected to Wingrave's first Parish Council, and within three months the P.C. was asking to inspect the contents of the parish chest and also "to take charge of anything supposed to be the Council's". The Vicar agreed reluctantly to an inspection, but denied the P.C.'s right to any documents, and added,

In case you may elect Mr Joseph Bonham to this committee, I beg to state that I should decline to hold any intercourse with him until he can exercise more self control. One may have to submit to insults in public, but obviously one need not expose oneself to them in private. [24]

The P.C. then challenged the Vicar's administration of the Charities "as no accounts have been rendered to the Parish". This resulted in a Public Enquiry by the Charity Commissioners in 1897. Meanwhile Joey and the Vicar were in conflict again.

In 1786 a villager called Elizabeth Theed lost her way in the local fields during a storm, but was directed home by the sound of Wingrave's church bells. In gratitude she left a piece of land to the Church so that every year, on Feast Day, [25] the aisles of the church could be strewn with rushes. People came from miles around to see this unusual spectacle, and even wandered round the church during the services. This incensed the Rev. Lockhart who, in 1896, asked the Bishop "if anything could be done to stop the strewing of grass in our church on Festival Sunday". Receiving no support, he took direct action. When Joey and his compatriots went to carry out this ritual on the evening before Feast Day, the church doors were all locked. Determined not to be beaten, they returned next morning with large armfuls of grass which they scattered not only in the aisles but also in the pews.

The public enquiry into the parish charities found "very little to look into", but it did give Joey a chance to air his reservations about the administration of the charities, while the Rev. Lockhart was able to complain about the strewing of grass. [26]

Strewing grass is a nauseous and offensive practice, actually discolouring the light-stained oak pews and floor blocks. Nothing was said about grass in the bequest. The charity was left for the purpose of providing clean rushes for the sake of cleanliness. Let dirty ways disappear. Cleanliness is next to Godliness, and Feast Sunday should be observed in a rational manner.

Despite all this, the custom still continues, but using hay instead of grass. And by 1906 the Bucks Herald could report, "the thoughtless and irreverent behaviour in past years has now ceased, and not an objectionable feature occurred to mar the order and conduct of the service".

or a clubroom for young men in the evenings, with perhaps a billiard table and an opportunity for games. He asked Lord Rosebery to sell him a piece of land, next to the school on the Recreation Ground.[27]

I would gladly give £100 towards the cost of such a room. I also have an offer of another £100 from friends outside the parish. The chapel people have rooms attached to their chapels for small meetings. Men of all denominations would naturally be welcomed in the Men's Clubroom. We make no distinctions.

At the same time he voiced another concern: the churchyard. Ten years previously the Rev. Lockhart had reported, "There is a pressing want of fresh burying ground. No vacant spaces are left in any part of the present churchyard for any more interments. Its present state is indecent, amounting often to a desecration of the dead". Lord Rosebery's agent replied,[28]

His lordship is going to give a third of an acre at the back of the schoolyard and opposite the churchgate to the village. He will also give the portion of ground that we discussed for the parish room (36 ft x 50 ft) with a proviso that it is for the benefit of all denominations, the management to be in the hands of the vicar and his churchwardens and two members of the parish council.

Although this was a very generous offer, the Vicar rejected it because any ratepayer, whether chapel or church, could vote in the election for churchwarden at the Easter Vestry.[29]

I fear the proviso makes my scheme quite hopeless. The majority here are Non-conformist, and they can always prevail on the Parish Council, and can, if needs be, elect a churchwarden who would be hostile. I could be left in a minority and might lose practically all control of the room. I wanted it for church purposes: for my class, for mothers' meetings, as well as a recreation room for the lads. I know the sort of feeling Lord Rosebery has, and can partly sympathise with it, but practically it does not work. We should raise all the money, and all the work would be done by the Vicar, who would be left at the mercy of others as to management. We already have an undenominational Temperance Hall which is practically in the hands of Nonconformists, and has rules as to Total Abstinence which make it impossible for me to work there. Only total abstainers are allowed to speak which, though I am one myself, I object to strongly.[30]

The Vicar also declined Lord Rosebery's offer of land for the churchyard.[31]

At a meeting of parishioners (May 1910) most were opposed to a burial ground opposite the church. It was simply a meeting of Nonconformists with a small sprinkling of church people, and though I managed to keep them from active and open unfriendliness, there is little doubt there was a good deal of fire waiting to break out had occasion offered. I have no wish to try and go on with the matter in the face of their feeling. My thanks to Lord Rosebery.

The Rev. Francis tried hard to ensure that fire did not break out! He continued the Rev. Lockhart's policy of making the provident clubs open to all parishioners irrespective of religious affiliation. Also the Nursing Association which he established. "The District Nurse costs us £42-10s a year. In practice, church people will pay it all. But all parishioners benefit equally, and Nonconformists being poorer, benefit the most".[32] The Rev. Francis also tried to damp down the concerns of Nonconformist parents for whose children the only local school was Church of England. "The senior teacher is Primitive Methodist. I got her appointed with a view to making special provision for

Nonconformists, but it has never been desired. A few scholars are withdrawn from Catechism; but none from other religious instruction."[33] His policies certainly avoided a conflagration, but didn't satisfy everybody. "I was told yesterday that I greatly favoured dissenters as against church people", the Vicar confided to Lord Rosebery. "It's not true, but it does go to show that I have no grudge against them".

It was six years before the Rev. Francis had another opportunity to provide a church room for his parishioners. In 1916 it seemed very likely that Lady Rosebery's School would be closed. The matter was brought up at a Parish Council meeting and it was proposed that the Vicar should be the first to be consulted. Would Lord Rosebery allow it to be used for parish purposes? No record of the negotiations has been found. All we know is that the Reverend Francis acquired the freehold of the property, and in 1918 transferred it in trust to the Oxford Diocesan Board.[34] He had at last achieved his ambition to provide a Church Room for the parish.

In 1919, when he retired to Norfolk, the Bucks Herald commented:

The Rev. Francis won the respect and affection of all classes of the community by his kindness and generosity to all. The Nursing Association, which he generously support- ed from its inception, has proved itself again and again of great value. The Provident Clubs, too, which he encouraged and improved, have been a real help to the working classes. Only recently he presented the village with a Church Room which will eventually be a great social benefit in the village. It was his own special wish that there should be no collection on his behalf, and no public presentation. However, it was felt that he should not be allowed to depart without some slight recognition of his work and goodness. The churchwardens and friends therefore, on behalf of the parishioners, presented him with an address framed in oak, and the Sunday School children presented him with two framed views of the church, both presentations being made privately.

These comments emphasise that in addition to initiating and organising parish projects, the Rev. Francis generously supported them.[35] Thus, he not only founded the parish magazine (in March 1907), but for twelve years personally paid at least half its cost, so that even the poorest cottagers could enjoy it. In 1918 alone this cost him about £14. In the same year the annual Choir Treat cost £14, while the church collections which were intended to cover the cost contributed only £2-8s-3d. These two items alone absorbed a quarter of his annual stipend of 100 guineas. Neither was it an exceptional year. In 1912, ignoring the Provident Clubs and the Nursing Fund, the parish expenses were £96-14-9d, while the church collections intended to cover these expenses, provided only £48-15s-10d. Donations from ten parishioners brought in a further £25, leaving the Vicar to find the balance. "It is the same with most of our funds", the Vicar reported. "The money contributed is quite inadequate and I must often either leave undone what seems to me useful, or find the money myself".[36] He was very good at 'finding money', for a massive annual bonus of 30% was added to each Provident account. Just how this was managed was not revealed, but it is perhaps significant that his successor, the Rev. Milner, had only one complaint: the difficulty of following a rich and generous vicar!

What the Bucks Herald did not mention is the Vicar's workload, of which we know only because he was the first of Wingrave's vicars to publish a church magazine. This reveals that quite apart from baptisms, weddings and burials, he conducted well over five hundred services each year, and was always game for more. Although there were communion services on Easter Day at 7 a.m., 8 a.m., and noon, "an additional celebration at 6 a.m. could gladly be arranged". He also had financial responsibility for the church, the burial ground, the Nursing Association, and the Sunday School, besides having to raise funds for the twenty-six charities supported by the church. He chaired the managers of the Parochial Church School, regularly visited the school and sometimes taught and tested the pupils. He took on the whole of the burden of collecting and paying out the deposits in the parish provident clubs. There were also all the usual parochial duties such as visiting the sick and the elderly.

Vic Rickard (1903-1989)

With such a workload, a conscientious vicar must have been delighted to find that a popular Wingrave sportsman was also an enthusiastic member of the congregation. Both Vic and his wife Sybil were closely associated with Wingrave Parish Church for most of their lives. Sybil was church organist for twenty years. Vic started as a choirboy, became a keen bellringer, was a founder-member of the Parochial Church Council, and after a spell as sidesman became churchwarden, a post he held under six incumbents. Together with his father, and later on his own, Vic was always doing odd repairs to the church. For over fifty years he wound up and maintained the clock on the church tower. One way or another he spent so much time there that one village wag said, "If the church ever fell down, you'd be sure to find Vic Rickard sitting amongst the rubble". For many years he was also the secretary and treasurer of the United Charities, and for thirty years was a governor of Wingrave Church of England Combined School. In 1987 the Bishop of Buckingham wrote:

Your record of service through so many years is, I think, almost without parallel in this archdeaconry. You have been a tower of strength to successive vicars and the whole Christian community in Wingrave.

THE CHURCH ROOMS

The building included a very large room and a smaller room. At first they were used almost exclusively for the club which had figured so prominently in the Rev. Francis' plans. Eventually they were also used for church and parish council meetings; concerts, whist drives, socials and dances; and for wedding receptions, being the only hall in the parish where alcoholic drink was allowed. And as the rooms could be hired separately, the church 'room' gradually became known as the church 'rooms'. Chairs, tables, lamps etc. were in very short supply at the end of World War One but, a year later, funds had been raised, furniture obtained and the club formed for youths and men. By 1924 it had a hundred members, and was open nearly every night. It flourished for many years, as a place of relaxation, where games such as snooker, cards and dominoes could be played. The Rev. Milner claimed that he spent three nights a week there, and practically ran it. During World War Two it served as a First Aid Post, as the H.Q. of the local Home Guard, and as a school for the London evacuees billeted in the village.

Jack and Iris Tompkins, who were the last caretakers and occupied the adjoining schoolhouse for 39 years, recalled their New Year's Eve socials.

We organised lots of games and refreshments. We had a Christmas Tree and, of course, Father Christmas. He used to prepare in our house, walk round the building and enter by the front door. The piano was played, everyone singing carols. Then three cheers for Father Christmas and the raffle prizes were taken off the tree. In the huge fireplace there was an enormous fire. Just before midnight those who rang the bells went up to the church and rang the Old Year out and the New Year in. It really was a most enjoyable evening.

In 1978 it was felt that the Church Rooms were no longer needed. The old parish school had been replaced by a modern building, and had become a Community Centre for social activities. The Church Rooms were sold and eventually converted into two

48. The annual strewing of hay in the church on Feast Sunday.

49. Church garden party held in Mr and Mrs Luck's garden (now the Hollies) in Leighton Road. The Rev. Wadsworth bowls determinedly, under the watchful eye of Vic Rickard, while the lads of the village look on anxiously. From the left: David Hewitt, Barry Fleet, Joe Henley, David Holt, Alan Timms and friend.

dwellings. But that was not the end of the Rev. Francis' gift, for the interest on the Church Rooms' Account has already helped towards various church needs, including the provision of a kitchen and toilet in the parish church itself.

CHURCH ACTIVITIES

The poor were always remembered, particularly at Christmas and New Year. Page 95 provides some examples.[37] Treats and outings for Sunday School scholars and the choir were eagerly anticipated. In 1887 a very special outing was arranged for the Choir and Mr Rees, who was both the church organist and parochial school master.[38]

The cheap excursion train to Brighton was taken advantage of, and they started for this Queen of Watering Places at 6.30 a.m. under the supervision of the Rev. Lockhart. They arrived at Brighton at 10.30, and the day turned out to be a glorious one. After visiting the various places of amusement and interest, not forgetting a 'Dip in the Briny' and a 'Sail on the Ocean Wave', the Choir returned home having enjoyed a most delightful holiday and for most of them their first sight of the sea. The choir, which numbered 20, voted their thanks to Mr Joseph Rickard, for the loan of his van, which took them to and from the station.

Often the annual Treat took place in a field lent by a local farmer. In August 1890 a procession of children carrying banners and led by a brass band made its way to a field lent by Mr James Gibbs. The Vicar, their teachers, parents and friends followed.[39]

Various games were indulged in until 4 o'clock when tea was announced. We need hardly say that the youngsters, who numbered nearly one hundred, did ample justice to the good things provided: in fact the bread and butter and cake seemed to vanish as if by magic. Parents and friends then had their tea, after which all seemed bent upon making the little ones happy. Games and sports continued and toys and sweets were distributed. At nine o'clock a fine display of fireworks was witnessed by the village. The playing of the National Anthem brought a most pleasant day to a close. On leaving the field a bun was presented to each child.

Recollections: Singing in the Choir — Vic Clay

I remember joining the choir in 1918. From 1919 Mr Stubbs, the headmaster, was also choir-master and organist, so there was no escape from school discipline. I remember singing anthems at Whitsun and Harvest Festival, the same each year. Mrs Griffin and Hilda Gibbs sang the ladies' solos, and Alfred Rogers sang the boys'. I remember singing at the funeral of Mrs Freeman of the Old Manor House, and at the wedding of Miss Mary Paine. We boys were each paid one shilling. We were also paid five shillings if we didn't miss any services or practices for a whole year.

CHURCH GOVERNMENT

In 1920 the church authorities finally determined their response to the formation of the Parish Council in 1894, when it had taken over the Vestry's civil responsibilities in the parish. A parochial church council was elected by those on the church electoral roll to administer church affairs in the parish. Henceforth, decisions on church matters would be made by those committed to the Anglican church rather than just any resident of the parish.

Chapter Eleven

The Independent Chapel

THE STRUGGLE TO WORSHIP

Nonconformism in Wingrave dates back at least to the mid-17th century. Thus, in 1669, Roger Hitchcocke, Vicar of Wingrave, reported to the Archdeacon of Buckingham that "for many yeares past", an Anabaptist Assembly, said to be composed of "inferior tradesmen and meane inferior people", was holding weekly services in Rowsham. And Quakers worshipped at Wingrave at the home of John Lucas, yeoman. Their Monthly Meeting, attracted "sometimes an hundred, sometimes many more", and was the largest Quaker assembly in North Buckinghamshire.[1]

Over a century later Nonconformists were still meeting in Wingrave, in buildings licensed for preaching by the Archdeacon of Buckingham. In turn the homes of William Bonham (1788), Rebecca Rodwell (1800), John Edwards (1801), and William Honor (1803) were used. Then, in 1813, Richard Fleet (a Wingrave carpenter) died, and his workshop was sold. It stood in a large orchard on the eastern side of Church Street, and had far-reaching views across the Vale towards Waddesdon. William Cox, one of Wingrave's leading farmers, purchased it, had it licensed for preaching and offered it to the Nonconformists, who accepted it with much rejoicing. In 1817, under the guidance of the Rev. Thomas Hunt of Tring, they declared themselves an Independent Church, though they were also known as the Union Chapel because they were a union of Baptists, Quakers and Congregationalists. They demolished the workshop and erected a meeting house on the site.[2] William Cox then transferred the ownership of the property to the Rev. Hunt and the Trustees of the Chapel, on the understanding that it was "to be a place of public religious worship for promoting the Christian religion as professed by Protestant dissenters". It is said that the Rev. Thomas Hunt was the Nonconformists' minister from 1780 to 1828.[3] If so, then for nearly fifty years, in all weathers, he regularly rode or drove the eight miles to Wingrave and back. Just why he remained so loyal to the fledgling Wingrave chapel remains a mystery.

The year 1828 was the beginning of a new era. Firstly, a new minister, the Rev. Aston, arrived. Then in October 1828 William Cox offered to give the piece of ground adjoining the meeting house for a burial ground and for the erection of a new meeting house. The members unanimously accepted 'his kind offer', but it was 1832 before the new chapel was completed. It opened on September 12th, when three services were held, and the Rev. Aston was supported by eight visiting ministers, three of them from London, despite (in the absence of railways) an extremely uncomfortable journey of at least five hours by stage-coach. The minute book records, "This concluded an interesting day: the weather was fine, the congregation was large, and the collection amounted to £28-1s-3d".

The new chapel was essentially the building we see today: almost elegant in its simplicity, and very suited to its purpose, being both commodious and acoustically excellent. There is no record as to how such a small congregation managed to finance it, but a few clues have emerged. Clearly, even the poorest members of the congregation contributed their mites. Then there is a story of one member helping with the roofing, and contributions of labour may well have been widespread. Farmers usually contributed generously to appeals by the clergy for church projects and it would be entirely in character if Mr Cox had once more loosened his purse strings. Certainly William Griffin of Manor Farm contributed at this time, for he reminded his family of it every year, when he was always asked for a contribution to the chapel's upkeep.[4] Loans also had to be raised, and they were still paying off these debts in November 1835 when "they did a special collection for the debt upon the church and the Rev. Aston preached: 'Let us not be weary in well-doing, for in due season we shall reap, if we faint not' ". Poor little faithful flock! They certainly needed those words of cheer, be-cause by 1842 the deacons had decided to

50. *William Griffin (see also page 106)*

pay £3-5s-3¼d for land in Church Street, on which to build a manse for their minister.

The new chapel adjoined the earlier building, which became a vestry and schoolroom for Sunday scholars. Large shutters were installed between the chapel and the schoolroom so that they could be opened on special occasions to provide extra seating. Including the gallery, there was extensive free seating, but pews with opening doors cost £3 or £4 a quarter. Presumably they were rented by gentry and farmers with Nonconformist sympathies. Several local farmers were strong chapel supporters: John Grace of Church Farm, William Cox of Windmill Hill Farm, and William Griffin of Manor Farm, for example. In addition, the trustees included two gentlemen and five farmers. Some came from such a distance (Hillesden, Chesham and Quainton, for instance) that they were probably not regular attenders. Even so, their pew rentals alone would make a major contribution to the chapel's work. Agricultural labourers simply couldn't afford such fees. In any case, their sons favoured the gallery, enjoying the clatter of their hobnailed boots as they raced up the stairs.

"FIRST IT MUST BE MY CHAPEL !"

The love and loyalty which people felt for their chapel in those days is illustrated by the story of a Wingravian grandfather who helped to tile the chapel roof when it was built. In later life he became almost blind, and eventually made the long journey to London for an operation. Some sight was restored and his son went to bring him back home. As they approached Wingrave, he asked, "Father, what are you looking forward to seeing most?" The answer came promptly, "My chapel". This rather distressed the son. "Oh, Father, I expected you to say, 'Mother'". "No," replied the old man. "Of course I want to see your mother, but first it must be my chapel".

The standards required for full membership of the chapel were high. And mem-bers not only had to accept those standards, but also had to put them into practice. Thus in 1834 the meeting felt obliged 'to exercise the painful part of its discipline', and John Goodger of Rowsham was "excommunicated for intemperance and inconsistencies after being admonished in vain". "May the Lord restore him again to the fold", wrote the Minister. This was one of a number of expulsions over the years, the grounds for which included profanity, intoxication, immorality, theft, and non-attendance at chapel. Only one of those excluded was subsequently re-admitted. This was George Griffin, the village baker, whose musical talent later brought so much benefit to the life of the chapel. He was excluded in 1846 for "neglect of religious ordinances and general misconduct". It was ten years before he was restored to the fold.

THE MINISTERS

The attitude of members to the chapel, and their response to its discipline, were very much a reflection of the minister's success in shepherding his flock, but also of each member's ability to respond to the varying strengths and styles of the ministers. And, as the records of the 19th century show, the ministers certainly did vary: kindly old men; fierce evangelists; a Doctor of Music, who was described as "a condensed orchestra"; and even one minister who was referred to as stern and arrogant.

The Rev. Thomas Hunt (1780-1828) and the Rev. Aston (1828-1860) stayed for a total of eighty years! Between them they transformed Nonconformism in Wingrave from a small group of Nonconformists meeting in private houses and relying upon one visiting minister into a substantial and united congregation with its own chapel, Sunday school, burial ground and a manse for its resident minister. The Rev. Aston clearly made a strong and favourable personal impression upon his flock, for a century later one lady in Wingrave could still recall her mother's comment, "The Rev. Aston was such a lovely man, with such a nice wife". A 40% increase in membership supports her view. Indeed, in the Rev. Butt's opinion, the Rev. Aston was a bit too successful!

The Rev. George Moore (1861-73) was long remembered as a loving and devoted pastor. He believed in visiting his congregation in their homes, and Monday was his favourite day for this. He said that when he saw the flags flying on the line, he knew the ladies must be at home. One wonders what sort of reception he got in the middle of washday. Presumably a welcome, for he must have enjoyed his time in Wingrave, since he returned to celebrate the anniversaries in 1879 and 1890 and the chapel's Golden Jubilee in 1882.

In sharp contrast to his predecessors, the Rev. John Pike (1874-78) was a very earnest evangelical pastor, who held many cottage meetings. His ministry was long remembered for his fervent preaching, his evangelical outlook, his 'conversions' and his 'mighty revivals'. Even thirty years later the theological press reported, "The effects can still be seen of the work of grace that then went on", and reported one conversion in some detail. The subject of the conversion was a local drunkard named Fred. His condition was so bad that the villagers had nicknamed him 'Born Drunk'. Meeting Mr Pike around the village one day, Fred demanded, "Why have you not saved me?" So Mr Pike 'set the word of God before Fred.' On the following Sunday evening, Fred was present at the chapel meeting. After the sermon, and a hymn, the meeting was thrown open for prayer. The first to stand up was Fred with the cry, "God be merciful to me". Subsequently, "he found peace and rest in the Lord, and became a companion of Mr Pike in the village work." [5]

It would be interesting to know what the Rev. Butt made of all this, especially as the Rev. Pike's four years in Wingrave doubled the chapel membership. Quite probably it simply left the Vicar speechless, for it even surprised some members of the chapel, one of whom recalled, "The Rev. Pike was a big wild-looking man: a missioner from the slums. When preaching, he used to shout and sing, and we thought him a bit odd for a minister. He was definitely a bit out of the usual, but he was a most successful evangelist".

The Rev. J.S.White (1883 -1889) was another contrast. He was a devoted pastor, but a quiet preacher. Even so, he could make his point effectively. At the end of one sermon he announced that he would tell the congregation a little verse, which they must remember as it would help them at all times. The congregation sat expectantly, awaiting

51. The Manse, home of the Congregational ministers, was built in 1842. Beyond is the end of Church Row, now demolished. Opposite is Church Farm, of which the wall and cowshed have been demolished.

52. Members of the Congregational Chapel gather at its front door for a 'likeness' to be taken. On the lefthand side of the doorway, with the impressive beard is the Rev. White 1883-89.

some fine poem, but the preacher just repeated:

Go on, go on, go on, go on;
Go on, go on, go on;
Go on, go on, go on, go on;
Go on, go on, go on.

He appears to have been the first of Wingrave's Nonconformist ministers, whose family actively supported him in his work. His wife worked hard for the chapel. She took a very active part in the Sewing Circle, and always went visiting with her husband. She became President of the Temperance Society. This was much more of an achievement than it sounds today, for at that time a Nonconformist wife usually walked very much in her husband's shadow. For example, women were not allowed to speak at the deacons' meetings. This was challenged in 1884, because women who visited candidates for membership needed to report their findings to the meeting. Despite the value of this work, the deacons decided that in future women should not visit candidates, thus avoiding the necessity of their speaking. The White's two daughters also helped in the Temperance Society.

After 1887 the chapel's finances were in a sorry state and poor Mr White was receiving his stipend in odd bits and pieces: £8-7s-5d, £7-6s-7d, £5-1-5d, etc., which must have been most trying for Mrs White's housekeeping. The deacons applied to the North Bucks Congregational Association for financial assistance but, for some unknown reason, the Association was unwilling to recognise the Rev. White as a minister. And so in 1888 he gave notice to the deacons that he would leave. Despite the Congregational Association's attitude, the Rev. White seems to have been genuinely popular.

The next incumbent, the Rev. John Barton (1892-1924), was a great worker and a good man, but rather stern and domineering. He insisted that women should be kept in their place. Mrs Barton was a sweet, gentle, motherly woman, but at the Ladies Sewing Meeting it was her husband who always took charge, saying that Mrs Barton's place was in the home. On one occasion when she was present and dared to say something, he at once told her, "Please be quiet and sit down". It is also said that if the organist was playing too loudly for the minister's liking, he would descend from the pulpit to push in the stops. In 1898 he announced that he had been invited to accept another church, "which was a strong temptation". Clearly the temptation to leave Wingrave must have been overcome most successfully, as he stayed for another 26 years!

Undoubtedly it took time for the members to adjust to some of these ministers, but the minutes of the business meetings suggest that congregations did adjust, and developed a regard and even a fondness for them despite their idiosyncrasies. Kind and appreciative words were minuted at their departure, and sometimes there was a more tangible acknowledgment. Shortly before the Rev. White left, about 120 people sat down to a public tea, at which he was presented with a purse containing £14, contributed by "upwards of one hundred families in Wingrave, Rowsham and Aston Abbotts, both conformist and nonconformist".

FAITHFUL WORKERS

However, it is not just the ministers who make a church or chapel successful. Ordinary men and women, faithful workers over the years, do much to maintain the standards and routine of a chapel, especially when ministers come and go more and more frequently. What follows is just a small selection of the many faithful workers who have selflessly served both ministers and congregations over the last two centuries.

William Robinson (1816-1898) is remembered as "One of Nature's gentlemen.

He was tall, but slightly bent when elderly, and with a saintly face that made one feel he possessed an inner holiness. He was a very dependable man, a living example of Christian piety". In addition to serving in the Wingrave chapel and Sunday school, he used to preach at Rowsham, Aston Abbotts and Burcott, sometimes walking great distances after doing his Sunday farm duties. He was a member for 58 years, and for nearly 54 years a deacon of the chapel.

John Dimmock (1822-1904) was an expert shoemaker, who *made* shoes rather than mended them. He entered the Sunday school at six years of age, and was a teacher at twelve. He became superintendent at thirty-three, and held the post for twenty years. He celebrated his 50th birthday by giving a tea to the Sunday school teachers, "after which an enjoyable evening was spent, praising God and singing hymns".

George Griffin (1817-1902) was first the village baker and later its postmaster. He was a man of great musical ability, and was the chapel's first organist and choir-master. He composed many anthems, hymns and choruses. When he became the village postmaster, he often sat in the little office attached to his house, on the corner of Nup End and Winslow Road, with little to do. On such occasions he would sometimes pick up a Post Office form, rule some lines on the back, and compose a new hymn or anthem, usually complete with words. His most notable work was the oratorio, 'Samuel', which was sung in many local towns and villages. George conducted the chapel choir, but it was very much his own choir, and a very good choir it was. Wingrave was noted for good singing, and George had the choice of the village singers, for it was looked upon as a great privilege to be included in his choir. George resigned his post of organist and choir-master on his 82nd birthday, after sixty years of service.

Joseph Humphries (1837-1912) had a ruddy complexion, the result of many years of hard work on the land. A border of dark brown whiskers, which grew from ear to ear, and were neatly trimmed, added dignity to his appearance. He was a comfortable sort of man, whose contented expression assured you that he was kindly disposed to life. He was a great influence for good, for he and his wife were Sunday school teachers all their long lives and it was said that Joseph carried that teaching into his everyday life.

Ralph Smith (1892-1972) was a baker and confectioner and a craftsman in the art of cake decoration. He gave loyal and devoted service as Congregational Church Secretary for 49 years, serving under nine ministers. In addition to his clerical duties he performed countless small tasks behind the scenes. These included coping with an aged and temperamental boiler, lighting fires, arranging pulpit supplies, and representing the church at County Union meetings, and on the Executive Committee.

In some families such dedication has continued from generation to generation. Daphne Rickard (1922-1977) was born into a Wingrave family of Nonconformists. Her maternal grandparents, William and Emily Gurney, were keen members of the Congregational Church, and William was the principal undertaker for its funerals. Daphne's mother, Gladys Rickard, was the church organist for nearly fifty years, and secretary and treasurer for twenty-five years,

53:Gladys Rickard (1896-1961)

54. *Connie Bignell playing the original organ in the Congregational Chapel gallery. The large doors at the far end could be opened up to accommodate the choir on anniversaries and other special occasions.*

55. *There were plenty of helpers at the Congregational 'Fair' in 1963. From left rear: Nora Rickard, Avis Cousins, Gwen Taylor, Jennifer Bignell, Janice Cole, Linda Brinded, Wendy Gurney, Betty Jarrott, Pamela Kirby. From left front: Marjorie King, Mrs G. King, Doris Peters, Ivy Bignell, Doreen Honor, Win Ellis, Mrs E. Ellis, Daphne Rickard, Betty Carter, Mrs F. Philbey, Mrs A. White.*

in addition to serving as a deacon for twenty-two years. Soon after being received into membership, Daphne became Sunday School Superintendent, continuing until incapacitated by illness thirty-five years later. She was also very active in taking the church into the community. She was a lay preacher, a great visitor of the sick and elderly at home and in hospital, a regular contributor of poems and short stories to Christian periodicals, and village correspondent for the Bucks Herald. Her sister, Pamela Kirby, continued the tradition, and at her death held the positions of Elder, secretary and treasurer. However, for sheer length of service, few are likely to match the late Connie Bignell, who was organist for seventy-four years.

THE CONGREGATIONAL SUNDAY SCHOOL

The Sunday school flourished for well over 150 years. Sunday was a demanding day for children, as Frank King recalled:

It was Sunday school on Sunday morning from 10 to 11. We assembled in the big schoolroom where we sang hymns and said prayers, and were tested on the text we had been given to learn on the previous Sunday. Then we were divided up by age and went into the three little classrooms for Bible study. We returned at two o'clock for another half hour of Sunday school and then went straight into chapel for afternoon service 2.30 to 3.30. We really did have to go 'straight into chapel'. It was not an option. We had to go through the internal door: no-one was allowed to go through the outside door! Then home for tea and back to chapel from 6 to about 7.15.

Knowing that the children faced nearly four hours of school and service, the superintendent and his teachers would try to maintain their interest and enthusiasm, by involving them in Missions, and encouraging them in district scripture examinations and singing competitions.

Everyone, but especially the children, looked forward to the Sunday school treats and outings. Every year the Sunday School Anniversary took place on the first Sunday and Monday of August. The chapel, beautifully decorated with flowers, would be packed, with extra chairs placed down the aisles. Even the gallery at the back of the chapel was usually full up at anniversaries and special occasions, mostly with boys. The children in the choirs, dressed in their Sunday best, would sing their hymns, especially prepared for the occasion. 'Amazing Grace', 'Love Divine', and 'Guide Me, Oh Thou

---

Recollections: The Anniversary Services – Joy Harries

My most vivid memories of Wingrave are of the Church Anniversary Services in August, when I was collected in a pony and trap with my parents and brother Ken. What a thrill to jog from Linslade along the country lanes through Mentmore to Wingrave. We came over every year to spend the day with Mr and Mrs Ellis, so that my father could play on his violin for the services in the Congregational Church. He was a professional violinist and sat by the organist, Connie Bignell, and someone was in the back "pumping" the organ. Rather different to organs these days! My father did this for many, many years, and when he was playing, I also sang in the choir with the children. Eventually buses ran from Linslade, so in later years we came by bus, and walked up from the crossroads.

My father was Tom Watson, and my mother was originally Mabel Griffin, sister of Ted, the baker. So I am a great-granddaughter of the composer George Griffin, and as a small child I remember visiting Stewkley and other villages to hear performances of 'Samuel', the oratorio that he composed, being given by local choirs and orchestras.

Great Jehovah', were great favourites. When the congregation joined in it was enough to raise the roof! Sankeys hymns were very popular, and one was always included in each service. It always followed the prayer, and for some unknown reason was called 'The Chant'. Past scholars often attended these events, some even travelling back to Wingrave from afar, for they welcomed the opportunity to renew old friendships and happy memories. In July 1864 and 1866 the Rev. Griffiths of Hitchin, who had himself been a scholar in the Sunday school, preached to crowded congregations. On the Monday a tea was given to the children at 3 p.m., and to 350 parents and friends at 4 p.m. Prizes were then distributed. Back in 1879 the Minutes tell us that:

£5 worth of books were presented to the children as rewards for good conduct, diligence and punctuality. The singing, speaking and Tea were of an excellent quality, the collection over £11, and all seemed to enjoy themselves. Many old scholars came home, (i.e. to Wingrave) notwithstanding the awful tempest and terrible storm of August 2nd.

At Christmas there would be a Christmas tree, small presents and a special Tea, followed by games and perhaps an entertainment. For some years lantern slides were very popular, and in 1908 the children enjoyed listening to a phonograph.

Before World War Two, many Wingrave families could not afford summer holidays, unless they had conveniently situated relatives. So for many villagers the highlight of the year was the Sunday school summer outing to places like Velvet Lawn (near Ellesborough) and Ashridge Woods. George Ellis would provide free transport in his waggonette, and local farmers would lend their carts and waggons. As they passed along the country lanes, enjoying the scenery, the passengers would sing well-known tunes, or George Griffin's hymns and anthems, or their favourites from Sankeys. Often they would have to get out and walk up the hills to ease the weight for the horses. At Ashridge the children played in the woods, had donkey rides, climbed the Monument, picked ferns and flowers, and had a tea of bread and butter, slab cake and shiny buns. Hilda Roberts remembered, "Under the trees someone would begin to sing an anthem by George Griffin, perhaps 'How Beautiful Among the Mountains', and all would join in, the lovely cadences rising and falling against the background of the wooded hills".

Recollections: The Outing to Margate - Grace King

In 1928 the three Wingrave Sunday schools combined and booked a special excursion train to Margate. Families and friends were encouraged to join the party, for two hundred full-fare passengers were needed to cover the cost of hiring the train.

When the great day arrived, everybody was dressed in their Sunday best. For these special occasions, I always had a new dress and a new pair of knickers to match. Bert Rickard ran his motor coach up and down the Tring Road to Marston Gate Station, and at six o'clock in the morning the train set off. Being a special train it went all the way to Margate without stopping. It was a corridor train too, which was lovely. Everybody enjoyed the beautiful countryside, which was so new and exciting to most of us. When we got there, families did their own thing until tea-time, when we met at a hall for a splendid tea: the children first; then the adults. Most of us slept on the train on the way back. When we awoke, it was dark like the middle of the night, and we were back at Marston Gate, with Bert Rickard waiting to ferry us back to Wingrave.

Such days were a big thing in our lives. They caused great excitement in the village, especially on this occasion, for Fred Bignell and Bosy Bateman missed the train home and sheepishly came back the next day, having had to walk all the way from Tring Station.

When he was a schoolboy, Frank King's father loved the Ashridge outings. Then he left school and his first job was at Upper Wingbury Farm. They wouldn't let him have a day off to go to Ashridge, and on the day of the outing he was given a horse and told to go down to a field to do some swarth-turning. When he got to the field, he decided that he would go to Ashridge, so he tied the horse up to a sapling in the hedge, and off he went. Next morning came the reckoning. "Where was you yesterday?" So he told them. "Well, you'd better get back there again today then", was the reply. And that was the end of his first job.

"As the years went by," wrote Daphne Rickard, "the outings went further afield: to London Zoo; and a park near Kettering. Outings to the seaside started in the nineteen-twenties with visits to popular resorts like Southend, Clacton and Eastbourne. It was often the only day that most children ever saw the sea, and as we left and the blue sea disappeared into the distance, we would wave out of the window, and sigh, 'Goodbye till next year'."

EXPANSION AND CONTRACTION

Much earlier (in 1904) it was realized that the old schoolroom was quite inadequate for the increasing numbers attending the Sunday School. Two new classrooms needed to be built and furnished, and an ancient heating system replaced. At the Annual Church Meeting the Rev. Barton urged, "It is our duty as well as our privilege to leave things better than when we found them, and to provide for our children as our fathers have provided for us." [6] The church had always been admirably self-sufficient, raising funds by all sorts of events, so once again the congregation set to work. Eventually £300 was raised, but a further £70 had to be borrowed at 4%! In our present age of easily available credit it is difficult to appreciate how painful such a debt was to many self-respecting people, quite apart from the interest draining away at a worrying £2-16-0d per year! Four years later the Treasurer (T.W. Heley) could bear it no longer and donated £10 with the promise of a further £10 if the remaining £50 could be raised. It was, but only because the Rev. Barton broke with tradition by appealing to such as Lord Rosebery and Leopold de Rothschild.[7]

I do not think we have appealed to your Lordship before. We pay our way without aid except for such special objects as this. I sincerely hope therefore that your Lordship may be able to help us now . . . .

By 1990, Sunday School attendance was so reduced that after much discussion and with great regret the Sunday School was disbanded. "Numbers are now very few on a Sunday morning. Children have so many other commitments".

RATIONALISATION

The number of adult members was also declining, and with it the finances of the church. It was both a local and a national problem. One solution was to close the buildings and sell them. Another was to retain the buildings but enlarge the pastorates. Wingrave had long shared its minister with Aston Abbotts, and (from 1870) with Rowsham, but eventually both the latter closed. By 1945 Wingrave was grouped with Burcott, and later with Burcott and Winslow. In 1972 a much more radical solution was agreed at national level. Subject to the views of the individual (and fiercely independent!) chapels, Congregationalists and Presbyterians combined to form the United Reformed Church. Wingrave Congregational Church agreed to a joint pastorate with St. Marks Church at Aylesbury. In future the minister would live at Aylesbury, and so in 1974 the Wingrave manse was sold.

Chapter Twelve

The Primitive Methodist Chapel

Little is known as to how Methodism spread to Wingrave, but it was probably the result of Methodist evangelism in a wide area around Aylesbury. Apparently, a Primitive Methodist mission of 1836 made a significant impact in the village.[1] Certainly, by 1839 there is a reference to a Primitive Methodist Society in Wingrave in the records of the Aylesbury Primitive Methodist Circuit.[2] In 1841, Thomas Fleet, a local carpenter, provided the Primitive Methodist Connexion with a plot of land in Nup End Lane, and a chapel was completed that year at a cost of £260.[3] Only two of the seven trustees lived in Wingrave: George Fleet, a carpenter, and James Kirby, a shoemaker, who was soon to become a strawplait dealer. His daughter, Mary Ann, was the first child to be baptised there in 1844. By this time the membership had reached 41, but it had declined to only seven by 1850, when the Circuit Report noted:[4]

This chapel has sixty-five seats which let for 6d each per quarter. The first quarter or two they all let, but since then a great number have given them up and others we can't get the money from. There are no 'managing men' in the place. The Society which was once so flourishing is lamentably scattered. We wish it may again rally.

Within a few years this hope was realised. By 1859 a new chapel had replaced the earlier one, and by 1864 the membership totalled 134.

THE VERY GATES OF HEAVEN

Hilda Roberts, who entered the Sunday School in 1881, and was a life-long member of the chapel, described the interior of the building, and some of the ministers and members in her Recollections of Old Wingrave.[5]

There was one big room for the meetings, similar in size to the present room, but with a gallery at one end, and the communion table and a round pulpit at the other end. The pulpit had a bare wooden seat for the preacher, a plain wooden bookboard and was reached by two steps which elevated the preacher above his flock. A medium-sized harmonium, which stood just below the pulpit, wheezed and squeaked its way through the hymns with the help of the organist, a self-taught but capable musician gifted with a memory for music so that, if by chance he forgot his book, he could still play the tunes. The chapel divided itself into two distinct sections. The front half had a boarded floor, and fairly wide wooden seats. The back half had a floor of red bricks and the seats were forms with slatted backs. On the right-hand side, where the brick floor began, was a tallish combustion stove with a pipe which lost itself somewhere in the region of the roof. Lots of folk actually preferred the less comfortable seats so as to be near that stove. It burnt mostly coke, and I wonder we weren't ill with the fumes. Oil lamps provided the lighting, so all the lamps had to be individually lit and extinguished, in addition to being filled, cleaned and trimmed. By 1906 the chapel lamplighter was being paid 25/- (£1.25) per annum. At the back was the gallery, which was the width of the chapel. It had quite a good-looking front, and in the middle panel was a clock, which suffered from long bouts of unemployment. Mischievous youngsters would some-times drop articles over the front of that gallery onto unsuspecting elderly heads. A door beside the pulpit led into a narrow scullery running the width of the building. It had a small window, and was just large enough to hold a trestle table at one end and a copper at the other. There were several other similar tables stacked on the beams above, and the trestles for them were stacked in one corner of this scullery place, ready for use at tea meetings.

Great times were experienced in our humble little chapel. To the congregation it was often the very Gates of Heaven, for God was very real to the men and women who worshipped there. The fervour and enthusiasm, and the warmth and earnestness of those early days seem to me to be entirely absent from present-day worship. Our senior steward was James Kirby. His conversion was his constant topic. He had been a wild character when younger, but was converted about the time of the building of the chapel. However, I remember him as a venerable old man with a long white beard and a snowy fringe surrounding a very bald pate. But he was still quite a character. He was a worthy Methodist of the old school and gloried in calling himself a Ranter. I remember him often shouting "Hallelujah" and "Praise the Lord" in the middle of the preacher's sermon, whether it fitted what the preacher was saying or not. He always occupied the aisle end of the front row, and was a stickler for time. Woe betide any preacher who was late. Brother Kirby would pull out his large silver turnip watch, and compare it with the chapel clock. "It's time we began," he would say. "The man's not here, so we will have a hymn". We knew exactly which hymn it would be for he always chose number 223, "Father whose Everlasting Love", in which the fifth verse ended,

> To all, to all, thy bowels move
> But straitened in our own we are.

I didn't understand its meaning then, and I don't think I understand it now. I had heard my mother speak of "bowels moving", and I considered it very rude to sing about it. Number 223 is still in our hymnal today, but without the fifth verse. Just as well! A prayer would follow, always commencing, "O Holy One of Israel". In his enthusiasm he would get so worked up that he would pick up a seat with both hands, and bang it down.

One of the preachers on our circuit was Caleb Sheffield from Whitchurch: a big, stout, ruddy-faced man, with merry twinkling eyes, and a perpetual smile, which visibly broadened at the sight of us children. What interested us most was that the right sleeve of his coat almost covered a hook, like a meat hook, which had to serve as a hand. Many a time he told us the story of that hook.

"Ah, my friends, I've bin a rum 'un in me early days! It's a wonder the Lord had patience with me wicked ways. I had a pious mother as loved and cared for me, but I left home as a lad and went to the great city of London, and after trying lots of jobs I got in with some chaps as led me further into sin. I worked in a brewery and I got to like the stuff as we brewed. I looked after one of the engines and one day I was a bit frisky, and I thought I was about master of that engine, but I went a bit too far and my arm got caught and it was whipped off in a second. When I was in hospital I thought on me evil ways, and a kind minister as visited me pointed me to the Saviour, and I determined to give up my sins and here I am today the livin' monument of His mercy, with this hook to remind me of the pit from whence I was rescued."

Caleb made a living as a drover, taking farmers' animals to market for the sales, and as a dealer at the various markets: in garden produce, and anything else that came his way. He kept an old pony and a small cart, which he used as his means of transit. He *was in the habit of saying it was the Lord's pony, because it always took him to Chapel on Sundays. On one occasion Caleb arrived very late for morning service. James Kirby had announced a hymn, and as the congregation was singing the last lines, in stalked Caleb, mopping his brow with a red handkerchief all the way up the aisle. He went straight into the pulpit, and as soon as the steward had finished the prayer, he rose,*

"Dear friends, I can't abear to be late, but the Devil played me a trick this morning. He didn't want me to come here to preach today, so 'the old en-e-my' got into my old pony and sent him into the furthest field, and catch him I couldn't. But I've bested 'the old en-e-my' ye see, for here I be!"

Caleb's sermons were memorable. Even the children looked forward to them. His simple, homely language, and the vivid way in which he expressed himself created a lasting impression. For instance, Wingrave had a reputation for lusty singing, and so Caleb would often introduce a new or unfamiliar hymn when he visited Nup End. "That went well," he would say afterwards. "I always makes it a rule to put my new horses in the shafts here. I knows that if they'll go at all, you'll make 'em go." When preaching he would sometimes burst out singing, even in the middle of a sentence: perhaps "There's not a friend like the lowly Jesus", or "Sunlight, sunlight in my soul today".

To the end of her life, Hilda Roberts could still remember several of Caleb's sermons. And it is said that no-one who was there ever forgot the open-air meeting which he led on the Green, when he chose as his subject, 'And they put the Ark on a new cart'.

Not all preachers could provide such memorable sermons. Indeed, the preachers varied a great deal in quality. Hilda Roberts recalled a disastrous sermon by William H. of Aylesbury.

He was a flashy sort of person with a smattering of education, and a lot of confidence. He had heard of the 'New Theology', a sort of religious reform proposed by a prominent preacher of that time. While he floundered amongst the facts he had got hold of, Brother Kirby fidgeted and frowned, and at last said, "Brother H., you'd better 'give out' (meaning 'leave off'). You seem to have got all muddled up. PREACH THE GOSPEL!" Needless to say, Brother H. did 'give out' at once, and sat down like a deflated balloon. That was his finale at Wingrave.

Ron Bignell also has recollections of preachers who were less than inspiring.

Some of the old local preachers were long-winded. They would preach for two hours and say nothing worth listening to. Mothers used to bring their babies into chapel and, of course, the little ones would get hungry and tired, and cry. To keep them quiet, mothers used to breast feed them. It was nothing to see three or four babies being breast fed while the service was going on.

Seventy years later, Minnie Rickard, whose parents had often entertained visiting preachers, recalled others who were 'real characters'. (Recollections: page 132)

DEAR LORD ROSEBERY

Eleven new trustees were appointed in 1889, this time seven of them from the village and all working class: five bricklayers and two bakers. In 1905 their ranks were augmented by six more bricklayers and labourers. Amongst these were some of the 'managing men' that were so needed: Thomas Jones, Thomas Mead, George Bignell, William Roberts and William Fleet, for example. Active and enthusiastic, they furthered the work of the Chapel, its Sunday school, the Temperance Hall, and the musical and

56. *Minnie Jones (later Rickard) was organist for the Methodists for 65 years, and trained the school and Methodist choirs.*

57. *"The three stalwarts" : Will Fleet (standing, left), Will Roberts (standing) and George Bignell (seated). They had great ambition and energy, which they applied both to business and the Methodist chapel.*

Recollections: Entertaining the Preachers – Minnie Rickard [6]

What a difference in preachers of long ago from those of today! In those days we had both morning and evening service, so it meant the preacher staying to dinner and tea, and when I was a girl, my family usually provided this. One preacher, from Aston Abbotts, was very short and had a very bent back. He always walked with his left hand supporting his back and his eyes to the ground. Fortunately, there was not much traffic in those days. He needed a little platform to stand on when in the pulpit, so as to see his congregation! His favourite theme was the Israelites. And he always saucered his tea.

A preacher from Stewkley used to bob down in the pulpit and all of a sudden pop up like a Jack-in-the-Box. When offered the cake at tea-time, he took the remainder of the cake instead of the piece cut. Imagine me trying to keep a straight face!

Some preachers came for a fortnight or even a month's evangelistic services, and often stayed with us. I think it was Mr Dykes who, during every meal would break into singing several times, always the same hymn, "I've a message from the Lord, Hallelujah. This message unto you I give." We got used to it after a time.

During a sharp wintry time, with much snow, two young men (Mr Green and Mr Hull) arrived on a mission. They had a van in which they were supposed to live, but because of the weather they lived with us. They were very nice young men, and I remember the jolly time we had together. When the time came for them to move to Aston Abbotts, my sister and I sewed up their pyjamas. It was too bad of us, really, because it was cold and wintry and they had to sleep in their little van. I know it took quite a time to unravel the pyjamas. They both became ministers. The Rev. Green was minister at Stewkley for several years, and sometimes came to Wingrave to preach. He well remembered the pyjama game!

Mr Sale, an old gentleman from Aylesbury, kept a grocer's shop, and always brought some sweets which he gave us just before he left in the evening. One Sunday I whispered to mother, "Isn't it time for Mr Sale to go home?" Mother tried to hush me up, but with no effect. Mr Sale said, "What does she say? I think I know what she wants". Straightaway he fetched the sweets, saying, "Now can I stop?" "Oh, yes," I replied. After that he always gave us the sweets as soon as he came into the house.

social activities connected with them. By the beginning of the 20th century it was very clear that larger premises were needed if all their hopes and plans were to bear fruit. Their concern was increased in 1903 when a very successful mission added significantly to their numbers. Should they start on a new site, or appeal to Lord Rosebery for extra land to build an extension? Three young wives, Hilda Roberts, Polly Hannah Fleet and Bessie Bignall, who were all members of the chapel, felt strongly that a new chapel was needed, situated on the Winslow Road, the old one being somewhat hidden down a side road. The site they favoured was in a field belonging to Leopold de Rothschild, the largest landowner in the Vale of Aylesbury with a total holding of nearly ten thousand acres. Hilda described their visits to Leopold's home at Ascott.

We decided to visit this gentleman and ask him in person to give us a piece of ground for a new chapel. There were no buses, so we had to walk the four miles to Ascott where he lived. We were well received, and Mr de Rothschild listened sympathetically and promised to consider our request, and see us again in three weeks' time. Then we were given refreshments, and started the four mile walk home, buoyed up with the hope that our request would be granted. Three weeks later we made a second journey to Ascott, this time by appointment. Many enquiries had been made, and the farmer who rented 'our' field had strongly objected to the field being cut up, saying it was his best grazing land. So we couldn't have that, but Mr de Rothschild told us he would give us a donation and help us to obtain ground for our extensions, which he did. So our efforts were not all in vain. Two years later we had our schoolroom, kitchen and vestry to the great joy of us all.

Undoubtedly, Mr de Rothschild talked to his relative and neighbour, Lord Rosebery, for it was the latter who eventually provided the site. What the three young wives never knew was that their request for a main road site was not ignored solely due to the objections of a local farmer. The Rothschilds and the Roseberys were extremely generous to the local community, but they were definitely not "a soft touch", and Lord Rosebery had asked his land agent to look into the matter. The agent replied,[7]

The original request some years ago was that you should grant them a piece of land directly at the back of their existing chapel. This has now been dropped in favour of the new scheme. I think their real objection is that the present surroundings are not sufficiently aristocratic for them as they are opposite a small farmyard, and Nup End is off the main road, from which the chapel is not visible. The chapel they now use is certainly somewhat out of repair, but simply because ordinary repairs have been neglected. The brickwork is good enough and it would be infinitely cheaper for them to repair and enlarge instead of building a new chapel.

Financially, he was probably right and saved the chapel a good deal of expenditure. It probably saved Lord Rosebery a lot of expenditure as well for, having obtained the additional land, the chapel's next problem was to raise £400-£500. Soon an urgent appeal for funds was made. "Dear Lord Rosebery . . . .

ENLARGEMENT AND REFURBISHMENT

Building work commenced in 1905, and the foundation stones were laid in October, each one representing a contribution of at least £5. A schoolroom and kitchen were built on the land at the back of the chapel. Beneath the kitchen a stokehouse was constructed, and a central heating boiler installed. The chapel was renovated as well. The gallery was removed, new pews and windows were installed and a removable partition was constructed between the chapel and the schoolroom. Eventually, at Easter 1906, Mrs Mary Ann Butt, the wife of the Rev. George Butt,[8] performed the Opening Ceremony. Mary Ann was the daughter of James Kirby, a founder member of the chapel. She had run a small drapery shop in Wingrave, and taught the older girls in the chapel Sunday School for many years. In middle age she became a local personality, and astonished the parish by marrying the Rev. Butt, who was a Methodist missionary in South Africa, and a widower with two sons. She travelled to Cape Town for the wedding and then joined her husband in missionary work, thus fulfilling a life-long ambition. When they eventually returned to England, her husband became President of the Primitive Methodist Conference, and they made frequent visits to Wingrave. There is no record as to what the Rev. Butt thought of his father-in-law's rather eccentric behaviour in chapel. But perhaps James Kirby was on his best behaviour when the President of Conference was visiting, for the majority of chapel folk seem to have been somewhat in awe of the

58. *Caravan-based 'Mission' held on the recreation ground. The building on the right is the first pavilion to be built on the 'Rec'.*

59. *The Primitive Methodist Chapel before its refurbishment in 1959. The large wooden partition between the chapel and the schoolroom could be removed to provide extra accommodation on special occasions: see picture 62, page 137. The refurbishment dispensed with this facility.*

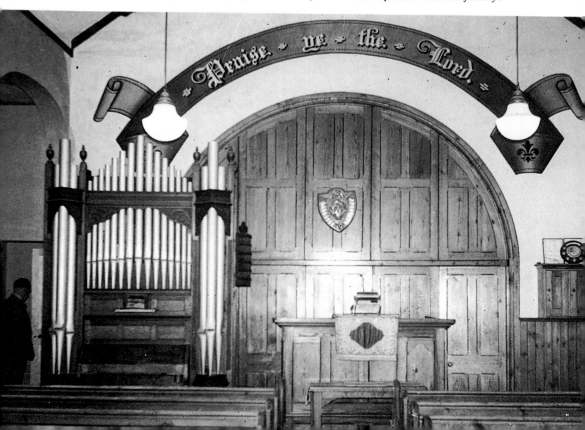

Butts. Even Hilda Roberts thought it a great honour when the Rev. Butt baptised her son Leslie, after preaching at the 1912 Sunday School Anniversary service.

CHAPEL LIFE

In 1929, with so many social functions in progress, the Trustees decided to replace the inconvenient oil lamps and solid fuel water heating by electric lighting and electric tubular heating. At the switching-on ceremony, the Chairman of the Aylesbury Electrical Committee congratulated the chapel on its enterprise, for it was the first public building in the Aylesbury area to be so equipped. Mrs Annie Woodward Jones, the village postmistress, and the longest serving member of the chapel, was chosen to switch on the installation. The chapel was filled with people, all sitting in darkness. Then Mrs Jones proclaimed, "Let there be light". She turned the switch and, suddenly there was light and heat everywhere. Finally, the choir sang a rousing anthem, for Wingrave people would sing at every opportunity.

Every Autumn the chapel would be decorated with many and varied gifts for the Harvest Thanksgiving services. The next day a 'Tea' would be held in the chapel schoolroom, and after a short address, bidding would be keen for the vegetables, fruit and flowers sold by auction in aid of chapel funds.

60: Mrs Mary Ann Butt

On Tuesday afternoons the ladies met for a Sewing Meeting. Sometimes all manner of handiwork was produced for the next sale of work, and sometimes shirts for Africa were sewn to be sent to the missionary societies. Great gossiping was enjoyed at these gatherings, and if any particularly choice piece of news turned up (such as Mary Ann marrying the Rev. Butt and going out to Africa) then the gossiping and the sewing went on faster than ever!

In the 1920's a Guild was formed with weekly meetings classified as Devotional, Social and Literary, each group encompassing a variety of activities. Thus the Literary Group meetings included quizzes, spelling bees, debates both within the group and against other groups, and at one stage every member gave a talk on his job.

As well as Teas and Social Evenings, when competitions and games were played, other more original activities were gradually introduced. For instance, one Ladies' Evening was undertaken solely by the ladies, even to the smaller duties of organ blowing and pew opening. The audience was entertained with "duets, quartets, part songs, monologues, recitations and several old camp meeting songs of fifty years earlier". Another very novel concert, given by the ladies, was called 'The Launching of the Fleet'. The cast, dressed as fisher girls, gave an excellent programme consisting of shanties, sketches and duets, all depicting some aspect of life at sea. At the end, small ships were presented to every member of the audience. Not to be outdone, the men decided to form a concert party, which they called 'The Prim Dozen'. For six years or more they gave variety concerts in the local towns and villages, always to packed houses. They all played an instrument, and were all completely self-taught. Between them they played the piano, cello, violin, clarinet, guitar, banjo, mandolin and drums, but Horace Bignell conceded that one of the chapel's accomplished women pianists would have been a great asset! All the popular songs of the day were sung, with 'Red

Sails in the Sunset' and 'Just a Song at Twilight' being particular favourites. Between the musical items they performed amusing little sketches. In one of them, Bert Sandall sat stroking a ferret, "scaring some of the audience stiff".[9]

Wingrave was renowned for its singing and the Methodist Choir led by Mrs Minnie Rickard was particularly active and successful over a very long period, visiting many of the chapels in the area. For example, in May 1937 the choir performed at Aston Abbotts' chapel:

On Good Friday evening the Choir gave a very credible rendering of the cantata, King of Glory', conducted by Mrs Minnie Rickard with Miss Joan Bignell at the piano. Mr Fred Bignell (violin) and Mr Horace Bignell (cello) also ably assisted in the success of the evening, which will live in mind and memory, for the choir sang with spirit and understanding too. Just what we should do without the very generous help from our friends at Wingrave we cannot say.[10]

In the days when the chapel was still lit by paraffin lamps, there was "quite an excitement" when the choir won a prize and spent the money on new lamps. These were used successfully for many years, until electric lights were installed.

In 1967, at a concert to celebrate her 80th birthday, Minnie Rickard arranged a programme which included recitations, choruses, and songs 'grave and gay'. At the close, she was presented with a beautiful bouquet in appreciation of her many years as leader and conductor of the choir, as well as her 65 years as chapel organist. She died in 1968 at the age of 81.

THE PRIMITIVE METHODIST SUNDAY SCHOOL

The Sunday school started in 1869, and has continued to the present day. From the late 19th century until the Second World War it was run by George Bignell, William Fleet and William Roberts who were, arguably, the most outstanding of the 'managing men' in the village. They had been childhood friends when they had all attended the Independent Chapel's Sunday School. They eventually moved to the Primitive Methodist Chapel, where they courted and later married three young Prims', who were also close friends. The young ladies argued that it was the attractions of Methodism, which were responsible for the young men's move to Nup End, but not everyone agreed. Religious affiliations were treated very seriously in those days, and it is said that Will Fleet's sister, Mary Ann, never forgave Polly Hannah Jones for 'poaching' her brother, or her brother for marrying Polly Hannah. For that matter, it is also said that Polly Hannah never took kindly to Mary Ann!

Their conversion to Methodism was a great loss to the Independent chapel for the three young men became Sunday school teachers almost at once. They soon gathered others around them until at one time there were thirteen male teachers on the chapel's register, which was a record for the Aylesbury Circuit. The group worked hard and imaginatively to make the school a success, and weekly attendances of thirty to forty young people are said to have been the norm before World War One. In particular, they realised that it was vital to encourage and train their young charges to the full. So once each month the young men of the Bible Class would take charge of the whole Sunday school, whilst the Superintendent and the regular teachers would go into the Bible Class. This gave the young men an insight into the workings of the school. Similarly, to give their young instrumentalists confidence and experience, they encouraged them to take turns as organist each week at morning Sunday school. The girls who attended Sunday school were sometimes made responsible for refreshments at the adult fund-raising socials, and also encouraged to contribute to sale-of-work stalls. Minnie

61. *Primitive Methodist Sunday School: winning team in Circuit Elocution Contest. From the left: Colin Marsh, Graham Horwood, Barry Simpson, Clive Mildred, Humphrey Bignell, Roger Mildred, Josephine Rickard, Carol Simpson, Margaret Taylor, Beryl Taylor, Yvonne Roberts, Susan Bignell, Kathleen Sandall, Gillian Rickard.*

62. *Primitive Methodist Pageant: Women in History.*

63. *"We're off to the Sea!"* *Will Roberts (with ball). Other men from the left: Colin Bignell, Dennis Rickard, Alfred Rogers, Vic Clay, Donald Bliss, Lionel Fleet, Ken Rickard, Leslie Roberts, Maurice Rogers, Tom Rickard, George Bliss, Harvey Roberts, Clifford Woodruff. Women from the left: Renee Bliss, Joyce Fleet, Joan Bignell, Hilda Bliss, Marjorie Rickard.*

64. *On the beach: Hilda Roberts and family. From the left: Harvey, William, Leslie, unknown, Hilda.*

Rickard was one of the few women teachers at this time. She not only trained the choir, but also ran the children's Bright Hour, and successfully coached them for the Circuit scripture examinations. For the rest of their lives the three friends, and their wives and families gave much of their spare time to the Nup End Chapel. Will Fleet, for example, was a chapel steward for 33 years, and taught in Sunday school for 43 years, eventually becoming assistant superintendent and then superintendent.

The highlight of the Sunday school year was the Anniversary, always held on Whit-Sunday and Monday. The partition between chapel and schoolroom was removed and replaced by a platform of tiered seats extending some way back into the schoolroom. This was for the choir. The youngest knelt at the front, and the rest sat in rows behind, higher and higher, so that it was quite unnerving for those perched on the top row. The chapel was always packed for this event, with extra seats down the aisles, others behind the choir in the schoolroom, and some people even standing outside. Afterwards the platform was dismantled and packed away until the following year.

Teas, sports days and outings were greatly enjoyed by the youngsters. Before the First World War the woods at Ashridge were a popular venue. In 1905, free transport in the form of horses and farm waggons was provided by a local farmer. The main cost was food for the picnic tea, which typically included: 26 loaves, 8 lbs of butter, 27 lbs of cake, 4 lbs of granulated sugar, 5 lbs of loaf sugar, 1 lb of tea and 3 tins of condensed milk. From 1919 to 1922 the venues were still local, but transport was by two horse brakes. For the remainder of the Twenties and Thirties they ventured far and wide by rail, usually to the seaside: Llandudno, Brighton and Eastbourne, for example. So some serious fund-raising was required each year, and the irrepressible Hilda Roberts wrote this poem to encourage the silver to flow at one such fund-raising event:

> We're off to the sea! We're off to the sea!
> This is the thing that pleases me.
> For a whole long summer's day
> We are off on the sandy beach to play
> On our yearly holiday.
>
> We will gather shells and sail on the sea,
> And catch in our net some shrimps for tea.
> We'll watch the big ships come sailing in
> With their sirens making a cheerful din
> On a sunny summer's day.
>
> We're off to the sea! We're off to the sea!
> But our Super says we must wait and see!
> For money is scarce and the funds are low.
> But I hope we shall gather enough to go
> To the sea on a summer's day.
>
> So we children will bring you the boxes round.
> You've brought big collections, I'll be bound,
> And just you be thinking this all the while
> That lots of children will laugh and smile
> On that sunny summer's day.

LATER CHANGES

For the centenary of the Wingrave chapel in 1959, the interior of the chapel was completely redecorated and largely refurbished; the organ recess was built; the old three-seater pulpit was replaced with a more modern pulpit with a plaque, hand-carved by Douglas Dunker, a leading member of the congregation. In addition, a new communion table and rail were installed, and the partition between the chapel and the schoolroom was boarded up as diminishing numbers made the tiered platform unnecessary. Fortunately, "loyal men and women continued to serve God and their chapel with love and devotion", including descendants of 'the three stalwarts' of earlier days: Horace Bignell and his sister Joan; Christine Fleet and her husband Douglas Dunker; and Leslie Roberts and his wife Pat. Despite this continuity, things have changed, as Horace Bignell observed:

For good or ill, the services have completely changed. Fiery, off-the-cuff preaching has turned to academics; hymns with harmony are now sung in unison. Other attractions gradually drew more people from regular worship, until we were few in number.

Happily, in the 1990's, a new generation of worshippers has increased congregations and begun fund-raising to repair and improve the buildings.

64. The heart of the village, circa 1935, viewed from the church tower. Windmill House (to the right of the pond) was built in 1742. Between it and the background of mature trees are the kitchen gardens of the Old Manor House (extreme top right). The war memorial marks the corner of the Green, and the school entrance is just visible (extreme bottom right). On the edge of the graveyard are the Parish House and Hilda Gibbs' Old Post Office. See also page 278.

Chapter Thirteen

Schooling

LAISSEZ-FAIRE IN EDUCATION

Before 1833 the existence of schools depended entirely upon voluntary funding and enterprise, the leading organisations[1] being the British Society (from 1808) and the National Society (from 1811). From 1833, their income was boosted by an annual subsidy from public funds of £20,000, shared between them. Even so, the chance of a working class child receiving any education at all depended upon whether a school existed locally. Often it didn't. Even if one was available, attendance was still voluntary, and remained so until 1880. The decision was left to parents, and many didn't like the idea: a child at school was a child not earning! Worse still, parents had to pay for the schooling. It was 1891 before fees were abolished.

By 1851 the two societies had established 18,500 schools attended by nearly 1¼ million children, and by 1857 the parliamentary grant was £541,000. This sounds impressive until one looks behind the figures, which included Sunday schools, providing at best two or three hours of education per week. Not more than 10% of working class children attended school full time. It was difficult to obtain trained and competent teachers. The educational standards achieved were very low. This last was not too surprising. Huge classes, poor teachers, and lack of equipment made effective education very difficult.

In the 19th century there was much support for the provision of 'Christian Education', to improve the character of the Poor. It was thought that it would reduce lawlessness, immorality and idleness. It followed that reading should also be taught, to give access to the Bible and the Book of Common Prayer. Beyond that, views differed considerably. Social reformers and many Nonconformists wanted the poor to develop their talents, and "better themselves". Some advocated the extension of education to writing, arithmetic, and even to history and geography. Others, including the government, the established church and the upper classes, saw education primarily as a means of social control. This meant developing in the labouring classes docility, submissiveness, and reasonableness; providing sufficient education (but no more than sufficient) to serve the needs of their employers; and ensuring that they accepted their present situation as their divinely ordained "station in life".[2] As late as 1862, Parliament was told, "We do not profess to give these children an education that will raise them above their station and business in life".[3] Too much education might make them wonder why the Good Lord should expect them to accept poverty as their inevitable destiny. Dissatisfaction among the masses was greatly feared as memories of the French Revolution were revived by the numerous revolutions in Europe in 1830 and 1848.

The 'social control' viewpoint limited educational development until 1862, when a combination of sharply rising costs and abysmal educational standards led the government to make its payments to schools 'performance related'. In future, two factors would determine a school's grant: its overall attendance figures; and the pupils' performance in annual examinations of the 3 R's (Reading, Writing and Arithmetic), conducted in person by Her Majesty's Inspectors (H.M.I.'s). However, in order to test results, subjects had to be identified and standards set. This was done in the Revised Code of 1862, which established the 3 R's as the first national curriculum. It is doubtful whether its supporters realised what a big step they were taking, for it was the beginning of state intervention in the details of education. Once a national curriculum existed, it could be (and it was) extended, and any school which neglected it in favour of religious instruction could find itself with poor examination results and a reduced grant. Payment by results was followed by a significant improvement in educational standards, though the means of achieving those standards sometimes left much to be desired.

The 1870 Education Act was soon to promise even more state involvement!

THE EARLIEST SCHOOLS OF WINGRAVE

William Grace's Charity

The first school that we know of in Wingrave was set up under William Grace's will of 1720. His piece of meadow ground at Rowsham called The Ham would provide the churchwardens with £2 each Ladyday:

for the instruction of the poorest children of the parish, aged 7 to 9 years, in the word and fear of God, in writing and arithmetic, and such handiwork as might be beneficial to them towards getting an honest and lawful living.

We do not know just how the money was used, until the early 19th century when the churchwardens selected five children, aged 7 to 10, and paid a schoolmistress to teach them reading and plaiting. There was an outcry in 1832, when the money was paid instead to the master of the Church Sunday School, and so in the following year it reverted to the schoolmistress.[4]

Plaiting Schools

As explained in chapter four, most plaiting schools were just sweat-shops designed to get the highest possible output of plait from the 'pupils'. The schoolmistress was probably illiterate.

Sunday Schools

In 1819 the Independents[5] used their recently-built chapel in Church Street to establish the first Sunday school in Wingrave, and provide local children with religious knowledge free from Anglican doctrines. It was another eleven years before the Parish Church founded its own Sunday school. Together they attracted about 150 children each Sunday. The Primitive Methodist Sunday school came still later.

The principal concern of the schools was religious education, but in addition they probably taught the alphabet, reading, writing, and enough about numbers to enable the pupils to understand the stories in the Bible. Most children attended both morning and afternoon sessions, and after one of them would join the adults for the normal adult service. For many working class children, this two or three hours per week was their only contact with education. In 1851, in the parish of Wingrave with Rowsham, it seems likely that between two-thirds and three-quarters of the children aged 3 to 16 years took advantage of it.

Wingrave's First Day School

In 1846, Joseph Lucas, the farmer and brewer, and his brother Edward Munday Lucas, both of Rowsham, gave a piece of land in Church Street, opposite the parish church:

for the purpose of having erected thereon a schoolroom to be used for the education of poor children in the principles of the Christian religion according to the doctrines of the Church of England, and also, if it be requisite, a house for the master or mistress.

The building was completed by August 1847 at a cost of £154. It is now the East Room of the present Community Centre. On either side of the entrance door, two bricked-up arches indicate where windows once overlooked the churchyard. The room was heated by an open fire, with no fireguard until the 20th century. At the back of the room a doorway led outside to the two privies, which were simply earth closets. Though thoughtfully separated by a partition, they were unroofed, and adjoined the schoolroom just below opening windows! Despite the obvious consequences in terms of smells and flies, and their appalling condition when flooded by heavy rain, it was twenty years before an Inspector recommended alterations to the windows, and the provision of a roof. Even with a roof, the 'offices' were pretty grim. "Either the roof leaked or the lavatories leaked, for everything seemed damp and nasty."

At first the schoolroom seems to have been used only for the Church Sunday school, for no 'scholars' are identified in the 1851 Census. It was probably 1853 when the day-school opened with Henry Peter Pearson as schoolmaster, and an enrolment of twenty-five boys: only 27% of the 3 to 12 years age group. We know that poverty was the hallmark of the agricultural labourer, and remarks recorded in Wingrave and elsewhere in Buckinghamshire confirm that it was the loss of the child's income, and the fees charged for school attendance (Fig. 16), which deterred parents from sending their children to school.[6] It cost 5d a week to keep four children at school, a significant sum if you earned only 10s-0d. Even with double that income, every penny counted.

Sent some children home for their school Pence, and they did not return. (Elizabeth Montague, infants' schoolmistress, Wingrave)
I didn't attend very much. You had to pay a penny (per week) for school. If you didn't have a penny, you didn't go. (Mary Ann Alcock of Wingrave[7])
Fanny Bateman's mother refused to pay one week's school fee as the child had attended one day only. (James Wyatt, schoolmaster at Wingrave[8])
The boy is at farm work. I wish he could have kept on (at school), but we can't do without his 2s-6d with bread so dear. (George Stokes, labourer of Great Horwood [9])
I would like to keep my girls at school, but how are we to live if they ain't at work? (Mrs Clarke, labourer's wife of Thornborough [9])
I send my little girl (of 6) to school, but I can't send more. It grieves me, but I can't send but one. (Mrs Hawks, labourer's wife of Long Crendon[9])

Fig. 16: Fees At Wingrave Day School, 1875

Farmers' children: 6d per week each
Tradesmen's children: 3d per week each
Labourers' children: 2d per week for the eldest, and
1d for each of the others in the same family

WINGRAVE PAROCHIAL SCHOOL: THE EARLY YEARS

Between 1854 and 1872 we know very little about Wingrave's parochial school, for the first log book (1863-1872) is missing. However, from the Vicar's brief comments in his Diocesan Visitation Returns, two things are quite clear: competition for the hearts and minds of Wingrave's children was intense; and the majority of them were still receiving their only education in Sunday school. The initial low recruitment of the Day School proved to be the norm. Over the next fifteen years less than 25% of the relevant age group was enrolled. However, in 1858 a Royal Commission on Education estimated that only 12.5% of the nation's children attended a day school.

SCHOOL VERSUS WORK

In 1867, in an effort to reduce child labour, and increase educational attendance, Parliament passed the Workshop Regulation Act. This forbade the employment in workshops of children under 8 years of age, and imposed a "part-time" system on those of 8 to 13 years. Henceforth they could only be employed in a workshop if they had received ten hours' education in the previous week. Inspectors enforced the Act, but it had major loopholes. When an inspector was sighted in a village, word spread like wildfire: time for a sharp exit! Plaiting schools were just rooms in ordinary cottages, so the illegal plaiters left through the back door, scurried across the gardens and alleys and were soon back home, where they could plait legally. Moreover, the classification of plaiting schools as workshops was challenged. It took three years and two test cases before the Queens Bench ruled that plaiting schools did come under the Act. The effect was remarkable. School enrolments rose sharply. 105 children were recorded as scholars in Wingrave's 1871 Census. This was encouraging. Unfortunately, a large proportion of these children were part-timers, attending for only ten hours per week. Neither was this the only problem.

THE PROBLEM OF INCREASING NUMBERS

Even allowing for part-timers and substantial absenteeism, the 1871 Census proved that Wingrave School's one small room was totally inadequate. By this time the 1870 Education Act was already the law of the land. One of its main provisions was that the control of education would remain with the churches only if they could provide enough schools for the nation's needs. Otherwise School Boards, elected by the local ratepayers, would be created with the power to build and manage schools financed from the rates. This would be welcomed by Nonconformists, who regarded the Wingrave Parochial School as mainly a nursery for the Church of England. A Board School would be non-denominational. Its pupils would be given simple Bible lessons, but would not be taught the creed of any one sect. Of course, Wingrave's Vicar viewed the matter quite differently: Board schools would be a disaster. To the Rev. Butt it would seem obvious that the doctrine of the established church must be taught. It mattered not that School Boards would represent the majority. They were obviously wrong or at best deluded. "We are doing all we can to avoid a School Board," wrote the Vicar, "but on account of the prevalence of dissent (i.e. of dissenting religion) it is a matter of great difficulty to raise funds". And funds had to be raised, if Wingrave School's accommodation was to be increased. Yet the Vicar was correct in thinking that local Nonconformists would not pay for the new classroom. One resident, a Mr Griffin, actually wrote to the Board of Education asking that no public funds be provided for it. Moreover, the Vicar had only just finished raising £350 for the new combined chapel and schoolroom in Rowsham. It was undoubtedly a boon to Rowsham's aged and infirm, and to its children, for both groups wanted to use Church of England facilities without trudging across the fields to Wingrave in the cold and mud of winter. However, the number of children at Rowsham was so small that it did little to ease the accommodation problem at Wingrave School.[10] Could the Vicar raise still more money to build another classroom at Wingrave? Remarkably, he did, though he had to go outside the parish for most of it. Known as the North Room, it was built in 1871 by Joseph Fleet of Wingrave. The trustees of the school (the Rev. Butt, with Mr Bennett, Mr Buckmaster and Mr Lucas, three local farmers) contributed £65. The remaining £115 came from the National Society, the Oxford Diocesan Board, the Mercers' Company and, of course, the Rothschilds. The Board of Education refused to make a grant.

SCHOOL VERSUS WORK: THE CONFLICT CONTINUES

Early in 1872 a new schoolmaster was appointed. James Wyatt was 39 when he took up residence in the detached, three-bedroomed schoolhouse, which had been erected in 1859. It was fortunate that it was available, for Mr Wyatt came complete with a wife and six children, and another seven arrived before the family left Wingrave. He taught all the pupils of 7 years and over. Hannah, his wife, taught the infants and the girls' needlework. Mr Wyatt soon made his presence felt. In 1873 the H.M.I.'s annual report on the school was very positive. "Order in the school is good, and the results of the examination (especially in spelling and penmanship) are very creditable to the energy and diligence of Mr Wyatt". It was remarkable that he was achieving so much for he was working under very difficult conditions. He had sixty-three children in his class, of whom thirteen were twelve years and over, and the eldest was sixteen. They were of all abilities, and many of the older children were illiterate, having only recently started school. Some of them were half-timers who attended for only two hours per day, but not necessarily for the same two hours! Their intermittent attendance disrupted the teaching and held back the full-timers. Because they spent such long hours plaiting, they were often tired and listless. Some were helping out at home. Others only attended "when they fancied. Here today and gone the next two". The school log book illustrates some of the problems:

9.8.1872:   *There has been a better attendance this week, but few half-timers present.*
21.10.1872:   *Several children (who had left to go to work) have been readmitted lately who are very backward and prove a great hindrance to the progress of the third class.*
13.9.1873:   *Reopened school with bad attendance due to late harvest.*
8.4.1873:   *William Higgins played truant and was temporarily dismissed.*
18.11.1873:   *Several boys absent, having followed the fox-hounds.*
23.6.1874:   *William Higgins, John Honor, Walter Bateman and George Badrick withdrawn at 11.30 to carry meals into the hay fields.*
28.9.1874:   *Some boys absent – engaged in the potato grounds.*
9.3.1875:   *Some boys have left school for work again, after few attendances.*

Some parents would connive at their children's absence from school, usually to help out at home, or for the additional income it provided. Similarly, some farmers would employ schoolchildren when they needed cheap casual labour, especially at harvest time. Even so, it was unusual for adults to show both blatant and persistent contempt for the attendance laws. However, the Smiths were such a case. In 1876 Agnes and Ann Smith, aged eleven and eight, who had been attending Wingrave School for two hours per day, were withdrawn to work full-time at their father's plait school at Floyds Cottage in Mill Lane. In June 1877 their father, Mr Thomas Smith, and three other parents were charged at Linslade Petty Sessions with refusing to produce a certificate of school attendance. Smith was ordered to pay a fine of 6d plus 11-6d costs!

The problem of absenteeism came to a head when the 1880 Education Act made attendance compulsory for children until the age of ten, while children aged between 10 and 13 could leave only when they had passed Standard IV. The 1880 report on the school merely noted the "very bad" attendance, but the next year's was very blunt:

The school continues to improve in the face of considerable difficulties. Mr Wyatt's efforts to teach are still thwarted . . . by the supineness and inattention of the School Attendance Committee, or their officer or both. The irregularity of the attendance is proverbial, and unchecked in any way by the responsible authorities.

The Inspector might also have had a quiet word with the Vicar, whose generosity in lending out the schoolroom caused constant interruptions to the teaching. The schoolroom was regarded as being the only suitable venue in the parish for public events, so half-holidays were given for meetings of the Temperance Society, the Mentmore Flower Show, the British and Foreign Bible Society, the Evening School tea, the Sunday School tea, and the village feast, while two whole days were allowed for the local Agricultural Society's Dinner. There were also occasional closures for such things as a meeting of Sunday School teachers, and a public tea to celebrate the marriage of Leopold de Rothschild. In addition, half or whole day holidays were given for Ash Wednesday, Ascension Day, Whit Monday, Shrove Tuesday, the Patronal Festival, the Harvest Thanksgiving and the Aylesbury Choral Festival. And sometimes the master decided (with the Vicar's permission) to close for a holiday, "as a bad attendance does far more harm than a holiday in counting average attendances for Grant".

THE CONTENT OF TEACHING IN THE 1870's

The range of subjects taught was very limited. The Church insisted upon Religious Instruction, and regarded Needlework as essential for the girls, but until 1879 Reading, Arithmetic and Writing (the latter including Penmanship, Dictation and Spelling) were the only government requirements.(Fig.17) The H.M.I. left Mr Wyatt in no doubt about this in 1875/6 when he ventured outside these basic subjects. "Had he confined himself to the Elementary Subjects only, I think better results would have appeared in the schedule", was the terse comment in the annual report. Writing did not include individual expression until Standard VI, and in the 1870's Wingrave went no further than Standard IV. It was 1875 before Grammar and Geography are mentioned in the school log book. There were no practical activities, like painting, drawing, modelling, music, drama, physical education or games.

For the financial health of the teachers and the school it was essential that the 3 R's were drilled relentlessly ready for the yearly ordeal, when an apprehensive and subdued class, and a worried master (clad in his best suit), listened for the sound of the Inspector's horse and trap approaching the school. The H.M.I. would examine the scholars and, according to the results, determine the government's annual grant to the school. A cut in the grant could reduce both the master's salary, and the school's expenditure upon books and equipment. So rote learning was used to teach almost everything: multiplication and weights and measures' tables were chanted and tested; number bonds were drilled and tested; spellings were taught and tested; and penmanship and dictation (considered as ends in themselves) were constantly practised. The youngest pupils even had to chorus their reading: 'simultaneous reading' it was called. Older pupils had to read aloud before the class, and the brighter pupils waited impatiently while less fluent readers hesitated and stumbled over passages in the spectacularly dull class reading book. These methods were still in use in the 1920's and 1930's as Frank and Grace King remember:

We used to learn our tables in the infants. We had to say them parrot fashion day in and day out. And you never forget them. That was a good way of teaching. You sit there saying them in a singsong tone, and don't know what you're saying, but you never forget them. We used to have dictation and if you spelt the words wrong that was your misfortune. You had to write them out fifty times each. And that was another good way of teaching.

Religious Instruction, the first lesson of each day, was still very important in Church schools. Pupils studied the Bible, the Prayer Book, the order of church service, and the Seasons of the Christian Year. The difficult words in the Litany would be explained, as

Fig 17: The New Educational Code of 1879

	Reading	Writing	Arithmetic #
Standard I*	To read a short paragraph from a book not confined to words of one syllable	Copy in manuscript character a line of print, on slates or in copy books, at the choice of the managers; and write from dictation a few common words.	Notation and numeration up to 1000. Simple addition and subtraction of numbers of not more than four figures, and the multiplication table to 6 times 12.
Standard II	To read with intelligence a short paragraph from an elementary reading book.	A sentence from the same book, slowly read once, and then dictated. Copy books (large or half-text) to be shown.	Notation and numeration up to 100,000. The four simple rules to short division (inclusive)
Standard III	To read with intelligence a short paragraph from a more advanced reading book.	A sentence slowly dictated once from the same book. Copy books to be shown (small hand, capital letters and figures).	Notation and numeration up to 1,000,000. Long division and compound addition and subtraction (money).
Standard IV	To read with intelligence a few lines of prose or poetry selected by the inspector.	Eight lines slowly dictated once from a reading book. Copy books to be shown (improved small hand).	Compound rules (money) and reduction (common weights and measures). **
Standard V	Improved reading.	Writing from memory the substance of a short story read out twice; spelling, grammar, and handwriting to be considered.	Practice, bills of parcels, and simple proportion.
Standard VI	Reading with fluency and expression.	A short theme or letter; the composition, spelling, grammar, and handwriting to be considered.	Proportion, vulgar and decimal fractions.

Notes:

\# The work of girls will be judged more leniently than that of boys.

* Standards roughly correspond to age. Six-year-old children are expected to reach Standard I. Standard VI is the expected level of an eleven-year-old child.

** The "weights and measures" should be only such as are really useful, such as: Avoirdupois Weight, Long Measure, Liquid Measure, Time Table, Square and Cubical Measure, and any measure which is connected with the industrial occupations of the district.

Source: The Victorian Schoolroom, Trevor May, Shire Publications, 1995

would be the archaic language of the Bible, the morals to be drawn from its stories, and their application to everyday life. There would also be little talks to illustrate such virtues as thrift, temperance, punctuality and the value of the Ten Commandments. Like all the other lessons much of this had to be memorised by constant repetition, because every year the Oxford Diocesan Inspection took place in the presence of the Vicar and the managers. When the children had sung their hymns, and recited from memory the Catechism, the Collects and the Apostles' Creed, the Inspector questioned them carefully, to check their understanding. Finally, there was a written test. The pupil gaining the highest marks was awarded the Diocesan Prize, generally known as the Bishop's Prize. Hilda Mead (later Roberts) - whose recollections of Wingrave feature in this volume - took the prize in 1888. It was a rule that it could only be presented once to any particular pupil, but this did not deter Hilda in the least. Prize or no prize, she still topped the list for the next two years.

Rote learning meant that the pupils spent most of the school day sitting (or squirming!) at the uncomfortable wooden desks, in rooms which were inadequately heated, and so poorly lit by oil lamps that by November the school had to start and finish earlier. Otherwise, by the end of the afternoon, reading and written work would have been impossible, and the field path back to Rowsham dangerously dark. Only at midday was there a real break (of two hours) when the "lucky Wingravers" went home for 'dinner', leaving the Rowsham children to eat the cold food which they had brought to school, and warm themselves up playing games in Church Street, or sliding on the pond when it froze.

Equipment was minimal. In 1883 there was no cupboard for schoolbooks, and not even sufficient desks. Being cheaper, slates were preferred to paper for written exercises. Only the more competent scholars had copybooks, and used pen and ink. To blot your copybook was a serious matter, which might well justify a caning. Her Majesty's Inspector was forever recommending "more books and apparatus".

It is impossible for the mistress in charge (of the Infants' Class) to teach them thoroughly without the necessary materials. There is no gallery, there are but few reading cards, no box of loose letters, no colours, no primers, and no picture cards for object lessons. (H.M.I: 1873)
A fresh set of books is required for each standard, also some textbooks of Grammar and Geography.(H.M.I: 1875)
The supply of maps is insufficient: Geography cannot be taught unless this deficiency is remedied, and at once. (H.M.I: 1879)
The supply of books wants replenishing. Most of those now in use are old, torn and practically useless. New reading books should be provided." (H.M.I: 1880)

It is clear from the above that at times the H.M.I.'s patience was wearing thin. This is not surprising. Ten years later he was still demanding that "a full and sound supply of books must be provided without delay". Even by 1904 the school had no clock, no piano, no chair for staff or visitors, no fireguard and insufficient cupboards.

ENTER MISS DE ROTHSCHILD

In his Visitation Return for 1875, the Vicar wrote, "There is still no School Board, *and we hope to avoid this*". Perhaps Hannah de Rothschild had already discussed with him her plan to build a new infant school in Wingrave. Otherwise his optimism is surprising, for the school's numbers were still rising: at about 10% per annum. And later that year, the numbers rose even faster when Hannah Rothschild provided gifts of caps, pinafores, scarves and belts for the boys, and hats, cloaks and scarves for the girls. Wingravians were not backward in coming forward when school offered advantages like that. In consequence, the school's accommodation was once again overflowing, and the Inspector noted that its educational standards were falling. He produced the ultimate threat:

The first class are not very forward in the elementary subjects. My Lords will look for improvement in the first class of the infants' school as a condition of an unreduced grant next year.

So the opening of Hannah de Rothschild's new infants' school in January 1877 was a Godsend. It was purpose-built on the corner of Dark Lane and Moat Lane, and provided the infants with much larger and better accommodation. It also freed the East Room at the old school for the older children. Mr Wyatt quickly reorganised, creating two extra groups working to standards V and VI, the highest in the educational code. Six months later the Inspector's approval for these changes was received as part of a satisfactory report on the whole school.

CHANGES AT THE HELM

By the end of 1885 both the Rev. Butt and Mr Wyatt had departed.

Throughout his thirty-four years as vicar, the Reverend John Molesworth Butt had devotedly managed the village school. He was a frequent visitor, checking attendance registers, helping occasionally with the teaching of Reading, Arithmetic, Scripture, and Dictation, and even supplying materials for the Girls' Needlework. He was instrumental in the building of the school house, and raised funds for the north extension to the school, as well as contributing generously from his own pocket. He was buried in Wingrave churchyard in September 1887, aged 73 years.

The Wyatts had arrived in Wingrave with six children. By September 1881, seven more had been born, but four had died in childhood. Then in February 1882 tragedy struck again: two more children died on the same day. Mrs Wyatt was ill for months after this, and Mr Wyatt seemed to be a changed man. The Inspector obviously suspected that the attendance registers were being falsified, and the 1885 Report was critical of Mr Wyatt's conduct at the annual examinations:

The general results of the examination are not very satisfactory. The worst of it is, however, that I am not at all sure how far the work is honest; there is so much prompting and attempted copying that it quite takes the gloss off anything one might say in the way of commendation. What I should like to see would be perfect silence and honesty, and much better paperwork.

Mr Wyatt left Wingrave School at the end of 1885.

CHARLES REES

Mr Wyatt's successor arrived in January 1886. After testing the school, Mr Rees pronounced the scholars very backward in Reading, Writing, Spelling, Sewing and Geography. Only five children in a class of over forty could answer the question, "What is an island?" He realised, "It will only be with very hard work that we shall be able to present a tolerable appearance at the Examination." Mr Rees saw discipline as the key to progress. "I am determined to get good discipline," he wrote, and went into action.

Jany 18th: Was obliged to use the cane today, the culprit being Owen Ludlow. When told to hold out his hand he was very impudent and wanted to know, "What for?" etc.. As he would not open his hand, I rapped very sharply over his knuckles, which soon brought him to attention, but not before he had shouted out to his sister to run home and tell his father.

Jany 25th: I was obliged to cane three boys rather severely – two cuts on hand. Clarke would not hold out his hand so served him the same as Ludlow above. The boy shrieked loudly and a Mrs Hedges ran into the school asking, "Was that my nephew?" She left after using abusive language. Mrs Clarke next came up and was very outrageous when she found her boy had been caned. She took the boy to Mr Lockhart, who found she had no cause for complaint.

By the end of February Mr Rees had recorded seven canings, all of boys, after which things seemed to settle down and, though Mr Rees was still not satisfied, the reports by both the government and diocesan inspectors (H.M.I. and D.I. respectively) were complimentary:

The tone of the school is good and it is in excellent order. (D.I: May 1886)
There are signs of improvement about the work. (H.M.1: July 1886)
The discipline is very good. (D.I: May 1887)
I am glad to see still further improvements in the work and tone of this school (and) am prepared to recommend the merit grade 'Good'. (H.M.I: May 1887)

Other things were also going well. Mr Stewart Freeman, a London auctioneer, whose wife had a private income, was leasing the Old Manor House (now Macintyre Homes) from Hannah de Rothschild. He became a churchwarden and a school manager, and with his wife began to visit the parochial schools. They offered general prizes for good attendance and good conduct, and six prizes in Needlework for each standard. Mrs Freeman also provided the school with sewing materials. Not to be outdone, the Managers decided to encourage attendance by returning the fees of the four pupils with the least absence. In 1887 teaching conditions were vastly improved by the addition of a third classroom, the West Room, plus a new porch and cloakroom. Mr Freeman was a prime mover in this: he helped the Vicar with the initial planning; shared the £120 cost with Mrs Leopold de Rothschild, and may have helped persuade Lord Rosebery to give

66: Wingrave Parochial School, probably very early 20th century

the land. Also on the horizon was the bright star of 12 year old Arthur Robinson, a pupil at Wingrave from the age of 2½ years, who just a year later would become the school's first pupil teacher, and prove what could be achieved with a parochial education. These were all excellent carrots to complement Mr Rees' stick!

In the midst of all this good news it comes as a surprise to find the Rev. Lockhart and Mr Rees in conflict, with the former objecting to such things as: Mr Rees' forceful manner, "which rendered it unpleasant for a Manager to discharge his duty"; Mr Rees' boisterous manner when teaching; and (by implication) his caning of girls, which in future was forbidden "under any pretext". Over the next two years the log book does not hint at any further conflict. Then in June 1889 Mr Rees really overstepped the mark.

On Tuesday afternoon I punished John Badrick of Rowsham for carelessness by giving him three strokes on the back with my stick. In the evening his father brought him up and complained very much that his back was bruised. I was sorry that the punishment showed as it did, but I showed the father that the punishment was necessary, and accounted for the bruise that the blow fell on his shoulder bone. The father was satisfied with the explanation. I do not acknowledge that the punishment was excessive.

The Vicar's view was rather different:

Neither the father nor the mother were at all satisfied with the explanation of Mr Rees. Mr Rees admitted to me that the punishment was very excessive. I saw the boy stripped, and his back was covered with bruises. The boy has not been to school since Tuesday. The parents say they will summons.

There is no further direct reference to this in the log book, but in July an intriguing entry by the H.M.I. records that he tore out two pages because, "An entry in Mr Rees writing contravened Article 8".[11] Only as the year ends do we learn the fate of Mr Rees.

I was presented with a splendid Gladstone bag by the teachers and scholars this morning. I suppose now that my work in this school is over, I must say that I leave with much regret. I thought to have stayed here some time longer.

Mr WILLIAM BAKER

When Mr Baker arrived in Wingrave in October 1889 he was 43 years old, married though with no known family, and the first Head Teacher of Wingrave School to possess a first-class teaching certificate. His salary was £110 per annum plus rent-free accommodation in the school house, and free coal.

In his second week at the school, Mr Baker described the pupils, as "very backward, very restless and disorderly". His conclusion was remarkably similar to that of his predecessor, but his remedy was very different. If Rees was a flogger, then Baker was a tester. Every standard was tested in every subject. Having tested and found deficiencies, he looked for causes, personally gave remedial lessons, and then re-tested again and again to ensure that a satisfactory level of attainment was both reached and maintained. He obviously had considerable skill in handling his classes, for after only two months, and long before the children's academic skills improved, the Rev. Lockhart was impressed by the improved tone of the school. So was the H.M.I. in his next report.

The school has vastly improved under Mr Baker. The improvement is so general and so satisfactory that, in view of all the circumstances, I think that the Excellent merit grant has been earned. (H.M.I: 1890)

This was the first time in the school's history that the coveted 'Excellent' had been received, and with it the higher cash grant. The 1891 report was just as complimentary,

151

and even noted that "the children have evidently been taught to think for themselves". The Rev. Lockhart was so delighted that he pinned a notice to the school door inviting parents to inspect the report, and three weeks later had copies printed for circulation amongst the scholars.

ATTENDANCE

At this time average attendances were generally high. The 'work versus school' battle continued but on a smaller scale, for the attendance officer was now functioning more effectively, mainly calling on parents and issuing warnings, but from time to time taking out a summons against a persistent offender. The fine, usually 5s-0d, now sounds trivial, but it did represent about a third of an agricultural labourer's weekly wage. The irregular attenders were more difficult to deal with. Bad weather noticeably reduced attendance, but some children had no coats, few had raincoats and many had only light shoes. The walk across the fields from Rowsham in wet weather, or even just within the village through heavy rain or snow, left them wearing sodden shoes and socks for the rest of the day, for most of them simply didn't possess spare clothing to change into. At such times a parent might reasonably consider it best for the child to remain at home. Illness also had a significant effect on attendance. Illness which is now regarded as trivial, such as measles, was then a serious matter. Whooping cough, for instance, was a potential killer. Children's illnesses quickly became epidemic, due to close contact in large families and crowded classrooms. In 1894 an epidemic of scarlet fever lasted for over three months, and there was an average of 27 scholars absent with it. Eventually the Medical Officer of Health ordered the school to close for over a month.

Meanwhile the number of occasional holidays granted by the Managers grew by the year. National events entered the list. Queen Victoria's Golden Jubilee (1887) and the Duke of York's wedding (1893) merited a day apiece, while for Queen Victoria's Diamond Jubilee (1897) there was a full week's holiday. To celebrate the relief of Mafeking (1900) the whole school visited London at Mr Freeman's expense. The school was closed for use as a polling booth in the Parliamentary, county, district and parish elections. All this was in addition to the traditional events: the Band of Hope's outing; a choir trip to London; the Sunday School teachers' picnic; a Sunday School outing to Windsor; the Freemans' annual treat for day and Sunday School pupils; etc., etc., all of which required the school's closure for a day, even if the actual event took place at the weekend! Half-day closures resulted from the school's use for the Oddfellows' Fete, the Allotment Holders' Dinner, a Women's Tea, and a village Rummage Sale. Even the Inspector of Weights and Measures had the school for a whole day. Add in the closures for Church Holy days, and the continuity of teaching was at such risk that one wonders how the staff could maintain the high standards for which the school was regularly praised. Wonder turns to disbelief when one learns that for a whole year the managers failed to replace an assistant teacher, leaving Arthur Robinson and Mr Baker to teach classes which, at maximum, averaged 66 pupils of all abilities, and with a six-year age range. Disbelief turns to irritation when one learns that "for years past" the Managers had refused to change the way of promoting pupils from the Infants School despite it being "the worst arrangement both for scholars and schools that could be devised." In spite of all these problems, Mr Baker's five years as headmaster transformed the school. Year after year the compliments flowed:

The order and tone of this school is excellent. The whole of the work done deserves very high praise. (D.I: 1892)
The style, accuracy, and intelligence of the children's work are again highly satisfactory. They are in capital order and sing unusually well. (H.M.I:1892)

152

This (school) shews a completeness of teaching which is very desirable, as well as a general interest among the scholars in what is taught. (D.I: 1893)

The school has scored another genuine success in its examination through sound, neat and intelligent work. All the classes afford evidence that they are being thoroughly well taught. There is no better singing in the County. (H.M.I:1893)

The school is in capital order, and has come out very well in examination. Mr Baker is leaving it in a very creditable state of efficiency. (H.M.I:1894)

At this point Mr Baker left. Within a month an assistant teacher had been appointed. Within a year an additional classroom had been built. Within four years the boys' playground was surfaced and drained.

Mr LEMUEL JONES

The new headmaster arrived in September 1894, and stayed for almost 25 years. Some of the senior citizens of today's Wingrave were taught by him. Horace Bignell was a pupil at this time: see Recollections below. Mr Jones' arrival was followed by other important changes. Gradually the pupils' day became more active and varied as more subjects were added to the Educational Code: Singing, Military Drill (boys), Musical Drill (girls), Clay Modelling for the younger pupils, Drawing and Painting for the

---

Recollections: Attending Wingrave School 1911 to 1916 _ Horace Bignell

Mr Jones was the Head. He was a good schoolmaster really. He was quite strict, and there was no jiggery-pokery up there in those days. You didn't dare do anything you shouldn't at school, or you had the stick. One day in February 1914, as the bell was being tolled for afternoon school, some of us scholars ran into a neighbouring field where hunters with hounds were gathering. When the Hunt set off, seventeen of us boys played truant and followed it. Next morning we all had the cane.

I remember the Inspector visiting, and asking our class some questions. "How many pennies weigh an ounce?" was one. Vic Rickard gave the right answer, and the inspector gave him a penny. Then he asked, "How long will it take for the sound of the Aylesbury hooter to reach Wingrave?" (Wingrave folk used to fix their clocks by the hooter at Rivetts Works, which we could practically always hear). I knew how far sound travelled in a second, so I worked it out in my head, and he gave me a penny too, and that was something in those days.

When I was eleven I got a scholarship to Aylesbury Grammar School. I never liked it, but my Dad pushed me. Mr Jones gave me evening lessons before the written and oral exams., which were held in Aylesbury. I was the only boy in Wingrave to get a scholarship. There were only twenty for the whole county. I came seventh. I got to Aylesbury by push-bike. There was no bus.

---

upper standards, Science, and Cookery for the Girls.

The school-leaving age was raised to eleven years in 1893, and to twelve years in 1899. The compulsory attendance required by the 1880 Act was now enforced much more rigorously by the attendance officers. This and the decline of straw plaiting encouraged attendance, but there were still occasional reports of boys truanting to work in the fields. For instance, in the summer of 1897 the school log book records:

Mr Manning of West Park Farm has six boys at work on his farm under age. One, George Goss, is not eight years old. Notices have been sent to the parents.

67. *Schoolmaster Mr Lemuel Jones and his two assistant teachers with a group of 'scholars'. It appears that the girls' school uniform was a pinafore. Third from the left on the back row is Minnie Jones (later Rickard), who became a monitress, pupil teacher and eventually an assistant teacher in the Wingrave School.*

68. *Mr Jones with another group of 'scholars'. Some sort of headgear seems to have been compulsory for the boys.*

Fortunately, most farmers now preferred full-time to casual labour, and this reduced absenteeism. Of course, with increasing numbers additional accommodation was needed, but with Stewart Freeman deeply involved in church affairs there seems to have been little problem in finding funds. In 1895 the new South Room came into use, finally completing the cruciform plan of the school buildings, which remained unaltered for the next fifty years.

Fig. 18: The School Plan 1895

Room	Built	Standards
East	1847	I and II
North	1871	III
West	1887	Collective & Reading
South	1895	IV to VI

The Education Act of 1902 made the County Councils responsible for elementary education. They also had to finance it, so the Vicar no longer had to worry about raising funds. County set allowances for furniture, apparatus and books, which were simply requisitioned by the school. A County surveyor inspected the buildings. County officials, rather than the Vicar, checked the register; County determined the holiday dates, not the needs of local farmers; and County advisors made recommendations on educational matters, though H.M.I.'s. continued their inspections. The school became known as the Wingrave with Rowsham Parochial School. In 1905 the school was brightened up in the first recorded re-decoration since 1847.

All staff present at 8 a.m. to begin replacing maps etc., after the cleaning and beautifying of the school. The new floor in the East Room is a great boon and comfort after the rickety unsafe boards that have been removed. Colour washing (of the walls) and lime washing of the ceilings, painting and varnishing of all the woodwork and the complete renovation of the lobby have all been well carried out and the school presents a clean and bright appearance.

New furniture and equipment usually came due to the comments of H.M.I.'s. The report for 1911 criticised the "old-fashioned, cumbersome, long desks" which forced the children "to adopt injurious attitudes of body". It also demanded that "a larger and more powerful stove should be substituted before another winter comes round". By the end of August the chairman of the County Council's Building Committee had discussed the heating problems with the school, and by mid-September nineteen new dual desks were installed. However, even the County Council's resources did not guarantee that problems were actually resolved. In 1917 Mr Jones was still reporting, "Only 37° at 10.50 a.m.. The stove is ineffective for heating. No amount of stoking does much good".

THE DEPARTURE OF MR JONES

In 1919 Mr Jones left to take charge of Bierton School. Throughout his twenty-five years at Wingrave very pleasing comments were a feature of the annual reports:

The Master is not afraid to try educational experiments. The quietness of the teaching in every class commends itself strongly. The bearing of the children and their attention to lessons are all that can be desired, and things go pleasantly and smoothly. (H.M.I: 1909)

Things are going well here. The teaching is full of earnestness and care, and the good conduct of the children and their steady interest in their lessons contribute materially to the success achieved. (H.M.I: 1914)

I understand that the Master is leaving the School after many years of successful service. He leaves it in a very high condition of Religious Knowledge, due to his own efforts and those of his colleagues. The School is one of the best in the Deanery, and is just as good as when I last inspected it. (D.I: 1919)

JOHN HENRY STUBBS (1919-50)

John Stubbs had taught at four other schools before he became Headmaster at Wingrave. With his wife and two young sons, he moved into the School House in June 1919, and soon after a daughter, Margaret, was born.

The H.M.I.'s report for 1920 hinted at some development of the timetable, schemes of work and syllabuses and, on the whole, it was a satisfactory report:

There are some gratifying signs of life in this school. The Headmaster deserves credit for the intelligence and zeal with which he is performing his duties. He is assisted in the Senior Division by two industrious teachers, both of whom, according to their abilities, are doing loyal and useful work. The Infants are in very capable hands, and are lively and promising.

One of the "two industrious teachers" was Mrs Minnie Rickard. A native of Wingrave, Minnie Jones (as she then was), entered Hannah de Rothschild's Infant school at the age of 2¾ years. She transferred to the Parochial School at seven years, became a monitress at 14, then a pupil teacher, until in 1907, aged 19, she was appointed Assistant Teacher. She remained in this post for over thirty years. In addition to teaching general subjects, she would take charge of the school in Mr Stubbs' absence. She was also responsible for music and singing, and under her direction the school choir had considerable success:

At the Herts and Berkhamsted Annual Musical Festival at St Albans the School Choir was again first in Class IV (schools with average attendance under 100), and was awarded the Challenge Banner. (May 1927)

The "capable hands" in charge of the infants belonged to Mrs Ivy Stubbs, the Headmaster's wife, who continued to teach that age-group for nearly thirty years. She was clearly an exceptional teacher, and throughout her time at the school the reports on her work with the infants were always very complimentary:

Number, Reading and Writing are all well taught and practised with obvious gusto and highly creditable proficiency by the children. The outlook here is distinctly encouraging. (H.M.I: 1921)

The capable and industrious teacher of the Infants' Division is over-weighted with 37 children of ages varying from 4 to 8 years. (H.M.I: 1925)

The lowest class were delightfully spontaneous and well-taught. It was gratifying to find they had so much enjoyed their missionary lessons. (D.I: 1927)

It was hard work to tear myself away from the infants. (D.I: 1928)

The work/school conflict which had once so affected attendance was now largely a thing of the past. Unfortunately, in the Twenties and Thirties, epidemics of children's diseases still occurred. They, and the absences they created, often dominated the log book. For example, in May 1920 there was an outbreak of measles, which affected the whole school, but especially the infants where the attendance was cut by 50%. By the middle of June there were twenty-one cases, after which the epidemic subsided. Only two months later one of the infants was found to have diphtheria, which then had a high mortality rate. The child's brothers were excluded from the school, the staff observed all the pupils carefully, and notices were sent to the parents of absentees. Concern grew when the child died, and increased when a few days later her brother also died. However, there were no further cases. Then, just a few months later, the District Nurse reported that two pupils had been suffering from scarlet fever, and had reached the 'peeling' stage. At this time it was also a highly infectious disease with a high mortality rate. Thus when a case was reported, any other children from the same house were excluded from school. By the end of April almost a third of the school was absent, and it was closed for two weeks. As all this happened within one year, with children constantly coming and going, the teaching was greatly disrupted. Neither did it stop there, as the H.M.I.'s Report for 1923 reveals:

This school has been conducted during the past two years under conditions which must have been at least unsettling, if not actually depressing, to both teachers and children. A succession of epidemics has seriously affected the attendance and another outbreak seemed imminent at the time of the inspection. These circumstances have considerably affected the work of the school, and it says much for the energy and industry of the Master and his assistants, that the attainments of the children reach such a good level.

In the 1920's and 1930's illness was probably no more prevalent than in the 19th century, but it was more identifiable and more quantifiable due to compulsory schooling (the leaving age was now 14 years), better medical knowledge and services, and a greater concern to avoid epidemics. The School Medical Officer, the District Nurse, the School Nurse and the teachers were all on the alert for the early symptoms of contagious diseases. If any were found, the children were immediately sent home, and each case reported to the County Medical Officer. Other children from the same house, or even from the same area were also excluded from school, as being potential carriers

69. *Musical Festival Winners 1926. Back Row (from left): Minnie Rickard, Joan Gibbs, Ruby Woodruff, Minnie Kirby, Ethel Clay, Doreen Honor, Susie Bock, Gladys Goldney, Eddie Bignell, John Stubbs. Second Row Down (from left): Denis Rickard, Ivy Kempster, Molly Bandy, Edna Bateman, Freda Clay, Connie Hugget, Phillys Paxton, Cyril Beilby. Third Row down (from left): Olive Bateman, Edie Bandy, Beatrice Goldney, Win Rickard, May Coleman, Ivy Goldney, Chrissie Clay, Hilda Bliss. Crossed-legged (from left): Dick Sandall, Maurice Rogers, Basil Stubbs, Clifford Woodruff.*

Fig. 19: Epidemics Affecting Wingrave Parochial School 1920-1926

Infectious Diseases	First Reported	Length (weeks)	Peak Absence	Days school closed Other information
Measles	May 1920	8	26%	
Diphtheria	Sept 1920	2	3%	2 children died
Scarlet fever	April 1921	23	40%	Closed 16 days
Influenza	Jan 1922	Not known	19%	Closed 5 days
Whooping cough	July 1922	20	29%	
Scarlet fever	Dec 1922	7	21%	
Mumps	Jan 1923	21	17%	
Measles	Jan 1924	7	44%	Closed 19 days
Influenza	Feb 1924	Not known	Not known	
Measles	Mar 1925	Not known	23%	
Chicken pox	May 1925	29	18%	
Whooping cough	Feb 1926	8	51%	Closed 3 weeks

of the disease. The following extract from the school log book illustrates the process.

Received information that Edgar Bignell is suffering from Scarlet Fever. Excluded James Bignell. Tom Sandles and Edith Bandy in bed with sore throats. Regarded them as suspicious and excluded Dick and Willie Sandall, and Harold and Molly Bandy.

The diseases most common at this time were spread by droplet infection, and crowded classrooms greatly increased the chances of an epidemic. Measles was particularly dangerous, but almost always conferred immunity for life. So to prevent an epidemic, every child who had not had the disease was sent home and excluded from school for a specified period. If such exclusions severely reduced attendance, the County Medical Officer could instruct the Head to close the school. Decisions about exclusions and closures sometimes had to be discussed with County officials, and as there were no telephones in the village the Head had to get out his bicycle and pedal into Aylesbury. Especially when there were exclusions, epidemics had a disastrous effect on attendances and thus on the teaching.

Recollections: Excluded! - Mrs Ethel Perkins

Each Monday I was given a ha'penny. I spent it on sweets at Mrs Gibbs. One Monday I chose 'ballsers' from a big jar. Mrs Gibbs put them in a twist of paper, and I went off to school with them. At school Mr Stubbs came into the classroom, and said, "All those who have not had measles, come to the front". About ten of us hadn't. We were all told to go home, and stay away from school until we were told to come back. Mary Reynolds and I were from Rowsham and we walked the 1½ miles to school and back each day. So we started off. It was a beautiful day. We played in the fields. We used my 'ballsers' as marbles, and when we had finished, we ate them! Then we got out our packed lunches and ate them. I always carried my younger brother's lunch to school, and I'd still got it, but he was still at school because he'd already had measles. So we ate his lunch as well! Oh, we had a lovely time. But when we got home at long last we found that the others had got there before us. That took a bit of explaining.

70. *John and Ivy Stubbs, headmaster and infants' teacher 1919-1950.*

71. *Joyce Whipps in 1952. It was the first of her 32 years as infants' teacher at Wingrave school. She is in the East Room with windows overlooking the churchyard. The bottom half of the classroom walls was unpainted cement, and above that was whitewashed. There was just one very damp (built-in) cupboard, and no other storage. The room was lit (to misuse an expression) by one bulb high up in the rafters (there was no ceiling), and heated by a coal-burning stove, the front of which kept falling off.*

The 1920's saw a real increase in the medical provision for Wingrave's school-children. Examinations at school by a County Medical Officer began in 1908. In 1923 the first vaccinations against Diphtheria appear in the log book. There were no more cases at Wingrave School until 1931, by which time an isolation unit had been established at Ledburn. By 1930 school dental inspections had begun and shortly afterwards treatment was also given on the school premises. A nurse visited the school several times a year to examine the pupils' hair for nits (the eggs of lice). At Wingrave it was always the girls whose hair which was infested, presumably because it was fuller and much longer than the boys'. "The usual families received notices," was the tactful comment in the school log in January 1930. It was 1933 before an "all clear" was noted "the first time for fourteen years". After that it became the norm, and the nurse concentrated on the pupils' general cleanliness, which still caused exclusions as late as 1939.

WORMS' EYE VIEW

What was school like from the pupils' viewpoint in the brave new world of the Twenties and Thirties? Fortunately personal recollections reach back to those days: see Recollections pages 158, 160, 162. One thing is certain. Some aspects of school, which were perennial occurrences then, would be unacceptable today. Even in the 1930's, the school regime was much more autocratic, being based on punishment and particularly on the fear of corporal punishment, which is now illegal in schools.

Recollections: Discipline At School -- Frank and Grace King

Grace: Mr Stubbs used to go into Aylesbury one day every month to collect the wages. He used to be gone all day. On such occasions, Mrs Stubbs, the infants' teacher, was in charge of his class. She had the door of the Infants' room open, and if we made any noise she'd come in and shout, "Hands on heads, you monkeys", and we had to sit there until she said, "Put them down", hopefully before 'Johnny' (Mr Stubbs) returned.

Frank: In Minnie Rickard's class, when we had English, I would always say, CONTRO-versy, and she used to insist that it was con-TRO-versy. Well, I kept on saying CONTRO-versy and one day she got really mad with me. She went to the cupboard and got her cane out, which had a knob on the end of it. And she came tearing down the gangway between the desks, until she was behind me and fetched me such a fourpenny one across my shoulders. I never said CONTRO-versy again!

Grace: Everything was so quiet, and I suppose I just wanted to make a noise. I had my ruler, and I poked somebody's pencil box from the ledge underneath the desk, and it clattered down. Johnny looked up. "Who did that?" "Grace Honor, Mr Stubbs." And I had to go out front and have the cane _ on the hand. Quite a few girls had it. I doubt if there was a week went by, but what somebody had the cane. Buller Rickard said his mother used to say to him every night when he came home from school, "What have you had the stick for today?" And if he said he hadn't had the stick, she wondered what was the matter.

Frank: Charlie Horwood reckons the lads used to put Mr Stubbs' canes down the knot-holes in the floor. Not that it made much difference. If he didn't have a cane handy, he would go and cut a stick out of the lilac tree in the schoolhouse garden. That's probably how he cut Ivan Gurney's thumb. One of the little knots, where he cut the twigs off the side of the stick, must have hit his thumb. Anyhow, sixty years later Ivan still had the scar. But parents didn't complain, not like they do now. They used to say, "Well, you must have deserved it".

In winter the school could be so cold that writing was impossible.

Bitterly cold morning. Not one of the thermometers registered above 28°F (Infants 24°F).No coal in the store house. Impossible to work. Desks moved and children warmed by Xmas games and dances. (Log: Dec 1920)

A deep snow this morning and snow continued falling. At 8.45 a.m. the fires were black, not having been lighted long, and the temperature in all rooms was 2° below freezing. Penmanship and such-like were out of the question. Dancing was taken at intervals to keep the children warm. (Log: Jan 1926)

Still bitterly cold. Temperature (in school) at 8.45 a.m: 24° F. Physical exercises taken on the pond (sliding). (Log: Feb 1929)

Lighting from the old oil lamps was completely inadequate. Even after electric lights replaced them in 1930, reading and writing were still very difficult on winter afternoons, because too few bulbs had been installed. Twenty-five years later the East Room still had just one bulb hanging from the rafters. For many years the playground was just compacted earth. In dry weather it became very dusty, and the dust was blown into the school making everyone uncomfortable. Heavy rains flooded the playground, making it difficult for the boys to reach the 'offices' as the urinals were officially known. Any rain made the surface of the playground too muddy for P.E. and Netball, besides ensuring that a lot of dirt was carried into the school. These problems were not solved until 1934, when a drain was replaced and the playground was asphalted. It took even longer to bring the lavatories to an acceptable standard. Early 'improvements' made little difference. Thus the new earth pans fitted in 1906 were "much handier", but "lay too low to catch the liquid", and were still not emptied regularly. In the Spring of 1937 they were not emptied for over five weeks. It took the Managers a year to raise the funds, but by the end of 1942 the school drainage and sanitation scheme was completed. At long last the earth closets were replaced by water closets.

Fig. 20: Attendance Perfect

1930-31 Aubrey Badrick, Ray Deller, Avis Rickard, Daphne Clay, Cyril White.

1931-32 Beryl Gibbs, Gerald Goldney, Clarice Bignell, Norman Brackley, Daphne Clay, Avis Rickard, Victor Gurney.

1932-33 Avis Rickard, Daphne Clay, Annie Higgins, Thomas Reynolds, Jean Deller.

1933-34 Avis Rickard, Daphne Rickard, Jim Kirby, Victor Gurney, A. Badrick.

1934-35 Daphne Clay, Edward King, Frank King, Jim Kirby, Fred Kirby, Norman Brackley, Peter Kempster, Evelyn Goldney, V.Gurney, J. Rickard, D.Higgins, Clarice Bignell.

1935-36 Daphne Clay, Victor Gurney, Fred Kirby, Jim Kirby, Norman Brackley, Peter Kempster, Connie Goldney, Violet Bignell, Irene White, John Fleet.

1936-37 Norman Brackley.

1937-38 Norman Brackley, Fred Kirby, Peter Kempster, John White.

1938-39 Olive Wiltshire.

1940-41 Joan Holden, Betty Cook, Betty Spore, Iris Hurlock, Jean Leonard, Dorothy Soskin, Joyce Smith, Betty Smith, Cynthia Lewis. (includes evacuees)

1941-42 Mervyn Roberts, Ian Roberts, Iris Dell, Joan Bottero, Gordon Bonham, Pamela Rickard, Joyce Smith, Betty Smith.

1945-46 Rose Pearce.

Recollections: Attending Wingrave School - Daphne Rickard

Mrs Stubbs was in charge of the infant class. She was an excellent teacher, but strict by today's standards. Naughty children stood in a corner, face to the wall. Bad work or bad behaviour got you a slap on the hand and, if we talked too much, she ordered, "Hands on heads", and there we babies sat silent for what seemed like eternity, but which was probably only five minutes.

I can still see the picture alphabet on the wall: A in apple, B in ball, C in cat, D in dog. I've never forgotten: THR in thrush, EIR in their, ERE in there. And even now I can hear us droning away at our "tables". We quite enjoyed it. After all, one 3 is 3, two 3's are 6, three 3's are 9 was just as much fun to us as a nursery rhyme, or anything else to repeat. And if some didn't understand what it really meant, doubtless it came in useful later. And we of that generation have no doubts that nine 9's are 81, or seven 12's are 84: you just try us!

The walls of the classrooms were just plain brick, and no bright paint. But the coal fires were always cosy. In winter weather, in the infants class we would change places so that we all had our turn nearest to the fire, well hidden behind a big strong guard. I remember morning prayers. Did we always sing, "Children of the Heavenly King"? That's the only hymn I can remember. We used to say a prayer before going home, "Thus may we abide in union with each other and the Lord". Unfortunately, as a five-year-old I always said, "NURSE may we abide in union". I thought it was something to do with the District Nurse who came into the school to see us every week.

In the middle class I was taught by Mrs Minnie Rickard. I can't ever remember NOT being able to read, and I loved dictation, but I didn't excel in practical things. Boadicea's chariot never would stay stuck together, when made from cardboard. Winding wool ended in a frightful muddle, and sewing afternoons were made bearable only by the Enid Blyton stories read to us by Mrs Rickard. And I never did understand singing lessons, because she taught us tonic sol-fa with all those weird hand signals that denoted doh, lah, te, soh, whereas I thought it much easier to understand black blobs _ on five lines _ going up and down!

And so up into the top class with Mr Stubbs, who was also strict. Rarely a day passed without a boy having the cane. I remember hot Horlicks in mid-morning break. And I can see those dilapidated old lavatories. Either the roofs leaked, or the lavatories leaked, and everything seemed damp and nasty. There were also good times in the playground: games, and country dancing to Gathering Peacocks and Sir Roger de Coverley.

Then came the scholarship examination, and I went off on my lonely way to Aylesbury. In spite of all I learned there, it is the old Wingrave School which has a special place in my heart.

THE SCHOLARSHIP EXAMINATION

By the 1930's there were many more candidates for places at the secondary schools (Aylesbury Grammar, and the Cedars at Linslade, both then being coeducational). Thus in 1933 twenty-two Wingrave children sat the Entrance examination held at Wingrave School. Not many passed, but this was not surprising, as a former pupil explained,

I can remember sitting the exam. We just went in one morning, and we had these

papers given out. We'd had no preparation for it. We had what must have been an intelligence test, but we'd never seen one before. There were different symbols down there, and then the question, "What comes next?" Well, I hadn't a clue! I so wanted to go to the Cedars. We had a letter to say that I was one mark short, but that my parents could pay, but that was impossible. I was so disappointed.

On this occasion, only two free places were awarded: to Donald Rand from Seabrook's Farm at Rowsham, and Daphne Rickard from Wingrave. Both these places were accepted, but the parents of children offered fee-paying places often felt that they could not afford it. Even if the place was free, there was the uniform, the sports kit, the books, the bus fares, and for the last year or two the cost of food and clothing with no earnings to pay for them. Or perhaps they could have afforded it for one child, but not for several, and were not prepared to favour one more than the others. Some parents felt that extra education was a waste of time: it was better to get a job. Some pupils preferred to stay in Wingrave with their friends. They did not want to suffer the taunts of those who remained behind, or travel alone to school each day, to join a class of strangers.

Recollections: The Scholarship Examination -- Prudence Goodwin (nee Rickard)

I well remember the time, halfway through one morning, when Mr Stubbs gave me an envelope, saying, "Take this home, and give it to your parents. They'll be very pleased". I guessed that I had passed, and I was so relieved that when I got to Church Alley I burst into tears. I had been under such pressure to pass from both the school and from my parents that I was still crying when I reached home. My grandmother greeted me. Knowing that the exam result was due, she assumed that I'd failed. "Sit on my lap, ducky", she said. "Don't cry. We'll pay. We'll send you to a private school". Of course, that only made me cry harder. Then my mother came in, opened the letter and said, "She's passed!" At that I sobbed even louder, but eventually they managed to calm me down.

CHANGING ATTITUDES

At the outbreak of war, in September 1939, one hundred and seventeen children, eighteen mothers and four teachers from a London County Council junior school were evacuated to Wingrave. They were all billeted on the villagers, who had no choice in the matter. They all became pupils of Wingrave School. Not surprisingly there were difficulties. "Wingrave at War", edited by Geof. Aldridge, is a collection of personal stories of this period.

Mr and Mrs Stubbs retired in 1950, having served the school for a total of over sixty years. Before Mr Stubbs' time one gets the impression that parents only visited the village school to complain. It was still a church school, which didn't recommend it to chapel folk. And the repeated raising of the school age, now rigorously enforced by the attendance officers, had upset many who were now parents. Then, in the 1920's, a small but increasing number of parents began to visit the school when their children had medical and dental inspections and treatment. However, it was after Mr Stubbs began to invite parents and friends to an annual Open Afternoon, that the barriers really fell.

Although a wet afternoon, all the available space was occupied, about 80 being present. The children sang and danced, all classes contributing an item. The rooms had been decorated by the children, and calendars, cards and other articles made in the Handwork lessons, were on view. Each child received a present from the Christmas tree, together with an orange and sweets. The children surprised the staff by presenting the Headmaster with a shaving set, and the lady assistants with bottles of scent. The Vicar spoke a few words of appreciation, as did Mrs Roberts. (Log: Dec. 1922)

In the 1930's this event attracted even more parents, for it was used to present the 'Attendance Perfect' certificates awarded to pupils who had attended both morning and afternoon sessions for a whole school year: see Fig. 20, page 161.

By 1934, such was the improvement in attitudes towards the school that the Methodist concert party, The Prim Dozen, provided the Xmas tree for the Open Afternoon. Perhaps the main factor in bringing village and school together was the Stubbs themselves. When they retired in 1950, Hilda Roberts reviewed their time in the village.

Mr Stubbs soon interested himself in the general life of the village, and in many capacities proved his gifts as an organiser. He was church organist from 1919 until 1946, a member of the Church Council from its inception in 1922, and its secretary from 1933. He was Clerk to the Parish Council for seven years, National Savings group chairman and secretary up to 1950, and as secretary of the Allotment Society organised the first Flower Show. He was also a founder member of the Tennis and Bowls Clubs, a member of the British Legion and chairman of the village branch for five years, and secretary of the Recreation Ground Committee for seven years. A keen and talented football player (he played for Aylesbury United in 1924), he played for the village football team and was its secretary for eight years. He organised events to raise funds for improvements to the school, notably the school playground and sanitation scheme. From 1924 onwards he led and conducted 'The Scarlet Ramblers', a very successful concert party, which gave pleasure to many people in the district. Mr and Mrs Stubbs will be greatly missed in the village, not only as the respected, highly esteemed schoolmaster and mistress, but as friends and willing helpers in so many varied ways. They have become a real part of village life.

A NEW ERA

In 1946 Wingrave School became a primary school with its pupils transferring to a secondary school at the age of twelve. It was the beginning of a reorganisation, which (for Wingrave) was not completed until 1974, when the school moved out of its old building into a brand new school, large enough to accommodate not only the children of Wingrave and Rowsham, but also those bussed in from the nearby villages of Aston Abbotts and Cublington, when the old village schools were closed down. It was the end of an era, in which so many changes had occurred: from the daily trudge across the fields from Rowsham, to the gleaming luxury of the school bus; from slates to computers; from playground drill to P.E. in a properly equipped hall; from hand-me-downs to school uniform; from one schoolroom for 3 to 12 year olds to a purpose-built school for 5 to 12 year olds.

72. Joyce Whipps, with headmaster Brian Ellis, rings the school bell for the last time at the old parochial school, July 1974.

73. Margaret Morley with Year Seven pupils, winners of the Bucks Herald 150 Years Anniversary Competition, 1982. 'Editor' Emma Bowes, the daughter of our publisher, displays the class entry, a front page which could have appeared 150 years ago in 1832.

74. *Winners of the Aylesbury Vale Middle Schools' Netball League, 1977. From the left – top row: Paula Slingo, June Page, Susan Page, Kate Inns; bottom row: Rebecca Watkins, Laura Hicks, Rachel Hickman, Julie Wesley.*

75. *Deputy Head, David Lewis, with the Wingrave School football team,1977. From the left – top row: Robert Walker, Chris Smith, David Roberts, Nicky Holt, Tim Kempster; bottom row: Michael Smith, Charlie Snow, Kevin Lovell, Paul Brackley, Gary Megram, Graham Alcock*

Chapter Fourteen

Hannah's Infant School

This much-needed and greatly appreciated gift to the village opened in January 1877. Despite its close connections with Wingrave Parochial School it was built and operated entirely at Hannah de Rothschild's expense. It included a four-bedroomed schoolhouse for the schoolmistress, as well as a large schoolroom (55 feet by 18 feet), and a Reading Room for adults. A glass-panelled partition separated the two rooms. Children entered through the cloakroom at the back. There were earth closets at the end of the yard, and to the side was the playground, which tended to be overgrown with weeds. The schoolroom was heated by an open fire, but even a quarter of a century later there was no fireguard. Oil lamps were used for lighting. Along one wall stood the 'gallery'. This was tiered seating, constructed so that the infants could see the mistress, and the mistress could keep a watchful eye on her fidgety charges. She needed to. As an old man, Fred 'Buller' Rickard could still remember sitting cramped on the back row, using his pea shooter and catapult to great effect. The remaining floor space was taken up by four cumbersome nine foot long desks, with no backs: not at all suitable for infants.

When the school opened in January 1877, the Reverend Butt, Elizabeth Montague, the newly appointed mistress, and her ten-year-old monitress were there to greet the thirty infants transferred from Wingrave Parochial School. There followed a steady influx of new pupils so that, by the time of the first government inspection, eighty pupils were on roll, all being taught in the one schoolroom. Miss Montague soon found a very wide range of abilities and attainments. It was an uphill struggle to classify and group the children and instil some form of discipline. It became clear that extra help was essential and, in May, Hannah agreed to appoint Elizabeth Rickard as a pupil teacher. Whilst admitting the school's problems, the H.M.I.'s report was encouraging.

This school, recently opened and attended by infants who seem to have been under no sort of discipline before, is naturally enough in a backward state at present. It is, however, superintended by a mistress who seems anxious to improve its condition and it is conducted in peculiarly well-built and substantial buildings, and everything which can contribute to its improvement is willingly supplied. (H.M.I: 1878)

This latter comment was very true. The overall welfare of the pupils was close to Hannah's heart. Every Tuesday and Thursday during the winter months she provided them with a dinner of rabbit stew, with milk to drink. Each summer the children looked forward to her 'treat', which was usually a special tea. Every few years at Christmas, they were measured and later presented with fine new clothing: red plush cloaks and white straw hats for the girls; and black caps and red scarves for the boys. Even three years after her death, this tradition continued. The teachers, too, were given cloaks. Hilda Roberts, a pupil teacher there in 1893, treasured hers for many years.

By the 1880's there were about 100 pupils enrolled, and the single schoolroom was very crowded, providing ideal conditions for the transmission of coughs, colds and the infectious diseases of childhood. This was well demonstrated in April 1886 when Wingrave suffered from a widespread outbreak of a particularly virulent strain of measles. Eventually the attendance fell below twenty, and the school was closed for several weeks. In all, nine young children died between April and July, including six year old Edward Jones, the only son of Thomas and Annie Jones (the village postmistress), and three infants from the Ridgway family. When the school reopened the mistress reported,

Those who have returned look very white and ill, and there is a small share of crying from the babies. The singing lesson was very badly done, so many of the children are suffering from colds and weakness left by the measles. The children are to have one soup dinner per week.

Hannah involved her school in her family's celebrations and sorrows. The celebrations (of marriages, comings of age, etc.) usually merited a day's holiday and a free tea at Mentmore. Lord Rosebery's pride in his wife's efforts was demonstrated when he brought Mr Gladstone to see the school, and by his continuation of the gifts, holidays and teas for some years after Hannah's death in 1890.

By this date the 102 children on the school roll, were divided into three classes, all sharing just one schoolroom. Two years later the H.M.I. recommended separate accommodation for the Babies (the two to three year olds) where they could chatter and play, or cry their way throughout the day, as did many newcomers before they became accustomed to their new environment. Meanwhile, the older ones would have some peace in which to work. The Reading Room had not proved popular with the villagers and, in 1894, Lord Rosebery agreed that it should become the Babies' Room. This appeared to resolve the school's problems, and the 1894 Report was very favourable.

This is a very good Infants' School where the elementary subjects are well taught, and where everything is done in the way of Varied Occupations, Musical Drill and the like to make the children intelligent and happy in their school lives.

Unfortunately, when the babies were moved out of the main schoolroom, the old gallery was reduced in size and transferred with them, though it was still much too large for the tiny tots using it. Amazingly it was eight years before His Majesty's Inspector noticed that the babies had to sit all day with their feet dangling in the air, and asked for something to be done about it. Foot-rests were quickly provided, but only solved part of the problem. Six years later the H.M.I. once more took up the matter.

The gallery in the Babies' room is a thoroughly bad one in every way. The little ones are stacked on it with scarcely room to move, and it is impossible for the teacher to have, as she should have, ready access to each child. Furthermore, it covers about two-thirds of the floor space, and in the limited area that remains, Games, Exercises and Marching, features so essential in a Babies' class, are impossible.(H.M.I: 1908)

Finally, at long last, the problem was resolved.

The classroom has been wonderfully improved by the removal of the gallery, and the substitution of very suitable tables and chairs. These babies are in the right hands and their teaching merits a word of praise. (H.M.I: 1909)
This is a very happily conducted school. The children are bright, and appreciate the interest their teacher takes in them. (H.M.I: 1910)

Staffing

The Infant School usually had a staff of three. One was a certificated teacher, who was in charge of the whole school, but also taught the oldest children. She was assisted by a pupil teacher and a monitor. Thus, in 1887, an enrolment of 94 was divided into three

Lady Rosebery's School, Wing...

76. *Hannah de Rothschild's Infants' School in Moat Lane, Wingrave. After her marriage she was Lady Rosebery.*

77. *Miss Edward's class at the infants' school circa 1907. Notice the hobnails in the soles of the children's boots. The road on the right is Moat Lane, leading to the Anchor pub. In the hedgerows mature trees abound as everywhere in the Vale. From the left: standing - Horace Woodruff, Vic Rickard, Fred Fleet, Joe Clay, Fred Bignell, — —, — —, May Higgs, Dora Stent, Queenie Mead; seated – Myrtle Rickard, Connie Fleet, Violet Clay, Win Bateman, — —, Nellie Bandy, Harold Bandy, Hannah White, Arthur White.*

classes: the certificated teacher had forty 6-year olds; the pupil teacher had twenty-two 5-year-olds; and the monitor looked after the thirty-two 'babies'. The use of a pupil teacher and monitor was essential to reduce staff costs while coping with the large enrolments. The pupil teacher was, in effect, apprenticed for five years to the certificated teacher, who supervised his/her teaching and provided additional instruction designed to raise both academic levels and teaching skills. In 1883 this involved an hour's tuition before school from 7.30 to 8.30 each morning! At the end of each year the pupil teacher sat a government examination at Fenny Stratford and if the result was satisfactory both pupil and tutor received a government grant. At the end of the apprenticeship the pupil teacher sat the Queen's Scholarship examination which enabled the most able candidates to attend training college for three years. Those who didn't reach that standard, but whose examination marks were sufficiently high, were awarded a certificate and an annual grant towards their salaries. At a time when schools depended so much on voluntary subscription, the system seems to have served Wingrave well.

At least eight Wingrave children entered the infants' school (seven of them at under 3 years of age), progressed through the Parochial School and became monitors. Of these, five became pupil teachers, and four of the five were subsequently appointed as assistant teachers in the village schools. In addition, although Edith Woodruff never progressed beyond monitress, she taught the Babies for eleven years. Typical of these local 'prodigies' was Hilda Mead. She started school in 1880 when 2 years 10 months old, became a monitor when 13, and by 1893 was given three mornings a week for study. By 1897, at the age of twenty, she had passed the Queen's Scholarship Examination, and was immediately 'retained' by the school as an assistant teacher. She taught at the school until 1907, by which time she was married and beginning a family.

In 1915, a year after the outbreak of World War I, the County Education Committee closed the Babies' class "for the period of the war". By 1916 it had transferred the rest of the pupils to the East Room of the Parochial School, thus closing Hannah's school. By 1919 the building was in use as the Church Room (see page 114).

78. The earliest known photograph of children attending Hannah's school.

Chapter Fifteen

Farming

At the end of the 18th century agricultural pioneers, large landowners and ambitious farmers were unanimous as to the deficiencies of the 'open field' system of farming, and were convinced of the superiority of the large enclosed farm. Its much larger fields, hedged all round, would protect the farmer from interference by his neighbours, or by his neighbours' animals, and leave him free to raise crops and/or animals in whatever proportions, and by whatever means, he felt most likely to boost profits.

In 1798, a private act of Parliament permitted the enclosure of Wingrave's four vast open fields, and their hundreds of small unhedged strips were consolidated into the fields we now know.[1] It was a great upheaval for everyone. Even those with large holdings found that the costs of hedging, ditching, seeding pasture and administration were a considerable drain on their capital. Everyone lost land to compensate the tithe-holders, but some small farmers even had to sell part of their land to finance enclosure. This and the loss of grazing rights on the fallow and the commons made their small acreages uneconomical. Even so, they struggled on, maintaining their numbers and the illusion of a stalwart peasantry, despite being reduced to a mere 6% of the parish area.

By the end of 1798 three-quarters of the parish was cultivated by just eight farmers, and most of the rest by eleven smaller farmers. This suited the large landowners, for it greatly simplified the administration of their estates. Some landowners left their tenants to their own devices, knowing that they were local men, who knew the local climate, the land and the labour force intimately. Some tenants even had land of their own in the parish. Other landowners required quite specific changes spread over several years "in order to put the farm into the proper proportions of arable, meadow and pasture land". For example, in letting out 248 acres to Joseph Lucas of Rowsham, the Mercers' Company of London provided detailed instructions for the creation of twelve new fields, with hedgerows, hedgerow trees (as named!), and then were equally specific as to how the land was used.

The supporters of enclosure did not advocate it lightly. The large landowners often lived far from Wingrave. They saw land mainly as a safe investment for their capital. During the 18th century, convinced that land would provide a moderate but reliable income in the form of rent, they had bought out many of Wingrave's smaller farmers. Consequently, between 1753 and 1797 they considerably increased their holdings (Fig. 21). The ambitious farmers, who rented the land from them, viewed land differently. To them, land was part of a business in which they could use their enterprise, farming expertise and marketing skills to produce food on a large scale, for sale at a price which would not only cover the rent, but show a profit. If, thanks to enclosure, they adopted new crops or breeds, new methods and machines, and could be sure of ready buyers for their produce, then their profits should be substantial.

THE CHANGE TO A PASTORAL REGIME

Having extended and consolidated their holdings, and established forward-looking and profit-hungry farmers on them, the landowners' next step was to decide to what use the land should be put. Of course, farmers who were owner-occupiers could decide for

Fig. 21: Parish of Wingrave with Rowsham
Occupation of Land by Size of Holding

Year	0.25 to 1 acre No. of Occupiers (% of Farmland)	1—10 acres No. of Occupiers (% of Farmland)	10—100 acres No. of Occupiers (% of Farmland)	Over 100 acres No. of Occupiers (% of Farmland)
1753	---------------36 (6.6%)**-------------		17 (39.5%)	8 (53.9%)
1797	7 (0.8%)	18 (4.2%)	17 (30.3%)	9 (64.7%)
1798	14 (1.0%)	18 (4.8%)	11 (18.5%)	8 (75.7%)
1832	21 (1.0%)	11 (1.9%)	12 (19.7%)	7 (77.4%)
1876	6 (0.2%)	17 (2.8%)	4 (7.3%)	9 (89.7%)
1910	3 (0.2%)	19 (2.9%)	7 (11.4%)	12 (81.9%)
1926	8 (0.2%)	21 (3.8%)	14 (31.0%)	9 (65.0%)

** For 1753 it is not realistic to use Land Tax figures to distinguish between cottagers and small-holders. However, by using enclosure and other records, this distinction is possible from 1797.

themselves. In any case, as figure 22 shows, there was considerable agreement that for the parish of Wingrave with Rowsham the future lay in pasture, and by 1801 it dominated the landscape. From a farming viewpoint the commercial logic was clear. London provided a rapidly growing market for meat and butter, while the climate and soils of the Vale of Aylesbury could produce some of the finest pasture in the country. If the soil was thoroughly prepared, well drained and re-seeded with suitable grasses, meat and milk yields would be high. So the land would yield the substantial profits which the farmers sought, and from which the landowners could expect increased rents.

Fig. 22: Parish of Wingrave with Rowsham – Land Utilisation

Year	Arable		Pasture	
	Acres	% of Parish	Acres	% of Parish
1797	1764	73.8	624	26.2
1801	386	16.8	1909	83.2
1810	746	32.5	1549	67.5
1876	828φ	36.0	1467φ	64.0
1905	507*	18.4	2255*	81.6
1918	**	24.0	**	72.0
1994	1173	43.3	1537	56.7

* The area of the parish was increased in 1886, when a detached area of Drayton Beauchamp was absorbed.
** Based upon 8 farms and one Bucks County Council holding, so arable and pasture are stated as percentages of the total farm area, not the total parish area.
φ For land utilisation maps for 1876 and 1994 see Appendices I & II

THE ENCLOSURE OF MERCERS' FARM, ROWSHAM
Much of the above can be illustrated by the following account of the enclosure of Mercers' Farm, Rowsham.[3] It belonged to the Mercers' Company of the City of London, and had been leased to the Lucas family since at least 1570. At the time of enclosure, Joseph Lucas was just coming to the end of a 21 year lease. The reports and recommendations which follow were the work of a committee of the Mercers' Company aided by Mr Bull, the Mercers' agent.

172

79. *Joe Hedges in Windmill Hill farmyard in the early 20th century.*

80. *"A lovely bit of ploughing." The picture was taken during a plowing match, so the horses are walking on the stubble, not in the furrow, which would damage the land still to be ploughed. The 'forest' (i.e. foremost) and 'body' (i.e. middle) horses are driven by 'the lad', just visible on the right. The 'filler' (i.e. rearmost) horse is controlled by the ploughman, using a pair of reins.*

On the 6th September 1798 we went to Rowsham and visited the two homesteads, houses, barns, stables and cow-houses late in lease to J.Lucas. We found one of the homesteads and other buildings in decent repair. The other homestead and buildings are in indifferent repair. We also viewed the allotment of land amounting to 248 acres, 1 rood, 11 poles, partly enclosed in 1798 [4] . . ., and as far as we could form an opinion of the land in its present state, it appeared to be of good quality. Joseph Lucas should have leave to repair the present buildings, except a part which we give permission to be taken down and a cow-house erected with the old materials. We are also of the opinion that one of the homesteads may be converted into an habitation for one or more poor labourers employed on the business of the farm.

Joseph Lucas is to lay down (to pasture) 100 acres, and to keep the same during the term of his lease: 21 years from Michaelmas 1798, at £320 per annum. The Company to allow him in three years £350 viz. £200 towards the subdivision fences, mounds, quicks, etc., and £150 towards the substantial repairs of the respective buildings. The tenant is to form the subdivision fences and proper gates for the convenience of the farm, and he is to plant the quicksets, and to plash the hedges when of sufficient growth to become mounds.[5] Young timber trees of oak, ash, elm and willow to be planted in the subdivision fences.

Fields 1 and 2: Now arable. To be laid down to grazing in 1800.
Barley in 1798; fallow in 1799. To be well-dunged and sown in Spring of 1800 with barley or oats and grass seeds, viz. equal quantity of Dutch white clover and trefoil, and an equal quantity of rye grass and may seeds. To be hollow-drained after being seeded down.
Field 3: Now arable. To be laid down to grazing. Fallow in 1798. To be well-dunged. Barley in Spring 1799 subject to the same proportion of seeds as 1. above. A pond to be made.
These three fields will make excellent grazing ground, either to fatten oxen and sheep, or to be used as dairy ground. The tenant should be compelled by his lease to hollow drain where necessary in the first five years.

Fields 4,5,6 and 7: To remain as arable. Fields 4 and 5 require hollow draining.
Rotation to be: 1st Year: wheat; 2nd Year: beans; 3rd Year: Barley; 4th Year: Fallow dressed or sheep folded.

The instructions continued so as to cover the entire farm.

THE EFFECT OF THE FRENCH WARS: 1793-1815

Even as the parish settled down to this pastoral regime, the French Wars cut Britain off from continental supplies of wheat, and between 1796 and 1820 its price rose spectacularly, as figure 23 shows. Although wheat farming could be enormously profitable in the period 1796 to 1820, and although most of the parish could grow good crops, it was not easy for farmers to take advantage of it. Many Bucks farmers, like Joseph Lucas, had leases which restricted cropping perhaps by restricting the rotation. One farmer at nearby Hardwick received notice to quit his farm, simply "because he had deviated from the specific terms of his lease in sowing clover".[6] Some, being owner-occupiers, had no leases to worry about, but were naturally reluctant to plough pasture, which had only recently been laid down at considerable expense in plowing, dunging, draining and seeding. Farmers also had to consider the condition of their land, and the needs of the whole farm. For example, in addition to what he rented, Joseph Lucas had 112 acres of his own land, but almost half of it was water meadows with names like Duck Lake Meadow, Big Meadow, and Brook's Meadow. This committed him to a

Fig. 23: Price of Wheat in England and Wales per Imperial Quarter 1771-1845 [7]

Years	Average Price Shillings	Maximum Price Shillings	Minimum Price shillings
1791-1795	42.24	54.75	36.75
1796-1820	83.25	126.5	51.8
1821-1845	57.4	68.5	39.3

certain amount of grazing, but in winter (to avoid poaching the pastures) that grazing would have to be replaced by fodder crops like oats, barley and roots. If he devoted too many acres to wheat at the expense of fodder crops, he could find himself making a large profit on wheat only to lose it buying-in expensive fodder for his animals, when they had to be stall-fed in winter. In addition, there was no guarantee that there would be a large profit on wheat for, as figure 23 shows, during and just after the French wars the price of wheat was extremely volatile. Even so, as figure 22 shows, in the parish of Wingrave with Rowsham, some farmers did plow up pasture. By 1810, compared with 1801, the area of arable had almost doubled. However, the parish was still committed to grazing as the dominant activity. Moreover, as the years rolled on, it seems that the parish and the whole of the eastern Vale remained committed to grazing. We know that from 1833, when the Rothschilds, with their passion for hunting, began to settle in the Vale, they regarded its extensive pastures as one of its attractions. This was still the situation in 1876, (Fig. 22) and thirty years later it was said of the Vale that,

one may travel mile after mile and hardly see a plowed field. Many acres have been laid down to grass, and many more are being laid down every year; for though the land will yield fine crops of wheat and beans, grass gives a better return. [8]

THE PRODUCTS OF A GRAZING ECONOMY

In the early part of the 19th century butter was the dominant product of the eastern part of the Vale of Aylesbury, where the parish of Wingrave with Rowsham is situated. The grazing, especially when improved, was excellent for cattle. Generally, one cow would provide milk for five pounds of butter per week for about forty weeks in the year.

The cows were milked twice daily, usually out in the fields, and the milk carried back to the farm in pails hanging in pairs from a yoke. The milk was poured into shallow containers, and left until the cream rose to the top, when it was skimmed off. In the Vale, this process was repeated several times. On the larger farms butter was made twice a week. It was processed in churns, usually turned by a horse. Each churn held about eight dozen pounds, and one horse could turn several churns at the same time. Marketing the butter was quite simple. It was patted up into lumps of about two pounds each and packed into baskets made of osiers. These were known as 'flats', and held from 36 to 120 lbs. of butter. Having come to an agreement with a butter factor as to quantity and price, the farmer only had to deliver the flats to the nearest point where the factor's carrier passed and leave them by the roadside. Then every month or so the factor would send payment.

Butter-making provided a good and reliable income, and every farm in the parish seems to have taken advantage of it.[9] The dairy was usually part of the household accommodation, but whitewashed brick walls, and a supply of rain-water from a strategically placed tank were the main concessions to hygiene. At Seabrook's Farm in Rowsham the dairy included a churn room where the churn was turned by a horse in the yard outside, the two being connected by a shaft through a hole knocked in the outer wall. Butter was certainly made at Baldways Farm in Wingrave, for Hilda Roberts re-

175

*81. Horse-driven Churn at Broughton, near Aylesbury
(dating from the late 18th or early 19th century)*

membered her father telling the tale of Farmer Buckmaster, who rented it in the 1840's:

*How Farmer Buckmaster went to the Fair
At Aylesbury one Michaelmas Day,
And hired a dairymaid young and plump
That came from Amersham way.*

*And how he helped her to skim the milk
And make the butter come,
And strain and press the curds and whey
When the missis weren't at home.*

*And when next hiring time come round
He thought 'twas time to speak,
And so they set up housekeeping
On just eight bob a week.*

Pigs were a very profitable sideline in a pastoral economy. They were usually bred in Berkshire, 'stored' in Oxfordshire, and 'finished' in the Vale on the by-products of butter-making: skimmed milk and buttermilk.[10] Without refrigeration, people were careful not to eat pork unless there was an R in the month. So from Michaelmas to Spring, 'Porkers' were killed on the farm and either sold to local butchers or (especially when rail transport became available) sent to London to be sold at market. At other times the pigs were marketed as bacon. Another by-product of dairying was beef, for cows which had ceased to be profitable as 'milkers' could be sold for meat.

However, while dairy farmers were glad of the extra income from selling redundant calves and milk cows for beef, some farmers specialised in rearing beef cattle specifically for the meat market. In fact, the best grazing in the Vale was devoted to this. The grass was so good that it was possible to fatten the animals without much additional feeding stuff, except in winter when they had to be stall-fed. In the parish of Wingrave with Rowsham most farmers kept some beef cattle, but it was usually subsidiary to dairying. Sheep were also important. The production of lamb and mutton for the London market was profitable, with wool as a by-product. In addition, farmers valued sheep as manure providers, both when grazing and when folded on crops such as young growing wheat or turnips. As Vale farmers put it, "A sheep's fart is better than a cow's turd!"

From 1810 to 1876 about a third of the parish was devoted to arable. (Fig. 22) Although the bakers and brewers provided a local market for wheat and barley, its main use was for animals. As one farmer explained, "Farmers must have straw for their cattle, and they grow wheat and barley because it provides the best straw for their purposes".[11] In this context the grain was a valuable by-product, either marketed or fed to the cattle.

The best waterside meadows yielded two tons of hay to the acre, and much was sold. Some went to London, where milk cattle were stall-fed underground, so as to produce milk close to the market.

THE SOURCES OF WINGRAVE'S SUCCESS

During the first seventy years of the 19th century farmers in parishes like Wingrave with Rowsham were especially favoured. Not only did they have excellent grazing land, but they had access to London, at that time the largest and fastest growing urban market in the world. Moreover, after 1839, this trade was expedited when Aylesbury was linked to London by rail due to the construction of the first branch-line in the country. It even included a station (at Marston Gate) just two miles from Wingrave. The agriculture of the parish also benefited because, by the time of enclosure in 1798, ambitious landowners and farmers had already bought out many of the smallholders, so that Wingrave rapidly became a parish of medium to large farms. It was the larger farms which flourished during the 19th century, whereas the smaller farms (even the smaller dairy farms) barely paid their way.

THE WORLD MARKET AND THE GREAT DEPRESSION

From the 1870's the development of railways and steamship lines enabled the grass-lands of the New World to export farm products cheaply and in huge quantities. Other European countries stemmed the flood by imposing import duties. Britain alone remained free trade, because cheap food meant cheap labour, and that meant cheap exports of manufactures. Figure 24 shows how one import of foodstuffs after another came to harass British farmers. For example, between 1861 and 1895 imports of wheat and wheat flour almost trebled and the price of wheat in Britain halved. It was a disaster for farmers with large acreages of wheat. The parish of Wingrave with Rowsham, like most

Fig. 24: Annual Average Net Imports Into The United Kingdom (Million Cwts)

Years	Wheat and Flour	Meat	Butter	Cheese
1861-65	34.7	1.6	1.0	0.8
1891-95	96.6	10.4	2.4	1.3
1932-36	112.7	30.9	8.4	2.9

of the eastern Vale was less affected directly, for the acreage of wheat was small, and any surplus could be fed to livestock. However, the low prices caused farmers everywhere to consider reducing their acreage of arable. Mr Elliott of Hulcott, whose 316 acres had included 60 of arable, had converted it all to pasture by 1885, and was very forthright when questioned by the Tariff Commission in 1905:

Questioner: *Gradually throughout the district has there been a conversion of arable land into pasture?*
Mr Elliott: *A great many farmers have laid down a portion (to grass). Not all, but they have laid down a portion.*
Questioner: *About what period did the conversion of arable into pasture take place?*
Mr Elliott: *In the eighties I would say. Agriculture began to go wrong about 1878 or 1879. That was when I had my first remission of rent, I know.*
Questioner: *What, in your opinion, has been the cause of that change?*
Mr Elliott: *Because the corn was not worth growing. You could not make a profit.*
Questioner: *Is the conversion into pasture directly traceable to the inability to get a profit from corn growing?*
Mr Elliott: *Quite so. You can farm pasture with less labour.*
Questioner: *Would you agree with the last witness that at present it is impossible to grow corn profitably?*
Mr Elliott: *Certainly I do. Most decidedly.*

Farmers were still reeling from the chaos in the wheat market, when the cold storage steamers and the railways with their refrigerator cars began to bring vast quantities of chilled and frozen meat to England. Previously only canned meat could survive the journey from the New World, and it could not stand comparison with home-produced meat. "Canned mutton from Australia was coarse and stringy, each can containing a lump of overdone and tasteless flesh, flanked on one side by a wad of unappetising fat, and surrounded by a great deal of gravy."[12] Even so, from 1866 to 1871 English imports rose astronomically. Later, chilled and frozen meat began to arrive. Shipments of beef from the Americas in the late 1870's were followed by Australian and Argentinian mutton in the early 1880's. Although not up to the standard of first quality English meat, it was much more palatable than the canned variety, and much cheaper than English meat. Between 1861 and 1895 imports of meat rose from eighty thousand to 500,000 tons. By 1895 even the price of top quality English beef had fallen by 25%, mutton by 17% and pork by 10%. In particular, the chilled beef from the Americas, being of much better quality, dominated the British market until well into the 20th century, and reduced the profitability of farming in the Vale of Aylesbury, as elsewhere. However, the farmer's loss varied with the size of the farm, with the farmer's ability to produce the most marketable goods, with the farmer's relationship with his labour force, and with the willingness of the landlord to share his burden. The following three cases show the extent to which fortunes could vary in the Vale.

Home Farm, Wingrave [13]

John Gibbs rented the 54 acres of Home Farm from the governors of Berkhamsted School. In 1879 he asked for a reduction in his annual rent of £96. They granted a token cut of 6.25%, and they also agreed to pay the land tax. In 1886, he tried again:

Dear Sir
I take the liberty of writing to ask the governors of the school to give me something back out of the rent I have sent them as my neighbours are getting 30% back. Things was bad when I agreed to keep on with the land but they are much worse now with me as I have had a very bad year. I do not ask them to sink my rent but to give me something back for

a time till things are better with farming as it will be no use my kepin on without they can help me in some way

> *Yours truly,*
> *John Gibbs*

Presumably he got some help because he continued to occupy the farm, but a photograph suggests a man racked by the strain of work, worry and insoluble problems. By 1891, at the age of 46, he was dead. His son (another John) took over the lease, but did no better than his father. In 1896 the school's solicitors were about to sue him for arrears of rent when, at long last, he managed to make a payment:

I have enclosed a cheque for £50-3-0d the amount I made of the wheat. I have not thrashed the beans yet nor have not sold the hay . . . .

The Gibbs appear to have had five problems: the small size of the farm (54 acres); the large proportion of arable (60% in 1864 and 1875) in an area ideal for grazing (the same fields are now 100% grass); the growth of crops for sale rather than fodder; the growth of the wrong crops for sale (the price of wheat had halved since John Gibbs senior took the farm); and a landlord, prepared to reduce rent by only 6% when other landlords were conceding 30% to 50%.

Mr Elliott's Farm, Hulcott, Bucks.

Mr Elliott's farm (only two miles from Home Farm) was also in a prime grazing area but, with six times as much land, was a very much better-sized holding. However, it had not profited him, as he explained to the Tariff Commission.

Questioner: *What has been your experience with grazing in recent years?*
Mr Elliott: *Very bad indeed.*
Questioner: *Has there been any diminution of profits?*
Mr Elliott: *There has been a great loss the last two or three years especially.*
Questioner: *That is in beef?*
Mr Elliott: *Yes, beef and mutton, but beef principally.*

Sensibly, Mr Elliott had concentrated on grazing. Unfortunately, he was grazing beef cattle, when market prices clearly favoured milk production. It appears that he had an inflexible attitude to labour problems. "We used to milk over sixty cows, but the men went on strike, and my father sold some of the cows and we diminished (the herd) gradually until I do not milk at all."

Mr J.Treadwell's Farm, Upper Winchenden, Bucks.[14]

At the other end of the Vale, (six miles to the west of Aylesbury) Mr Treadwell rented two farms, of which the "little farm" alone was of 200 acres. His rent on the larger farm had been "very much reduced", but only by 10% on the smaller one. He had also had some labour problems.

Mr Treadwell obviously studied the market, and adjusted his farming accordingly. He had previously made butter, but it became unprofitable, largely due to the cost of labour, and he now sold the milk. Instead of buying cattle cake, he used his own barley, oats and beans as fodder. "I have made a good bit of money with my milk," he told the Royal Commission on Agriculture. "Dairying has been the next best thing to sheep". For he was also a well-known sheep breeder. "I have been able to sell a good many sheep, besides five rams to go abroad for breeding purposes, so that I have made a good deal of money with my sheep." With a large holding, at least one sympathetic landlord and a flexible response to the market, the Depression had not yet touched him. Even so, he was already anticipating the effect of a fall in the price of mutton.

THE DEPRESSION DEEPENS

Farmers viewed the Great Depression as "a great national calamity" and were unanimous as to its chief cause: "the heavy and progressive fall in the prices of agricultural products".[15] However, falling prices reminded the farmer of other problems such as the weather, disease and – particularly – taxation.

The end of the 1870's and the beginning of the 1880's were both cold and wet, which damaged crops and caused an epidemic of liver rot in sheep and foot and mouth disease in cattle.[16] Fortunately, though they would grumble, farmers regarded such things as "a visitation of the Almighty" which they just had to accept. "The grievous burden of local taxation" was not regarded so philosophically. Through levies both obligatory and voluntary, the farmers and landowners were amongst the chief supporters of the poor, the insane, elementary education, the police, the local judiciary, the parish highways, sanitation, etc..[17] A meeting of farmers at Tring in the 1890's passed a resolution demanding "that the poor should be maintained and educated out of Imperial Taxation, and the highways should be maintained by a wheel tax". However, the extension of voting to the labouring classes by the Reform Acts of 1867 and 1884 had considerably reduced the former power of landowners and farmers. Cheap food pleased both labourers and manufacturers, for whom it kept down the cost of labour.

Meanwhile, for the farmer, the Great Depression was compounding a labour problem, for it savagely cut the farmer's income just as his labour force (reduced by emigration and the greater availability of jobs in the towns) began to appreciate its increased bargaining power. And, as if all this was not enough, the butter trade – a critical element in the Vale's economy – was decimated by competition from Ireland and Europe. These aspects of the Great Depression are considered below.

Labour Relations in the Late 19th Century

In 1848 farmers in Wingrave, Rowsham, Aston Abbotts, Hulcott and Bierton joined forces to form an agricultural association to promote:

habits of industry, self-reliance and skill on the part of the labouring classes connected with agriculture. Hence prizes are awarded to labourers who excel in ploughing and hedging, as well as those who display the greatest amount of practical knowledge in the art of rearing stock, and who bestow most attention and attain the greatest success in that important department of agriculture. Prizes are also awarded for long service, and presents of smock-frocks and gowns are given to old and deserving men and women. In fact, the association has at heart the welfare of the labourer, and the amelioration of those who bowed down by age, are worthy recipients of relief.[18]

The speeches at the Association's 1872 dinner displayed a similar benevolence. The chairman, Mr E.M. Major-Lucas, farming 470 acres and letting out a further 207 acres, all in Wingrave and Rowsham, told members:

It is said that agricultural labourers have not been paid sufficiently and I agree with the general truth of this, but in these parishes as the price of provisions increases the pay of the labourers also advances, and I say without fear of contradiction that farmers now give what they think is due from the interest of their capital, and if necessary they will give still more. (cheers) I have been a farmer for some years, but have never seen my labourers more kind to me; and I hope I act in the same spirit to them.

Later, Mr Alfred Roads, farming 360 acres in the parish, spoke in similar vein:

If you want good men you must pay good wages. Let the masters act properly by the men, and there will be no strikes. In these parishes farmers give 13 or 14 shillings a

WINGRAVE, ASTON ABBOTTS, BIERTON, & HULCOTT

Agricultural Association.

THE ANNUAL PLOUGHING MATCH

WILL TAKE PLACE AT

WINGRAVE, on THURSDAY, OCTOBER 31st, 1907,

When the following Prizes will be awarded :—

TO PLOUGHMEN.

Half an Acre of Land in 4½ hours.

Class 1 (Winners of Prizes in previous year).—First Prize £1, Driver 3s. 6d. ; 2nd ditto 15s., Driver 3s. ; 3rd ditto 10s., Driver 2s. 6d. Five teams to start or 3rd Prize will not be awarded.

Class 2—First Prize £1, Driver 3s. 6d. ; 2nd ditto 15s., Driver 3s. ; 3rd ditto 10s., Driver 2s. 6d. ; 4th ditto 5s., Driver 2s. Five teams to start or 4th Prize will not be awarded.

5s. will be given in addition to the best Ploughman of the day, 2s. 6d. to his driver.

To the best-managed, cleaned, and cared-for Team and Harness, the property of Members competing in either Class—1st Prize 15s., Driver 4s. ; 2nd ditto 10s., Driver 3s. ; 3rd ditto 5s., Driver 2s. ; 4th ditto 2s., Driver 1s.

FOR HEDGING AND DITCHING.

Two Poles to be executed in a workmanlike manner in 4½ hours. Competitors to be regularly employed by the Members who send them.

Class 1 (Winners of Prizes in previous year)—First Prize 15s. ; 2nd ditto 10s. ; 3rd ditto 5s. To be five Competitors or the 3rd Prize will not be awarded.

Class 2—First Prize 15s. ; 2nd ditto 10s. ; 3rd ditto 5s.

5s. in addition to be given to the best Hedgecutter of the day.

TO SHEPHERDS.

Having reared the greatest number of Lambs till 1st May. The whole number of Ewes put to the Tup to be entered. (Tegs not to be entered.)

Class 1—From 80 Ewes and upwards—£1 ; 15s. ; 10s. ; and 5s.

Class 2—From 40 Ewes and up to 80 —17s. 6d. ; 12s. 6d. ; 10s. ; and 7s. 6d.

TO COWMEN.

Class 1—Having milked regularly the greatest number of years for the same Master, or on the same Farm, in radius of Association.—Four Prizes of 12s. 6d. each. Receivers since 1905 not eligible.

Class 2—Cowmen under 40 years of age, having milked regularly the greatest number of years for the same Master, or on the same Farm, in radius of Association. —Four Prizes of 12s. 6d. each. No Prize to be awarded under two years' service. Receivers since 1901 not eligible.

Class 3—Cowmen under 20 years of age, having milked regularly the greatest number of years for the same Master, or on the same Farm, in radius of Association. —Four Prizes of 5s. each.

FOR LENGTH OF SERVICE.

Class 1—To Labourers having worked the greatest number of years for the same Master, or on the same Farm, in radius of Association.—Four Prizes of 12s. 6d. each. Receivers since 1898 not eligible.

Class 2—To Labourers, under 40 years of age, having worked longest for the same Master, or on the same Farm, in radius of Association.—Four Prizes of 7s. 6d. each. Not again eligible in same Class.

TO THE OLDEST, MOST NEEDY, AND DESERVING MEN.

To be recommended by Members. Eight donations of 5s. each.

TO THE OLDEST, MOST NEEDY, AND DESERVING WOMEN.

To be recommended by Members. Eight donations of 5s. each.

☞ After the Match, the ANNUAL DINNER will take place at the BELL INN, WINGRAVE, at 4 o'Clock. H. G. LEPPER, Esq., will preside.

week besides extras. As long as I pay my men well I have no fear of Mr Richardson (of the Agricultural Union) coming amongst them. (hear, hear)

This was an eye opener! It is the only mention of agricultural wages varying with the cost of living that we have encountered anywhere at that time. With rising prices, such a scheme would be welcomed by the labourers of 1872, but how would they react when imports cut prices dramatically? Sadly, no details of the scheme have been found.

Although they were somewhat better than the starvation wages reported by the 1867 Royal Commission into Agriculture, the 1872 wages of 13/- or 14/- per week were not princely. In any case, in practice, no more than a third of the men got full rate. Another third got a shilling, two shillings or even a half-crown less, at a time when just a shilling a week made a world of difference to life. The rest were lads on two to five shillings a week. At hay-time and harvest the wages bill rose considerably, but most of the extra went to the mowers and reapers who were on piece work, and to the extra men who were taken on. For the rest there was the same pecking order, and pay was still by the day: four days' work got four days' pay.[19]

So perhaps it is not so surprising that within 18 months Mr Richardson was leading striking labourers from Wingrave and elsewhere on a march through the local villages, in pursuit of more pay! And between March 1873 and October 1874, emigration (much of it from the Vale and some from Wingrave and Bierton) removed nearly eight thousand people from the Aylesbury area to Queensland alone. Indeed, from the 1870's, due to emigration and migration to the towns, farmers became concerned about 'the flight from the land'. Not without reason, for between 1871 and 1911 the proportion of the national workforce employed in agriculture nearly halved. Wingrave, separated by a wearying six miles from Aylesbury, was slower than some parishes to lose its labour surplus. There were still unemployed labourers there in the 1890's, but they were fewer, and mainly single young men and lads.

82. *Extract from George Griffin's Wages' Book for 1865. Allen was off work sick and so received no pay.*

The 'flight from the land' also affected those who remained, as the Royal Commission into Agriculture was told by their commissioner for the eastern counties, which included Buckinghamshire:

it seems that the attitude of the labourers is one of the least satisfactory features in the farmer's prospect. There seems to be a spirit of restlessness and of a desire for change, amongst the labourers; and a marked want of confidence between the farmers and their labourers. The farmers can no longer command labour when they especially want it.

What especially irked the farmer at this time was that, while his income was severely reduced by the Depression, almost everything that the labourer required (his meat, drink and clothing) were much cheaper than before. Yet he could not reduce his labourers' pay without the likelihood of the man leaving him. He also complained about the quality of the labour, and the smaller amount of work done by each labourer, which increased his costs. And he had to watch his P's and Q's! Farmers were still employers, and could hire and fire as they pleased, but they no longer monopolised the job market. And the younger labourers were beginning to realise this! Mr Treadwell explained the new relationship to the Royal Commission of 1895:

Questioner: *Is there a tendency for the best men amongst the labouring classes to leave the district?*

Treadwell: *I find it just this, that now those young fellows get so pert that you cannot speak to them, and if you see anything going wrong, and say anything to them, they say, "Give me my money. I will go." They do not trouble about getting work about home, many of them, but go right away. They like change.*

"They like change!!" Yet only thirteen years earlier (in questioning a witness before a government enquiry) Lord Vernon had asked in some astonishment, "Am I right in assuming that you want the labourers to raise themselves out of the condition of labourers to something better?" Of course, Jack was still by no means as good as his master, but he was certainly anxious to narrow the gap.

We have no direct evidence as to how these changing attitudes affected Wingrave and Rowsham, but the election of the new parish council in 1894 provides a clue. The 1894 Local Government Act not only required the replacement of the Vestry by a parish council, but gave everyone who paid even the smallest rate in the parish a vote in the election. So a Parish Meeting was called, and on the evening of December 4th the old elite turned up in force: the Vicar, the Reverend Lockhart, was asked to chair the meeting; Stewart Freeman, the local squire, prepared to become chairman of the new council; and seven farmers had been nominated for the seven places on the council. Were they surprised when a further ten candidates (seven tradesmen and three labourers) were nominated by the large attendance of villagers? Probably not! More likely they assumed that they were the only people competent to administer the parish, and that most people realised this, and sat back waiting for the forelock-tuggers to vote them into office. It didn't happen! Four tradesmen, two labourers and just one farmer were elected. The 'squire' was narrowly defeated in the vote for the 'chair', which went to Mark Finch, another local farmer. It was a social revolution. However, it was short-lived. By 1904 there was a small attendance at the Parish Meeting, there were only seven nominations and the farmers were back in force. But at least everyone knew that the balance of power had swung towards the labourers who, when it came to a vote, had the advantage of numbers, and no longer depended entirely upon the farmers for jobs.

The Demise of the Butter Trade

In 1895 a witness reported to the Royal Commission on Agriculture:

In the Vale of Aylesbury the production of butter has been given up to a great extent. The farmers say that the prices for butter are too low. I asked one farmer, "Why does foreign butter sell better than yours?" He said, "Because ours does not keep so well". I believe it is simply a question of the making. If the English butter is made properly it will keep just as well as any foreign butter. In the case of one or two farms where I went, where they still make butter, the butter is evidently not of the best quality.

Investigation showed that Vale butter was often made in a sloppy, unscientific way, and without experiments or proper records. In some cases the buildings, the surroundings and the animals themselves were in an unhygienic condition. Generally, the dairy cows were fed according to the various ideas of the farmers, or according to the food that might happen to be on the farm, rather than upon scientific principles. Consequently, the butter varied in texture, colour, flavour, quality and availability. Meanwhile, butter from highly efficient co-operative dairies in Denmark, Ireland, Brittany and Normandy was cornering the English market. For instance, the centrifugal cream separator, invented in 1856, was adopted by continental creameries much earlier than by England's farmers. It was more efficient and labour-saving than skimming by hand, and greatly reduced costs.

When he took over Manor Farm[20] in Wingrave in 1864, George Griffin used the milk from his dairy herd to produce butter. His annual average income from it (1869 to 1873) was just £229 per annum. In the first ten months of 1874, due to a combination of low output and low prices, receipts plummeted to £129. With a wages bill of about £400 a year there had to be changes, and George switched to selling raw milk to the London market. In the next five years his income from milk averaged £552 per annum: a clear vindication of the change, which also reduced his labour costs.[21]

By the end of the century the commercial production of butter had virtually ceased in England though, in the Vale, barn butter (as the farmhouse product was known) was still produced by a few farmers who had private customers: small grocers in London or the local towns; or private families. The latter were especially valued, as the farmer got the retail price. The decline in butter production (and thus the availability of skimmed milk) was followed by a serious decline in pig rearing. In 1867 there were nearly 53,000 pigs on Bucks farms, while in 1904 there were only 34,339.

Other Effects of the Great Depression
One writer[22] considered that the Vale "was little damaged" by the Great Depression due to its predominantly pastoral farming, its option of selling arable crops or using them for fodder if market prices were low, its several sources of income (milk, beef, lamb, mutton, wool, bacon, pork and hay), and its easy access to both the London and local markets. Undoubtedly these advantages saved Wingrave and Rowsham, and many of the other Vale villages, from the worst effects of the Great Depression. But then the worst effects were very grim indeed. Farm incomes for the United Kingdom, which averaged £47 million per annum between 1860 and 1874, were down by 40% to £28 million between 1875 and 1904, with an all-time low of £13 million in 1879.

Even if the Vale suffered less, reduced incomes caused a variety of problems. Small farms had a particularly lean time. For the factors and dealers who serviced the industry it meant either giving extended credit or accepting bad debts. It was difficult for farmers to get loans, and this plus lack of capital meant, for example, continued use of old equipment, inability to improve the land by installing drainage, and difficulty in converting arable to pasture. Some farmers had even sold stock to pay off debts or cover unavoidable expenditure. They were then unable to re-stock and, due to understocking, the pastures could not be maintained in a first-class condition. Many farmers could not afford to hire labourers for jobs like weeding crops, and hedging and ditching. Some arable went out of cultivation and gradually reverted to rough pasture.

The low prices received for other agricultural products persuaded some small farmers to enter the duck trade. Duck rearing and fattening was originally confined to Aylesbury, but by the end of the century it had spread to Haddenham in the west and Leighton Buzzard in the east. So considerable was the trade that the railway provided special facilities and freight rates for carrying the ducks to London. From May to October 1894 nearly 18,000 ducklings were sent to London from Aylesbury, Marston Gate and Cheddington stations. Strangely, despite its many moats and ponds, no clear evidence of 'ducking' has been found in Wingrave and Rowsham. Perhaps this reflects the relative prosperity of the parish, for ducking required a great deal of work for a very modest return. Moreover, the incubation and early rearing usually took place in the home, much to its detriment. With the onset of the Great War the trade disappeared, never to return.

THE MARKET FOR RAW MILK

By the 1880's, with a well-developed rail network, and a considerable demand for milk from the urban areas, many English farmers abandoned wheat and meat and turned to dairying, even when it meant the expense of converting arable to pasture. This was particularly noticeable in Buckinghamshire where the number of cattle rose from 57,448 in 1867 to 75,992 in 1904. Of course, the extra production did not help the price of milk, but at least there were no imports to worry about, and demand was increasing.

More importantly for Wingrave and Rowsham, the eastern Vale of Aylesbury still had the special advantages of soil and climate which so favoured dairying. Another great advantage was the Aylesbury branch railway line (with a station only two miles from Wingrave), which brought London's massive and rapidly growing market within easy reach – in theory, at least. In practice, a number of technical problems had to be overcome. At first the milk was transported in a variety of containers, in open railway trucks, and thus exposed to summer heat. Early consignments were often soured or partly curdled by the time they reached London. It was not until the late 1860's that a mechanical cooler and a new design of metal churn greatly improved the quality of rail-borne milk and enabled the trade with London to develop.

That solved the transport problem. Actually marketing the milk in London was more difficult. It had to go through a wholesaler, and one farmer's output was simply not worth the attention of a London firm. In 1894 the Dairy Supply Company of London bought over 33 million gallons. Fortunately, at that time, the Rosebery Estate had a dairy at Mentmore, and Knight Bruce (Lord Rosebery's agent) sent the milk to Cheddington Dairies at Notting Hill. It seems that Bruce also acted as agent for some of the larger local dairy farmers. Thus in 1896 Mark Finch of Rowsham wrote to him:

Here I shall milk 40 cows and at Astwell Park 50 to 60, and can deliver by either L.& N.W., Metropolitan, or G.W.R.. If you are in the market to buy, I shall be glad to treat with you. You can rely on purity and quality.

However, what transformed the situation was the decision of the English Condensed Milk Company (now Nestles) to open a factory in Aylesbury only a few hundred yards from the High Street station, the terminus of the Aylesbury branch line. By the 1880's, as the Anglo-Swiss Condensed Milk Company, it was consuming 1¼ million gallons of local milk annually. By the early 20th century fifty churns a day (roughly ¼ million gallons a year) were sent from Marston Gate alone. In addition, some farmers used their own specially designed horse-drawn milk floats, which had low floors to facilitate the loading and unloading of the churns. The drivers were usually lads from the local farms and if several met en route, they would race one another into the town. Later, in the 1930's, the milk was collected from the farms by lorries which called daily and usually picked up the churns from a roadside platform.

By this time the production of condensed milk had ceased, but the Nestles factory continued to collect milk from local farms, and send it to London by rail in large ventilated milk vans. In addition, until 1961, local milk was pasteurised and bottled for local retailers, while from 1928 to 1941 cheese was produced. Nor was this all! By 1911 Dominion Dairies was established in Bicester Road, Aylesbury, where it processed a considerable gallonage of milk into cheese and butter. Much of its Golden Acres butter was also shipped out by rail.

THE INTER-WAR YEARS [23]

Leopold de Rothschild died in 1917 and most of his Wingrave property was sold the following year. At about the same time the Worshipful Company of Mercers, Berkhamsted School, and Mrs Fountaine, the owner of Mitchell Leys, all decided to sell their Wingrave holdings. These sales put 1155 acres of the parish on the market: over 40% of its farmland. It was the biggest change in land ownership in the parish for sixty years.

By modern standards the farms were sold at incredibly low prices.[24] For example, Thistlebrook Farm's 144 acres fetched £3300, the 84 acres of Parsonage Farm went for £2175, and the 91 acres of Floyds Farm were sold for £2700. So prices per acre were as little as £23 per acre, and never exceeded £30: and in each case this included the farmhouse and the farm buildings. Such prices indicate the extent to which the Great Depression had destroyed the confidence of both landlords and farmers. Only twenty years earlier Stewart Freeman had paid Lord Rosebery £150 per acre just for farmland.[25] In 1918 the only landlords to show a little interest were Mrs Freeman who, with her daughter in mind, made a successful bid for Floyds Farm; and Bucks County Council which bought Mitchell Leys and Windmill Hill farms, but only because (under the Smallholdings Act of 1908) it had a statutory duty to create smallholdings. The remaining six farms went to owner-occupiers, including three sitting tenants. However, even tenant farmers didn't show much enthusiasm. Although his family had tenanted Manor Farm for three generations, Frank Griffin didn't even consider the possibility of ownership. He thought that, if the Rothschilds were selling, they must know something adverse about the future of farming.[26] Financially he made a wise decision. Although, during the Great War, farming enjoyed a rare period of prosperity, by 1922 farm incomes in the U.K. were collapsing, and did not begin to recover until the beginning of World War 2 in 1939.[27] Meanwhile, farming was so depressed that it became difficult to sell farms at any price. Thus Home Farm at Rowsham, which was put up for auction in 1936 and again in 1939, didn't find a buyer on either occasion. It was finally sold to a private buyer a little later.

Although the 1918 sales transferred about 30% of the farmland of the parish to independent farmers (i.e. owner-occupiers) much of the remaining farmland continued to be owned by landlords leasing their properties to tenant farmers. In consequence, the majority of farmers still could not make improvements to such things as drainage, access roads and buildings without fear of losing their investment, if the landlord refused to renew their lease.[28] In addition, depending upon the precise terms of their lease, tenant farmers might find management of their holdings constrained by restrictions on such things as crops, crop rotations, the proportion of arable to pasture, the use of buildings, how much hay could be sold, the maintenance of hedgerows, the mowing of pasture, manuring, etc., etc.. While, in a period of prosperity such restrictions might be perfectly reasonable, and entirely in the long-term interests of farming, they were often not suited to a period of economic emergency such as farmers faced in the inter-war years. Of course, in theory, everything in a lease was negotiable, but no tenant could force a landlord to modify a model lease designed for more prosperous times. A comparison of Wingrave leases dated 1899, 1930 and 1998 (all for the same farm) suggests that over the years, landlords' requirements have gradually become more realistic, but this was obviously no help to tenants in the inter-war years, when every initiative and the utmost flexibility were needed to cope with overseas competition and changing markets. If, for instance, the markets showed an increasing demand for fruit, vegetables, poultry, pig products, improved milk supplies, etc., a delay or impasse between landlord and tenant as to what could be done, or 'who would pay for what', was to no-one's advantage. The experience of Frank Hows of Straws Hadley Farm gives some indication of the need for flexibility, though as an owner-occupier he had no lease to constrain him.

FRANK HOWS AND THE STRAWS HADLEY / BETLOW FARMS [29]

In the Twenties and Thirties, despite the expansion of the London market, and the continued demand for milk from the Dominion Dairy and Nestles, things were little better in Wingrave or the Vale, once the wartime boom had evaporated. The demand for milk had increased, but so had the supply. The railways were now bringing milk to London from distances of up to 130 miles away. With the Vale's rich meadows as their prime asset most local farmers divided their attention between beef, dairy cattle and sheep, varying the balance as prices fluctuated, and experimenting with anything else that seemed promising. In Wingrave in the Thirties "everyone milked", except Filmer Kidston of Manor Farm, who just kept a house cow. The size of the dairy herd varied from farm to farm. Floyds Farm had only five dairy cows in 1928, Windmill Hill Farm kept about a dozen, and Church Farm had 20 to 25, while just over the parish boundary Oxleys, Upper Wingbury and Lower Wingbury Farms usually had larger herds. Dairying was popular partly because milk brought in 'the monthly cheque', which helped to ease cash-flow problems.

Frank Hows had two farms: Straws Hadley in Wingrave, and Betlow Farm, two miles to the south, near Long Marston. Both were mainly on the clay of the Vale, and with their emphasis on cattle and sheep both were typical Vale farms. (Fig. 24)

Fig. 24: Farm Stock – Straws Hadley and Betlow Farms

	1928	1931	1933	1940
Cattle	1 bull 98 beef / dairy	1 bull 68 beef / dairy	1 bull 93 beef / dairy	1 bull 86 beef / dairy
Sheep	1ram 148 sheep	2 rams 240 sheep	2 rams 238 sheep	4 rams 256 sheep
Pigs	--	9	21	1 boar 126 pigs
Poultry	--	194	588	--
Horses	10	8	5	3

The regularity of the milk cheque could be relied upon, but unfortunately its value varied with the amount of milk which dairy farmers sent to market at any one time. Figure 25 illustrates the problem. Sales of beef and mutton earned £725 in 1928, and £868 in 1931, but over the same period the return from dairy produce dropped from £579 to £373. Fortunately, due to good planning or good fortune, Frank had moved into pigs and poultry. He had also trimmed his expenditure. In 1928 he had bought-in £220 of feeding stuffs. In 1931 he had eighteen acres producing fodder crops (roots, wheat and beans). Helped by generous applications of manure and basic slag, he even had a small surplus for sale. In consequence, his total income actually increased.

Frank was obviously encouraged by this outcome for by 1933, in addition to his cattle and sheep, he had more than doubled his herd of pigs, and had a flock of nearly six hundred poultry. By 1940 he had abandoned poultry, and was concentrating on breeding pigs for his herd, which now numbered 126. It was a sensible decision because pigs are ready for sale at 5½ to 7 months, and a steady income can be obtained by

83. Cat Street (now Castle Street) at the beginning of the 20th century. Mrs Ann Gibbs, seated outside Home Farm with son Tom (always known as Dodder) and daughter Martha (known locally as Pat), who also appears in 84 below as Mrs Chapman.

84. Maltby Farm between the wars: Vic Chapman, farmer and milkman (on the right) with his wife Pat.

Fig. 25: Main Sources of Income: Straws Hadley and Betlow Farms

Source	1928	1931
Cattle for meat	£235	£634
Sheep and lambs for meat	£490	£234
Dairy produce	£579	£373
Wool	£39	£19
Eggs	--	£107
Pigs	--	£40
Fodder	--	£35
Total	£1343	£1442

selling small batches at intervals throughout the year, with obvious advantages for the farmer's cash-flow.

Of course, the amount of effort that went into all this was considerable. The dairy herd, usually between 14 and 18 cows, had to be milked by hand twice daily, every day of the year. Eggs had to be collected, cleaned, graded and packed. Cattle and sheep had to be moved around the pastures, while lambing and calving were great times for hyperactive insomniacs. So it is to be hoped that Frank enjoyed his work, for it certainly wasn't making him rich! In 1928 his net profit on an investment of £5250 plus stock and equipment (for Straws Hadley alone) was £12-6s-5d. It rose to £19-13-11d in 1931, which didn't even re-pay a loan of £20 to the business from his wife. We know that in 1927/8 his wages bill totalled £502. However, he employed at least five men full-time and their minimum wages of £1-11s-8d for a 50-hour week would cost £410 per year without national insurance, overtime, piece work and harvest extras. It appeared to leave very little, if anything, for Frank.

MAKING ENDS MEET

So how did farmers survive? Firstly, in determining a farmer's profit and loss, some creative accounting was possible. For instance, much depended upon the valuations of livestock and feeding stuffs. Very conservative valuations could trim a lot off profits. Secondly, many of the things which could be charged against profits as business expenses also had non-business uses. Protective clothing such as boots, gumboots and overalls, are examples. So are cars and petrol. Not that the amounts were large. Frank's first car was bought second-hand in 1928 for £8, and replaced by another in 1931 for £17-10s. Still, every little helped! Thirdly, farm produce, such as meat, poultry, eggs, milk, butter, bacon, vegetables, and timber for the fires were available at cost price. In fact, if Mrs Hows ran out of milk, she would simply dip herself a jugful from the churn that was awaiting collection. Some farmers even made butter and cheese for family consumption. Fourthly, farm labour was very cheap. In 1928, though the rate was gradually increasing, farm workers still got only a minimum of £1-11s-8d for a 50-hour week. Later, when their pay went up from £1-12s-9d to £1-14s-2d, the men rubbed their hands with glee. Usually, the annual rise was less than a shilling a week. "An extra 1s-5d per week! Marvellous!" Even at these very low wages only the larger farms, like Thistlebrook, Straws Hadley, Bell Leys, Heselthorpe and Manor Farm (Rowsham) employed four men, while the smaller farms, like Parsonage, employed just one or two, and six farms had none. Fortunately, for a few shillings a week village lads would come in before school, arriving at 6.30 a.m. to do jobs like stone picking , 'crow-starving' and even milking. At the weekend and in the holidays they would take on whatever jobs were going. They rolled the oats, kibbled the beans, cut the chaff, chopped up mangolds

189

and swedes in large and potentially lethal 'root pulpers', carried sacks of chaff and moved hay as it was cut from the rick. And all that was just to *feed* the livestock! Sometimes school friends made up a gang and went round the farms doing jobs: see Recollections page 194. Fifthly, to trim their expenditure, farmers went to great lengths to avoid 'buying-in', which saved them the dealer's mark-up. Farmers went to Tring or Aylesbury on market days, not only to check prices at the auctions, and news at the taverns, but also because this was where a good deal of bartering and trading went on. If a farmer bewailed a shortage of fodder, another farmer might well help him out with the qualification "Pay me with a load of rough hay, back end". This actually meant, "Pay me with a load of your best hay in the Autumn". Or if a farmer's thrashing machine had broken down, someone might volunteer, "Let us have a couple of loads of mangolds, and I'll bring me box over and we'll have you sacked up in no time". Many were the unrecorded bargains struck on market days. Thus, after threshing, someone might well have a few loads of good straight straw that would solve a neighbour's thatching problem far more cheaply than buying from a dealer. Needless to say the cash for that would go straight from back pocket to back pocket. As mentioned earlier one could reduce the bill for feeding stuffs by growing one's own, and reduce it still further by 'folding' animals on the growing crops. Turnips were often grown for this purpose. The sheep not only ate the tops, but also totally consumed the roots while they were still in the ground. In Wingrave and elsewhere in the Vale, starting in February, in readiness for the Easter market, some farmers would fatten the lambs by folding them on the young corn, and they would eat it out of sight. In the course of this they consolidated and manured the ground, while the corn (prevented for the time being from shooting upwards) would spread sideways, and from these 'tillers' send up more shoots than usual, producing a field of corn so dense that it looked as if you could walk on it. Finally, some of Wingrave's farmers increased their income by retailing milk in the village and supplying shops in the local market towns with meat, poultry, eggs and butter. By cutting out the wholesaler, they got a better price. Tom Horwood, who worked Church Farm, sold milk from door to door. He delivered on foot to customers near Church Farm, but he also had a bicycle with a carrier in front, which would just take two of the oval buckets from which he served the milk straight into the customer's jug. Eventually his son Charlie took over the round, going from door to door in his white milking smock. People remember how from time to time he would swill the milk round the bucket, partly to see that everyone got a fair share of the cream, but also to ensure that the milk had at least the minimum fat content, if an inspector took a sample for testing when the milk was low. At this time milk was about 'tuppence ha'penny' a pint, and someone living on their own could ask for "a pennoth o'milk", which was just under half a pint. Vic Chapman of Maltby Farm, a contemporary of Charlie, similarly clad in the traditional smock, also walked and biked round the village selling milk.

None of the above ploys got to the heart of the problems facing agriculture between the wars. Low prices for farm products were certainly a major problem, but so was the largely unrecognised problem of the low productivity of small-scale farming manned by ill-paid labour using mainly hand tools. The labourers might be hardworking and skilful, and the results picturesque. Unfortunately, the low productivity meant low profits and little capital with which to mechanise.

MECHANISATION

Pitstone Green Farm [30] which is only five miles from Wingrave, acquired its first tractor during the Great War, though it was mostly used as a stationary engine for powering other machines. The same farm bought a Fordson tractor during the 1920's, and this was

85. *Job King trenching in the fields below Windmill Hill Farm.*

86. *Bert Harwood puts new life into an old hedge.*

used extensively for ploughing, and pulling the binder. However, even in the Thirties, horses were still the dominant source of power on most British farms, and certainly on Wingrave's farms. They pulled the plough, the drill, the harrow, the swarth-turner, the tedder, the haycart, the reaper and also powered the elevator. They backed the water carts into "Town Pond" so that if the water was deep enough the tank would fill all by itself, and they transported people and materials wherever they were wanted. Not only was this source of power dated, but some of the machinery can most charitably be described as 'well past its sell-by date'. One villager, looking back to the Thirties, can remember a farm which used a two-horse reaper which had to be followed by men and women who bound the corn into sheaves before they 'shocked' them. That machine had been superseded over fifty years earlier by the self-binding reaper which was worked by just one man. Windmill Hill Farm had one in the 1930's. Even the self-binder lagged far behind the most efficient equipment then available, for the tied bundles of corn still had to be shocked until the corn had dried out, when they were loaded into waggons, and carted to the farmyard to be barned or ricked while awaiting threshing. And whether the shocks were piled up to the rafters in the big barn at Windmill Hill, or built into ricks and thatched at farms which had no barn, the cost in labour was formidable. Another villager remembers in the Twenties leading a horse round and round to power the elevator which raised straw to the top of the ricks, though on progressive Bucks farms this was a process that was being transferred to steam power seventy years earlier.[31] Steam power was certainly used in the parish in the inter-war period (and earlier) mostly by agricultural contractors. In particular, their steam plows could cultivate the lower land of the parish which was heavy gault clay. On Wingrave's higher ground the soils were lighter. It was 2 or 3-horse land and the farmers' own horses could cope. Even after the Second World War steam or tractor-powered thrashing machines were still in use in the parish usually by agricultural contractors, though Jack Masters of Bailey's Farm at Rowsham acquired one and hired it out. Although when first introduced in the 19th century thrashing machines saved labour, they were still very labour intensive: one manufacturer recommended using a team of eleven men. By contrast, in the United States reapers and threshers had long been superseded by the combine harvester which required only two men: one to drive the combine and one to drive the lorry into which the grain was automatically transferred. Some models also tied the straw into bundles! Combines were in general use in the United States by the end of the Great War.

By comparison, in the parish of Wingrave with Rowsham (and most of Great Britain) the introduction of modern machinery was very late and very gradual. In part this was due to the small size of British fields. As late as 1976, Wingrave's fields had not changed since enclosure nearly two centuries earlier. In part it was due to the lethargy of British manufacturers. In 1926 Browns of Leighton Buzzard were still producing the Bedfordshire drill, invented at the beginning of the 19th century, and not until the 1950's was a combine manufactured (by Massey-Harris) especially for the farmer with small fields. On some farms the problem was lack of capital. It was not until the mid-Thirties that Wingrave's farmers began to appreciate the economy in labour, the flexibility in use, and the greater speed obtainable by substituting tractors for horses. For example, on the heavy clay of the lower parts of the parish two men and a horse drill would sow ten acres in a day, whereas one man and a drill pulled by a tractor could sow fifty to seventy acres a day. Moreover, the occasional maintenance of a tractor was less expensive and time-consuming than the daily foddering, watering, bedding, and equipping (with a complex harness) of a horse. Frederick Bignell of

87. *Church Farm between the wars. A hay cart is got ready to go out to the fields.*

88. *Building the ricks. On the left a hay rick has been completed and 'pulled'. On the right a straw rick is well under way.*

Recollections: Helping On The Farm – compiled from material supplied by Vic Clay, Norman Brackley and Frank King.

I was the youngest of a gang of village lads, which included Harvey Roberts, Lionel Woodruff, Vic Rickard, Frank Pargeter, and my brother. We worked on local farms on Saturdays and in the holidays. I got a shilling a day, six shillings a week in the holidays, and most of my earnings went to my mother, for with a large family, things were 'tight'. Still she usually gave me back a whole sixpence for myself. We trimmed banks with fagging hooks and cleaned the weeds out of ditches. Sometimes we 'thistled', which meant cutting down thistles, nettles and docks. We helped to build the hay ricks. When I was the youngest member of the gang, and an elevator was being used to raise the hay to the top of the rick, my job was to lead the horse round and round to power the elevator. By the time I was ready to leave school I was working on farms which had no elevator. Sometimes I worked standing halfway up the rick in a pitch-hole, using a long-handled pitch fork to throw the hay to the top. A really tall rick might have to have two pitch holes, one above the other, to get the hay to the top. After that the rick still had to be thatched and 'pulled'. Rick builders liked to leave a rick looking neat and so went round it pulling out the bits of hay that stuck out. Another job was picking stones off the plowed fields, for large stones could break farm implements. The stones were dumped in gateways and on farm tracks which in winter were usually poached into mires. When I started working on farms, what I particularly disliked was going home on dark nights, all alone across the fields and allotments. I carried a stick, but I was still scared. I was only nine years old!

Later, before I left school at 14, I worked for the Pargetters, who rented Glebe Farm down Leighton Road. They had eight cows, and I enjoyed milking. In cold weather the cow kept you nice and warm, but it could be a very dirty job. The cows brought in from the fields in wet weather would be plastered with mud, and first of all the milker had to get the worst of this off their udders and undersides. I was supplied with a couple of buckets of warm water and a cloth and washed off as much as possible. They were all washed with the same cloth, but at least the buckets of water were changed every four cows or so. But cleaning the cows got me dirty, and the cows didn't help by kicking me with their filthy feet and flipping me with their filthy tails. And their tails were not just muddy! In the early summer when the grass was fresh and plentiful, their tails were heavy with green cow-shit. So I not only had mud round my ears and shoulders. . . . !If the cow was a persistent tail-wagger, I would tuck its tail between my leg and the cow's leg. Combined with a sharp, "That's enough of that", this usually settled the beast, though it would often turn its head, and give one a long, long, stare, as if to say, "All right, I know who's master." The Pargeters were very kind. They used to give me a lovely crusty pudding made from Bisning, the second milking of a cow after it has calved.

After the corn had been harvested, there was always the 'leasing', when families went into the fields to collect the ears which had broken off or been left behind. It continued into the Thirties. You were supposed to wait until the last shock had been cleared from the field before you went in, but if the farmer was slow to remove it, people would say, "It's been there long enough," and go in anyway. Some had their leasings ground into flour, others fed the wheat to the chickens, and the oats to the pig. A family might get as much as 28 lbs of flour from their leasings. It was a great help to a large family. It also helped the farmer to avoid the seed from this year's oats coming up in the middle of next year's wheat: a volunteer crop as they called it.

89: The slower pace of life in the Thirties. Ern Ellis, in his pony and trap, returns empty milk churns to his smallholding down Cat Street, where he milked.

Helsthorpe Farm is said to have been the first in the parish to acquire a tractor: a ten-year-old "International". That was in the mid-Thirties. Frank Hows bought one a couple of years later, while Stan Ellis of Floyds and Jack Masters of Rowsham acquired tractors in the early part of the war. As smaller tractors came onto the market, the incentive to change became irresistible. Besides, it was now wartime and there was more money about. Nationally, by 1941, farm incomes had trebled in just three years. Increased production of wheat was a national priority. There were subsidies of 50% of the cost of drainage improvements, and £2 per acre for plowing up grassland.

SOME POST-WAR CHANGES

By 1950 farm incomes, nationally, had increased six-fold in twelve years. With agricultural subsidies for 1964/5 running at £365 million, the government was criticised for 'feather-bedding' the farmer. Indeed, the government raised agriculture to a level of national importance previously unknown in peace-time. In return farmers revolutionised their industry with a combination of mechanisation, factory farming and fertilisers. Snippets of information from around the parish show that Wingrave and Rowsham's farming was also changing. Frank Hows was the first to acquire a combine, and he offset some of the cost by hiring it out to farms at Wingrave, Rowsham and Tring. Oxleys Farm installed the first machine milking parlour in Bucks., though the milk still went into churns. At first Jack Masters powered his threshing gear with a steam engine

195

(he had two!), but later used a large tractor. Filmer Kidston used a combine drawn by a tractor. Some land, compulsorily converted to arable during the war, was re-seeded for pasture. With fast access to London, property values in Wingrave rose sharply. Frank Hows sold out for a very good price and bought a farm cheaply in Devon.

By 1965 British farmers were using half a million tractors and sixty thousand combine harvesters. Productivity rocketed, for output was raised despite a reduction in the labour employed. Hay can now be cut, turned, baled, loaded and transported to the barn before any manual handling is necessary. The production of silage is totally mechanised, and sixteen acres can easily be cut, crimped and shrink-wrapped into black, cylindrical bales in one day. It turns into silage in six or seven weeks, when a JCB equipped with a spike will effortlessly trundle a bale out to the fields. All the driver has to do, before dumping the bale into the feeder, is to strip off the black plastic. Manual hoeing to 'single' root crops was replaced by single planting machines. Machine spraying, instead of hoeing, is now used to clean the ground of weeds. The resultant economy in labour has been essential to Vale farmers who now have to compete with the high wages and labour shortages created by the post-war industrialisation of Aylesbury and Leighton Buzzard.

Some changes have had unexpected results. Hand milking was replaced by machine milking, partly to save labour. Stricter regulation of milk production in the interests of hygiene meant the replacement of old sheds and barns by modern milking parlours. The long-winded and strenuous handling of milk in heavy churns was replaced by the pumping of milk from farm tanks to road tankers, which required substantial access roads. These requirements created a significant change in Wingrave's farming, for many farmers and landlords were not prepared to fund such expensive facilities. Indeed, on small farms, the small output of milk could not justify such expense. In consequence, in the last thirty years, ten farms in the parish have abandoned milk production and now concentrate on beef, lamb and arable crops.

In the first half of the 20th century, the number of larger farms in the parish was reduced, while the number of smaller farms (of 10 to 100 acres) doubled. This was partly due to the Smallholdings Act of 1908, and partly due to chance. For instance, Charles Paine's semi-retirement divided his 192 acres into three farms. In the second half of the 20th century this miniaturisation was reversed, as farmers began to appreciate the economies of larger-scale production, and realised the labour-saving potential of modern machinery. However, so as to modernise farm operations, while avoiding investment in expensive equipment which would be given limited use, some farmers (in the parish and the Vale) have continued to use contractors. They are well-suited to operations like harvesting and making silage, where there is some leeway as to time. On the other hand, hay is usually made by the farmers themselves, because decisions on cutting, drying and storing are critical and cannot be delayed.

By 1990 the eighteen largest farms in the parish were worked by just nine farmers. This left nine farmhouses with their farm buildings both vacant, and rapidly dilapidating. Usually, the farmhouses found ready buyers while developers snapped up the farm buildings and converted them to housing. In addition, the farmyards at Parsonage and Church farms have been used to build entirely new housing. All this has provided landowners and the owner-occupiers of farms with some additional capital, removed potential eyesores from the village scene, and added substantially to the parish housing stock, in most cases without creating the feeling of urbanisation. Within the parish only Rowsham has had farm buildings converted to industrial units, though this has also happened at Upper Wingbury just outside the parish boundary with Wing.

Today, Wingrave is no longer dominated by its working farms. Whereas, in the 19th-century, thirteen farmsteads were situated within the village, half of them scattered amongst the houses and cottages, there are now only three left, all situated on the southern boundary. In consequence, Wingrave is a very different village to what it was. It is 25 years since a flock of sheep was driven along the main road through the village, and cowpats are no longer a menace to pedestrians.

MARSTON GATE STATION

In its heyday Marston Gate was a busy little station, and a great convenience to farmers. Like Cheddington and Aylesbury it had cattle pens. On Wednesdays the 9 a.m. passenger train collected cattle for Aylesbury market. There would be one van for cows and a second one if there were also sheep. A little later the farmers, in their best tweeds, would line the platform, headed in the same direction. Each week about ten waggons of 'London Sweepings' arrived, for the horse droppings swept up from London's streets were so popular that local farmers competed keenly for a load. Another regular delivery was the chaff of barley, which Aylesbury Brewery Company sent to Long Marston, for local farmers used it as cattle feed. Hay and coal were other regular loads. Wingrave's newspapers also came via Marston Gate. Mrs Harwood used to cycle to the station, collect the papers for the village shop, and then deliver them. Each year fifteen tons of seed potatoes would be delivered for the Allotment Society, and Michael Higgins would bring them up to Wingrave in a trailer drawn by a tractor.

Recollections: Marston Gate – Christine Dunker

The road was bleak, the hedges starkly bare
With icy flakes in frosty morning air
And we exhausted, wearily we strode
Down winding stretch of stony Marston Road
A two mile walk for early morning train
When cry would be 'She's running late again'.

She always was. We sat by fireside heat
With fingers numb and chilblains on the feet
And asked for papers, 'None' was terse reply.
No morning papers. Nothing to inspire
The roving eyes, save battered wooden clock
Precisely stating time with tick and tock
Until the noise was drowned by piercing scream
As train arrived with hissing spouting steam.

A sudden rush, no waste of precious time,
The doors flung wide, and high athletic climb
To smoke-filled carriage, dimly dark and grey,
With corner seat, and crumbs of yesterday.
And once inside we heaved contented sigh
And leaning back waved Marston Gate goodbye.

Then eyes would peer for black-faced sheep
In distant meadows where, from wakened sleep,
They scattered wide as the monster hurtled by
Disrupting peace, with smoke-disfigured sky.
Then going slow, terminating tossing,
Red for danger, nearing Broughton Crossing.
Points manoeuvred, sight of Aylesbury town—
"We're nearly there. Be careful stepping down."

90: Post-war view of Marston Gate Station looking towards Cheddington.

Despite Christine Dunker's rather sombre account the Cheddington line was quite a friendly affair. Regular passengers knew one another quite well. The stationmaster also knew them, for he was very much in evidence. When a bell rang to indicate the approach of a train, he closed the gates across the Marston Road, went into the box and set the signal, and came down to the platform to take the tickets. Then he flagged the train off, though he would usually 'hold' it for a minute or two if a breathless late-comer appeared in the distance. Finally, he went back into the box, re-set the signals, and opened the gates. Only then could road traffic go. Hard luck for the car or cart which arrived just as the gates closed, especially on a day when there were cattle to load. You just had to be patient. The train driver also got to know some of the travellers. Mrs French, who lived at Betlow Farm close to the line, but a good mile's walk from Marston Gate, would be picked up, or dropped off, at her front door.

A few Wingravians commuted to work via Marston Gate. In the Thirties a Mrs Wilkins used the trains to get to and from Berkhamsted where she had a job at a clothing factory. Her monthly return ticket cost 12-6d. Then, during the war, the factory put on a special bus to bring in the workers, and Mrs Wilkins switched to that. It was this competition from motor vehicles that eventually killed off the rail traffic. In the Thirties, Nestles began using lorries to collect the milk churns direct from the farms, and passengers used the more accessible buses, and the very much cheaper bicycles. Marston Gate was simply two miles too far from Wingrave. The passenger service closed in 1953 and ten years later the line was closed, and dismantled.

Chapter Sixteen

The Hamlet of Rowsham

In 1798 the open fields of Rowsham had been enclosed together with those of Wingrave, and its inhabitants had undergone the same great upheaval. After enclosure the eight principal landholdings were worked as just six farms.

Fig. 26: Rowsham – The Post-Enclosure Landholdings and Farms

Farm	Acres	Owner	Farmer
Mercers' Farm	248	Mercers' Company	Joseph Lucas
Baileys' Farm	112	Joseph Lucas	
Allotment of Sarah Lucas	15	Sarah Lucas	Joseph Lucas
Allotment of New College	14	New College, Oxford	
Hale Farm	211	John Parker	Charles Fleet
Higgs' Barn Farm	116	Earl of Chesterfield	William Higgs
Seabrook's Farm	45	Robert Seabrook	Widow Seabrook
Fenn Farm	25	Ed. Monday Lucas	Ed. Monday Lucas

THE LUCAS FAMILY

The Lucas family had leased Mercers' Farm for over three hundred years. During that time they had played a significant role in the parish as good employers and generous benefactors to the parish church and other worthy local causes. Back in 1620 Robert Lucas was one of three parishioners who had given the parish church its treble bell. Over the years, various members of the family established charities: for the poor at Xmas; for the church organist; and towards the parochial schoolmaster's salary.

Joseph Lucas senior (1751-1832) was probably the most notable member of this family. He farmed half of Rowsham's farmland (fig. 26), and was also a maltster and brewer, supplying beer to forty-three licensed premises. He is mentioned in Dr Lipscomb's 'History of Buckinghamshire':

Mr Lucas became very opulent as a brewer and eminent as a grazier. He built a commodious house at Rowsham (Mercers' House), in which he resided with great hospitality, and enjoyed as long as he lived the respect of his neighbours for his benevolence of disposition, kindness and generosity.

Thus, when Joseph died in 1832, it was typical of him that he bequeathed £10 -16s per year for life to the widow of his late servant William Badrick, while his labourers with ten years' service received £10 cash, with two to nine years' service £5, and the rest £1. A fulsome tribute by the vicar, Isaac Denton, is recorded on a wall plaque in the parish church (see page 200). The next generation (another Joseph) was equally benevolent. He and his brother Edward gave the land for the construction of the parochial church school in 1846 and it was the same Joseph who, in 1855, provided the parish church with its first organ. "An organ such as very few churches can boast of."

The family's property then passed to a nephew, Edward Munday Major-Lucas, who for many years had helped to run the estate. A year later he married his cousin,

Recollections: Joseph Lucas (1751-1832)
– Rev. Joseph Denton

Pause and reflect with reverential awe;
Kind-hearted Lucas lies entombed below.
Loved through long life, revered unto its end,
The widow's succour and the orphan's friend:
Nor gave a poor man grief but when he died.
In every action of his life you trace
The splendent feature of some Christian grace.
Now cold's that breath, which warmed the poor before.
His cheering voice, alas is heard no more.
The mourning peasants as they raised his bier,
Rolled down their cheek the tributary tear.
The vicar with their grief his own combines,
And sheds a tear as he endites these lines.
Yet why prolong the melancholy strain:
His death, though loss to us, to him is gain.

Mary Montague, who lived nearby at Fenn Farm (now known as Home Farm), and set up home at Mercers' House. Its ornamental gardens were known for their magnificent rhododendrons and azaleas. Here they were living in 1875 with their seven children and a resident governess, nursemaid, cook and housemaid. Edward employed the majority of Rowsham's workers, for he not only owned the malthouse, the brewery, the Red Lion public house, the smithy, and three farms, but also leased Mercers' Farm. It was therefore a considerable shock to the small community, when he decided to leave Rowsham due to ill-health. The estate was sold, and the family moved to Willesden. For Rowsham it was the end of an era. No longer would landed gentry live there. When Edward died in 1899, his family gave the parish church an eagle lectern in his memory.

THE NEW CHAPELS

1870 was an important year for Rowsham for two new public buildings were erected: a Congregational chapel and an Anglican 'school-chapel'. Since the 1830's Independents had worshipped in a cottage, licensed for the purpose, but they had long felt the need for a proper place of worship. Their nearest chapel was in Wingrave, a long cold, muddy trudge across the fields in winter, especially for the young, the elderly and the infirm.

Sir Anthony Rothschild gave a plot of land at the end of Wingrave Footway (now Brewhouse Lane). More than half the estimated cost had been raised by Good Friday, the day the foundation stone was laid. It was a beautiful day and over 450 were present, including friends from Wingrave and Aylesbury. During the ceremony it was said, to cries of approval from the audience, that this would be "an independent church unfettered by state control, a place where all may worship as their conscience dictated". The building was soon completed and the opening services took place in June. So many attended that "the congregation adjourned into the open air", for the chapel had only been built to seat one hundred. Later four hundred sat down to tea in a large marquee, 'trays' of food being donated so that all the profits would go to the building fund.

Ethel Perkins (nee Higgs) lived in Rowsham as a child and attended Sunday school at the chapel "from 10 until 11 in the morning, 2 to 3 in the afternoon, and then straight into Sunday service. We had anniversaries and Wingrave folk walked across the fields to join us".

91. Home Farm, Rowsham (formerly Fenn Farm) circa 1906-7. Mabel Gurney (later Rickard) on the right and her cousin are in donkey baskets specially constructed to hold small children.

92. Manor Farmhouse, Rowsham. Bob Higgs says his father, Sam, and his brothers, used to catch sparrows roosting in the ivy by using a net fastened to two long poles. Times were hard, and his grandmother made sparrow pudding for her large family.

93. *The Anglican combined school/chapel. "The handsome building of fancy brickwork and latticed widows" was completed in July 1870. A century later it had fallen into disrepair, and was put up for sale. Subsequently it was converted into a private house.*

94. *The Rowsham band pictured in front of the Red Lion. From the left, standing - unknown, J.B.Bates, Joe Badrick, unknown, Joe Goldney, Harry Higgs, unknown, Will Bennion (drummer); seated – Tom Higgs, Fred Ashpool, Harry Badrick (son of publican), Fred Goldney. Before World War One it played at many local events, and every Boxing Day it circulated Rowsham playing carols.*

The problem of cross-country travel between Rowsham and Wingrave obviously affected Anglicans as much as Nonconformists. Moreover, the Anglicans were responsible for education as well as worship, so the Rev. Butt was doubly concerned at the lack of an Anglican building in Rowsham. A dual-purpose 'school cum chapel' was decided upon and Mr Lucas and Mr Bennett, another local farmer, gave their full support. 'The handsome building of fancy brickwork and latticed windows' was completed in July 1870 at a cost of £350. On the day of the opening ceremony Mr Lucas gave the Sunday school scholars "a capital dinner of boiled beef, vegetables and plum-pudding". Later a thanksgiving service was held in the new large room of the school-chapel with its ingeniously designed pews, which could easily be converted into school desks. A tea for two hundred was provided in a large marquee, waited upon by Mr Griffin of Wingrave "in a most obliging manner". The vicar then thanked God for permitting him to help in building it. He rejoiced that "those who had the means had bestowed them ungrudgingly, and that now a building uniting convenience, strength and beauty had been brought close to the poor man's door, planted in the midst of their cottages, for the use of themselves and their children for ever."

We know very little of this small school, for the log books have only survived for 1891-3. Miss Mary Ann Keen, living on the Recreation Ground with her widowed mother, was schoolmistress. According to the vicar, she was a very respectable young woman who diligently and faithfully performed her duties, but with academic results rather lower than the Vicar's and the H.M.I.'s expectations. In 1874 the scholars aged between 6 and 8 passed Standard I satisfactorily, but the older ones knew practically nothing. Consequently in 1875 the Vicar expressed the view that Rowsham School should be for infants only, for the older ones were not only learning nothing, but were impeding the progress of the younger ones. This made sense, but some parents were reluctant to send their children across the fields in all weathers, despite a more suitable education being provided at Wingrave. The pupils used a path well-used by agricultural labourers, but often arrived cold and wet, shoes soaked and muddy, for very few had boots. No wonder so many suffered from chilblains, sometimes so severely that they were unable to walk, or even to wear their shoes. Wingrave scholars went home for the long dinner break, but those from Rowsham took packets of food which they ate in the classroom. Afterwards they played on the Recreation Ground, or in icy weather slid on the pond until afternoon school began.

So older pupils still continued attending the Rowsham 'infants' school, even after education was made compulsory in 1880. In 1886, the vicar instructed that all girls from ten years old, and all boys from 8 were to come up to Wingrave, and in no case to be received at Rowsham without special application to the manager. But by 1891, after Miss Keen's untimely death in 1890, it had been turned into a mixed school, teaching up to Standard IV! In 1892 the H.M.I. commented, "The presence of a few older children, especially boys, robs the infants of the attention due to them." Finally, in 1893, the school was reported 'Inefficient' and it closed at Christmas. So from 1894 all Rowsham children had to attend the Wingrave Schools. Ethel Perkins well remembers the tramp to school.

We all walked together. In summer we had lovely times, playing in the hay, never afraid of cows. We clambered over stiles, came up the Knolls into Church Street, and so to school. It was very different in the winter. It didn't matter whether it rained, hailed, or snowed, we __had__ to go to school. So we walked along the road. Two miles it was. We had no raincoats or wellingtons in those days, and had to sit in our wet shoes all day. Mrs Stubbs hung our wet coats over the fireguard. One day my little bobble hat got scorched, but I still had to wear it. Money was short in those days.

ROWSHAM BREWERY

Once Edmund Munday Major-Lucas had announced his retirement, it was arranged that the brewery would be auctioned in the autumn of 1875. It was conveniently situated beside the main Aylesbury to Leighton Buzzard road. At the front, double doors allowed a horse and cart to be backed in for loading. Hinged shutters on the upper windows and louvred 'lanterns' on the roof brought in air and light. There were extensive storerooms, stabling and coach-houses at the back, for as the advertisement put it, this was 'an important lucrative concern, carrying on a large trade'. The forty fully-licensed public houses and three beer-houses supplied by the brewery were all within ten miles of Rowsham. They included the 'Red Lion' at Rowsham and the 'Bell' and 'Carpenters Arms' at Wingrave. Private households were also supplied, for some people preferred beer to suspect well-water. And beer was cheap

95. *Rowsham Brewery*

enough. Around 1850 table beer cost 3d a gallon including local delivery. Farmers, too, were good customers at harvest time for large quantities of free beer were one of the labourers' perks.

The auction never took place, for the brewery was bought privately by William Kempton Gurney, who had been general manager since his father's death in 1869. He also bought the Brewery House next door and the adjoining cottage. All this must have been very reassuring to the employees, especially when he announced in the Bucks Herald, "It is my intention to carry on the business of a brewer, and I trust, by paying strict attention to the same, to receive a share of the public patronage." Besides the manager a team of twelve men were employed, including two stokers, two storemen, two maltsters, two draymen, a coachman and a groom.

The malt needed for the brewing of beer was processed on the other side of the road at the malt house, easily identified at that time by the large cowl perched on the roof directly above the furnace. The barley was first soaked in water, which was pumped up from the Thistlebrook! After 24 to 96 hours the barley was spread onto large ventilated floors, where it was turned and raked for several days until it sprouted. It was then dried in the kilns for 2 to 3 days. The processed grain, now called malt, was 'shot' into sacks. Those destined for the Rowsham brewery were carried along a path through Mercers' orchard, and then straight across the road. The late Phyllis Norman, whose father owned Mercers' Farm (by that time re-named Manor Farm), well remembered the strong pungent smells on days when malting and brewing were taking place.

After storage for between four to eight weeks the malt would be ready for grinding, followed by mashing. In the mash tub, water and cereals would be added to the malt, and as the mixture was brought to a temperature of 54° the brewer stirred it consistently with his mashing stick. When he stopped stirring, the solids settled, and the liquid, called wort, was drained off. It was then boiled in a large-lidded brewing copper

96. *The Old Malthouse, Rowsham.*

97. *The Rowsham Brewery (on the left), and the Gurneys ivy-covered house.*

for two to three hours, hops being added to give flavour as well as to prevent spoilage. Once filtered and cooled, yeast was added to start fermentation. William Gurney was the tunman: in charge of the final process of the filling of the casks. When William died in 1906 and his son took over, a valuation of the brewery included:

Fourteen hogsheads, each of 54 gallon capacity
Ninety-eight barrels, each of 36 gallon capacity
Twenty-three firkins, each of 9 gallon capacity
Four casks, each of 6 gallon capacity
Twenty-five half-firkins, each of 4.5 gallon capacity

TWENTIETH CENTURY CHANGES

Until the 1920's life in Rowsham did not change greatly. The horse was still the main source of power on the farms, with the steam engine as its principal rival. The hamlet's situation on the main Aylesbury to Leighton Buzzard road meant that soon after the Great War it had a bus service and, very occasionally, a motor car chugged past. But there was very little traffic and most of it was horse or pedal-powered: workers from the villages going to and from Aylesbury; the horses and carts of Aylesbury's traders looking for business in the villages; and cattle and sheep being driven to market. Tom Woodruff, Wingrave's blacksmith, walked across the fields twice weekly to the small smithy, which still stands in Bennett's Lane, but now garages someone's car. Of course, if William Norman's prized shire horses needed attention he would drive up to Wingrave and bring Tom back in his car. For Tom was a good farrier, and had a wonderful way with young horses. Jack Masters is said to have been the first farmer in Rowsham to acquire a tractor, just in time to help with the ploughing-up that the government demanded as part of the war effort.

The Anglican school-chapel continued as a place of worship after the closure of the school in 1893. At first its weekly Sunday afternoon services were well-attended, as was its Sunday school. Harvest festivals and concerts took place in the 'Mission Hall' as it became known. However, numbers declined, and it was last used for worship in the 1960's. In 1975 it was converted into a private house. Attendances also dwindled at the Congregational chapel. Sunday services were last held in 1957, after which it gradually became a ruin.

The closure of the brewery in 1939 passed off quietly, probably because everyone was too worried about the chances of war. Not much remains. The pump-house has crumbled into a ruin. The malthouse drying sheds were used for a time for occasions like whist drives, but have now been demolished. Even the brick-built part has lost its distinctive cowl. The brewery has been converted into a private house, though the old louvred vents still crown the roof. The pond, hidden away behind the malthouse, is still a delight, though only visible to trespassers. The reaction was quite different when, in 1957 Benskins decided to close the Red Lion. There was a real outcry. A petition which attracted over a hundred signatures was supported unanimously by the Parish Council. The hamlet had no shop, no proper meeting place and this was their only social centre. The Red Lion had a good main road position, and in summer there was plenty of passing trade. There had been a pub there at least as early as 1768 when Roger Kempster was its licensee. The regulars were most unhappy about cycling to Wingrave. "When you get over 70, your bike won't carry you very well if you've had above a pint," commented Will Bennion, a regular for over fifty years. The brewery replied that the pub would need complete re-building. As trade was limited, this would not be financially viable. The Red Lion was demolished in 1958, and the licensee, Mr Percy Higgs, moved to a council house in Wingrave.

98. *Customers gather outside the Red Lion, Rowsham, for a press photograph, during a campaign to prevent its closure. Pictured (from the left): Percy Higgs (landlord), Ralph Goldney, Don Rand, Ray Higgs, Charles Ellis, — Ellis, William Bennion, Cyril Reynolds, Harry Perkins, Ted Reynolds, Charles —, William Alcock, Arthur Bennion, George Reynolds, Joseph Higgs.*

99. *Despite the protests, and its main road position, the brewery closed the Red Lion in January 1958, and so destroyed Rowsham's only social centre.*

LORD ROTHSCHILD'S STAGHOUNDS AT ROWSHAM NEAR AY

100. The Hunt and Lord Rothschild's staghounds assemble at Rowsham in the middle of the
Aylesbury/Leighton road: now the traffic-laden A418.

101. On a very different occasion, the fox has just been dug out and the followers gather round.
The photograph was found amongst the effects of the late Percy Fleet of Thistlebrook Farm.

Part Four: Everyday Life

Chapter Seventeen

The Business Life of Wingrave

LIFE IN THE 1880's

The lack of transport still made it necessary for the parish to be self-sufficient in most respects. Only the better-off could afford to maintain a pony and trap, or to hire a horse, and even for this fortunate minority a journey to Aylesbury or Leighton was a time-consuming affair: most ponies needed continuous urging and a touch of the whip to maintain a steady jog-trot. It was slower still by Shank's Pony, which was the only option for most villagers. Even the post was brought from Aylesbury on foot each day. Of course, from Marston Gate you could get the train to Aylesbury, but that was too expensive for most people. Frank Griffin, who attended Aylesbury Grammar School, travelled to school by train in the 1880's, but his father farmed 367 acres and could afford the fare. Even so, the station was over two miles from Nup End, and in a wet winter the road was often blocked to pedestrians for several weeks when Langdale Brook (known locally as 'Langles' or 'Old Langle') flooded for quite a distance, sometimes to a depth of eighteen inches or more. Even cyclists were defeated by this, as Joyce Sinnott discovered:

There were times when, by pedalling very fast from the Thistlebrook bridge, and then putting your feet on the handlebars, the boost got you through, but more often than not it didn't work, and you ended up wading through the flood.

Of course, if a cold spell followed a wet spell, the whole lot could be frozen over, as Sybil Rickard recalled:

One morning when Nellie and I were trying to get from Wingrave to Cheddington there had been a severe frost and the road was very icy and slippery. The water at Langles was frozen over and Mr Ellis, who was taking us in his brougham, had to get out and break the ice to enable the horse to cross the flood safely.

Shopping and Services

In 1881 as in 1851, Wingrave had five carpenters, four butchers, four publicans, three grocers, two wheelwrights and a blacksmith.[1] The women could still turn to at least four dressmakers, while both Widow Fleet and Mary Ann Kirby had added drapery to the attractions of their grocery shops. However, by 1881 there were only (only!!) two bakers, two tailors, two dealers and four cordwainers, in each case just half the numbers of 1851. Only the building trade had expanded, with the emergence of two builders, and a more than doubled workforce of nine bricklayers and four brickies' labourers. This probably reflected the activities of the Rothschilds, contracts for substantial private houses, and the demand for cheap terraced housing as an investment by the few people, like James Kirby and Josiah Fleet, whose businesses had proved particularly profitable. With this exception, business activity in the village had at best stagnated since 1851.

This was not too surprising, for in general the purchasing power of the parish was no greater. Emigration had limited the increase in population to just ninety in thirty years. Agriculture and straw-plaiting still provided most of the employment, but both were in depression in the 1880's. The contribution of children to the family income was drastically reduced by the 1880 Education Act's requirement for compulsory full-time attendance at school to the age of ten years. The twenty or so destitute villagers, mostly aged 60 to 80, received from the Aylesbury Union an average of only £6-10s per household per year: a derisory 2s-6d per week.[2]

Diversification

Wingrave's tradesmen responded to the lack of business in the traditional way: by looking for income from more than one source. Thus when Josiah Dimmock left the family business on the Green and established his own bootmaking business in Nup End, in the cottage now called Dean Leys,[3] he also started (in the same cottage) a shop selling a wide variety of goods, and with the help of his wife ran both businesses. Similarly, in 1851 James Kirby was a plait dealer, but within ten years had also established a grocery business in his front room with his wife and later his son in charge. In the 1880's his daughter, Mary Ann, took over and the grocery became subsidiary to the drapery and dressmaking which was her speciality. Likewise, William Higgins, who established a butcher's shop in Chapel Street, also used the premises for his wife's grocery business, and his daughter's dressmaking.

This combination of diverse activities under one roof provided an insurance policy against the death of the main breadwinner, for the widow knew her side of the business, and a great deal about her husband's side of it. So, when William Higgins died in 1883 at the age of 47, his widow Caroline somehow found the money to buy "the house between the graveyard and the pond"[4] from Thomas Newman, the retiring wheelwright. Here Caroline and her daughter, Mary Ann, continued to make a living from butchery, groceries and dressmaking. Josiah Dimmock's wife, Sarah, was not so lucky when he died in 1895. Bootmaking was a skilled craft and Sarah had to abandon that side of the business, but she continued to run the shop for another twenty years.

The pursuit of several different activities, plus the need to stock all those items which were most in demand, also resulted in a rather bizarre selection of goods. Mrs Mary Ann Fleet's shop next to the blacksmith's is said to have "sold anything from pepper to peppermints, and cottons to kettles". From her Rothschild cottage on the corner of Nup End and Main Street, Harriett Gibbs sold "a variety of useful commodities", including nobs of salt, lamp glasses, paraffin and the pork which was butchered by her husband, John, a former pig dealer. Hilda Gibbs (no relation to Harriett) once observed that her mother's shop, between the graveyard and the pond, "stocked everything from a frying pan to an elephant". Her stock certainly included hardware, dustpans, brushes, lamp glasses, groceries, cigarettes and tobacco, and lots and lots of sweets of every shape and size in boxes on the counter, and glass jars on the shelves: liquorice laces and rounds; sweet cigarettes; gobstoppers at a farthing each; etc., etc.. With the school so close to the shop, it was a very profitable line.[5]

HIGGLEDY-PIGGLEDY PLANNING

In the 19th century there was no planning authority to regulate where a business was located and what constituted suitable premises. Consequently, Wingrave's businesses and shops were housed in a wide variety of buildings mixed up higgledy-piggledy amongst its homes. Indeed, many homes doubled up as business premises. If one had practically no capital, the "shop" might well consist of just a pair of scales and a few shelves in one's living room or wash-house to accommodate the stock, with the family table to provide a counter. Of course, some occupations demanded buildings dedicated to a particular use: Joseph Rickard's steam-driven corn mill; the village forge; the Griffins' bakery; William Gurney's brewery at Rowsham; and the village pubs, for example. The requirements of carpenters, wheelwrights and butchers were not so critical, though a reasonably-sized and weather-proof working space was essential. Purpose-built sheds of brick or timber at the bottom of the garden were popular, but so were old farm buildings and outhouses. Those adjoining Baldway House[6] had been used by Henry Keen, the wheelwright, and were currently occupied by Thomas Reynolds, a mealman. Until his retirement, Thomas Newman, the wheelwright, had his workshop in the outhouses of "his house between the graveyard and the pond". Most of the rest used their own living accommodation as their shop, and even as their workshop. Wingrave's tailors, cordwainers, drapers, grocers and two of its butchers operated in this way. Indeed, in the 19th century the Rose and Crown appears to have been the only butchery with dedicated buildings: a large thatched wooden shed at the roadside for the slaughtering and jointing, and a proper little shop at the side of the pub.

THE BUSINESS CENTRES

Although enterprises of various sorts were scattered all round the village, there were two business centres. One was round The Green, where George Higgins had recently replaced Charles Mortimer as publican of the Rose and Crown. He kept the butcher's shop going, with his wife selling the meat. Nearby lived John Dimmock. Like his brother in Nup End, he was a boot and shoemaker. He made them rather than mended them, and did a good trade, because he saved people walking to Aylesbury to buy their shoes. Further along, opposite the pond, Thomas Newman, assisted by four men and a boy, built carts and wheels in the outhouses, while his son ran a drapery shop from the house. Thomas would shortly be retiring to a substantial new house in the Leighton Road, leaving James Stranks, who had recently established a wheelwright's in Chapel Yard, to look after Wingrave's wheels. On the other side of the Green the smithy stood under the spreading chestnut tree (both still there today). The smith was Freddie Brandon, a short, stocky man, whose family had run the smithy for at least half a century. Joseph Kempster helped him, for there was plenty of work to do. Next door was Mrs Mary Ann Fleet's drapery and grocery shop, while the other end of that row of cottages was used as a carpenter's shop and had a saw-pit at the side. In later years James Stranks converted the shop into a wheelwright's. Beyond that was the cottage where James Gibbs, the tailor, lived and worked.

The other centre was Nup End, where Hilda Roberts lived as a child:

In Nup End we had two or three quite fascinating shops, all differing very much. On the corner of Winslow Road [7] and Nup End lived James Kirby, the plait dealer. His daughter, Mary Ann, kept a little draper's shop in one of the downstairs rooms. She also sold grocery, sweetstuff and the accessories for plaiting straw. That was a shop to linger in! A large iron knocker on the door announced the customer and in a few minutes Mary Ann, a small plump smiling woman, appeared from a remote doorway, and enquired your business. While she leisurely weighed or searched for your requirements, you had time to feast your eyes on all the wonderful things stacked around the yard of space where you stood. A moveable flap blocked the way to the dark interior, but close by were shelves full of rolls of calico, and shirting, and other materials, and in a small glass-fronted case were delicate ribbons and laces and other things, which in my childish eyes were the longed-for but unobtainable. Mary Ann deserved a halo, for she was all that was dutiful and sweet, in addition to being an amateur milliner and dress designer. She advised, produced the required materials, and eventually provided the finished article at a moderate price. Mary Ann and her father combined the various branches of the little family business, and many a plaiter worked out her liabilities to Mary Ann for dress material or shirts or what not by the tens of plait she sold to James.

On the opposite corner was George Griffin's little post office, and next to it John and Harriett Gibbs kept a small shop. Harriett wore a black mob-cap, and encompassed her scanty grey locks in a curly black net. There would often be a neighbour in the shop, listening to Harriett's grumbles and recollections. "Ah, what times we've seen . . . ," she would begin. She had never seen a train or a motor vehicle, but just before she passed on she saw a girl riding a bicycle. I shall never forget her tirade of wrath about the indecencies of the bold female who dared to sit astride "one of them iron thing-a-me-gigs!". If Harriett could have had her way, the offending female would have been burnt as a witch.

Further down Nup End was Dimmocks. Josiah was a bootmaker and mender and a good one at that! He seemed old as long as I can remember him. He wore a little round cap to cover his bald head, very thick spectacles which made him look very owl-like when he peered at you over them, and a leather apron smelling of wax: a peculiar piney leathery sort of smell. It was a quaint little shop with white sand sprinkled over the clean red bricks, so that there was a scrunchy sound as you walked on it. It had an L-shaped counter, which left a narrow passage to the door into his shoe-making shop. The front door of the shop had no latch on the outside by which you could enter. Instead, a long string was fastened to an inside latch and brought alongside the window to a nail on the further side of the counter: very primitive, but effectively excluding any unwanted intruder. You knocked and continued to knock until Josiah could leave his last and come to pull the string. Once inside there was plenty to interest you. A screen of fine wire netting kept your fingers from straying into the wide-necked bottles which housed clear knobbly delicious looking sticks of sugar candy, which Josiah broke with a tiny hammer, letting the candy fall with a bump into the tiny hanging brass scales. A nice lot you got for a halfpenny! Behind the counter were rows of small drawers containing shoelaces, whipcord, tape, string, boot buttons, cottons, needles and dozens of other things. Flanking the side counter were stacks of besoms, buckets, brooms and, on the window ledge, lamp glasses and small dicky-lamps. It was a little chemist's shop as well, and on a side shelf were bottles of hair oil, senna leaves, senna tea, chair oil, Daff's syrup of rhubarb, and Hort's horn and appedeldock for rubbing.

Nup End also housed the Griffins' bakery, the Bell Inn, the Carpenters' Arms, Thomas Mead the baker and plait dealer, John Kirby (yet another shoemaker), and William Mead, the carrier.

PROBLEMS

The intermixing of business operations and residences was convenient for both traders and shoppers, but it had some serious disadvantages. Blacksmiths were notoriously noisy, and usually worked with their doors open. Some of the wheelwright's processes were also noisy, especially as they were often carried out in the yard rather than the workshop. And the neighbours soon discovered which carpenter was undertaking a particular burial. "Joby's got that one!" they would say, when the sawing and tapping came from Joe Rickard's workshop. For the interment was not a thing to be delayed (especially in summer), and the noise sometimes went on late into the evening as the coffin was hurriedly constructed.

Vermin were a considerable problem. The barns and outhouses of the farms were their prime breeding places as Edward Griffin explained:[8]

In the days before Warfarin and other modern poisons, rats were an ever-present pest on the farms. My grandfather, Frank Griffin, used to describe how, when anyone went into the barns, the rats used to run down the beams of the barn in an almost continuous stream. When he and his brothers were boys they used to sit in the barn with a gun and shoot them. About the only effective way to reduce the number of rats and mice was to keep numerous cats. The cats lived wild about the farm, and were not fed but left to fend for themselves. At times the cats became almost as numerous as the rats and their numbers were also kept down by shooting them. Occasionally, a mistake was made and one of the lads would shoot a domestic cat. They were probably not very careful which cats they shot! Eventually, an anonymous notice was put up in the church porch saying, "The indiscriminate shooting of cats must stop".

Rats were attracted to the premises of butchers and bakers like flies to a dung hill. Michael Higgins, whose grandparents, George and Annie, took over the Rose and Crown around 1890, remembers their roadside slaughterhouse (where they also made sausages) being over-run by rats, and littered with their droppings. They also raided the chicken runs, which were kept in many private gardens, eating the eggs and killing the chicks. They scavenged the pig styes, and gnawed their way into stores of fruit and vegetables. They were a constant threat to household food, and were one of the reasons for the popularity of food safes, though these had to be suspended from a wall bracket or ceiling hook, rats being agile climbers. Despite the use of cage traps, spring traps and poisons, and the experience of rat catchers like old William Gurney and in later years Harry 'Ratter' Gurney, they were impossible to eliminate.

Whatever your need, someone would be anxious to try and satisfy it, and to earn a few pence in the process. Joey Bonham was one of several villagers who would sweep your chimney. Will Gurney would buy your rabbit skins. Joseph Humphrey was a gardener by trade, but on Saturday evenings his tiny old cottage was filled with men waiting for a twopenny haircut. Sarah Hart, a spinster with two young children, would be pleased to assist with your cleaning while Susan Fleet would look after your laundry. Most folk could use a few extra pennies! Gipsies occasionally passed through the village, and they knew just what would extract a few coins from the housewife's purse.

One old woman was a big tall specimen, brown as a berry, with black wavy hair, and wearing a tattered bright shawl over a very shabby black skirt, with a bright old hand-kerchief tied over her head. She walked along with her hands very busy making string potato nets, which were popular in most households in those days, when the whole of the meal was cooked in one large pot over a coal fire, and the various vegetables were kept separate in these nets. The gipsies were experts at making them. They also made clothes pegs from wood they gathered from the hedgerows. These were known as gipsy pegs, and very long-lasting they were, and very secure in windy weather. Less welcome were gipsies selling sprigs of heather: "Bring you good luck, m'dear."[9]

LIFE IN WINGRAVE IN THE EARLY 20th CENTURY

Occupational Changes

At the beginning of the 20th century the dominant occupation for men was still farming, but it now employed only 110 of the village men, and another twenty farm labourers were unemployed.[10] Most of the latter were in their late teens or early twenties. As there was no Social Security, they were fortunate to be in families where at least one member had a job. Otherwise there is no indication as to how they supported themselves. The

213

number of women still plaiting straw in the parish of Wingrave with Rowsham in 1901 is unknown,[11] but the Bucks workforce had been decimated, falling from 3412 in 1871, to a mere 173 in 1901, as cheap imports massively undercut local prices, and reduced earnings to a pittance. Twenty years later the trade had almost vanished. The redundant children were absorbed by education, for in 1893 the school leaving age was raised to eleven, and by 1899 to twelve. Even so, for women alone, about 65 alternative paid jobs were required between 1891 and 1914, and the parish simply couldn't provide them. About 30% (mainly teenagers) remained at home, or went to relatives, helping with the housework. 20% turned to dress-making, though there is no indication as to what they earned. A few more found paid jobs in the parish: teaching, nursing and delivering mail. Of the rest some obtained live-in jobs outside the village as domestic servants, others continued to plait despite the extremely low wages, and a few just retired.

COPING WITH CHANGE

The demise of straw-plaiting was a major change, which reduced the incomes of many families. Fortunately, as detailed in earlier chapters, there were some compensations: for instance, allotments, the Temperance movement, Wingrave's provident clubs, old age pensions, cheap imported foodstuffs, national health insurance, Wingrave's Nursing Club, the increased availability of jobs, and the reduced competition for them. So life was easier than it had been. Even so, for many its problems were considerable as a few examples illustrate. The week's holiday away from home was unknown, unless relatives could provide board and lodging. Most children received no more than an elementary education. There was little social and economic mobility. The percentage of paupers had fallen, but was still over 2% just before World War I: for the infirm the workhouse was still their last resort; while the able-bodied, both male and female, were a familiar sight, tramping the roads in search of shelter and food, as Connie Bignell recalled:

An old tramp came to our house frequently. If my brother Fred saw him he'd run and tell mum, "Not Loving God is coming. Put the kettle on," because he always used to sing, and it ended up every time with "Not Loving God".. The first time he came he asked if he could have something to eat. Mum said, "Yes, I'll give you something to eat if you'll eat it here". Because lots of tramps took the food away with them, and it was not really what they wanted. So he became a regular customer. Mum made him tea, and gave him bread and something, and he always came in and had a good feed. We used to love him. He came for several years. There were lots of tramps about at that time.

SELF-SUFFICIENCY CONTINUES

What did not change was the gap between Wingrave and its nearest towns. Ordinary folk still had no easy way of bridging it, so self-sufficiency continued to be a feature of the village. However, the turn of the century did see a number of deaths and retirements amongst the traders and artisans, and doubtless some people shook their heads and muttered that things would never be the same. It was understandable. The village was used to stability, and even a change of faces was a major event. In 1895, after 39 years as postmaster, George Griffin retired. His replacement, Ann Woodward Jones, would notch up 40 years in the job before handing over to Hilda Gibbs, who held it for another thirty-six years! Just three postmasters in 115 years! And there were plenty of other examples of long service. The Mortimer family had run the Rose and Crown for almost a century before handing over to George and Annie Higgins at the end of the 1880's. The Higgins only stayed for forty years! The Dimmock brothers were both dead by 1905, ending a family tradition of boot and shoe making that went back into the 18th century. However, people had plenty of time to get used to their replacement, for Frank Rogers served the village for the next thirty-five years. The village also acquired a new smith. Around 1890, after half a century at the smithy the Brandon family was replaced by the Woodruffs, who occupied it for nearly seventy years.

In the early 1900's even more shops and businesses were opened. One of the longest lasting was Phil Rickard's butcher's shop. It was located in what is now the garage of Lawndale, his house on the corner of Winslow Road and Twelve Leys. With his trilby crammed down onto his head, and his large blue apron flapping in the wind, he was a familiar sight around the village, delivering meat to customers' homes, on a very solidly-built bicycle with a stout oval iron frame attached to the front, into which his oval delivery basket fitted nicely. He also came round the village on Saturdays, selling meat from door to door. As was usual at that time, Phil bought his meat "on the hoof". He slaughtered the animals on the premises, and their dying cries could be heard clearly by the neighbours in Winslow Road and Mill Place. He was helped by Walter Stranks, a little old deaf and dumb man who lived in a house along the lane, opposite the chapel. Walter was a bit like Charlie Chaplin, with a black moustache, and could get very angry when teased by the children, chasing them and waving his walking stick. One of his jobs was working the sausage machine in the shop. The older folk still remember him: "Excellent sausages they were, and good meat Phil had too!"

Round about 1912 a general store was established by people named Wood. It was located in a timber building opposite the present village shop, which was then a private house, in which the Woods lived. It may well have been the forerunner of the present village shop, but little else is known about it except that on one occasion it was broken into by two of the village lads.

In 1900 William Gurney junior, lived with his wife and widowed father in their home next to the Mill House, which was the last building on the Winslow Road going towards Aston Abbotts. He was a carpenter, and in his workshop, at the bottom of the garden, he made such things as ladders, barrows, parts of carts and farm equipment, and wheels. Stacks of wood stood at the side of the house to season, including the oak and the elm that he needed to make coffins, a speciality which eventually established him as an undertaker. For funerals he discarded his working clothes, covered his ginger wig with a top hat, put on a tail coat, and pushed the bier - the long-handled, flat-topped cart on which the coffin rested - to the chapel, with the mourners following on foot. William and (later) Frank Rickard, his son-in-law, were keen Nonconformists and did most of the chapel funerals, while Joe Rickard junior, another carpenter, usually did the parish church funerals. William's sober demeanour and religious associations made him an ideal choice for village constable, a thankless task, which he fulfilled so conscientiously that he always slept with his truncheon at the side of his bed. Until her death in 1920, William's wife, Emily, ran a little draper's shop in their front room. Her father, Reuben Honor, had been the village tailor, and she was skilled at sewing. Many younger women in the village went to her to learn

102: Frank Rickard (1895-1969)

215

dressmaking, after which they tended to buy the materials, trimmings, cottons, buttons, etc., which she sold.

Very small businesses were not dignified by an entry in Kelly's Directory, but they could be a great convenience for villagers, and a useful addition to the family income, as Connie Bignell recalled:

My mother made shirts for a lot of the villagers. She charged 8d each! She worked from morning to night. She had a sewing machine just inside the front door, and every time you went into the house, there was this machine going. I had to deliver the shirts, and when cotton went up she said, "They'll have to go up". And I was so upset that I'd got to tell people that they'd be 10d!

Various people had little shops tucked away in their houses, but they weren't shops as we know them: just a shelf or two in one of the rooms. The Jarrotts, who lived at the far end of Fleet's Row ran a little shop from their front room. They sold sweets, treacle, cheese and things like that. People took along a pudding basin and had "a penn'orth o' treacle". If their daughter, Maggie, was selling sweets and couldn't get the weight exactly right she would bite one in two, add one half to the scales and put the other half back in the jar!

LIFE BETWEEN THE WARS

Overall, at the end of World War One, Wingrave was still a 19th century village. But change was on the horizon in the unlikely form of the bicycle. For the personal mobility which the bicycle provided marked the beginning of a new era. Throughout the early 1900's bicycles were increasingly seen in Wingrave, but it was some years before they became commonplace: many people just couldn't afford them. During the Great War, and for some years after, there were no buses, and Horace Bignell push-biked into Aylesbury each day, at first to the Grammar School, and later to Webster and Cannon, with whom he served his apprenticeship. He insisted that he had to thank his father's membership of the Temperance Movement for the possession of a bicycle.

It was probably the war and the increasing use of push-bikes around the village that got villagers used to the idea of travelling outside the parish. By the end of World War One, George Paine had acquired a horse-drawn waggonette and would take people down to Marston Gate station. 'Old Langle' still crossed the Marston Road by a ford, and in winter it still regularly flooded. "As we approached the flood, Georgie would cry out in sepulchral tones, 'We shall never get through', but somehow we always did". George Ellis also had a waggonette in which he would take a few people to Aylesbury. From a distance the passengers in these waggonettes looked like a flock of huge black crows, for the going-out attire of adults was almost always black from head to foot. People said that black was handy for funerals!

It was the Great War which introduced a large portion of the male population to motorised transport: vans, cars and motor bikes. This, and the growing enthusiasm for push-biking, was bound to persuade someone to open a business catering for "these new-fangled thingumajigs", and it soon did. In 1919 two Wingrave cousins, Bert and Charlie Rickard, both of whom had been apprentices in the motor industry, and had wartime experience of vehicles, established separate "garages" almost facing one another in Nup End, despite the fact that Nup End Lane was (and is) a dead end, the village was half a mile off the main road, and had a declining population of 700 inhabitants, most of whom did not possess even a push-bike.

Bert's 'garage' was the cottage known as Dimmocks (now called Dean Leys) in

Nup End where his sister Alice had been running a grocery shop. At the end of the Great War, she married Harry Coleman and transferred her business to Winslow Road where it was later run by her daughter May Banks (and where it still trades), and Bert moved into Dean Leys with his car hire, cycle and car repair business. A little later the old wheelwright and carpenter's shop on the Green became vacant. He moved there and it became "Rickard's Motor and Cycle Works". Of course, the villagers followed these changes with their usual deep interest, but what really excited everyone was Bert's acquisition of two small motor buses. These catered for people who were too frail, or genteel, or lazy, or nervous to use a push-bike, and they really boosted shopping expeditions to Aylesbury and Leighton. By 1924 there was another bus service, running double-deckers with open tops, between Leighton and Aylesbury. It picked up passengers on the main road, but never came into the village, and so was no competition for the Rickard buses. By 1931 Bert's service was so popular that it went to Leighton twice on a

103: Charlie Rickard (1894 – 1955)

Tuesday, and to Aylesbury three times on a Wednesday and eight times on a Saturday, which were all market days. In 1934, when he sold out to the Eastern National Bus Company, it was his proud boast, "We never missed a service in 12 years".

In the meantime, due to injuries received in two road accidents, Charlie had to close his garages. He converted the Wingrave premises into a grocery and greengrocery shop run by his wife, and a fish and chip shop which he ran.

104: Bert Rickard's bus parked outside the Rose and Crown in the early Thirties. Bert is on the far right.

Recollections: Charlie Rickard - based on information from Douglas Rickard

Charlie was born in Wingrave in 1894. In 1909 his father apprenticed him for four years to Leonard Henry London of Linslade, a motor and cycle manufacturer. He served in World War One as a despatch rider. After demobilisation he returned to Wingrave, and established a garage in Wendover, and a workshop in a brick out-house in front of his house in Nup End, which he at first called Laurels Motor Cycle Works, and then just The Garage. Charlie wanted to instal a petrol pump, but the competition would have upset his cousin Bert Rickard, so as a compromise he obtained a licence permitting him to store up to 24 gallons of petrol in two-gallon containers. To accommodate this safely he had to dig a large hole in the garden and line it with bricks. Charlie's main business was repairing bikes, cars and motor bikes. He could build up a new wheel from a rim and a handful of spokes.

Then Charlie had two accidents. In the first he was thrown through the windscreen of his Model T, and in the second an alsatian caused him to crash his motor cycle. After this his left arm was much shorter than his right. As he could not drive a car or do some of the repair work on the vehicles, he decided to give up the garage. So, in 1925, he converted it into two parts: a grocery and greengrocery known as Nup End Stores which was run by his wife, Nellie, and a fish and chip shop, (in which Charlie later installed electric burners), where he fried on Wednesdays and Saturdays. They also sold paraffin, which at that time was essential for both lighting and cooking. Charlie had a horse and cart. The cart was rather like a large box with wheels and shafts, and a flat top on which you could carry things like cherry skips. Twice weekly Charlie drove to Leighton Buzzard and picked up fruit, vegetables, groceries, flowering plants and fish from a Luton trader in Market Square, not only to restock the shop and prepare for the evening's fry-up, but also to sell on his round. This took him to Slapton, Billington, Cheddington, Horton and Long Marston selling door to door. As the driver of the cart, Charlie sat in front of the box with no protection from the weather, and in winter the 'round' must have been a pretty arduous job. But Charlie was well-suited to it. He usually wore a cap tilted at a jaunty angle over his left eye, and his customers appreciated his cheerful personality.

Judging how much fish to buy was a considerable problem. Small refrigerators were almost unknown in Britain in the 1930's, and if the fish "went off" in a hot spell there was only one thing to do: dig a hole and bury it! Fortunately, on Wednesdays, the Luton trader had a stall at Aylesbury and would call in with fresh supplies. At that time it was taken for granted that children "lent a hand" when there were jobs to be done, so Douglas (their only child) would deliver paraffin and groceries, fetch water from the well and from the village pond if necessary, and if extra supplies were needed in midweek would cycle to Leighton after school on a push-bike with a carrier in front. After that there were always vast quantities of potatoes to be peeled! Early in World War Two the fish and chip shop closed due to the shortage of cooking oil (Charlie refused to use dripping for frying), but Nellie Rickard kept Nup End Stores going during the war, and for twenty years after Charlie's death in 1955. In addition to his business interests, Charlie was a member of the Parish Council, and the Wingrave branch of the British Legion. He also served as a Parish Constable.

105. May Banks in the village shop which she inherited from her mother, Alice Coleman. As late as 1974, bacon would still be sliced to your specified thickness.

106. Dimmocks (now Dean Leys), one of the oldest buildings in the village, is where Bert Rickard opened his first 'garage' after World War One.

106a. The only known picture of Bert Rickard's first bus, parked on his new site opposite the Rose and Crown circa 1923.

Visiting Tradesmen

The development of shopping excursions to Aylesbury and Leighton must have been viewed with some concern by the shopkeepers and tradesmen of Wingrave, for the population of the parish had fallen from 926 in 1891 to 632 in 1931, and they were also facing considerable competition from visiting tradesmen. They came by horse and cart. Some had a distinctive call, some rang bells and some just knocked on the doors of their regulars. The butchers included Grace and Bailey from Leighton, Stevens and Bates from Aylesbury, and Fred Ashpool, who came up from Rowsham. You went out to the cart, asked for what you wanted and it was cut up on the spot. Tring Co-op came round every week, and Aylesbury grocers such as Channels sent their representatives:

Every Monday their Mr Smith would visit Wingrave. My grandmother, Ann Woodward Jones the postmistress, would have her list all ready. He would sit down with his order book, she would tell him what she wanted, and it would all be delivered on the Wednesday.

Albert White came from Wing with fruit and vegetables, and Tommy Humphrey of Aston Abbotts delivered his "very nice bread" to Wingrave and Rowsham, at first by horse and cart, and later by van. Of course, Teddy Griffin was also delivering freshly-baked bread from his bakery in Nup End, but he only delivered on Monday, Wednesday and Saturday, so there was room for some competition. Certainly Teddy didn't lack custom. Like many bakers at that time, once the bread was out of the oven, he would bake anyone's cake for a few pennies. He would also cook the Sunday joint or the Xmas dinner. For the many folk with no oven it was a much-appreciated service.

Other visiting tradesmen brought cakes, meat, paraffin, drapery, milk and even fish. At this time Charlie Horwood from Church Farm was one of the local milkmen. He came round in a pony and trap with the milk in a big churn. Later he acquired an Austin Seven, and pushed back the passenger seat to accommodate the churn. The measures were hooked onto a bar on the inside of the churn, and with them he measured the milk straight into the jugs which were either brought to the door, or left in some convenient place. "Unhygienic?" mused one former customer. "Well, we survived". Several coalmen called from Marston Gate station, and the Wilstone and Leighton wharves. A talisman (selling goods on credit, to be repaid by instalments) visited the village, supplying such things as clothing, shoes, household goods, knitting and mending wools and needles. Mr Piper from Wing had a different system, which suited people who didn't like having goods on credit. He came round weekly, and each time he called you paid him what you could afford. When you had saved enough money, you could put in an order. Doreen Honor remembers her mother ordering the black stockings which were worn by most of the older ladies, who always kept a special pair on one side just for Sundays. He also sold hats, boots and shoes, dresses and dress material for those who preferred to make their own. Sometimes Doreen and her mother walked the three miles to Wing to choose something at his shop. A rag 'n bone man came from Leighton on a carrier bike, with large sacks dangling from the front of it. He also bought rabbit skins. Rabbits in their fur were often hawked from door to door by men who arrived with them tied to the handlebars of their bikes. At sixpence a time, rabbit was popular, for it made a good, cheap meal, and it was even cheaper if you sold the skins, as most people did.

King of the Road

Despite the commencement of motor bus services the bicycle was still king of the road. It provided transport precisely when its owner demanded it, it operated from home to destination, and it was cheap. You could get a new bike for £5 or so, and a second-hand one for much less. There were virtually no running costs, and at 10d for the return bus journey from Wingrave to Aylesbury, you recouped your £5 within six months. As the years went by, more and more people acquired one. The effects were considerable. No longer was the labourer tied to a job on the local farms, or the female domestic to a few of the more prosperous village families. Everyone now had a much wider selection of jobs of the sort that could only exist in a market town. The effect was especially marked on school leavers. In the Twenties and Thirties only half as many of Wingrave's lads went into agriculture as in the 19th century, while the number choosing building trebled. This was not surprising for at this time council contracts alone kept building firms very busy. The Wingrave firm[12] of Fleet and Roberts was employing about 130 men in the 1930's, though obviously the majority of them came from outside Wingrave. A small but significant number of lads entered factories, while a third of them entered a wide variety of jobs ranging from the delivery of milk to clerking in the offices of the County Council. Over 40% of the girls went into domestic service, more than double the numbers of 1891, much of the additional employment being in the surrounding towns. Ethel Perkins has fond memories of those times:

When I left school at 14, I did housework. I biked to Aylesbury to Youngs, who had the toy shop in Aylesbury. I had to set off in the dark on winter mornings, but sometimes I rode with Fred Pargeter, who worked at the County Offices. The Youngs treated me as one of their own. I was over ten years with them, and their daughter still keeps in touch.

Straw-plaiting was finished, but nearly a quarter of the girls found themselves factory jobs. Some of these were at a toy factory in the Hemel/Berkhamsted area, which was reached by cycling to Marston Gate and catching a train. About 10% of the girls found work as telephonists, clerks, shop assistants, etc: jobs which would never have come their way in the past. Of the remainder, over 20% remained at home, helping with the housework. By the 1930's the pushbike was the main form of transport for the daily journey to work: "One would see as many as twenty villagers come biking home to the village at the same time."

With so many people selling at the door, making shopping excursions to Aylesbury, and travelling to work one might suppose that the roads were crowded with traffic. In fact, by today's standards they were very quiet. There was so little traffic that farmers could drive their cattle even along the main roads. Will Fleet used to keep a few cattle in a rented field at the bottom of London Hill, just for a hobby. He "fatted them up", and then sold them. Every Sunday he would go down with his stick to look them over. It was George White, who looked after them, and eventually he would announce, "Them there cattle is ready to go, Master", and they would be driven to market through the village, down Handpost Hill, and along the main road to Aylesbury. This continued until 1939, when the government insisted that the field was converted to arable, as part of the war effort. Even as late as the mid-seventies the occasional flock of sheep would be driven through the village.

Despite the competition and the continuing fall in population, Wingrave's businesses continued to survive. In 1935, as figure 27 shows, the parish still had five pubs, three milkmen, two carpenters/undertakers, two butchers, two grocers, two builders, two boot and shoe repairers, a boot-maker, a baker, a brewer, a garage, a post office, a blacksmith, an electrical engineer, plus dressmakers, several amateur hair-dressers, sweeps, etc.. It looks very impressive, but sadly too many were living on borrowed time. Many proprietors were at, or nearing, retirement and, when they retired, their businesses usually retired with them, and were not replaced.

PHOENIX RISING?

By the end of the 20th century, five interacting factors (underlined below) had radically altered the pattern of 1935, destroying most traditional businesses, but creating a market for so many new businesses that, in 1998, they exceeded the total for 1935. The prime factor was probably the mobility conferred by <u>the wider ownership of motor vehicles</u>. By 1991, 86% of the households in the parish owned a car, and over 50% owned two or more cars.[13] This meant that, at last, villagers had a choice of shopping venue, which was independent of the availability and timing of public transport. This allowed factors two and three to operate: <u>the increased employment of women</u> (in 1991, 57% of Wingrave's women were "economically active"), which reinforced <u>a desire for one-stop, self-service shopping with massive choice and competitive pricing</u>. The fourth factor was a change in the <u>socio-economic balance</u> of the parish. By 1991, 59% of Wingrave's employables were classed as managerial, administrative, professional and technical, and thus had the higher incomes and increased purchasing power that these imply. Finally, although Wingrave's population has doubled since 1935, it is (on its own) <u>too small a market</u> for most businesses to operate profitably in.

Significantly, the three main survivors from 1935 have all managed to increase their markets. The one remaining pub now has a restaurant. The general stores is even more general, having added the post office, a video library, a dry cleaning agency and an off-licence to its attractions. The garage benefits from the massive increase in car ownership, but has added vehicle testing, and the sale of bottled gas to its services. A further 36 enterprises are based in the parish, while another eighteen, operating from outside the parish, see Wingrave as part of their market.[14] In total, these enterprises cover Building and Maintenance [14], Personal [9], Professional [9], Domestic [8], Garden [7], Accommodation and Food [7], and Car Servicing, Hire and Driving [3].[15]

Two striking facts emerge. Firstly, traditional enterprises like undertaking, blacksmithing, boot and shoe-making and repairing, butchery, and baking have disappeared from Wingrave. They cannot operate profitably if their market is limited to one or two villages. Subject to this caveat, higher incomes (and thus higher living standards) and technical innovation have increased demand and created new demands: landscape design, interior design, chiropody, office services, garden machinery, kennels and catteries, and mobile horse-shoeing services, for example. And how about unisex hairdressing for widening the market? Mention that sixty years ago, and it would certainly have generated some pithy comments in the taprooms of the local inns.

107. Bert Rickard's Motor and Cycle Works facing the Green.

Fig. 27: Parish of Wingrave with Rowsham
Termination of Businesses

Proprietor 1935	Trade/Occupation	Business Terminated
Thomas Gurney	Brewer/maltster	d. 1934: business to J. W. Gurney. Closed 1939
Joseph Rickard	Carpenter/undertaker	d.1938: business closed. Carpentry absorbed by Bates & Rickard, and Fleet & Roberts
Fred. Kent	Boot repairer	No dates for arrival or departure. Gone by 1939
Phil. Rickard	Butcher	Retired by 1939. Business closed. Died 1950
Bert Pidgley	Boot/shoe repairer	d. 1945. Business closed.
Frank Rogers	Boot/shoe maker	d. 1951, aged 86. Business closed.
'Teddy' Griffin	Baker	Business closed 1955 on death of wife.
Thos. Woodruff	Blacksmith	d.1957, aged 82. Business closed.
Henry Badrick	Publican	Old Red Lion demolished 1958.
George Young	Publican	Carpenters' Arms closed 1959.
Arthur Rickard	Builder	d. 1957. Business to sons Will and Joe: closed for financial reasons.
Wm. Bates and Vic. Rickard	Electrical engineers, carpentry, etc.	Partnership dissolved 1939, when Vic joined Fleet & Roberts (see below). Bates retired 1970, when business closed.
Mary A. Gibbs & Hilda Gibbs	Gen. Store and Post Office	Hilda retired and business closed 1971. Post Office continued on new site.
Wm. Gurney	Carpenter/undertaker	d.1949. Business to son-in-law Frank Rickard, on whose death (1969) it closed.
Fleet & Roberts	Builders	Creditors petitioned: firm wound up 1969.
Arthur Stone	Butcher	Business acquired by Fred Timms, and closed on his death in 1973.
Charlie & Nellie Rickard	Fish 'n chips, green-grocery and grocery	Frying ceased due to wartime shortages, and Charlie's death (1955). Shop closed on Nellie's death (1975): reverted to private house.
Almer Hart	Publican	The Anchor closed 1984: became a private house.
Edwin Turrell	Publican	The Bell closed 1990: demolished for housing.
Fred Bignell	Boot/shoe repairer	d. 1981: closed business earlier due to illness.
Vic Chapman	Dairy farmer	Milk round closed on retirement.
George Payne	Milkman	d. 1941. New occupier of Old Dairy did not milk.
Thos. Horwood	Dairy farmer	d. 1950. Son (Chas.) continued but sold farm 1965.
Albert Rickard	Car hirer, cycle and car repairer	d.1965. Son (Don) continued but died 1985. Business sold and continues.
Alice Coleman	Grocery, newspapers, cigarettes, sweets, etc.	d.1965. Daughter, May, replaced her. Business sold and continues.
Frank Gibbs	Tailor	Died in retirement 1948. Business ceased.
Len. Rickard	Insurance agent	d. 1972, aged 72.
Thos. Rickard	Insurance agent	d. 1953, aged 64.
Geo. Rickard	Matmaker	d. 1951, aged 55.
Fred. Rickard	Corn Merchant	d.1947, aged 77.

Chapter Eighteen

Home Life in Days Gone By

The parish of Wingrave with Rowsham had no electricity until 1927, no mains water until 1940, no mains sewage disposal until 1952, and no gas until 1988. Of course, not everyone had these services installed immediately they became available. The owner of each property had to pay for the installation of electricity and, if the property was let out, the tenant had the rent increased to cover the cost. For instance, for an extra 6d per week on the rent, the landlord might be prepared to have three lights installed. Not everyone could afford that. And most people could not afford electrical equipment. For that matter, most of today's appliances had either not been invented, or were high-priced luxuries only affordable by a minority. Consequently, for most families, housework in the 1920's and 1930's differed little from housework in the 19th century. There are still villagers who can clearly remember the Twenties and Thirties, and on one thing they are completely agreed. Housework in those days was a full-time occupation, and a very strenuous one.

WATER SHORTAGES

Water was a bit of a luxury. We had to fetch our water from a pump a good hundred yards away, and as there were no deep springs in Wingrave, it tended to dry up if there was a drought.

Many villagers shared Ron Bignell's problem. As late as 1936, when ten more council houses were built near the allotments in Winslow Road, the District Council took it for granted that all fourteen houses would use the well in 'Ratter' Gurney's garden, which had previously served the original four. Of course, in summer the well regularly dried up and each family had to make do with just two buckets a day from Tom Gibbs' horse-drawn water cart. A housewife remembered,

We had to save water for the weekly bath, which we had in front of the fire. Then we re-used the bath water for the laundry, and saved a pailful from that for cleaning the floor.

At about the same time, when Frank Hows deepened the well at Straws Hadley Farm, the well at nearby Chapel Row promptly went dry for a time. Fortunately, the local cottagers could get their washing water from the moat at the bottom of the Recreation Ground, though that was fifty yards away. For drinking water they had to go to the well at Waterloo Farm, a round trip of nearly half a mile. As late as 1948, there were still problems with the water supply, as Nancy Horsfield recalled:

In 1945 we felt extremely lucky to be offered the tenancy of a cottage directly behind the Mill House.[1] However, there was only one external door, and water had to be hauled up from the well and carried in pails through the living room to the kitchen. In the extremely dry summer of 1948, the well – which served all four cottages – ran dry. Mr Johnson, who lived in the Mill House, said that we could use the well in his garden: "Very pure water," he said. We were not so sure, for people told us that dead sheep had been put down that well in the past. So we contacted the Sanitary Inspectors in

Aylesbury. They tested the water and pronounced it "very definitely unsafe". Fortunately, the Council was building the houses opposite Twelve Leys, and the workmen had installed a standpipe. They let us use that, though it meant an even longer walk with pails of water. Not long after, we were connected to the mains, and we had a tap: it seemed like heaven!

BATH NIGHT

To get a bath demanded so much effort that in most homes it was at best a weekly ritual. Even then it meant carrying the water from the well or the water butt to the kitchen 'copper', stoking the fire, transferring the water into a portable galvanised bath, carrying away the dirty water for disposal in the garden or the nearest ditch, and cleaning the copper and the stoke hole. It is not surprising that one lot of water usually had to serve several people and sometimes the whole family: too bad if you were the seventh! Not all households had a copper in the kitchen, and that meant heating lots of kettles and pans of water on the kitchen range or the living room fire. With the expense of the fuel and the soap, and all the bother, some poorer families might observe bath night less regularly. Such families were easily identified: they not only dressed poorly, they smelt poorly as well.

THE WEEKLY WASH

Not every housewife followed precisely the routine described below. Some wives didn't even possess a mangle, and would pay a neighbour for the use of hers: old Sophia King charged a penny for mangling dry sheets. Much depended on upbringing. "I lived with my grandparents for a while," explained one Wingrave wife. "She taught me the 'North Country' way of washing." The fact that washing was hung out to dry in full view of the neighbours persuaded many women that their washing must be whiter than white. For a farm labourer's wife that meant a lot of extra hard work, for in pre-World-War-Two days the dirty wash was often dirtier than today's: with more manual labour, there were more dirty jobs; and clothes were worn longer! "Sunday was the day for a clean change," recalled one octogenarian.

The weekly clothes wash was a long exhausting affair which occupied the whole of Monday and most of Tuesday. Indeed, for many families washday began on Sunday, when water would have to be bucketed from the nearest butt, moat, stream, pond or pump to fill the copper in the kitchen, and whatever baths, bowls and tubs could be made use of. The copper was the centrepiece of the weekly wash. It was like a huge steel pudding basin, about three feet in diameter, set into a brick surround in the corner of the kitchen, and with space for a fire beneath it to provide the hot water that was vital for a successful washday. On Monday mornings some wives would be up at 6 a.m. to get the copper fire going. It was started with paper and sticks, with coal on top. But once it was going anything that would burn was put up the copper hole: wood, dried cabbage stems, coal dust, in fact anything that would get the water hot.

When the water was boiling, some was bucketed out, and carried across the kitchen, down the yard and into the wash-house, where it was poured into the dolly tub, and primed with shredded soap. The really dirty wash was dumped into the tub, pushed down into the water with the boiler stick, and left to get a good soak. After that it was ready to be dollied. This was done with a tool called a 'dolly' or a 'peggy-legs'. The old-fashioned ones looked like a milking stool with very broad legs and a broom handle rising from the seat. Grasping the handle, one lifted the dolly clear of the water, and then banged it down again and again, followed by a rotational movement from left to right and back several times. This alternate beating and stirring was intended to loosen the dirt and extract it from the pores of the material. Next, the dolly tub was pushed under the mangle, so that the contents could more easily be put through the nine inch diameter wooden rollers to get rid of surplus water, most of which (hopefully!) drained back into the tub. The sodden pile was then carried back to the kitchen and bit by bit dumped into a shallow sink, half-full of hot water from the copper. If the cottage did not have a sink, the family's galvanised bath would be used instead. Heavily soiled items were then rubbed by hand, using large bars of green soap and lots of elbow grease. For really stubborn dirt (the cuffs and collars of shirts, for example) a scrubbing board was used. This was stood in the sink at an angle of $45°$, and the dirty clothes held in place with one hand while they were scrubbed with a large scrubbing brush held in the other hand. The 'whites' were transferred to the copper, which had been topped up with water, plus a measure of washing soda, and a good helping of grated soap. With the wooden lid in place, the contents were left to come to the boil, and bubble for twenty minutes or so. Meanwhile, the coloureds were rinsed in clean water and mangled, ready to peg out on the washing line.

Everything was then hauled out of the copper with the aid of the boiler stick and heaped onto a slatted frame placed over the top of the copper, so that as much hot water as possible could drip back into it. This created space for a fresh load of washing without starting the water heating from scratch. It took a good deal of muscle to fish out and manoeuvre large items like sheets saturated with boiling water, especially with the hot steam billowing up into one's face. In fact, in cold weather such clouds of steam were produced that one could hardly see across the kitchen, and if the walls were of painted brick the steam condensed on them until they ran with beads of moisture, while the floor soon swam with the drips and splashes from the carrying of buckets and wet washing. It was damp, dangerous and debilitating. Having dripped for a time, the washing was transferred from the drainer on the top of the copper to the sink for swilling. As these were 'whites' they would be swilled a second time in water to which Reckitts' Blue had been added to ensure that they really did look white. And some items were kept aside for starching. Connie Bignell confessed:

It was alright when it was Robin's Starch, but not so easy if it was Reckitts', as that was all nobbly and a real job to mix. Making the starch included stirring the little 'blue' bag into it for a minute. Sometimes I left it in a little too long, and made it too blue, and mother wasn't too pleased.

Everything was again wrung out and items without buttons were carried to the wash-house for mangling. Mangling large items like sheets was strenuous work and really needed two people: one to turn the mangle, and one to ensure that the sheet was fed in evenly, and that fingers were not fed in at all! Next the wash was carried into the garden and pegged to the clothes' line. If the weather was fine, this was the time when the housewife could take a break and start getting the midday meal ready! If, however, it was showery weather she would keep one eye on the sky and one ear cocked for a neighbour's call. "Mrs Jones! Rain!" Then there was an almighty scramble to get every-thing under cover before it got soaked. That was when accidents could happen. A small item dropped on the ground could easily be rinsed clean, but a sheet dragging in the mud was sometimes 'the last straw'. A showery day was really hard work, while if the rain 'set in' most of the drying would have to take place on clothes horses placed in front of the living room fire. The ideal was to get the wash dry by the early afternoon so that it could be smoothed by being put through the mangle once more. This was usually the final process for items like sheets, but it was not the end of the Monday marathon. Many items still had to be ironed. There was also the not-so-little matter of clearing up.

The water remaining in the copper still had to be ladled out and disposed of either on the garden or in the nearest ditch. The copper hole had to be cleaned out. The walls of the kitchen might have to be wiped down, and the floor certainly had to be scrubbed. And if it was a rainy day, then the clothes horses needed periodical attention, removing items that were dry, and 'turning' items that were not.

Tuesday was the day reserved for 'airing' and ironing. Hopefully, the weather would be fine and warm so that items that needed airing could be pegged out on the clothes line once more. If not, out would come the clothes horses again around the fire. Ironing was done with flat irons which were usually heated by standing them on a bracket which was hooked over the front bars of a bright coal fire. The iron had to be just the right heat: not too cool, or the result would be poor; and not too hot for fear of scorch marks. Before use it was rubbed with a cloth to make sure that it hadn't been sooted by the fire. In addition, to get a good finish, especially after starching, the articles being ironed must not be too dry, and might need a sprinkling with water. What constituted 'the right heat', 'not too dry' or 'a good finish' were matters of judgement and experience and many housewives took a pride in the whiteness and crispness of their husband's shirts, and their daughters' dresses. To be content with the state of one's laundry was a great comfort, but a comfort hard come by.

Finally, for economy was the order of the day, came the darning and patching; and the folding and putting away.

SPRING CLEANING

Perhaps it was the open fires, which sometimes 'smoked', or the smogs which they created. Perhaps it was the haze from the oil lamps, and the oil stoves and the lack of extractor fans. Perhaps, in the days before tar was used to bind and waterproof the surface, it was the dust from the roads, for then they were finished with flint chippings consolidated by a steam roller, producing a surface that held the dirt, which blew into the homes via the ill-fitting wooden doors and windows. Whatever the reason, houses seemed to get more grimy in those days, and spring cleaning was a MUST. So, once every year, each room in turn was stripped of all its furniture and coverings. Every inch of floor was scrubbed or polished. Every bit of paintwork was washed down. Every ornament was thoroughly washed. Carpets and rugs were taken out into the garden, hung over the washing line, and beaten with a bamboo carpet beater. Sometimes the children were allowed to do this, and had a great time seeing who could make the most dust. They were the only ones to enjoy it. As Daphne Rickard pointed out, "No wonder that men dreaded spring cleaning , and women were worn out after it!"

THE JOBS THAT HAVE VANISHED

Many of the jobs that burdened the housewife earlier in the century have now disappeared. Before myxomatosis arrived, rabbits were a very popular dish, for they were plentiful and cheap. However, bought at the door, they were 'in the fur', and it was the housewife who had to gut, skin and joint them. Even the head was usually added to the stew, which meant removing the eyes!

Many families kept a pig and a few chickens, especially after allotments provided villagers with more land. For example, in 1910 when Lord Rosebery sold off the Rothschild cottages in Wingrave, George Bignell bought (for £200!) a four-bedroomed house just past the chapel in Nup End. It included half an acre of garden, and his son, Horace, remembered:

We had chickens and sometimes two sties of pigs, and we even grew some corn. The hens were kept at one end of the garden for most of the year, but before the winter we moved the wire netting so that they kept the weeds down in the garden and also manured it. A steam engine used to come up to the Bell every year to thrash. So everybody who had a little bit of thrashing took their corn up there, and came back with the grain, which was good feed for the animals.

Keeping animals created a lot of chores. The chickens were not too demanding. The husband might dig the run occasionally, trim the wing feathers, and put fresh straw in the nesting boxes, but it was most probably the wife who fed and watered them, collected the eggs, and preserved any surplus in waterglass in a large earthenware crock. Eventually, poor layers would be culled. The husband usually did the killing, or at least tried to, as Nancy Horsfield explained:

Benny Underwood still laughs at the time when Frank tried to kill a hen, which refused to die. To get some assistance, he had to walk up the road to Ben's house with the poor bird squawking under his arm.

Once the bird had been killed, the corpse was usually drawn and plucked by the wife.

All this paled into insignificance compared with the work of keeping a pig. Its sty had to be mucked out and its bed of straw replaced regularly. Pigs are voracious feeders, and although the vegetable waste from the kitchen was part of its diet, many extra hours of work had to be put in on the allotment and in the garden to produce the potatoes and barley, which were its staple food. Even the children had to work at the business of fattening the pig, and were sent out with buckets and baskets to collect windfall apples, acorns, grasses, dandelions and snails: anything to tempt its appetite. When the pig was ready for killing, it was usually despatched by Phil Rickard or one of the village pig stickers, who first cut the animal's throat, so as to bleed the carcase dry, while one of the family collected a jugful of blood, which was the essential ingredient of black puddings. Not everyone liked to see the pig killed, but it was the pig's 'screaming' as it was man-handled out of its sty to the place of execution that upset most people. "It frightened me to death," confessed Doreen Honor, whose uncle's pigs were killed only twenty or thirty yards from her home.

The pig sticker knew the anatomy of a pig. His cuts were quick and decisive, and when the carcase was opened, the multitude of organs (heart, liver, lights and tongue), not to mention the unmentionables, were all skilfully separated and removed. The carcase was then cut into halves, and the hams, gammons, flitches, spare ribs, haslets, griskins and rearings were cut. It was often the man of the house who "salted down" the hams and the flitches, in the large 'lead', which was reserved for just that job. However, it would most likely be the housewife who poured brine over them for the next few days, and she would certainly have to cope with the multitude of other jobs. There were few households that could consume all the offal from a pig before it went 'off', and much was disposed of to relatives and friends, especially those who had shared out the surplus from their own pig killing. Making up the portions took time, but a plate of offal, nicely arranged, with a cloth to keep the flies off, was always well received, and kept the exchanges going. That was only the beginning, for there were the tripes and 'chitterlings' to clean, and the pig's bladder to drain and blow out to its full size ready for storing the lard. And there were meat pies to be made, and faggots, and lard, and brawn, and pig's pudding, and sausages . . . . Connie Bignell's aunt and uncle kept pigs, "and when they killed one they had half and we had half, and we'd always got plenty of bacon". What DID Connie's parents do to deserve such a gift?

Without freezers it was very difficult to preserve surpluses, but people did their best. Fruit was jammed and bottled. Wine was made. Apples and pears and potatoes were stored in outhouses. One perennial task as spring approached was 'chipping' the potatoes, i.e. knocking off the sprouts to stop them from going soft. Some people even bought milk and made their own butter, "and very good it was".

Before electricity reached the parish, lighting was by lamp, candle and lantern. Lamps were for general illumination. However, there were lamps, and there were Aladdin Lamps, which gave a much better light. "An Aladdin lamp was something to treasure." Lanterns were for outdoor use, and you lit your way to bed with a candle or nightlight. Unfortunately, creating light created work. The lamps had to be cleaned, filled with paraffin, the wicks trimmed and occasionally replaced, and the glass chimneys polished regularly with newspaper with a spot of paraffin on it, for however carefully you adjusted the wick, they always got smoky.

If there was a coal-fired range in the kitchen this would provide the main cooking facility, but in some houses most or all of the cooking had to be done on the living room fire. This was why it was so important that wood be already chopped for starting the fire next morning, so that Dad could quickly get the kettle boiling and make the tea. Ron Bignell recalled:

The big oval iron pot on the fire might have clangers (bacon dumplings) in it, or a steak and kidney pud for the main course, with Brussels, cauliflower and potatoes (the greens in one net, the potatoes in another) to go with it, and for afters a roly-poly swathed in a cloth, all in the same pot. Provided you got the timing right and kept the water bubbling gently, they all tasted good. And we must never forget the swimmer: an odd bit of dough put in the pot for one of the kids. It was eaten with sugar on it. I could eat one now!

Cooking facilities varied from household to household. One lady told us that her first oven was a biscuit tin placed on top of an oil stove with the lid used as the oven door. Later, some of the more affluent villagers installed the paraffin-fired Valor Perfection, the very latest in cooking technology. Anyone who had a coal-fired range in the kitchen, *and* a fire in the living room was regarded as well off. Even then the rest of the house was virtually unheated. Joyce Sinnott remembered:

In winter the bedrooms were icy. At night one left the warm living room and ran upstairs as quickly as possible, and got into bed as fast as one could, for the only heating in most people's bedrooms came from the stone hot water bottle which had been put between the sheets earlier in the evening. This warmed the bed, but on a winter's morning the room was so cold that sometimes one had to break the ice which had formed in the jug on the wash-hand stand.

SHARING THE CHORES

For much of the 19th century the children of Wingrave's agricultural labourers had to contribute to the family income. At an early age they would do this indirectly by relieving their mother of some of the household chores, so that (hopefully) she could devote time to the straw plaiting which could make such a vital difference to the weekly budget. The children might be sent out to scour the hedges for dead stick, furze and briars for firing. They would have to fetch the drinking water from the well both morning and evening, which was a time-consuming job even if there was a well near the house, but a 'rotten old job' in bad weather, or in a drought when it had to be carried from the nearest pond or moat. Even worse was the washday water. So much was needed, and it not only had to be carried to the cottage, but also disposed of in the nearest ditch afterwards. There were always errands to be run: to the baker's for bread; to the shop with half a score of 'pearl' to pay off last week's owings; to Granny Smith to find out if Gramp was better, "and Mam says, 'Can she borrow a cup of sugar?' "; to old Uncle Harley with the rabbit skins. It seemed endless. The children would also be looked to for such things as minding the baby, feeding and dressing the younger ones, fetching vegetables from the garden, preparing them for the pot, making beds, sweeping floors, splitting straws, clipping plait, collecting manure from the roads . . . . Then there were the seasonal jobs like sorting out the pig potatoes, gleaning after the harvest, gathering fruit from the hedgerows, combing the hedgerows for snails (a delicacy for the pig), finding rushes for candles . . . . Parents expected these things as of right, and pleases and thank-yous would be in short supply. Indeed, if a girl baulked at changing a dirty nappy, or emptying the chamber pots she would be berated as a "fussy little madam" or "a proud little hussey" and told to "get on with it". Time saved on household jobs helped maximise the housewife's income from straw-plaiting, and this was the first priority.

As the children grew older they would contribute directly to the family income, the girls by plaiting, and most of the lads by working for one of the local farmers: crow-scaring and odd-jobbing. Just how much leisure they would get would vary from family to family but, if Hilda Roberts is to be believed, it wasn't much.[2]

> When I was a girl, why then
> It was work, work, work, from morn till night
> And next morning begin again.

> I learned to plait when I was six,
> There were nine in front of me,
> And Father worked on a farm all day
> For the sum of one and three.

> And when he finished his daily round
> He picked up his straws as well
> And we all used to plait by a dim rushlight
> And he'd always a tale to tell.

Even so, in most households there would be time for children to play. The list of jobs was not really endless, and there would be occasions when the younger children would be turned out of the crowded cottage if only for the parents "to get some peace". On a cold winter's evening, simple but boisterous games like 'tag', leapfrog, or hopscotch would keep the cold at bay. There would also be times when older children, in charge of younger siblings, would occupy them with games, amuse them with simple toys like a corn dolly, or pop across the road to the nearest farm, where there was usually something interesting to see.

The family life of agricultural labourers continued on this pattern with little real change until the Education Act of 1880 made full-time schooling compulsory for all children aged 5 to 9 years, while those of 10 to 12 years could leave only when they had achieved a specified standard of education. The census returns for the Parish of Wingrave with Rowsham emphasise the impact of the 1880 Act (Fig. 28). Subsequently, the minimum school leaving age was gradually raised: to 11 years in 1893; to 12 years in 1899; and to 14 years in 1918. This automatically made full-time employment illegal below the age of 14 years. Fortunately, as explained earlier, the economic tide was very slowly turning in favour of the labourer and, with the trend to smaller families, this often compensated for the loss of young children's earnings. In any case, it was only work during school hours which was prohibited, and this left time for children to help

108. *Ivy Dene, on the corner of Nup End and Winslow Road, was built in 1876 by Hannah de Rothschild as a combined house and shop (the three-windowed ground-floor part of the building). Under the Gibbs and later the Higgins the shop was a pork butcher's for many years, but when Tom and Minnie Rickard (nee Jones) moved in (in 1927) the shop became part of their living accommodation. They sold Ivy Dene in 1935 for £350.*

109. *This view of Hannah's Infant School (later the Church Room) illustrates the state of the village roads before they were tarred circa 1930.*

Fig 28: Parish of Wingrave with Rowsham:
Attendance of Children (5--9 years) at the Parochial School

Year	Total Children of 5 to 9 in Parish	No. Described as scholars	Scholars as % of total
1871	129	66	51%
1881	121	101	83%
1891	131	124	95%

in the home, or to get part-time work outside it. In the Twenties and Thirties children's hard-earned sixpences and shillings could still be important to larger families. In other cases, children were just keen to be working, especially with animals. Frank King thoroughly enjoyed the work that he was given at Church Farm.

We lived in the cottages opposite Church Farm. I used to get up just before seven and go over there in the mornings. I climbed over the wall where Coblers Wick is now, and where the houses are up that side there was a cowshed. The cows in their herd all had individual names: there was Old Curly, Tinker and her daughter Little Tinker, Beauty, Mack, Lazy, Ruby and so on, and they knew their names! When I was about nine, I was told, "It's about time you started milking". They gave me a bucket and a little three-legged stool, and I used to milk two cows before I went home to breakfast and school. You tucked your head into the cow's flank, stuck the bucket between your knees and it was not difficult, because cows didn't have such big udders as they have these days. In that time, if you had a cow that gave five gallons a day, that was an enormous amount. As soon as I came out of school in the afternoon I was back there, milking and foddering, and then Saturdays as well. I did anything that was going: chopping up mangolds or straw for fodder, for instance.

There were plenty of other lads who found time to work, and a ready market for their labour. And, of course, the Parochial School only operated on five days per week, so a full day's work could be done on Saturday. There was also a generous number of day and halfday closures, and the lengthy summer holidays usually coincided with the main harvest. When they did not, there were still complaints in the school log books of absentees said to be working on local farms, and of pupils withdrawn from school early to take refreshment to their father in the fields. Obviously, old habits die hard!

With the demise of straw-plaiting, it was not so easy for girls to get part-time work. The solution was to help with the household chores, either at home or with a relative. With cheaper food available, some households obviously felt that help in the house was worth the loss of a bit of income.

SOME ASPECTS OF HOME LIFE IN WINGRAVE 1900 – 1939

What sort of life you had depended on whether the breadwinner(s) of your family was a labourer, an artisan, an artisan with his own business, a shopkeeper, a farmer or the member of a profession. An artisan with his own business might well employ a live-in servant, whose contribution greatly improved the circumstances of the lady of the house. In 1914 Daisy Hill (later Higgins) came to Wingrave to work for the Fleets, and their three daughters at Windmill House.

There was all the work to be done by myself, up early in the mornings, light the kitchen fire, cook breakfast for the girls to get to school by 9, have my own breakfast, light the dining room fire, cook more breakfasts, then all the washing up and bedmaking. It was difficult to keep up with the tidying of the bedrooms, for it was a large house. At that time there were lamps to fill, and no hoovers or washing machines. However, I struggled on and stayed longer than I should have done because it was at Wingrave that I met my future husband.

The farmer, the property owner, and the member of a profession might well employ several servants, thus freeing the ladies of the house for a good deal of socialising. Phyllis Norman of Rowsham was fairly typical. Her home at Manor Farm had a walled garden sheltering peach and nectarine trees. There was an orchard and large green-houses producing flowers and luxuries like grapes. She enjoyed an active social life, playing hockey, tennis (on their own courts), and croquet, which were usually followed by some social event: a dance or a whist drive perhaps. Her friends were principally from the farming and land-owning families: 'the county set'. Only recently, when travelling down to the South Coast with an American friend, she surprised her with extensive recollections of families and places over the whole journey. Wherever they went Phyllis seemed to know someone.

The life of the labouring family, though much improved on the 19th century, was conducted at a much more modest level. For older folk the greater availability of food was a particular cause for rejoicing. There might be four meals in the day. Breakfast usually consisted of bacon and egg, or at least an egg, which most people could manage as they had their own hens. Of course, if the hens weren't laying, it would be bread and 'scrape' of some sort. Dinner at midday was the main meal, and the children would run back home from school for it. Bacon dumplings, known as clangers, and rabbit stew were popular dishes, probably because they were cheap. Father usually had to wait till the end of the working day for his main meal. When the rest of the family had their tea, something would have been kept over from dinner for him. For the rest of the family, tea was mainly bread and butter, perhaps with some jam to go on it. It depended on how much jam mother had made, and how many there were to consume it. At sixpence a pound bought jam was expensive and poor in quality. Perhaps better to spend a few pennies on half a pig's head, the meat from which would make a tasty brawn. With the ubiquitous bread and butter, and some salad from the garden, now that was really tasty. So was bread and home-dried lard, spread with golden syrup. One devotee assured us, "If you've never had it, you've never lived!" Cake was for weekends and visitors, and then as long as it would last. Homemade cake, that is! No self-respecting labourer's wife would *buy* cake. Tinned and bottled fruit was definitely for special occasions.

Dress was different. Very young babies were dressed in long petticoats for the first few months, after which they were shortened i.e. put into shorter clothes. Children wore more layers of clothes than today. In winter a girl would wear a vest, knickers, a liberty bodice and flannel petticoat plus a dress or jumper and skirt. For outside wear a coat, a woolly hat and a scarf would be worn. In many families clothing was still in short supply. In large families one change of clothes was the norm, and hand-me-downs were usual even for footwear, which was often unsuitable for country wear. Boots were preferred, for the village roads were flint-surfaced, rather muddy and almost entirely without pavements. Children's boots were as heavy duty as could be afforded, and the soles were often smothered in hobnails.

At least between some Wingrave families, a certain decorum was maintained. Thus Ann Woodward Jones, the postmistress, taught her granddaughters to address her closest friends as 'Aunt'. So Mrs Roberts was Aunt Hilda and Mrs Phil Rickard was Mrs Phil. But the ladies still addressed one another as Mrs Roberts, Mrs Rickard and Mrs Jones. On the other hand the men often indulged in the familiarity of nicknames.

There was 'Tickle' Bonham, 'Tosh' Gurney, 'Swimmer' Fleet, 'Chinner' Rickard, 'Gent' Gibbs, and 'Tapey' Payne, to name but a few. Some recognised a family hierarchy, as when a recent arrival in the village addressed Vic Rickard as 'Mr Rickard'. "There's only one 'Mr Rickard' in Wingrave", replied Vic, "and he lives in Cat Street. The rest of us are Vic and Joe and Bert and Don and 'Buller' and . . . . "

The chapels, the Temperance Hall, the Church Room and the pubs were the social centres for most villagers. The chapels were especially active. As well as the annual outings they regularly organised socials, faith suppers, sewing parties, concerts and services of song.

The chapel anniversary on Whit Sunday was a very important occasion. The choir had been practising for it for six weeks. To accommodate the choir a big platform was specially built at the back of the chapel. It started under the arch, and extended into the schoolroom behind. The chapel was packed, there were seats outside, and the singing was tremendous. Afterwards the staging was dismantled and stored for the next year. The Congs had the same sort of thing.

In addition, for many folk the family was important socially. Many families had three or even four generations living in the village, including a plethora of aunts, uncles and cousins. "All the Fleet family used to go to chapel on Sunday night," Connie Bignell recalled, "and afterwards they always used to congregate at Grandpa and Grandma Fleet's."

110. Packed into one of George Griffin's farm carts, "a flock of black crows" just about to set off from Manor Farm on some sort of outing, complete with fiddler. It must have been an important occasion: even the spectators are dressed up.

Recollections: Growing Up in the Twenties — Ron Bignell

One of my earliest memories is of gravel rash, which was painful even before they put some iodine on it. The trouble was the roads, which were surfaced with rolled-in gravel chippings and a liberal sprinkling of potholes. Children soon learnt to walk without falling over! The roads and the paths were so rough that almost everyone wore boots. Even most of the women wore boots, laced up with about ten holes and six hooks, or buttoned up. And the older women (especially widows) wore long dark frocks and black stockings. Their straw hats were painted black several times a year, and decorated with artificial flowers or fruit. They were kept on with hat pins. I used to think it must be very painful. As a child, I thought the pins were stuck through their heads, not their hair.

People today have the idea that children living then had nothing to do. In fact we were never bored. We had ball games, spinning tops, marbles, rounders, trundle hoops, etc., while evening entertainments included ludo, comics and a crystal wireless set with earphones. We could always play at Bliss's of Manor Farm. Everybody was welcome there, outside or inside the house. And if there was anything to eat around, we could have some if we were hungry.

Of course, we children were all little angels! We never did anything wrong! Well, not much! One night we might go out window tapping. Another time it might be gate-lifting: anybody's gate that could be lifted off was found the next morning upside down. When they tarred Wingrave's roads for the first time, me and my mate, Joe, found out that the tar would roll up off the old flint road, and we rolled quite a big bit up at the top of Cat Street, just like lino. We got into a hell of a row for it though! On the other hand we could do things that are not allowed now, like collecting birds' eggs: finches, tits, thrushes, blackbirds, robins, wrens, pigeons, crows, rooks, skylarks .... there were more birds about then than there are now! We could also search for moorhens' eggs. They were a great delicacy, for they tasted better than hens' eggs, and they were free. We also went blackberrying, mushrooming and picking wild flowers for our entry to the annual Village Show.

There were lots of things to watch: cows being milked, grain being thrashed, and horses being shod. This last was at the Forge, where Tommy Woodruff, working under the spreading chestnut tree, would fit a red-hot horseshoe, producing a smell of burned hoof, and wisps of smoke round his head. If we played around too much, he would catch one of us and give what he called a dry shave. He usually had about a day's stubble on his chin, and he would scrub your face with it. And it really hurt!

As we got older we could enjoy one of the highlights of the year, when the older lads and the younger men all met at Twelve Leys (now Chiltern Road) with sticks and dogs to turn over the rabbit pile at the side of the pond. There was a good chance of having a rabbit for dinner the next day.

At that time we had no street lamps in the village, so moonless nights were really dark. Not even light from Aylesbury or Leighton Buzzard reflecting off the clouds. Very good nights for courting they were, but if you didn't carry a lantern you could finish up with an ugly wife. And some of them did!

111. Tommy Woodruff, Wingrave's last resident blacksmith and farrier, at work in the old forge.

Chapter Nineteen

Red Letter Days, Recreations, and Other Relaxations

RED LETTER DAYS

The Village Feast

The parish church is dedicated to S.S. Peter and Paul, and its Patronal Festival, at the end of June, is known as Feast Sunday. In the 19th century the festival was celebrated in both a religious and secular manner. Today the *religious* celebration has not changed much. Hay is still strewn along the aisles of the church in accordance with Elizabeth Theed's bequest back in 1786: see page 112. Morning service is still held in honour of S.S. Peter and Paul. Maybe the church was always decorated with flowers on this occasion. It certainly is today, sometimes to such an extent that it has been advertised as a flower festival. And since such events tend to attract visitors, the parishioners have occasionally introduced a little fundraising into the festivities, by challenging the public to surround the church with pennies.

In contrast, the *secular* celebration has changed considerably. In the 1880's, for many people, it consisted of drinking and eating on the Sunday, and enjoying a fair on the Green on Monday and Tuesday. In later life, Hilda Roberts recalled this time, when she was about ten years old.[1]

I remember seeing large crowds drinking outside the village inns celebrating the Feast, and those villagers who could afford it always reckoned to feast a bit by having new potatoes, early peas and a nice bit of bacon, followed by a plum pudding.

What we called 'The Shows' arrived on Sunday evening and filled up the Village Green ready for the morrow. How excited we children were to see all the 'show folks'! By Monday morning the swinging boats and coconut shies had been erected, and the show women were busy making sticks of rock. The women didn't look too clean, but we children thought the half sticks of rock delicious! Mother was never willing for me to linger at the Fair, but we usually got a half holiday from school owing to the many certain absentees if we didn't. This meant that if I went home via the Green, I could steal a look all round the Fair. The shining brass gleaming through the open doors of the caravans always fascinated me and I longed to peep into the dim recesses of what seemed to me an enchanted dwelling place. One of the families of showfolks spent the winter in a house at Stewkley. David Mead, the father, had a van and a pony. He called this equipage 'Jumbo's Carriage' and gave penny rides as far as the Bell Corner and back. I once had a ride in it with some of my playmates, and we thought it wonderful.

Reports in the Bucks Herald help to fill in the picture:[2]

On Monday afternoon everyone seemed 'upon holiday bent'. The youngsters were to the fore in great numbers, and well supported the hobby horses and swing boats. In the evening there were many visitors from surrounding villages, and the coconut throwing, shooting gallery, and other stalls were well patronised. The Wingrave Brass Band paraded the streets, and considering the short time they have been established, played very creditably. Nothing happened to disturb the occasion, and happily there was an almost total absence of drunkenness.

It seems that the Feast Day fair continued to flourish over the years, but the next record of it comes in some notes by Joan Whitfield.[3]

When the war ended in 1945, the old custom of holding a fair on the Green after Feast Sunday was revived. Having obtained permission to use the Green from the Parish Council for a cost of £2 per year, Smith's Fair and Rose's Fair visited in alternate years. The vehicles were not allowed onto the Green until 8 p.m. on the Sunday evening, but the neighbouring roads were full of caravans and lorries much earlier in the day. The assembling of the fair was highly organised, and began with the setting up of suspended lights, and the starting up of the steam engine. The greatest area was taken by the Dodgem Cars. Owing to the unevenness of the Green, the platform had to be levelled with wooden blocks which were carried by the fairground children: even toddlers could carry a block. Old and young, boy and girl: each had a job to be done in sequence. Then stalls for rifle shooting, darts, hoopla, coconut shies, fish and chips and candy floss were set up, and the swing boat stands erected. Next day they were furnished with the necessary apparatus, and the glittering prizes were displayed. The fair opened at 6 p.m. on Monday and Tuesday evenings, when the youths from the neighbouring villages found their way to Wingrave guided by the sounds of the fairground music from the steam organ. Wednesday was dismantling day, when each one once more had a job to do. By midday on Thursday the last ones had gone leaving neither damage nor refuse as their legacy.

In the early 1960's old Mrs Rose died, her sons took over the fair, and asked the Parish Council to change the date of their visit to August Bank Holiday Monday. The P.C. refused, because there were parish events about then, and they did not want people's spare cash going out of the village. The fairs could only return at the original time. This offer was not taken up. Then the Green was levelled and in 1966 the 'tombstones' were put in.[4] As for having a special meal on Feast Day, most people eat so well now that something very exotic would be needed to distinguish the occasion from ordinary days!

May Garlanding

This custom almost died out but was saved for posterity by Hilda Roberts, who remembered the details and Joyce Whipps, a teacher at Wingrave School, who introduced it to the pupils. Hilda, looking back to 1885, when she was seven, recalled:[5]

Just before May Day, many children would canvass the cottages for flowers. Then, early on the 1st of May, they would make garlands of all shapes and sizes. Some decorated chairs with dolls seated in them, while others preferred crosses or hoops. They presented them at the doors of the cottages and chief houses, and sang the Mayday greeting:

> *Good morning, Ladies and Gentlemen, I wish you a happy May.*
> *I've come to show my May garland, because it is Mayday.*
> *The birds shall sing, and the bells shall ring*
> *And we'll all be Queens of the May.*

I do not think they were sent away without coppers or, at least, sweets and cakes. Their sweet little treble voices, singing so gaily on the morning air clearly found a tender spot in even the sternest heart and so drew money from pockets that were normally impregnable. My mother looked upon this as a sort of respectable begging, and only once do I remember her yielding to my entreaties to make me a garland, so that Bessie (my playmate) and I could go round our relatives. On this occasion, we visited all our local relatives, who gave us quite liberally in coppers: perhaps because they were so surprised to see us!

By the end of the morning we felt we had collected a small fortune: 2s-8d to be shared between us. With so large a sum we had to consult Mother. She promptly commandeered 2s-0d, one shilling for my moneybox and one for Bessie's. She divided the remainder between us. With such wealth we had long consultations as to how it should be spent. Bess was the older in age but the younger in self-confidence. Eventually, she gave in to a suggestion of mine. I had recently been a bit out of sorts, and Mother had administered a dose of Syrup of Rhubarb obtained from Dimmock's shop. It was sticky, sweet, and rather like treacle, with a fruity flavour. I really enjoyed it and planned to have a similar 'ache' sometime soon to obtain another dose. Well here was a good chance, so I suggested to Bess that we had 2d worth each, extolling to her innocent mind the delicious taste of this liquid. So, unbeknown to Mother, we borrowed two cups and visited Dimmock's with our twopences. Josiah looked over his specs at us a bit questioningly and suggested one cup but, with my usual audacity, I said, "No!" the other 2d worth was for Bessie's mother. So Josiah demurred no more. We watched with watering mouths as he poured the liquid into the cup reposing on the scale, wiping off the surplus from the edge of the bottle with his finger and popping it into his mouth. As he handed over the cups, he warned us not to spill it down us, which was just what we were about to do, but inside instead of out. We went into a quiet corner and sipped and sipped till the last drop was gone! Later we went to Bessie's home to take the shilling and tell of our success. When her mother heard the story she exclaimed, "Well, I'm glad Hilda had the sense for that. You (meaning Bess) never will take medicine, but it seems Hilda can get you to take it!" This version of our accomplishment rather took the wind out of our sails, because Bess felt she had been deceived, and I felt my initiative was somewhat misrepresented, but in later years we thought it a huge joke.

In Hilda Roberts' time the children carried their garlands round the village before school, and this continued well into the 20th century. Fred 'Buller' Rickard could remember how the children used to visit the Freemans at the Manor House to sing their songs and wave their posies and garlands. They had to get there soon after 6 a.m., though, if they were to receive a shilling from Mr Freeman. A whole shilling each! A real fortune! One year 'Buller' could find no flowers, so he carried a branch of plum blossom instead and, to his delight, Mr Freeman thought it a good idea.[6] As late as 1937, the tradition of calling at cottages and houses continued, as the Bucks Herald reported,

Evidently, the children were well received for many little faces wore bright smiles as they counted a goodly store of pennies. In these days of rush and hustle it is a happy thing to remember these quaint customs.

By the 1930's there was a formal crowning of the May Queen, but it was done in school time. Photographs taken in 1934, show a May Day procession on the Recreation Ground, with the May Queen and her two attendants on a wooden platform, the Boy Scouts on parade with the Union Jack flying, and a teacher (Mrs Minnie Rickard) is playing the piano. The old school was adjacent to the Recreation Ground, and parents would come onto it to watch the crowning ceremony, and the country dancing. At that time there was no maypole,[7] no procession round the village, and the participants were from the oldest age group in the school rather than (as now) from the youngest. So it is very likely that the children still did the rounds of friends and relatives before going to school. It meant being out and about by 6.30 a.m., when the menfolk were leaving for work, but it was the only way to make sure of those very important pennies.

The tradition seems to have ceased on the outbreak of war in 1939, and was not revived afterwards until Joyce Whipps took the initiative in the late 1950's. The modern version is similar to the traditional one, but is a group exercise in which the whole of Wingrave Primary School participates, and there is no door-to-door canvassing, as Joyce Whipps explains:[8]

A couple of weeks before May Day I did a "whispered vote" with my infants' class. One at a time they would come up to me and whisper the name of the girl they would like to see as the May Queen. The girl with the most votes became May Queen, and the next three in order were her attendants. I then repeated the process with the boys to find the Crown Bearer and his attendants. For the first few years the May Queen wore a long white robe I'd made out of some lining material, and a yellow silk cape and train. On May Day I was up at 6 a.m. making the crown with fresh flowers from my own garden wired onto a base. I found that the traditional flower carried in the Queen's posy was the Crown of Pearls flower, Crown Imperialis, which smelt so strongly of garlic that I had to wrap it up very well. The first year we just walked round the church wall and into the 'Rec.', and sang our little song whenever we saw people. I remember Mrs Horwood at Church Farm, running indoors and fetching sweets for the little ones, who were delighted! The following year a few people were ready to give the children money, but I said that I wanted the class to give memories and pleasure to the old villagers without reward coming into it! The dancing came later. At first we danced some simple country dances, and when we had a maypole made in the village, we were in our glory.

The Coronation of George VI

The church was crowded in the morning for a united service. Afterwards people listened to the Coronation on the wireless. In the afternoon a Carnival Procession took place, every child taking part receiving 1/-. Prizes were given for:

Best decorated bicycles: girls under 14: *1st. Daphne Rickard*
                       boys under 14: *1st. Peter and Paul Kempster*
Best decorated vehicle: *1st. Miss Coleman's Group*
Fancy Dress (Ladies): *1st. Miss Margaret Stubbs*; (Men): *1st. Mr Roadnight*
Decoration of Houses (daytime): *1st. Charles Rickard*; (night-time): *1st. Mr T. Brackley*
There were also prizes for sporting events. For example,
      greasy pole over the pond: *1st. John Goldney* and *Charlie Horwood*
      pillow fight over the pond: *1st. John Goldney* and *Doug Gurney*
      thread the needle: *1st. Mr Vic Clay* and *Miss C. Clay*

Souvenir tea packets were distributed by Guides and Scouts to everyone over sixty, and beakers were presented to all children in the village. A free whist drive in the Church Rooms and a dance in the Temperance Hall wound up a very happy day.

Empire Day

After Queen Victoria died, her birthday (May 24th) was kept throughout the Empire as Empire Day (now Commonwealth Day). Wingrave Parochial School celebrated it annually. All the scholars wore daisies and learned to chant:

    This little daisy that I wear, is emblem of our Empire fair.

On a typical Empire Day the normal timetable was suspended in the morning. In 1924, for instance, the school was open to visitors, and about seventy parents and friends were present. A group representing Britannia, the Home Counties and the Colonies was staged. The children were given a short address and saluted the flag at 11 a.m., after-wards singing patriotic songs. Empire messages from the King and Queen were delivered by means of a gramophone.[9]

Pancake Day

On Pancake Day, Hilda Roberts tells us, children used to go round the village singing:
    Ip pip the pan's hot, time to go a roving.
    A little bit of bread and cheese is better than nothing.
    Is the pan hot? Is the pan cold?
    I like pancakes hot or cold!

112. May Day: the Crowning. Colin Marsh crowns Celia Hazelgrove, the May Queen, in 1959.

113. May Day: the Procession in 1968. Kate Wells is the May Queen. Raymond Lovell and Mervyn Rawlings lead the procession. Ann Ellis and Sally Noakes are the train bearers. Sarah Roberts is in close attendance.

Only once do I remember singing this. I was with an older girl, and we were at the door of old Mrs Fleet's shop next to the blacksmith's. After a time she popped her head over the half door of the shop and handed us a farthing prize packet and told us to run away. It had a pinch of 'hundreds and thousands' in it, which we shared! Needless to say, Mother wasn't told.

The Slattery

This is one custom which has been entirely lost. Hilda Roberts could remember that it occurred at Old Michaelmas, but she had no idea what it signified.

What I do remember is a man coming round to our door with hot baked pears well-seasoned with sugar and cloves at 2d a basinful, which we bought and ate hot, and thoroughly enjoyed.

RECREATIONS

Cricket

So far, the earliest reference to cricket in the parish has been found in the Bucks Advertiser and Aylesbury News for 1854,[10] when a team from Aston Abbotts, Cublington and Wingrave was defeated by Quainton in one innings. The first mention of a wholly Wingrave team is in the Bucks Advertiser for 1872,[11] when Wingrave Juniors defeated Leighton Juniors. The venue is not mentioned: perhaps a friendly farmer lent a field. If there was a team of Juniors, then surely there was also a team of Seniors, though the earliest report of them yet located is in 1878, when they defeated Bierton.[12] In the meantime, Hannah de Rothschild had already given Wingrave parish the use of a recreation ground, "in the very centre of the village where our young people can engage in manly healthful sports after the toils of the day".[13] By 1888 there was a Wingrave Cricket Club, complete with President (the Rev. Lockhart), Secretary, Treasurer, and a printed set of rules. With 36 playing members and the patronage of Stewart Freeman and a number of local farmers, it appears to have been a well-organised club with an enterprising social side as well. It is noticeable that in 1892, when the Wingrave Manor House Amateurs were soundly beaten by Fleet's Professionals, the match was followed by "a very substantial supper at the Rose and Crown when Mr Stewart Freeman occupied the chair, and songs were given by several present".[14] Even regular cricket matches usually included a cricket tea, when an old man called Mortimer used to play the violin. The Wingrave team travelled to 'away' matches in a horse-drawn waggon, but Mortimer walked there, and afterwards walked back to Wingrave to ensure that he was there before the team arrived, when (if Wingrave had won) he would welcome them home by playing 'See the Conquering Heroes Come'. Strangely, it never occurred to anyone to offer him a seat in the waggon.[15]

However, 'the Rec' was still part of the Mentmore Estate, and it was not until 1904 that the Cricket Club plucked up courage and asked for an elm tree to be removed, as it was causing great inconvenience and occasionally even resulting in the cancellation of a return match. This was not surprising as the tree was in the centre of the playing area. The tree was removed. Lord Rosebery was thanked, invited to become Vice-president of the club, and asked for permission to build a pavilion.[16] Later, the Club appealed to Lord Rosebery for financial help in building it: members had already raised £15 towards the estimated cost of £30. Once more, his Lordship obliged.[17]

Judging by the number of stories of 'soaring sixes' it seems that cricketers were as prolific as fishermen in devising tall tales. Perhaps the tallest was of an 'away' match at Cheddington, when a colossal six is said to have landed in one of the waggons of a

114. Wingrave Cricket Club: Cup Winners 1912
 From the left: standing – R.Gadsden (with hat), T.Gurney, J. Bonham, F.Griffin, R.Higgins, F. Coleman, H.Jones; seated – F.Gibbs, E.Kempster, H.Kempster, P.Gibbs, A.Rickard, G.Levick.

115. Wingrave Cricket Club circa 1961:
 From left: back row - Jim Lewis, Jack Goldney, Don Rickard, Les Seaton, Steven Kopp, Frank Higgs, Doug Bateman; front row – Dennis Goldney, Jim Kirby, Terry Bateman, John Goldney, Alec Bignell, Fred Kirby.

passing train, and was swiftly carried off northwards. Rather more likely is one that Frank Griffin of Manor (later Bell Leys) Farm used to tell. Apparently, Wingrave won a competition in the 1890's. Their prize was a visit to Lords, where they met the touring Australian team including a famous bowler named Trott. The Aussies invited the Wingrave team to 'have a go' in the nets, and Trott bowled to Frank Griffin, who promptly hit him way out of the nets. Trott told Frank that he had never been hit so hard or so far in his life and presented Frank with the ball, which the family still possesses.[18]

Football

It is believed that the Wingrave Football Club was founded "around 1889". It was certainly in operation in November 1891, when a letter[19] was sent to Lord Rosebery, requesting permission to instal sockets for goalposts on the Rec., coupled with a promise to leave them flush with the ground. According to Frank Griffin, in the following season Gladstone, the Liberal Prime Minister, was staying at Mentmore with Lord Rosebery, and was brought to Wingrave by his host to watch a football match. Presumably, it was the link with Mentmore that persuaded the team to incorporate Rosebery's racing colours (red and green) into their kit. The visitors watched the match with interest for some time, but when Frank Griffin tackled someone perhaps more strongly than he should have done, Mr Gladstone asked Lord Rosebery whether this was allowed. On being assured that it was, the Prime Minister is said to have commented, "It seems a very rough sort of game".[20] It certainly could be: in more senses than one! The football team's supporters got quite upset if their team was losing. On such occasions the cry of "moat 'im" went up, and the referee would be shown the Moat at the bottom of the Recreation Ground, with the suggestion that he be a little more generous to the home side. Eventually, word got around about the Wingrave battle-cry, and some referees found they had a prior engagement when Wingrave was mentioned. We asked one of our informants, "Did you ever *see* a referee 'moated'?" "Oh, yes," was the reply. (see also Recollections: Moatin' the Ref.)

Fiercely loyal they might be, but the Wingrave football supporters definitely had a sense of humour, as Frank Griffin explained:[21]

Frank Gibbs never shaved in his life. In his younger days, when he played for the Wingrave football team, he had quite a long light-coloured beard. It used to show up when he put on his football jersey. We were playing Oving about Xmas time and when Frank had the ball one of the spectators called out, "Go on, Father Xmas". As the game continued all the crowd, of some hundred or two, took it up. Every time the ball went near him, there was a roar, "Go on, Father Xmas." Frank took it all in good spirit, but some time later the team noticed that he had had his beard trimmed a bit shorter.

Athletics

So far as we can discover there has never been an athletics club in the parish despite the fact that, in the past, village celebrations often included athletics, and not just for the youngsters! When Queen Victoria's Jubilee was celebrated in 1887, the programme was surprisingly varied with races over 120 yards, 200 yards, quarter mile and mile. These included a 200 yard race for men over 55 years, and a similar event for women over 55 years. There was also a 200 yards hurdles, a high jump, and a number of novelty races: sack; three-legged; potato; and wheelbarrow. To complete the programme there was a tug-of-war, and a greasy pole to be climbed.

Recollections: Moatin' the Ref' - Joyce Sinnott

Wingrave Recreation Ground (the 'Rec' as it is known locally) was usually the venue for local football matches. On this occasion Harry Bonham was playing in the Wingrave team, and Liz, his wife, was one of the spectators. Sometimes, when Wingrave was losing (or so it seemed to the opposition), Harry came over faint and fell to the ground. On such occasions, while Albert Alcock (the custodian of the First Aid bag) treated Harry, the Wingrave team got their breath back and had a little chat with the spectators about their defensive problems. On this occasion Wingrave was once again losing, Harry again came over faint and fell to the ground, but Albert was nowhere to be seen. The cry went up from the crowd, "Albert! Albert! Where is Albert?" Poor Lizzie was distraught. At that moment Connie Bignell arrived to watch the match. "Oh, Lizzie", she said, "whatever is the matter?" Without the slightest hesitation Lizzie replied:

> Well, it's like this 'ere Con,
> Our Harry's on the ground,
> But Albert's got the First Aid bag
> And he just can't be found.
> The bag should be available
> Our Harry's mortal bad.
> He's older than the rest of them.
> Our Harry's not a lad!

Just at that moment an argument broke out between the referee and some of the spectators, and the Wingrave battlecry of "moat 'im" was heard. At this Harry rose from the ground unaided, and joined the throng which was none too gently propelling the referee towards the edge of the moat, which at that time bordered Moat Lane. On seeing the water the referee agreed that some of his decisions had perhaps been a little biased, and the match continued. And Wingrave won!

After six happy years at Wingrave School, I went to Temple School in Aylesbury: a private school for girls. Part of the curriculum was a nature walk. On this particular day, a long crocodile of girls – with a teacher fore and aft to make quite sure that no girl raised her eyes to look at a boy – was making its way along the path from Aylesbury to Bierton. We were peering into the hedgerows in quest of nature, when along the road on a bicycle came Maurice Bonham from Bierton. He was a member of the Bierton football team, which had played at Wingrave the previous Saturday: not a very happy match! He recognised me in the crocodile. "Ah!" he shouted, "one of the Wingrave 'ooligans. 'OOLIGANS they are there. 'Moat 'im!' they shout, and 'Drown the ref!'" I was mortified, and the teachers were horrified. Back at school the headmistress demanded an explanation of my association with 'that young man'. Afterwards, on Monday mornings the girls clustered round me to ask if the referee had been drowned at Wingrave the previous Saturday. At first it embarrassed me. Then I realised that I could frighten them to shivering point, so I enlarged upon it until eventually I had the entire team being thrown into the moat.

116. Players and supporters 'snapped' outside the new pavilion (completed 1958), after a 'mixed' cricket match as part of a Fun Day on the 'Rec.', probably in 1959. The men had to bat and bowl with their left hand, and catch with their 'wrong' hand.

117. Wingrave Football Club's cup-winning team of 1926/7: see page 248. From the left: seated – Joe Clay, — Clay, Percy Gurney, Harry Bonham, Fred Pargeter; standing (middle row) – Vic Rickard, Horace Bignell, Reg Simmons, Harvey Roberts, John Stubbs, Bill Bignell.

118. *Wingrave Football Club 1934/5: Winners of the Oving Cup in the final against Wing. From the left (seated): V.Clay, D.Rickard, M.Rogers, I. Ellis, R. Goldney; (standing, middle row): P.Clay, L.Woodruff, L.Rickard, G.Reynolds, F.Horwood, G.Bignell.*

119. *Wingrave Football Club 1948/9: Winners of the Marsworth, Rosebery and Buckingham Hospital Charity cups. Players only. From the left (standing): Les Goldney, Ray Higgs, John Rickard, Bert Oakley, John Goldney, Frank Humphreys, George Reynolds; (seated) Jim Kirby, Dave Williams, Fred Kirby, Norman Brackley, Bill Clay; (kneeling) Irvin Mallinson, Basil Ellis.*

Vic Rickard (1903-1990)

Wingrave's versatility in sporting matters is well summed up in the life of Vic Rickard, a local athlete and all-round sportsman who won many prizes, medals and trophies. There are still a few folk around, who remember Wingrave's Peace Celebrations in 1920, when there was a public tea for everyone and a Sports Day culminating in the traditional Greasy Pole competition. With a shoulder of mutton as the prize many tried to take the flag at the end of the pole, but Vic was the first to succeed.

Vic was goalkeeper for the Wingrave Football Team, and a member of the team which in 1926/7 won three major trophies, including the Oving Cup, much coveted by players and supporters alike. Horace Bignell, the sole survivor of that team, recalls that in those days they travelled to 'away' matches in Bert Rickard's bus. They only lost one match in the season, and had several colossal wins: 26-0 against Cheddington; and 14-0 against Wing! Vic Rickard was the goalkeeper in the Final of the Oving Cup, played before a crowd of about two thousand. The Bucks Herald was full of praise for Wingrave's defence, and especially for,

V. Rickard in goal, who put up the best performance of any player on the field. But for the clever defence of Rickard, Long Crendon would have scored on more than one occasion. Not least when Long Crendon were awarded a free kick near goal and he brought off a spectacular clearance.

The team were driven back to Wingrave in triumph, with Vic Rickard seated upon the bonnet of Bert's bus. Incidentally, this was at a time when goal keepers had to take a lot of punishment, and it was not unusual to see Vic knocked flying into the back of the net. He could take care of himself though, and many a time he mistook an aggressive centre forward's head for the ball and punched it away. Vic was also an enthusiastic cricketer, playing as wicket keeper, and was later elected President of the club. In addition to playing for his village in established sports, Vic helped to found new sports, played in them, and also worked for the maintenance and development of sporting facilities in the parish. He helped form the Wingrave Tennis Club, and for years captained the club and looked after the courts. He was a founder member and president of the Wingrave Bowls Club; and a founder member and veteran champion of the Aylesbury and District Table Tennis League. For over 25 years he worked hard to keep the Recreation Ground in a good condition. He was Chairman of the Recreation Ground Committee for many years, and in the 1950's he was involved in the provision of a new pavilion.

The Sporting Scene Today

Seventy years later football is still the dominant sport in Wingrave with a first team, reserves, no less than three junior teams, and regular coaching sessions for juniors. Perhaps the most striking feature of Wingrave's football is the contribution of senior players and supporters to coaching and fund raising for the junior teams. Bowls still thrives, and over the years a policy of self-help has resulted in extensions to its premises and improvements to its green. With this sort of commitment it is not surprising that in recent years the club has represented Buckinghamshire at the National Championships and won the 'Famous Grouse' Bletchley League, in the face of considerable competition. The table tennis club still meets regularly. New interests include Golf, Netball and a Gun Club. Two clubs are in abeyance: Cricket due to legal objections to its venue; and Tennis while awaiting the construction of new courts. Perhaps the biggest difference to earlier years is the recent provision of an additional sports field with space for three football pitches, and plans for tennis courts, a multi-purpose all-weather hard-surfaced playing area, and a large pavilion with changing rooms and showers.

120. *Wingrave Bowls Club: founded 1925. The first annual prize-giving took place against the background of the first Rec pavilion. For its first year the club used a mown strip of grass on the Rec. Then the Parish Council gave permission for a green to be laid on the present site.*
Back row: Tom Rickard, George Bignell, Ivor Ellis, Ralph Higgins, T. Rixon, Percy Fleet, Arthur Rickard, Ralph Smith, Jack Randall, Frank Alcock. Front row: Will Gurney, Rev. Stuart, Frank Gibbs, Jim Fleet, Will Fleet, Fred Fleet, Rev. Stevens, J. Gibbs, Harry Kempster.

121. *Wingrave Bowls Diamond Jubilee, 1985. The present pavilion was built in 1966, and later considerably extended entirely by the efforts of club members. From the left:*
Norman Rickard, Pam Kirby, Jack Goldney, Shirley O'Brien, Joe O'Brien, Robin Perkins, Jill Roberts, Richard Clay, Joe Coombs, Carole Megram, Brian Bignell, Fred Kirby, John Rickard, John Goldney, Brian Ellis, Reg Cousins.

123. *From the front: Frank King, Ernie Bignell, Fred Peters and Bert Oakley take up the strain in the annual tug o' war on the Rec.*

124. *Improvised ice hockey on the village pond in the days before Leighton Road was infilled.*

Recollections: Wingrave on the Ice – Vic Clay

Cold spells and very sharp frosts remind me of schoolboy days in Wingrave over seventy years ago. When the duck pond was frozen over and quite safe to slide on, we used to have a long slide for the older children and a smaller one for the younger ones. We also played ice hockey at weekends when the young men were not at work. We stood around on the ice and picked two sides. One goal was opposite Hilda's shop, and the other was in front of the Old Vicarage. We played with walking sticks or cut hard-wood cudgels out of the laurels. I had many a knock on the shins when someone missed the old tennis ball 'puck' and hit me instead.

If we behaved ourselves, Mr Kidston of Manor Farm would let us use their moat. In our teens we managed to get a pair of wooden skates. They had a large screw which went into the heel of the boot and a strap to help keep them firm. Later we had steel skates which clipped onto the boot, and these were much better.

On Sundays I sang twice in the choir, and we played on the ice between services. I suppose we made our best suits a bit grubby, but the cassocks covered them up.

RELAXATIONS

Today, one can walk the footpaths around Wingrave regularly, yet rarely see a child, with or without parents. The recollections of our senior citizens suggest that it was very different in their youth. As Doreen Honor pointed out:

For children it was a limited, but placid and happy life. Parents felt no need to worry about children wandering around the village or the countryside. And such things as the picking of wild flowers, and the collecting of birds' eggs or butterflies were regarded as legitimate (and even praiseworthy) activities.

Others readily endorsed this view.

Sometimes my brother and I, and perhaps the children next door, would 'go down the fields'. There were old trees to climb, secret places in which to hide, and masses of wild flowers to pick. Closer to home, in Bell Field, you could pick cowslips and lady-smocks. Near Rowsham there's a water gate, and on hot days we used to bathe in this. We'd take most of our clothes off, and dry the rest on the hedge.(Connie Bignell 1905-1997)

Play days were magical in the fields surrounding the village. I lived opposite Parsonage Farm and could play with George Bliss' nine children. They filled my youth with joy. I played with them in pig sties, cattle barns and hay barns. I fell into ponds, went haymaking, drank warm milk from the cow, ate raw swedes, sat on top of ricks and slid down them. Hay ricks grew taller each day, and riding home on the last load with the farmer's family really was Harvest Festival. More often than not I was ankle deep in mud, and generally disreputable. My mother tried to keep me away from the farm, but by hook or by crook I was with the Bliss family. (Joyce Sinnott 1913--)

When I was a child we played 'down the fields' much more than children do today. We walked further too. Parents used to take their children out for walks, to Wing and Rowsham and back across the fields. We loved to sit by the Moat, with our sticks, string and poor little worms. (Daphne Rickard 1922-1977)

In general, children seem to have been much more active in their leisure time, and far less solitary than in recent years. For instance, girls enjoyed skipping, not only on their own, but with long ropes so that six or more could join in at once. Games like "Mary is A-weeping", "The Big Ship Sails on the Ally Ally Oo", and "What's the Time,

Mr Wolf?" were group games, involving a number of players, and a minimum of equipment. "Nellie" was a good example. A treacle tin was stood in an open space with someone's stone on top, and everyone stood about ten yards away each with their own stone. You threw your stone at the tin, hoping to hit it and knock the stone off. If you missed, your stone stayed where it landed. When you got the chance you had to run and recover your stone, before the person whose stone was on the tin managed to 'tag' you. If they did, then your stone went on top. It was a very popular game and adults would often join the children and play with enthusiasm. Such was the lack of traffic (and especially motor traffic) that games of this sort were often played in the road!

In the 1920's and 30's, as well as sports, and membership of national organisations like Scouts and Guides, the older youngsters could enjoy the varied activities provided by the club held at the Church Room "where – in three rooms – we played darts, billiards, dominoes, table tennis, cards, etc., under the strict supervision of the caretaker, Elijah Bonham". In the 1920's there was a girls' club, too, which met twice weekly and then at the end of the season gave a concert in the Church Room. By 1938 there were two lads-only nights, and the rest were mixed.

As indicated in chapters 9 to 12 Wingrave's socialising was very much centred on the church, the Church Room, the chapels and the Temperance Hall, while the five pubs "catered for the really wicked" (as one villager put it, with his tongue firmly in his cheek!) In fact, Wingrave offered a lot more. There were several concert parties. The Prim Dozen was active for a number of years. It tended to be associated with the Primitive Methodists, because most of its members were close friends belonging to that chapel. From 1924 the nine Red Ramblers entertained many folk in and around the Vale. As their founder and organiser was John Stubbs, the head of the parochial church school, the Ramblers were automatically associated with the parish church.

124. Two pages from the Women's Institute programme for 1933.

GENERAL COMMITTEE:
The Officers.
Mrs. W. Fleet. Mrs. G.P. Race.
Mrs. P. Rickard. Mrs. F. Alcock.
Mrs. V. Chapman. Nurse Oliver.
Miss D. Paine.   Miss D. Hows.

TEA COMMITTEE:
Mrs. J. Fleet.   Mrs. E. Ellis
Mrs. F. Rickard (Jun). Mrs. F. Ludlow.
Mrs. J. Tompkins. Mrs. W. Kirby.
Mrs. G.E. Griffin. Miss D. Paine.

ENTERTAINMENT COMMITTEE.
Mrs. Frank Rickard. Miss D. Honor.
Mrs. H. Bignell. Miss J. Bignell.
Mrs. J. Tompkins. Mrs. W. Higgins.
Mrs. F. Alcock. Mrs. R. Simmons.

Meetings in Temperance Hall.
first Thursday, at 2 p.m.

Thurs. JANUARY 5th.
"What is worth doing, is worth doing well."
CAKE COMPETITION.
Jolly afternoon of Games,
Solos, and Monologues,
arranged by the Entertainment Committee.

Thurs: FEBRUARY 2nd.
"A merry heart goes all the way."
BIRTHDAY EVENING PARTY,
for Members and their Friends.

252

In 1931, the Women's Institute also formed an Entertainments Committee, which established a tradition of W.I. entertainment which was to be maintained for over forty years. The Temperance Hall was where many of the concert party's shows were staged, sometimes for two or three performances. They also performed at the annual W.I. Birthday Party, invitations to which were greatly prized by non-members, while the members could only attend if they brought a male guest! There was always a delicious buffet supper, displayed on tables which ran the whole length of the hall, and this was followed by sketches, mimes, games, and dances, with a good sing-along to finish the evening. The Temperance Hall was also the venue for some of the village's larger musical occasions, as when the village choirs, augmented by musicians from the Leighton Buzzard Orchestra, performed oratorios and cantatas.

The Allotments Society concentrated on practical help for its members: the bulk purchase of seed potatoes, for instance. The highlight of its year was the Village Show held on August Bank Holiday Monday in the field opposite the Post Office, and later in Miss Paine's field where Baldways is now. In addition to the competitions for the best vegetables, fruit, flowers, cakes and wine, there were all sorts of sports, and the band came up from Rowsham playing as they walked. They were exhausted by the time they reached the Show, sometimes too tired to blow a note. No matter! Apart from the usual disagreement over the judging of the sponge cakes, everyone enjoyed themselves.

125. A float which took part in Wingrave's first carnival after World War 2. Half a century later many of the participants are still living in the village.

126. *Women's Institute 25th Anniversary Birthday Party. Maggie Paine (left) with Agnes Pargeter at the cutting of the cake.*

127. *'Passengers on a Bus' performed by the W. I. concert party. From the left: front row – Lily Rickard, Ada Deller, Ida Curtis, Bim Pullen, Doreen Honor, Christine Dunker, Betty Carter; back row – Minnie Rickard, Maggie Paine, Ivy Bignell, Barbara Ellis, Gwen Taylor.*

128. Menbers and their guests at the W.I. 25th Birthday Party in the Temperance Hall, 1950. Bim Pullen kneels beside a banner which she embroidered for the occasion.

129. W.I. Garden Party at Mrs Dix's in Castle Street, where members welcomed two Canadian visitors from Oak River W.I., Manitoba, after a correspondence of six years. Front row from left: Rose Camp, Betty Hatch (visitor), Mrs Dix, Myrtle White (visitor), Betty Carter, Marge Coltman, Joan Whitfield, Hilda Gibbs.
The barn in the background, converted and enlarged, is now a substantial private residence.

130. *A Conservative Party bazaar in the Church Room. From the left: Iris Tompkins, Christine Dunker, — , Mrs Tighe, Bim Pullen, the Countess of Essex, Joy Hows, May Banks, Flo Rickard.*

131. *Whist Drive and Tea in the Temperance Hall 1967. On the left: Will Philbey, Mrs King, Flo Harding, Herbert Harding, Gladys Horwood, Lucy Brackley, Bertha Kirby, Harry Kirby, Lizzie Horwood. On the right: Frank Rickard, Dick Kirby, Pam Kirby, Connie Bignell.*

132. In 1973, with this display, the Wingrave and Rowsham Gardens and Allotments Society won the Monro Trophy at the Royal Horticultural Society's Fruit and Vegetable Show at Westminster Hall. By 1977 they had won it four times! 133. Organisers (from the left) Alec Bignell, Robin Horwood, Sylvia Brackley, Norman Brackley and Dick Hewitt with the Monro Trophy.

Chapter Twenty

Some Everyday Stories of Country Folk

THE RICKARDS OF WINGRAVE

To the Wingravians of 1891 it must have seemed that there had always been Rickards in the village. Eleven families, a total of 58 adults and children, bore the name. In addition, the families of female Rickards provided a host of aunts, uncles and cousins with surnames which included Faulkner, Knight, Smith, Higgins and Goss: at the very least another thirty parents and children. This made a total Rickard brood of 88 out of a total population for Wingrave village of 811. In other words, the Rickards of 1891 were related to at least one in every nine of Wingrave's inhabitants.

The First Generation: William Rickard

Yet eighty-five years earlier there was not a single Rickard in the parish of Wingrave. It was 1808 when William Rickard, a bricklayer of Granborough, proposed marriage to Ann Stevens of the same village. The banns were called on three successive Sundays, and the Vicar prepared the entry in the marriage register so that it needed only the signatures of the happy couple and their witnesses. Then, at the last moment, the wedding was abandoned, and the Vicar put three lines through the marriage entry. There is no specific explanation of this, but in 1809 there is a significant entry in the Granborough Parish Register:

John Stevens (base born) son of Ann Stevens baptised 29th January

So, did William seduce Ann and then refuse to marry her? Or did Ann cuckold William, and both William and her lover reject her? We shall probably never know. What we do know is that, at about this time, William packed his tools and a few possessions and left Granborough. A morning's stroll of 8 miles, brought him to Wingrave, where he found work. He also found, and in August 1810 married, Susanna Paine, the daughter of Harley Paine, the publican of the Blue Anchor in Moat Lane.[1] William obviously maintained contact with his family in Granborough, for his elder brother, George, joined him in Wingrave and in 1810 married Elizabeth Paine, William's sister-in-law and settled down in the village at least until 1824.[2] By this time William's wife had borne him five children who, in the erratic spelling of those days, were variously surnamed Ricket, Rickat, Rickard and Rickhard. Then, in November 1825, Susanna died. Fortunately, William's eldest daughter, Mary, was 14 years of age, and so thought to be quite capable of looking after the family. Just over a year later, William remarried to Ann Bates, another Wingrave woman, who bore him five more children.

In 1841 William and his family were living in Windmill Street (now Mill Lane), where Wingrave's windmill had been standing for nearly thirty years. A bakehouse had been added to it, and it was now owned by John Gibbs of Aylesbury, who let it out to anyone who thought he could make a profit from it. Since 1837 it had been rented by William Burton. Despite extensive repairs and improvements, and round-the-clock working to catch up with the grinding when the mill had been becalmed, he gave up the struggle after five years. William Rickard lived in an excellent position to observe the miller's problems, and obviously thought that he could do better. In 1843, in partnership with Thomas Alcock of Lower End, he rented the mill, and very probably occupied the mill house[3] which came with it. By this time his two eldest children had married and left home, and two more had died. So only six children had to be accommodated, and by the standards of the day the house was no more than comfortably full. William and Thomas may have worked the mill for as long as nine years,[4] but by 1851 William and his family were living in Nup End and he states his occupation without reservation: bricklayer. He died there in 1855. His wife, Ann, outlived him by thirty-four years.[5]

The Second Generation: Joseph Rickard

Of William's eight surviving children, his youngest son **Joseph** was the outstanding member of that generation. He married at the age of 20, and rented a cottage in Cat Street [6] near to his mother and his elder brother George. By the age of 28 five of his children had been born, and the eldest three (aged 8, 6 and 4) had already started work straw plaiting. Like his father he was a bricklayer, and in 1864, aged only 31, he had the initiative, the resources, and the skills to build Mill House in what is now Winslow Road. This provided his rapidly growing family (seven of the ten had now arrived) with a solidly-built, well-proportioned and capacious property, its frontage embellished by those touches that only a skilled craftsman could provide, including the inscription "1864 T Rickard Bricklayer".[7] In such a house, Joseph's children would not have the privacy that today's children expect, but neither would they have to be sardined into their beds, as was so common in the large families of that time.

Joseph's brother George had been working the windmill in Mill Lane. He ceased using it in 1872, and a little later it was pulled down. Behind his new house, Joseph then built a large workshop, and equipped it with millstones turned by a steam engine. Immediately beyond that he built a pair of semi-detached cottages. George took charge of the steam mill and moved his wife and six children into one of the cottages. They must have been a bit crowded in the two-up, two-down cottage, but Joseph had re-housed his mother, and his sister, Elizabeth, in the adjoining cottage, so perhaps it acted as an overflow: such things were commonplace in the nineteenth century. Sister Elizabeth had never married, and remained at home with her mother until the latter's death. Together they scraped a living from the mother's parish relief and Elizabeth's straw-plaiting. Then, in the mid-1870's, George Goss became their lodger. He had been an apprentice bricklayer, and later a journeyman with Joseph and had lodged in his house for nearly twenty years. He must have seemed very much part of the family. So, it was quite natural that, when Joseph needed extra space for his family, George Goss should move in with the old lady and her daughter. Doubtless, it improved their finances. It must also have transformed Elizabeth's social life. At long last she kicked over the traces, and had a little girl of her own, whom she named after herself. After her mother's death in 1889 Elizabeth married George, and by 1891 young Elizabeth (now 14 years old) was stated to be George's own daughter.

In 1871 the area around Mill House was known as Mill Place, and later as Little Aston. It was quite a hive of industry. By 1881 the four Rickard families living there included one builder, three bricklayers, a carpenter, a labourer, two millers, a dress-maker, a pupil teacher, and eight scholars. Clearly, the emphasis was still very much on building. Equally clearly this was the direction in which Joseph senior expected future expansion, for in 1879 he committed his son, Joe, to a four-year apprenticeship as a carpenter with Samuel and Alfred Mayne, an Aylesbury firm of builders and carpenters. Events proved Joseph senior to be right. Corn milling declined as more and more corn was imported and milled in bulk at or near the ports. All over the country local mills closed. Some Bucks millers converted their mills to the production of cattle cake, or to crushing rubble for the production of building blocks, but there is no evidence that this happened at Little Aston. By, or before, 1898 the mill had ceased to operate. By 1891

Joseph senior either owned or rented enough land to feel that he could call himself a farmer. His total holdings are unknown, but included Short Nell, the field now called Shortnell, [8] and Aston Lea both adjoining the Aylesbury to Leighton Road. Maybe this is why (from 1881) Mill Place is recorded in the censuses as Little Aston. And Little Aston was getting bigger. Probably at some time in the 1890's Joseph or his sons built two more semi-detached houses on the Mill House site. Their distinctive design led to them being nicknamed 'the Swiss Cottages'. The plot of ground adjoining the Mill House was used as a rickyard, not only for Joseph's own ricks, but also for the small ricks of customers who had perhaps only an acre or so of corn to be thrashed.

Even after a century, when recollections fade, and have to be replaced by snippets from local newspapers, it is clear that the Rickards were very much involved in the life of the village. Thus in 1899 when Wingrave organised a bazaar in aid of the Church Restoration Fund, there were no less than fourteen Rickards amongst the members of the organising committee and the stallholders. On at least one occasion (August 1892) Joseph lent Shortnell Field to the Wingrave Total Abstinence Society for their annual fete, at which the assembled company rewarded him with three hearty cheers. In 1887, when there was a choir outing to Brighton, the party of twenty were transported to the station at Marston Gate in Joseph Rickard's (horse-drawn) van. Probably because his wife came from Aston Abbotts, Joseph also helped that village. For instance, in 1889, when there was a concert in the church to raise funds for an organ, Joseph erected the platform, free of charge.

By the time Joseph Rickard died in 1910, his family had long since grown up, and had families of their own.

The Third Generation: John, William and Joe
Three of Joseph's sons (John, William and Joe), and three of his grandchildren (Bert, Vic and Charlie) stand out particularly, because they became village characters, and contributed enormously to the life of Wingrave.

Joseph's son **John** was born in 1852. He became a builder and, for a time, also a butcher. He had at least eleven children including CHARLES who was always known as CHARLIE.

Joseph's son **William** was born in 1857. He married Thurza Thorne, and they went to live in Leighton Road. In 1881 he described himself as a bricklayer, and in 1891 as a bricklayer and shopkeeper. In 1895 he purchased one of the plots of building land on the Winslow Road from Leopold de Rothschild, and built his own house on it. When his father died in 1910 he took over his business of builder and contractor, a large part of the work being in connection with Ascott Estates. It seems that he was a successful businessman for he is said to have owned a large amount of property in Wingrave. He joined the Parish Council in 1901, he was an overseer of the parish, a trustee of Pratt's Charity, a steward and treasurer of the Methodist Chapel, and for many years superintendent of the Sunday School. He had ten children including ALBERT THOMAS, who was always known as BERT.

Joseph's son **Joe** was baptised in that name, presumably to distinguish him from his father, Joseph senior. In 1887, at the age of 24, he married Marie Mott and lived at Little Aston until 1895 when, like his brother William, he bought a plot of land from Leopold de Rothschild. It was a double plot on the corner of Winslow Road and Cat Street and on it he built not only The Firs, but also the large sheds for his workshops. Of their five children, three died in infancy. Marie died in 1899, and Joe re-married to Ada Gibbs from Cat Street Farm, who bore him three more children. Joe was a builder, master carpenter, house decorator, general contractor, and undertaker. As a young man he was one of the finest runners and jumpers for miles around, and a keen cricketer,

134. *William and Thurza Rickard with four of their ten children: see p. 259. From the left: Len; Frank, later a village carpenter and undertaker; Alice, later Coleman, who ran the village shop; and 'Buller', who became a popular village character, "genuine old Wingrave in the flesh".*

135. *Mill House in Winslow Road: see pages 259-260. The steam corn mill was in the outhouses behind the dwelling. Also behind it can be seen a pair of cottages, now demolished, which were part of what became known as Little Aston. The Swiss Cottages were built later. Note the state of the road and the absence of pavements.*

who was efficient with both bat and ball: later he umpired for several seasons. For some years he captained the Bowls Club. He was a devoted churchman and filled many offices in the church: he sang regularly in the choir for sixty-five years. He was Clerk to the Parish Council from 1904 to 1921. Yet he still found time for his garden, and won many awards for exhibits of sweet peas and other flowers at local shows. He was a genial, friendly person with a smile and a greeting for everyone. His nine children included VICTOR JOHN, who was always known as VIC.

The Fourth Generation: The Three Cousins
For much of the 20th century the three cousins, Bert, Vic and Charlie were deeply involved in the life of Wingrave, displaying the energy, enterprise and initiative that distinguished this family. Some of their contributions to village life are detailed elsewhere in this book: see chapters 10, 17 and 19.

The Fifth Generation:
Today, in stark contrast to 1891, there are only seven adults living in Wingrave who bear the name Rickard, and only two youngsters who may perpetuate the name.

POST OFFICE PEOPLE

George Griffin (1816-1902)
George was descended from a long line of bakers. He started baking in Cat Street at some time in the 1840's, while his father was still baking in Nup End.

According to family tradition, round about 1856, George also took on the job of village postmaster. Of course, with the low level of literacy at that time the job would not be very demanding, though some villagers did expect the postmaster to be able to read their letters to them. In any case by 1861 George was employing a journeyman baker, and his son John also worked in the bakery, which was now at the old Mill House in Windmill Street (now Mill Lane). Besides, George seemed to thrive on work. At various times he was also village constable, an assistant overseer of the poor, parish surveyor, and (for 27 years) the parish rate collector. In his spare time he composed a great deal of music, trained and conducted the Congregational choir and also conducted the occasional

136: George Griffin (1816-1902)

orchestral concert. In 1863 George moved into a substantial new house in Nup End (next to the Methodist Chapel) with a bakery and storage barn in a separate building alongside it: see picture 140 on page 267.

In 1876, George gave up baking and moved into one of Hannah de Rothschild's new cottages on the corner of Winslow Road and Nup End, where he established the village post office. The house and bakery were taken over by his son, George junior, and later by his grandson 'Teddy'. The new post office was really just the porch of his cottage, with a sliding panel in the door leading from the porch into his living room. Even the letter box was contained in that little porch, "and that arrangement had to answer for a good many years". At that time Wingrave's post was delivered from Aylesbury on foot, as Hilda Roberts recalled:

John Goodwin, the postman, walked each morning from Aylesbury, leaving letters at Bierton, Hulcott and Rowsham. He took the field path from Hulcott to Rowsham, and then the field way again to Wingrave, coming into the village at the Dean Stile, and up Nup End to the post office at the top, where George Griffin helped with the sorting. John then left for Aston with their letters, staying there for a meal, and returning to pick up the despatches from the same villages in the evening. With the help of a good stout stick, he carried all those letters and parcels on his back. I never heard that he was ever molested or interfered with in any way. He did this duty for many years and was as good as any clock to go by, for he was punctual almost to the minute all through the year. Holidays were almost unheard of in those days, and I don't think John ever had one.

In 1895, after thirty-nine years as postmaster, George senior finally retired. He was then 78 years old. When he died in 1902, his funeral was said to have been the largest ever seen in the village: "The chapel was filled in every part".

Ann Woodward Jones

Mrs Jones took over Wingrave Post Office after George Griffin's retirement. It is said that George was very supportive of her application for the job. She ran the post office from her home, 'Sunny Bank', which her husband, Thomas Jones, had just built on the Winslow Road, and onto the side of which he had added a small room to accommodate the post office. When Thomas died suddenly in 1905 his daughter Polly Hannah Fleet and her family went to live with her mother, and Polly assisted her in the post office. It was a good job she did! In the early 20th century the post office was open to the public from 8.30 a.m. to 7 p.m.. Moreover, the postmistress had to be ready at 7.30 a.m. to receive the postman, who now cycled the six miles from Aylesbury

137: Ann Woodward Jones (1856-1935)

with the post in bags in the large carriers on the front and back of the bicycle. If the post was heavy, he would also have a bag on his back, and if it was very heavy (at Christmas, for instance) there would be two postmen. As the years went by, Polly Hannah played an increasingly important role. For instance, the telephone came to the village in 1923, but Ann called it "a new-fangled thing", and refused to use it. So Polly Hannah took down all the telegrams.

Ann Woodward Jones was greatly loved and respected in the village for her warm, kind manner; generous spirit; and discretion. For instance, receiving and despatching everyone's telegrams she would know little bits of gossip, but she was a great believer in keeping everything confidential. Only in her daughter did she occasionally confide. Ann died in 1935, after being postmistress for forty years.

138. The photograph, probably taken at George and Mary Griffin's 60th wedding anniversary in 1901, shows them with their children and the children's spouses in front of Wingrave Post Office.

139. On the right Polly Hannah Fleet (nee Jones) with her daughter Sybil outside their home, Sunny Bank, to which Wingrave Post Office moved after the retirement of George Griffin.

The Post Lady

In 1921, when she was 16, Connie Fleet replaced her mother as post lady at a salary of £28-12s per annum. Seventy-five years later these were some of Connie's recollections.

I reckoned to get to Wingrave Post Office at seven o'clock ready for the post to arrive at 7.30. Then I had to sort it out and start delivering it. In summer, I finished the first delivery about 9 a.m.. Of course, the village was only half the size it is today. After that I went home, had my breakfast and helped mother.

While I was delivering the first post, the postman cycled on to Aston Abbotts where he delivered their post, and collected their outgoing mail. He returned to Wingrave at 11 o'clock, when another postman, who had also cycled from Aylesbury, handed him the second post. The first postman then delivered this second post in Wingrave, and went on to Aston Abbotts to deliver their second post. Meanwhile the second postman cycled back to Aylesbury with the outgoing mail from the two villages. Finally, at 6 p.m., the first postman returned to Aylesbury with the second batch of outgoing mail from both villages. In the winter, when the weather was bad, the routine was the same, but the mail was sometimes very late, and at the end of the day the postman would arrive back in Wingrave very tired. On such occasions Auntie gave him a hot drink and a piece of cake, and would worry greatly as he loaded up his bags to cycle the six miles back to Aylesbury.

One day Auntie said to me, "Be prepared tomorrow. You're going to have a visitor. Someone from headquarters at Aylesbury. They think they're paying you too much." At that time Babs Rickard used to deliver the letters for me down Thistlebrook (i.e. to Thistlebrook Farm). And I thought, "Well, if they want to lessen my money I mustn't let somebody else take the mail to Thistlebrook. I must take it myself." And that day it had been raining, and the fields were soaking wet. I had a sudden idea. I thought, "I'll take him across the fields." Well, when he arrived at the post office next morning, he was smartly dressed, and his shoes shone as if he was going to an office. Now that's quite a long way to Thistlebrook, and I took him across the fields, and over the stiles, and through the farm gates where the cattle had left a rich thick mud. By the time he got back the poor man was exhausted, and you could hardly see his shoes and the legs of his trousers for mud. He said, "I don't know about docking your money. I shall see if I can get you a bit more." And next week I had another shilling.

Wingrave Post Office was an ABC Telegraph Office, and received a lot of telegrams, which had to be delivered to neighbouring villages and outlying farms such as Burston Farm beyond Aston Abbotts, and Folly Farm and Red House Farm on the way to Long Marston. I had to deliver them. One day Auntie said to me, "Next time you take a telegram you've got to have it in a little case. You're not allowed to put it in your pocket." So I had this little case on the front of my bicycle where you put the lamp. I'd got to go to a farm on the Wing Road, and of course I'd got to turn the corner when I got to the Handpost. Now you went at quite a good rate down Handpost Hill, and I must have been going too fast to get round the corner. So instead of going round it I fell off my bike, and the telegram came out of the little case and was blown right up on top of the hedge. I wasn't tall enough to reach it, and I had to wait till someone came by. I was more careful after that.

The Alcocks, who used to live next door to us, had moved to Rowsham. Their son was a sailor and he brought this friend home. And my sister and I went down there to have tea with them. The next day I had to go down with a telegram. The day after that I had to take another telegram. Every day – he was home for a fortnight – I had to take a telegram. And when it came to the finish my auntie says, "I don't know whatever this man thinks of these telegrams, but they're a lot of gibberish. Not one of them makes any sense". So I spoke to him about the telegrams. "Well," he said, "I cycled into Aylesbury each morning, and sent these telegrams so that you could come and see me." He said, "I want you to write to me." I said, "I don't think my mother would like that." So it ended. But I often wonder what happened to him.

I used to do various jobs for people on my round. At one house, if the young lad who lived with his grandfather wasn't up, I had to shout up the stairs and tell him it was time to get up – his grandfather having left for work much earlier. His breakfast was always cooked and left on the hob. One particular morning I had to call and tell him his bacon and egg was covered in soot, and I can still recall the look on his face and the tears that followed.

Connie gave up the job in 1931 just before she married Horace Bignell. He was a staunch Methodist and she was a devoted Congregationalist, so they were married in the Parish Church, and retained their separate allegiances throughout their lives.

Annie Hilda Gibbs (1897-1993)

Hilda, as she was generally known, had always lived in the same house 'between the churchyard and the pond', and "I ain't thinkin' o' movin' now," she would say. She took over the job of postmistress in 1935, and the post office became part of the shop which she and her mother (Aunt Poll) had run for so many years. A visitor recalls it as "A lovely post office with all brown polished wood counters, and a great big brass scale with brass weights." Hilda ran the post office in her own inimitable way for 36 years. Villagers would sometimes walk there on a normal business day, only to find a note on the door, "Gone to a wedding". She was well aware that she was a character. "After they made me," she would say, "they threw away the mould."

Her finest hour came on New Year's Eve 1969, when masked raiders burst into the post office, knocked her over and made off with the day's takings. "I didn't have time to feel scared," she said. "They knocked me over before I knew what was happening." But she dialled 999, and the thieves were caught soon afterwards. For this Hilda received a certificate and a day out in London at the expense of the Post Office.

When decimal currency was introduced, it is said that she refused to handle fifty-pence coins. In 1971 she retired.

TEDDY GRIFFIN: THE MIDNIGHT BAKER

Until 1955 most of Wingrave's inhabitants still ate bread baked in the village, as their predecessors had always done. Wingrave's last baker was George Edward Griffin, who was always known as Teddy. He died in 1971, aged 93, and is still vividly recalled by many local people.

Teddy was the last of a long line of Wingrave millers and bakers dating back at least to the middle of the 18th century. In the Posse Comitatus of 1798, a John Griffin is listed as a baker. Teddy's most famous ancestor was his grandfather, another George Griffin, (see pages 123 and 262-4) who not only baked, but also composed music. Teddy Griffin spent the whole of his life living and baking in the same premises in Nup End. It is said that money was his ambition, and that throughout his life he worked really hard to make some. The bakery occupied most of his time. He baked on Monday, Wednesday, Friday and Saturday, and delivered each day, except Friday. He usually delivered in the evening, sometimes rather late: it would be nearly midnight before he finished his round. In those days no-one locked their doors, day or night. So, if you were up, he would just knock and come straight in, smiling as if it was the most

140. *George H. Griffin and his wife Agnes with their two eldest children, Teddy and Beatrice, circa 1888. The bakehouse, which still survives, is on the right. Note the sack of flour in the upper doorway, and the horse and cart with a basket of bread on top, ready to leave.*

141. *Teddy Griffin on his round in Nup End.*

natural thing in the world to deliver bread at ten o'clock at night. And if the customer had gone to bed he would just call, "Baker!" and leave the bread on the kitchen table. He knew exactly what bread each of his customers wanted, and he made sure that they had it. He usually delivered the bread on a tricycle with no lights on it, and a big box on the front to carry the bread. If you wanted bread on Fridays, you had to collect it from the bakehouse. The smell when you entered was out of this world. And there he would be: a tall, thin, wiry man with a smiling face, ginger hair (a family characteristic) going grey, and huge hands. Sometimes he would get the bread straight from the oven, using a 'pull': a sort of shovel on the end of a long pole. Teddy reckoned that it was good bread if when you cut it the crust flew and hit the wall on the far side of the kitchen: and it nearly did!

When he was not baking bread, Teddy always found something active to do. On Fridays, when the bread had been cleared out of the oven, you could take your cake along to be baked, while on Sundays he would cook people's joints, and at Xmas he would roast their turkeys and chickens. People would take cycles and motor-bikes to him to repair, and he would also refurbish old cycles and sell them to the many people who could not afford a new one. He would also re-charge the accumulators, which powered the early wireless sets. As a young man he was a keen amateur racing cyclist, and would cycle to races as far away as Birmingham and Herne Hill. He carried his racing wheels strapped to his back, and changed them onto his cycle when he reached the meeting. He often won, and his home was full of trophies and prizes.

Teddy would go anywhere for a bargain, which he then tried to sell to someone for a profit. And often he did. But sometimes he miscalculated, as when he acquired twelve pairs of white cricket boots, which occupied a cupboard for many a year. He often went to London for the day. When young he would cycle, but in his later years he usually went on his motor cycle, perhaps taking a friend in his sidecar. On one such occasion the friend found the sidecar half-full of great thick sticks of rhubarb. "What's all this?" asked the friend. "Oh", said Teddy blandly, "they like rhubarb in London." Off they went, with Teddy wearing an old cap with the peak turned sideways. His friend in the sidecar needed strong nerves, for traffic lights were in their infancy, and Teddy would totally ignore them, saying, "They don't have them where I come from. I don't bother with they blessed things." In due course they arrived at a garage near Baker Street Station, and sure enough they did like rhubarb in London. In exchange for the rhubarb, the tank was filled up with petrol, they were both given a cup of tea, and the motor-cycle was garaged free of charge. From there they went to the street market at Petticoat Lane. Teddy turned everything over on one stall, and then said to the stallholder, "Not today, Missus." However, at another stall he bought a pair of trousers, but asked the friend to pay. Teddy didn't want to get his wallet out, where anyone could see all his money.

Actually, Teddy just didn't like spending money. He always took sandwiches to London, but if he forgot them he would go without, saying, "If my head couldn't remember, my belly will have to go without." That day there had been a big cycle race on and he was anxious to find out who had won it. Badly as he wanted to know, he wouldn't buy a newspaper. Instead, he stopped someone with a paper, and asked to look at it, but the result wasn't in. So, later on, he stopped another person, and found what he wanted. Teddy walked his friend for miles round London, and eventually they got to the National Gallery, where they both sat down and fell sound asleep.

Teddy's carefulness with money extended to all sorts of things. When flour was delivered, he had to carry the heavy sacks up the open ladder outside the bakehouse to the upper floor. In later years he suffered from a hernia, but he would not have an operation to repair it, and refused to buy a truss to support it. Instead, when flour was delivered, he used to borrow a neighbour's truss to wear while carrying the sacks.

During the second World War the police were very alert in case German saboteurs were dropped by parachute, and they had 'stop and search' powers. Late one night Teddy was cycling through Leighton on his way back from a race meeting, when he was stopped by a policeman. The bobby was new to the area and so did not recognise Ted. Moreover, he was not very impressed by Teddy's answers to his questions, and so 'invited' him to come down to the police station. It was on Teddy's way home, and so he went along with this quite happily. They went into the station and the bobby announced, "Sergeant, I've brought along a suspicious character." "Oh, yes," says the sergeant, looking around, but completely ignoring Teddy, since he knew him well. "So where is this suspicious character?" "Here," says the new bobby indignantly, pointing at Teddy. "Not him!" said the sergeant, and everyone in the station fell about laughing, much to the discomfiture of the new bobby.

Teddy's wife died in 1955, sixteen years before him. On that day the bread had already been baked, but he would not deliver it, and Jack Tompkins and the baker from Aston Abbotts did it for him. After that he never baked another loaf. Towards the end, he had several heart attacks, and had to go into hospital, where he was given a hearing aid. One evening he gave it to a friend to adjust. The friend made the adjustment, and gave it back to Teddy saying, "Can you hear now?" "No, I can't," replied Teddy!

Teddy's death was a great loss to the village where, despite his idiosyncrasies, he was accepted as a wonderful man, a great character and, of course, a master baker. As one of his former customers put it, "A new crust off one of his cottage loaves, a lump of cheese, and a raw onion with salt: lovely! Royalty never had better!"

WILLIAM FLEET (1875 -1959)

William Fleet was descended from a long line of carpenters, and it was his great-grandfather who moved to Wingrave at the beginning of the nineteenth century. His father was killed when Will was a baby, and he had to leave school at twelve years of age without any practical training whatsoever. Despite this, he and William Roberts eventually founded the building firm which bore their names, and turned it into a successful and respected enterprise. In 1956, when he was eighty-one years old, William Fleet wrote a brief account of his life.

The story related today is that, due to excessive drinking, his father did not give his wife enough money for the housekeeping. Then one day he attended a mission meeting, realised the error of his ways and 'signed the pledge'. He returned home and told his wife that in future things would be different. A few days later he was dead! Evidence at the inquest revealed that he had been working at Mr Gurney's brewery at Rowsham. He was helping to remove the woodwork of an arch, which had been erected the previous day, when the arch collapsed and he was buried under three hundred bricks, probably weighing over half a ton. He was taken to Bucks Infirmary, but his spinal cord had been injured and several vessels ruptured, and four days later he died. At a time when the only social security was parish relief, and with six children to bring up, the family were very poor. Sarah plaited straw and as soon as they left school the children went to work, preferably where they could live in. Thus, at twelve years of age, William's sister Mary Ann became a domestic servant living with Farmer Biggs and his family at Old Manor Lodge, where the food and lodging was probably much better than at home. Sarah's father came to live with the family, but he had no stated employment, so perhaps he also received parish relief. William makes no pretence about the family's circumstances:

I was born in one of the cottages round the Recreation Ground in Wingrave. I was brought up very poor, and it was hard work for my mother. When I was twelve years of age I went on the farm working for Mr W. Griffin for three shillings per week of seven days. I stayed for about six years, and when I left I was having about fourteen shillings per week. I went to the London and North Western Railway stores at Wolverton Carriage Works and had two and a half years sending out the requirements to the stations from the stores. When I had saved £15, I used it to apprentice myself to the building trade at the firm of Webster and Cannon, Aylesbury. The first year I was paid 3d per hour, the next year 3½d, and the third year 4d. And 2s-6d per week if I lodged away.

After I finished my apprenticeship I was engaged to Miss Polly Hannah Jones, the daughter of Mr and Mrs T. Jones of Wingrave. I started my courtship in 1896, at twenty-one years of age, and we got married in 1903 at twenty-seven years of age. We went into one of those dear little cottages that the Countess of Rosebery had provided. About two months after I had served my time I went out to manage various jobs for Webster and Cannon. The first one was at the entrance leading to the Manor House (where Stewart Freeman lived). We had to get trees down, build piers, hang gates and put up fences. And in one of those piers is some information someone will find one day.[9] After I had completed the work at Leighton Road I was asked to go to Mentmore to Lord Rosebery to build the large peach houses. (It may have been this contact with the estate which resulted in invitations that William obviously cherished for the rest of his life.) *It was in 1903 when Lord Rosebery was 'at age' that I was invited to go to the Reception at the Riding School on the estate at Mentmore. I also had the pleasure of playing cricket on Mentmore Estate against Lord Rosebery,[10] and I had a chance to bowl at him, but unfortunately I didn't bowl him out. From Mentmore I went to (work at) St Luke's Church, Hampstead, London. From there to Oxted and Oxshot in Surrey and then back to Stewkley to help build the chapel. After that I went to the Grammar School at Aylesbury, (working) for a Northamptonshire firm.*

In 1905 the death of William's father-in-law had long-term repercussions for the family. Thomas Jones was foreman at Webster and Cannon, and his death from heart failure was completely unexpected. His wife, Ann Woodward Jones, who ran the village post office from their home, Sunny Bank (now Meads), on Winslow Road, was distraught and inconsolable. In typical village fashion, Polly and her family rallied round, and spent most of their time at Sunny Bank, which fortunately was only a few doors away from their cottage. This went on until 1910, when Lord Rosebery sold the estate houses, and they were put up for auction. William bought their cottage and the adjoining one for a total of £300, let them out, and the family moved permanently into Sunny Bank. Having made one difficult decision, William made another.

Finally, I started out on my own, and the work came in very fast, from different people that I knew quite well. Just as I was getting on, with lots of work, the government called me up for service (in World War One). *When I was discharged, I saw an advert in the paper for a job for the government near the Duke of Norfolk's estate at Arundel. And I stopped there for two years, and then came to Halton Camp to help Mr Roberts build the Record Office.[11] After that I went back to Aylesbury to have another start on my own. And in a short while Mr Roberts joined me as a partner.*

We made a proper dash for work, building anything that came along. The first important job was the Girl Guide Hall at Aylesbury. It was opened on 16th May 1926 by H.R.H. Princess Mary in the presence of the County Commissioner, the Aylesbury District Commissioner, the Architect, the Bishop of Buckingham, the Lord Lieutenant of

142. *The Fleet family in the garden of Moat House (opposite the village shop). From the left seated: Will Fleet, granddaughters Prudence, Janet and Gillian Rickard, Polly Hannah Fleet; standing: Douglas and Christine Dunker, Vic and Sybil Rickard, Joyce and Dudley Sinnott.*

143. *Some of the Fleet and Roberts' workforce at Southcourt. In the front row are Harvey Roberts and Jack Tompkins (2nd and 4th from the right) both from Wingrave.*

the County, and other dignitaries.

Will Fleet, representing Fleet and Roberts, was on the platform at the opening ceremony and was presented to Princess Mary. And it seems probable that the success-ful completion of this building gave the firm just the publicity it needed. William summed it up very modestly, "After building the Hall, Fleet and Roberts was very busy." Indeed, the contracts rolled in. There were many buildings for local authorities: schools at Buckingham, Bletchley, Dunstable, Queens Park (Aylesbury) and two large schools at Wycombe; 500 council houses at Southcourt in Aylesbury, and smaller contracts at Leighton, Winslow, Rowsham, Bierton, Wingrave and Whitchurch. There was also a lot of private building: 24 houses were erected at Wendover Road and sold quickly; and at least another 30 houses were erected for private clients, a number of them in Wingrave. Other contracts included the Conservative Club at Leighton, Stoke Hammond Chapel, a factory at Dunstable, the Jubilee Hall at Bierton, a ward block and operating theatre at Tindal Hospital, the Police Station at Leighton, a cinema at Princes Risborough and a hall at Wing Park for the War Office.

One reason for Will Fleet's success was the strict control that he exercised over the costs of labour and administration. His office was in extremely modest premises at 33, New Street, Aylesbury. For some years he used to cycle to work each morning and unlock the office door promptly at seven o'clock. His punctuality was such that people in Bierton would say, "There, 'tis a quarter to seven. Will Fleet's just gone by on his bike." He believed, "If the master isn't there, the men won't be there." Only later on was a car bought, and for some time that was shared with Will Roberts!

In the early 1930's Fleet and Roberts were employing about 180 men yet, in loyalty to Ann Woodward Jones, the family were still sharing Sunny Bank with her. So William bought an acre of ground opposite Sunny Bank, and designed a house for the family. He called it the Moat House, because one of the village moats bordered the property, and they moved in after Ann's death in 1935.[12]

Like many successful men he found time for a lot of other activities. He was a life-long member and for some years also a trustee of the Wingrave Primitive Methodist Chapel. He was a lay preacher at chapels on local circuits for 20 years. He was also a steward for 33 years; a Sunday School teacher for 43 years, rising to Assistant Superintendent and Superintendent; and President of the Temperance Hall. He pursued secular activities with equal devotion: he was a Parish Councillor for 14 years; manager of the village school for 30 years; a trustee of Pratt's Charities and a member of the Wingrave Charity Committee for 25 years; Captain of the Bowls Club for 15 years; and a vice-president of the Tennis Club. The firm of Fleet and Roberts often helped with village events. Without charge, they supplied such things as fencing, lorries to fetch and carry for the 'Rec' fete, marquees and men to erect them, and timber for platforms.

William and Polly Hannah had three daughters: Sybil, Christine and Joyce. In 1932, William's eldest daughter, Sybil, married Vic Rickard. He was a partner in Bates and Rickard, who were electrical engineers, and when Will Roberts died in 1939 he left Bates and Rickard and became a working director of Fleet and Roberts. Two of Will Roberts' sons also became working directors. Will Fleet retired in 1948, at the age of 72, though it was said that he had the energy of a man twenty years younger. At that date the firm employed 90 men. "There would be double the number if they could be had."

When Polly Hannah died in 1955, William wrote, "I miss her so much. She was everything to me she could be. We shall soon meet again." Shortly before his death in 1959 he wrote, "I have had a busy life, but a very happy one, and I thank God for it. He has been very good to me."

William's last recorded comments on Fleet and Roberts were made three years before his death. They reflect the fact that Will Fleet and Will Roberts had known each other for a lifetime: they were first cousins and had gone to school together. "I was grieved to lose my partner Mr Roberts sixteen years ago. He was a real good partner. I missed him very much in the church and out in business. We both had a wonderful life together. I am 80 years now. But the business is going on alright . . . as far as I can see". It was as well that he could not. Fleet and Roberts, with Vic Rickard and Harvey Roberts as joint managing directors, continued in business for another thirteen years, but eventually the firm's credit ran out. No-one in Aylesbury would supply them with building materials on credit. Then on June 5th 1969, its creditors petitioned for the company to be wound up. The petition was granted.

144: Arthur Bateman (on the right) and Will Bennion sheep-shearing on Wingrave Recreation Ground in the mid-Thirties. It was still very much an agricultural village.

145. *Baldway House. The garden extended right to Leighton Road, and was noted for its flower power. The daffodils were followed by a magnificent display of lupins. Most of the garden is now occupied by infill housing. In a field to the right, the Paines hosted the annual Allotments and Gardens Show for many years.*

146. *Subsequently, the annual Show moved to the 'Rec'. Seen here in 1947 are (from the left): Ern Underwood, George Horwood, Arthur Fleet, Mr Tighe, George Alcock, R.W. Ward, Sam Higgs, Rev.Cheeseley, Dick Kirby, Herbert Harding, Frank Rickard, Cliff Woodruff, Lionel Woodruff.*

PART FIVE

Chapter Twenty-one

The Great War 1914-1918

The First World War started on a note of optimism. To the clergy and the politicians it was "a moral issue and a just cause". To the Establishment it was "an opportunity to serve one's king and country". To many of the young men who would form the back-bone of the armed forces it was "high adventure, a chance to display 'pluck and dash', and a change from the drudgery of agricultural and industrial bondage." To those less committed, involvement was simply a necessity to avoid the charge of cowardice. All this was reflected in the extent of voluntary enlistment. The United Kingdom entered the war on 4th August 1914, and by the end of the year well over a million men had volunteered. Over the next nine months they were joined by a further million. As in villages all over the country, the men of Wingrave and Rowsham flocked to the recruitment centres. Over the four years of the war at least 122 enlisted, almost one third of the male population.

It was only when news of the war filtered back to Britain and the lists of dead and wounded lengthened, that civilians began to appreciate the appalling carnage, and the frightful injuries sustained by those fighting in the trenches. This generated an unremitting anxiety and fear. Imagine the concern at the Ferns, in Winslow Road, where William Rickard and his wife Thurza waited for news of six of their sons, including: Albert, who had left behind a wife and baby son; Ernie, who was later invalided out due to a weak heart (he lived to be 100!); and 'Buller' [1] who joined up in 1914 after falsifying his date of birth. Everyone knew that at any time a knock at the door might announce the delivery of a telegram with news of death or injury. And Wingrave's families received plenty of telegrams, for nineteen men were killed, and many injured, some suffering disablement for the rest of their lives. Wingrave's parish magazine is full of examples.

Two of the earliest to be sent to the front were Harry Bonham and James Alcock, who have been in France for fifteen months, and have indeed been in the thick of it. Together all the time, they were very seriously wounded on the same day, and in much the same manner: and they lay side by side in the Field Hospital to which they were carried. Most mercifully, they have done better than the surgeons anticipated, and are now safe in England. We hope and pray that their recovery may soon be complete. (July 1916)

We have to record the death of another from our parish who has given his life for his country and the great cause. Harry Bateman, aged 35, was wounded by the explosion of a shell on April 24th, and was brought to England on the following Sunday. He was in the Military Hospital, Bradford until his death on May 30th. His funeral was very largely attended, and was made the more impressive by the escort and firing party, with bugler, provided from Halton Camp. Only a few, probably, of those present had previously seen a funeral with military honours. There has been the deepest sympathy felt for his wife and child, and other close relatives. (July 1917)

We were grieved to hear of George Coleman, as very seriously wounded in France.

The injury to his leg was so great as to make amputation necessary. George Levick, who has lost an eye and was otherwise much hurt is doing well. Corporal Charles Green, who had charge of a gun on a merchant ship, is reported missing. The vessel was torpedoed and went down with all hands aboard. (September 1917)

Edward Reynolds is the second of his family to die for his country and for duty's sake. Ralph Goldney's name is in the first list of those who have been awarded the O.B.E. for conspicuous services in munition work. We congratulate him heartily on this honour. (October 1917)

We have lost Arthur Gurney, who a few weeks ago was at home on leave, cheery and in the best of health: now killed by a shell. As we write we hear of Mark Major, who has died in a hospital at Rouen, through the effects of a gas shell. William Goldney, too, has been so seriously wounded that one foot has had to be amputated. William Carter, who has been for long on the sick list, is to be discharged as no longer fit for service. There are others not actually posted as missing or prisoners, from whom no letters have come to their relatives at home for several weeks. Such suspense is most difficult to bear. (June 1918)

Fred Hedges has been killed. One of the earlier ones to join and three times wounded, he has now made the supreme sacrifice. (October 1918)

Even when congratulations are in order, one is conscious of the tragedy of the dead, and the plight of the wounded.

We very heartily congratulate Second Lieutenant Harold Jones on winning the Military Cross. He was in command of two platoons, during the raiding of enemy trenches, dealing successfully with the opposition and setting an excellent example of pluck and dash in attacking a crater, strongly held with machine guns. By his own example of indifference to fire, he encouraged his men to make great and successful efforts. His platoons were unable to return to their lines in the daytime, and he remained in the open with them until night fell, when he succeeded in collecting his men and brought them, together with all the wounded, back to the trenches. He was invested with the M.C. by the King at Buckingham Palace. His father, Lemuel Jones the schoolmaster, was given leave to attend. (July 1917)

THE HOME FRONT

With so many men serving in the armed forces, and others transferring to work on munitions, Wingrave suffered from a labour shortage, which was particularly noticeable at harvesting, which was always very labour-intensive. Due to a shortage of feeding stuffs it was difficult to maintain stocks of cattle and poultry. These problems with home production were compounded by the shortage of imported food due to ruthless u-boat attacks on merchant shipping and its use to move men and supplies for the army. "In Australia there are quantities of butter, corn, fruit, meat and wool just waiting for vessels to bring them to us." [2] For the towns this created shortages, but in Wingrave it probably made less difference. Provided there were men outside the age for military service, or agricultural workers exempt from war service, the allotments would supply vegetables and animal feed, so that chickens and a pig could still be kept. There was still game to be poached, which was distinctly easier if the keeper was on the Western Front; and if sufficient milk was available, many of Wingrave's housewives could even make their own butter. To the Rev. Francis this flouted the government's plea for voluntary rationing:

147. *Arthur Gurney: killed by a shell in 1918. See also page 276.*

148. *Tom Rickard in hospital after being gassed in the trenches.*

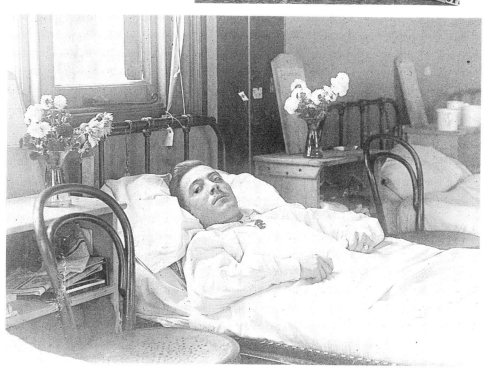

149. The heart of the village, circa 1914, viewed from the church tower. This is the view to the west of Windmill House, just visible on the extreme left: see page 140. The gathering on the Green is reputed to be of mounted troops.

150. Troops watering their horses in the village pond during World War One.

There are people everywhere, who have not yet learnt to play the game. Whilst there is food to be got, they mean to have plenty of it.[3] We have been asked by the government we have been put upon our honour for the country's sake and the sake of our soldiers at the front to deny ourselves in the matter of food ... It is our plain and manifest duty, as regards bread, meat and sugar to limit ourselves to the quantities suggested. If we do not do it willingly, it is quite certain that we shall be compelled.[3]

The Rev. Francis certainly made the need for economy clear to his flock: he preached about it; he wrote about it in the parish magazine; and he made sure that the children in school were well informed about it. Wingrave's school children responded by carrying out two successful projects. In March 1917 the school's Victory Potato Plot was launched. One afternoon, in school time, twelve boys and sixteen girls started clearing land belonging to the Vicarage. Then the boys dug the ground. By the end of May twenty square poles had been planted out. In June came the hoeing, and by the first of August all had been harvested. In September and October the school was closed at noon on nine occasions for the scholars and teachers to go blackberry picking. 604 lbs (274 kilos) were picked on just one afternoon! In all 1744 lbs (791.8 kilos) were gathered plus 8¼ cwt (419 kilos) of chestnuts, all for the National Economy Campaign. The blackberries were bought by the government to be made into jam. This tremendous effort did not go unnoticed, for in September 1918 the Ministry of Food decided to film Wingrave's pupils in action as an incentive to other schools.

There is no evidence as to whether the Rev. Francis' strictures about food economy had any effect upon the majority of the adults in the parish. Of course, the elderly, the widows and soldiers' wives with large families found little difficulty in complying: straitened finances saw to that! Certainly, the idea of putting the nation upon its honour to conserve food failed. In January 1918 rationing began with sugar, and soon included meat, butter, margarine, and nearly all important foodstuffs. In June 1918 the Vicar wrote:

It is rather wonderful, and much to the credit of people generally, that the restrictions as to food have been taken so patiently. It seems to be understood that rationing in the matter of meat and butter is absolutely necessary and fairer all round.

Throughout the war the civilians of Wingrave also worked hard fund-raising for the many organisations trying to relieve the suffering caused by the war: the British Red Cross, the Prisoners' Fund, Blind Soldiers, Belgian Relief, Armenian Refugees, French Emergency and the Minesweepers' Fund. Typical of these efforts was a sale of work at Easter 1917, which was very well-attended and raised £32-16s, far more than anyone had thought possible. It was used for Soldiers' Comforts. Already parcels had been sent out to seventy-six Wingrave men and grateful letters were continually being received. Soon, it was hoped, every soldier and sailor from the parish would have received a parcel. Only six months later even this effort was surpassed when an event in aid of the Red Cross raised £113-13s-6d.[4]

It seems that by the summer of 1918 disillusionment with the war was creeping in. "There are some here and there who, as our casualties increase, are inclined to rebel against the continuance of the War," wrote the Rev. Francis in June 1918. And three months later . . . . .

We were asked to make September 29th 1918 a day of special thanksgiving for the victory of our army in Palestine. The weather and prevailing sickness were against good congregations, but the church has seldom been so empty as it was on that particular Sunday.[5]

279

PEACE AGAIN

The Armistice was signed on November 11th, and the bells of the parish church were rung in thankfulness. Gradually the serviceman returned, much to the joy of their relatives and friends. Buller Rickard remembered that being a small village, everyone knew everyone else, so each returning hero was greeted and welcomed by all. Houses were decorated with flags, parties were held, and there was much eating, drinking and dancing. "I didn't go to work for a month," said Buller. "I was on beer. Everybody was happy. I shall never forget it."

Naturally, there was a great desire to honour and welcome these men at a special Peace Celebration. However, the men let it be known that they preferred not to be entertained apart from everyone else, so in July 1919 a special Tea was held at the school. Sports and games were played on the Recreation Ground, and everyone again decorated their homes with flags. To crown it all the school children were granted a Peace Holiday that year: October 20th to the 28th. For many years after that the school remembered the Armistice with a two minute silence. In 1936, for example,

The broadcast service from the Cenotaph was heard in school by all scholars thanks to the Headmaster's wireless set, and the two minute silence was observed at the correct time.

THE WAR MEMORIAL

The Parish Council considered the question of a suitable memorial to the men of Wingrave and Rowsham killed in the war, and presented their views at a public parish meeting. Afterwards the Vicar wrote: [6]

This Parish Meeting was by no means a pleasant one. It is pitiful that we should be wrangling over the graves of those who have died for us, and whom we wish to honour. . . . There is no need for bitterness and recrimination. In the parishes roundabout there seems to have been little of the difficulty we have ourselves experienced. We are united in our grateful and proud remembrance of the men who have given their lives for our country, and we should be careful not to dishonour them by unseemly strife, and an emphasis on our unhappy divisions. The Vicar is of the opinion that, outside the churchyard, the best place for the memorial would be the centre of the Village Green, where it might be accounted a real village cross. But so placed it would make it impossible to use the Green for swings and roundabouts at Feast Time.

Eventually, after taking advice from the Wayside Cross Society, a site at the edge of the Village Green was found to be generally acceptable. This would place the memorial at the heart of the village, where it could seen by all, but still leaving space for the annual Feast Day amusements. In 1921 the grey granite obelisk was erected, entirely at the cost of the parishioners. At a memorial service, Major-General Swann unveiled the memorial "to the memory of those men of Wingrave who gave their lives in the great cause of freedom":

Harry Bateman	Charles Green	Albert Reynolds
Charles Bignell	Arthur Gurney	Edmund Reynolds
John Bock	Fred Hedges	Joseph Rickard
Joseph Clarke	John Horn	Raymond Rickard
Fred Coleman	Thomas Kempster	Arthur Smith
William Fleet	Mark Major	John Thorne
	Kenneth Charles Jeffs	

VILLAGE GREEN, WINGRAVE.

151. *The War Memorial erected in 1921. There have been some changes around the Green since picture 149 on page 278 was taken. On the left, Bert Rickard's garage, marked by a petrol pump, is in operation. His bus is parked outside the Rose and Crown. To its right a large window has been installed in the building housing the butcher's shop.*

152. *Celebrating Armistice Day: 'Buller' Rickard leads the British Legion parade. Immediately behind him is the Earl of Essex. The cleric in the white surplice is the Rev. Barker, vicar of Wingrave.*

281

153. World War Two: Bert Rickard in Home Guard uniform. He had previously served in the army in the Boer War and World War One. His sons, Les (on left) and Don both served in the army in World War Two.

154. Hilda Gibbs in 1976. It was the 55th year that she had been involved in the Royal British Legion's Poppy Appeal.

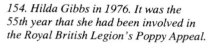

WEAR YOUR POPPY WITH PRIDE !

THE SECOND WORLD WAR

An account of World War II as it affected the parish of Wingrave with Rowsham is the subject of 'Wingrave at War', a booklet of personal recollections published in 1995 as part of the parish's V E Day celebrations. For this reason no further account of those times has been attempted here. However, we felt that the names of those who died for us should be recorded:

Cecil Goldney
Gerald Goldney
Edwin Irish
Clifford Stevens

155. Commemoration of V.E. Day 1995: the Wingrave and District Branch of the British Legion join the parade through the village.Those present include Len Scutchings (standard bearer), Tim Loader, Peter Wallis, John Goldney, Pat Stevens, John Dixon, Bert Oakley, Norman Brackley, Alan Rawlings, Margaret Camilleri, George Camilleri, Mary Rawlings. Next in the procession is Alan Frost's steam engine.

Chapter Twenty-two

Villagers and 'Strangers'

FRIENDLINESS

Even allowing for the golden haze which often colours recollections of times long past, Connie Bignell's assertion (Recollections page 285) that Wingrave was a much more friendly village "in the old days" may well be correct, simply because the sort of friendliness which she describes is encouraged by long and close acquaintance; common interests and problems; large extended families; and employment close to home. In the first half of the 20th century, and even more so in earlier times, all these were a feature of life in Wingrave, as in many rural communities.

In those days the population of the parish was about half its present size, so it was far easier to get to know people. In any case most villagers grew up knowing one another, for they had all attended the one village school, played with other children in the street, sung in one of the three village choirs, played games on the 'Rec'.... and always with other Wingrave villagers. Few ventured outside the village for their entertainment. A visit to Vale Park pool was 'a day's outing', while a day's trip to the seaside with two hundred of your neighbours from church and chapel was a holiday: something to be discussed, both in advance and in retrospect, with everyone you encountered. The area of the village being much smaller, it was much easier to encounter those that you knew, especially as (in those days) there were also far more people around the village during the day-time hours. For although the pushbike had freed men from the obligation to take jobs in and around the village, many still did. And whether they worked in the village or out of it, they walked or biked to work. So they were visible, and greetings could be exchanged. And they were known! Indeed, you didn't need a clock to tell the time, when folk like Stan and Arthur Pargeter, or Will Fleet went to work past your house. Although women might make an occasional visit to Aylesbury or Leighton Buzzard, they were generally 'somewhere around' the village. Perhaps shopping, for this was done mostly at the village shops. Since self-service was unknown, shopping was usually a bit long-winded, but it did provide an excellent opportunity to exchange the latest news of relatives, friends and events. It was very unusual for married women to have full-time jobs anywhere, and certainly not outside the village. Lacking modern household gadgets, they had no time for it. Neither did the household routine permit it. Dinner (at 12.30) was a cooked meal with a main course and a pudding. After morning school, Wingrave's streets were full of children walking (of course!) home for dinner. Dad might also be there, but most men had something kept over and steamed up at tea-time. Even the villagers who worked outside the village were usually back in Wingrave by the end of the afternoon, often biking home in pairs or groups. This timing was important, for after their meal most men worked in the garden or on the allotment in the lighter evenings. Gardens and allotments were a widely shared interest, which generated much inspection of growing crops, and discussions of their progress or lack of it. The men took a pride in their plots and their gardens, and loved to show friends and neighbours round them.

Most villagers were also connected with each other by marriage, religious affiliation, choice of pub, support for the Temperance Hall, etc.. As Figure 29 shows, of the married couples living in Wingrave, one or both had been born in the village in 75% to 85% of all cases. So the majority of couples began married life with access to a

Fig. 29: Origins of Married Couples Living in Wingrave

Year	Both born in the Parish	One born in the Parish	Neither born in the Parish
1851	28.7%	47.7%	23.6%
1871	43.1%	41.4%	15.5%
1891	45.3%	35.3%	19.4%

Recollections: The Good Old Days

Connie Bignell, Joyce Sinnott & Daphne Rickard

Connie Bignell had no doubts about it: the old days were the best.

I'd rather be back living in the old days, because I think the friendliness was lovely. Everybody seemed friendly to everybody. Then we were more like families than friends. Wingrave itself seemed more like a close-knit family in the old days. Of course, families were bigger; and a lot of couples married from within the village, and so had another lot of relatives just by marriage. Anyhow, one way or another, you knew everyone and everyone knew you. Nowadays there's so many strangers, you don't chat with everybody like you did. Some women would stand at the gate, and wait for people to go by, just for the pleasure of talking with them. And you used to go for walks more than you do now, and if you met someone you'd stop and chat with them. You really did talk to everybody. You knew everything that everybody was doing, and you entered into their troubles the same as you did your own. I suppose nowadays they'd call it nosiness, but it wasn't called that in those days. It was just friendliness. If you were in trouble, your friends would help you. I'd much rather be living in the old times. Lots of people tell us now that we had the best times, and we have to agree that we did.

Joyce Sinnott had "golden memories of Wingrave, because it had village pride and family pride", both of which were evident in the everyday life of the villagers.

Each Summer the Tring Show was held in the Rothschilds' Park. The day before, at the village forge, the fire burned brightly and the anvil clanged as Tommy Woodruff put new shoes on the magnificent shire horses from Manor Farm. At dawn the next day Prince, King, Duke and Samson, their manes and tails plaited with bright ribbons and their brasses gleaming, were led down the road to Tring. And at nightfall, as the proud farm workers led them back into the village, each one garlanded with rosettes, the cry went up, "Wingrave's done it again".

When my grandmother, Ann Woodward Jones, died after being the village postmistress for forty years, a long, long line of mourners followed the bier on foot to the churchyard, and the curtains were drawn over all the windows along the way. For that was the way of a funeral in Wingrave. Stewart-Freeman, despite his wealth and social position, was taken to the church in exactly the same way.

Daphne Rickard probably had the last word on things long past:

I'm still walking in the cornfields, running down Charity Gate, picking flowers in Bell field, wearing a new dress for the Sunday School Anniversary . . . But Wingrave's still here! Appreciate it! Love it! Try to make it as happy a village in the future as it has been in the past.

network of family and friends. In the days of larger families, this was really significant. Of course, not all was sweetness and light in days gone by. For instance, family relationships sometimes went wrong, and there were always those who, given a little authority, were convinced that they were 'superior'. (Recollections page 287) Nevertheless, it does seem likely that Wingrave was a very friendly village, with good and extensive social relationships. Consequently, for the first half of the 20th century, the increase in personal transport, and the improvement in public transport, had little effect on its social ethos. In the second half of the century the wider ownership of motor cars changed all that. And by 1991, 86% of all households in the parish owned at least one car.

It took the owners of motor vehicles some years to appreciate that they could move to a pleasant country environment like Wingrave, and still have within a radius of twenty miles a choice of employment at centres like High Wycombe, Luton, Dunstable, Milton Keynes and Hemel Hempstead, as well as smaller market towns like Thame, Tring or Leighton Buzzard. They could even, by car, park and ride to London and all stations en route. In practice the willingness to move home and travel long distances to work has been particularly shown by those in the managerial, administrative, professional and technical spheres and, by 1991, 60% of Wingrave's employed were in these occupations. Their appearance in the Wingrave housing market caused a mixture of disbelief and disgruntlement, for they could (and often did) outbid the resident villagers. As late as 1972, the news that an improved bungalow with superb views and five acres of land had fetched over £11,000, was greeted with cries of "Never!" "Absurd!" and "Ridiculous!". Worse still, new private housing tended to be designed (and thus priced) to the pockets of outsiders (i.e. the 'strangers' as the locals called them) rather than the villagers. Tales began to circulate of young married couples having to set up home elsewhere due to the high prices of accommodation in Wingrave. On the Floyds Barn development in Mill Lane, it is claimed that the first house to be completed was built for £80,000 and sold for £165,000.[1] At these prices not one of the properties was purchased by villagers. Fortunately, an extensive programme of council house building, and the development of an estate which included cheaper-to-construct terraced and semi-detached properties eased this problem, and some of the next generation have returned. Even so, the high price of housing is still said to prevent many from returning. The consequent reduction in the number of extended families and the sheer weight of numbers of immigrants makes it difficult to maintain friendliness at its old level. As Connie put it, "Nowadays there's so many strangers".

Too true! Between 1951 and 1991 Wingrave's population increased by 86%. By 1991 it had risen by 13% in just ten years.[2] Moreover, it seems likely to be still increasing. Yet every increase makes communication, and thus friendliness, more difficult to achieve. Twenty-five years ago, one stranger, Brian Hicks, appreciating this, established the Wingrave with Rowsham Communique, which in those days was printed on the old school Gestetner, and collated and stapled by hand. Every household in the parish still gets a free copy. Undoubtedly it helps, though no-one knows to what extent.

Of course, the influx of strangers has had significant pluses as well as minuses. Many of them are well practised organisers. More important, having come to Wingrave because they *want* to live here, they are prepared to devote much time and effort adding new interests to the list of existing village organisations. A Golf Club, Drama Group, Twinning Association, Music Group, Rambling Group, Art Club, Bridge Club and a very useful Community Association Transport Service come immediately to mind. In addition, many have joined enthusiastically in existing organisations, such as the Bowls Club, Table Tennis Club, the Cricket Club, and the Gardens and Allotments Society.

Recollections: Social Distinctions — Frank Griffin

An old lady of Wingrave had a daughter who worked in a lowly position in the kitchens at Mentmore Towers. One day she decided to go and see her daughter. She was walking up the drive to the house when she was overtaken by Lord Rosebery, one-time Prime Minister. Lord Rosebery had returned from London by train unexpectedly and, on arrival at Cheddington, as it was a fine day, had decided to walk home rather than wait for a carriage to be called. On seeing the old lady he raised his hat and wished her 'Good day'.

On her arrival in the kitchens the old lady told of her meeting with Lord Rosebery. Because he was not expected, the kitchen staff had no knowledge of his arrival, and told her it could not have been him. "It must have been a butler or a footman," they explained. The old lady denied it could have been one of those people. "None of those stuck up so-and-so's would have raised their hats to an old village woman like me," she said.

In particular, they have been major contributors to the Wingrave Community Association, which runs the Community Centre in the former Parochial School, not only helping to administer it, but fund-raising for building improvements, manning the bar, and redecorating the interior. The W.C.A. also acts as a clearing house for events put on by affiliated organisations. A clash of dates on fund-raising events is unlikely to raise the level of friendliness in any community!

Undoubtedly, Wingrave is no longer "one big family", yet especially amongst 'strangers' it retains its reputation as a friendly and caring village. Indeed, as house prices indicate, more people want to come to Wingrave than want to leave it. In practice, if they welcome it, most 'strangers' will soon be absorbed into one or more of the numerous social and recreational groups, usually based on common interests of the sort listed earlier. Because the membership of these groups is often overlapping, and often includes both villagers and strangers, they are an important means of promoting both acquaintance and friendship.

VILLAGE PRIDE AND FAMILY PRIDE

Joyce Sinnott (page 285) has 'golden memories' of village pride and family pride, but these are qualities that are even more difficult to define and to identify than friendship. Village pride is certainly reflected in Hilda Roberts' Remembrances, which describes the Wingrave of her childhood, well over a century ago.

Dear old Wingrave! As it appears in my memory it was almost an earthly paradise, in a perfect situation crowning the hill overlooking the lovely Vale of Aylesbury and the distant Chilterns. What changes have taken place! Roads which were over-hung with branching elms and oaks are now flanked with rows of houses, and the unsightly (though useful) telephone and electricity poles.

Clearly, Hilda is not so enthusiastic about the changes that took place in the Twenties and Thirties. Seventy years later, how well we know her feelings! What changes we have seen in the last twenty-five years. For the increasing population of Wingrave inevitably brings urbanisation with it. Creeping urbanisation too, as we realised when some friends visited recently, after a long absence from Wingrave. They made no comment on the major housing developments of recent years such as Parsonage Farm and Twelve Leys. Neither did they mention farmyard conversions like Manor Farm,

Straws Hadley, Essex Yard and Mitchell Leys. What really astounded them was the amount of infilling, usually on plots which at best could be graded 'small' to 'tiny'.

Fortunately, there are signs that people are concerned about their environment, and want Wingrave to be a place to be proud of. The forthcoming Millennium will be celebrated with a series of special events, sponsored and encouraged by the Parish Council and the Community Association. In recent years, public areas have been planted with trees, shrubs and bulbs, while recently three 'wild-life habitats' have been established. Thanks to the initiative of the first deputy head of the new school, its buildings now stand in a well-treed area. Much effort has been put into improving the village pond. A handyman is employed (when one can be found) to keep things tidy. Even as this is being written, a message has been delivered requesting assistance in "clearing up a corner of the village". Of course, these last two items are a sad reminder that not everyone has pride in the village.

At a more personal level, older villagers have memories which make it clear that in days gone by most Wingravians cared about the image projected by their family. Thus many villagers would help their children to prepare their entries of wild flowers so that they could make a good showing at the parish's annual Gardens and Allotments Show, one villager even taking his children all the way to Horton just to gather particularly good bullrushes. Some men liked to boast that their families had the traditional new potatoes and fresh peas on Feast Day, the first Sunday after St. Peter's Day (June 29th). "I have known gardeners dig up many more roots of potatoes than they normally would, just because the potato crop was late and very small," recalled Norman Brackley. "They were concerned that their families should keep up the tradition."

Villagers assure us that there were few feckless housewives in Wingrave. Most homes were kept clean and tidy. Apart from anything else, there was no knowing when the Vicar or the Minister might call. And to many people that mattered. Similarly, a farm labourer's clothes had to be appropriate to the dirty jobs on a farm, but come Sunday and there was a transformation. On page 191 Job King appears in his labouring role. Yet on Sundays, when dressed for chapel, he could well have been mistaken for the Chairman of the Board. This seems to have been fairly typical.

The industrious husband took a pride in providing his wife with a regular supply of vegetables: carrots were stored in the sand barrel, onions were strung up, potatoes were sacked, fruit was carefully stored and well-staggered sowings kept a steady flow of green stuff into the kitchen. He might go further, and raise vegetables and flowers for the annual Show.

We have no intention of trying to exemplify attitudes to family matters in recent years, but we have noticed that most parents take a keen interest in their children's progress at school and especially in the 12+ (now 11+) results; are very supportive of school events; cheerfully ferry their children to and from out-of-school activities; and are prepared to spend considerable time and money to advance their children's future.

WHITHER WINGRAVE?

We believe that the future will bring great pressures for further development of housing within the village, thus increasing its urban feel. There are already rumours that the ridge and furrowed Home Ground at Bell Corner will be built over, despite the fact that this is a field which the planners of 25 years ago were insisting should not be developed. More building means a further increase in population, and an even greater reliance on social and recreational groups for involving people with people. In these circumstances one can only commend the late Daphne Rickard's advice:

Wingrave's still here! Appreciate it! Love it! Try to make it as happy a village in the future as it has been in the past.

The Changing Village

156. The old Bell Inn was replaced by a
new Bell Inn (on the right). That has
now been replaced by housing.

157. In 1952 a mains sewage system was
installed. Beyond the excavations is
the Carpenters' Arms, long since closed.

158. Farm houses, yards and adjacent
paddocks have been developed for
housing. The aerial view includes
Manor Farm (upper right); Parsonage
Farm (upper left); and Church Farm
(mid-left).

WINGRAVE with ROWSHAM
LAND UTILISATION 1876

Based upon George Griffin's Map

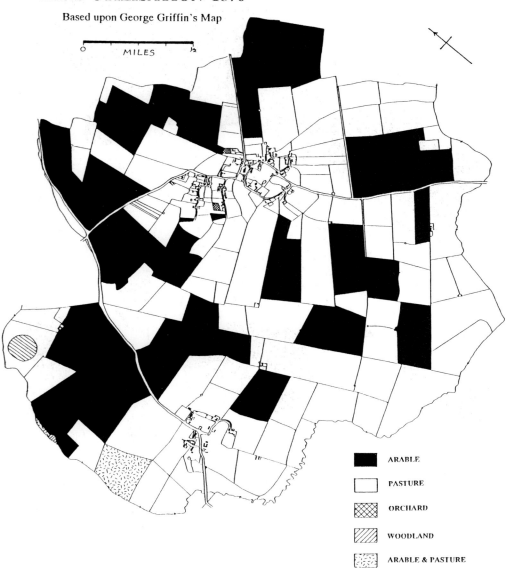

■	ARABLE
□	PASTURE
▨	ORCHARD
▨	WOODLAND
▨	ARABLE & PASTURE

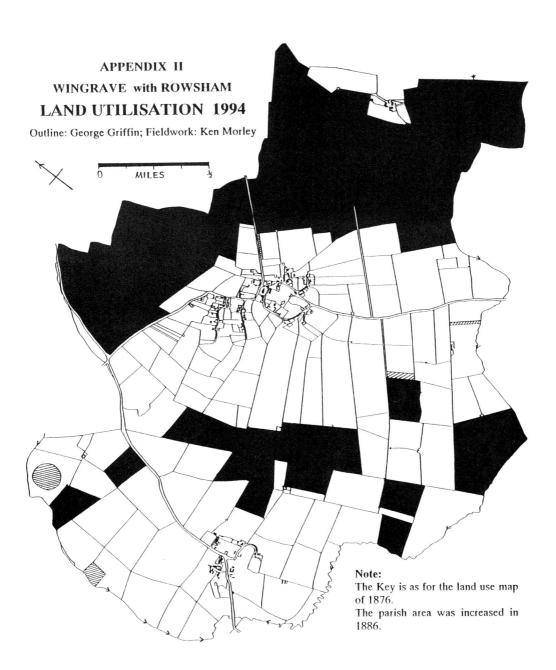

APPENDIX II

WINGRAVE with ROWSHAM

LAND UTILISATION 1994

Outline: George Griffin; Fieldwork: Ken Morley

0   MILES   ½

Note:
The Key is as for the land use map
of 1876.
The parish area was increased in
1886.

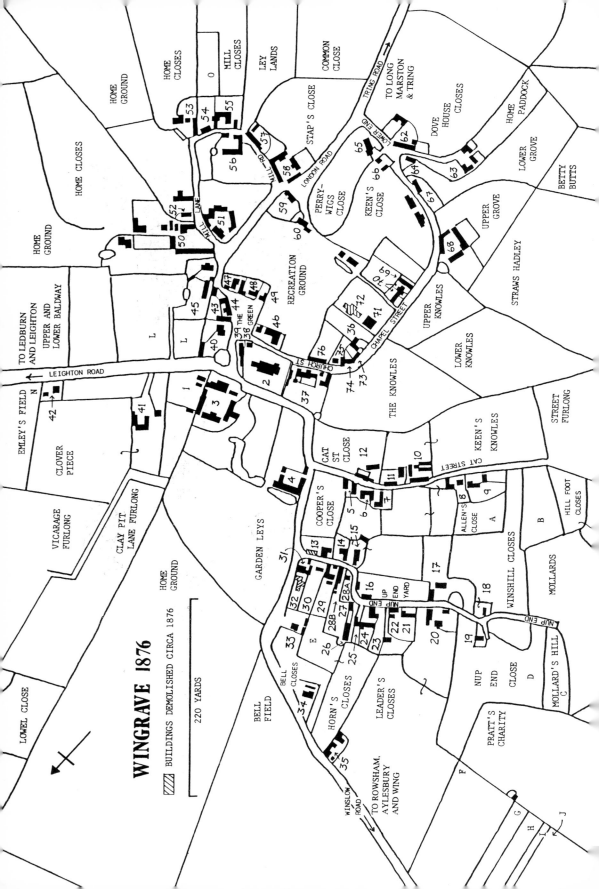

WINGRAVE 1876

▨ BUILDINGS DEMOLISHED CIRCA 1876

|————— 220 YARDS —————|

HOME GROUND

HOME GROUND

HOME CLOSES

HOME GROUND

HOME CLOSES

HOME CLOSES

MILL CLOSES

O

LEY LANDS

COMMON CLOSE

STAP'S CLOSE

53
54
55
56
57
58
59
60
51
52
50

MILL LANE

LONDON ROAD

PERRY-WIGS CLOSE

KEEN'S CLOSE

LOWER END

TRING ROAD

TO LONG MARSTON & TRING

62
65
66
64
63
67
68

DOVE HOUSE CLOSES

HOME PADDOCK

LOWER GROVE

BETTY BUTTS

UPPER GROVE

STRAWS HADLEY

EMLEY'S FIELD

TO LEDBURN AND LEIGHTON

UPPER AND LOWER BALDWAY

HOME CLOSES

RECREATION GROUND

LEIGHTON ROAD

N

42
41
1
3
2
37
45
43
44
47
48
49
46
39
38
40
L
L
L
THE GREEN

76
75
25
36
72
71
70
69
73
74

CHURCH ST

CHAPEL STREET

UPPER KNOWLES

LOWER KNOWLES

THE KNOWLES

CLOVER PIECE

VICARAGE FURLONG

CLAY PIT LANE FURLONG

HOME GROUND

GARDEN LEYS

COOPER'S CLOSE

CAT ST CLOSE

12
11
10
9
8
A
B

CAT STREET

KEEN'S KNOWLES

STREET FURLONG

HILL FOOT CLOSES

ALLEN'S CLOSE

31
13
14
5
15
4
6
7

LOWEL CLOSE

BELL FIELD

BELL CLOSES

HORN'S CLOSES

LEADER'S CLOSES

WINSLOW ROAD

TO ROWSHAM, AYLESBURY AND WING

35
34
33
E
32
30
29
28B
28A
27
26
25
24
23
22
21
20
19
18
17
16

NUP END

UP END YARD

NUP END

WINSHILL CLOSES

MOLLARDS

NUP END CLOSE

PRATT'S CHARITY

MOLLARD'S HILL

C
D
F
G
H
I
J

APPENDIX III: WINGRAVE
GEORGE GRIFFIN'S VILLAGE PLAN 1876

	Occupier	Property
1	Butt, Rev. John M.	Vicarage
2	Butt, Rev. John M.	Parish Church
3	Griffin, George	Bell Leys Farm
4	Griffin, George	Parsonage Farm
5	Rogers, John	2 cottages + gardens
6	Paine, Fred + 1 other	2 cottages + gardens
7	Honor, Geo. + others	Cottages + gardens
8	Stonhill, William	Homestead + land
9	Allen, Wm/Thorne, W	Cottages + gardens
10	Gibbs, John	Cat Street Farm
11	Mead, Thomas	Cottages + gardens
12	Paine,James + 3 others	4 cottages + gardens
13	Alcock,Hen. + 1 other	2 cottages + gardens
14	Mead.Wm.+Faulkner	2 cottages + gardens
15	Dimmock, Josiah*	House + land
16	Higgins,Thomas	House,coach-hse,etc
17	Alcock,widow +Hen.	House, bldgs + land
19	Bonham, John	Cottages + gardens
20	Fleet, Sarah	House + land
22	Bonham, Joseph	Carpenters' Arms
23	Gibbs,Jo. + 1 other	2 cottages + gardens
24	Paine,Th. + 2 others	3 cottages + gardens
25	Orlebar,Wm.+ 1 other	2 cottages + gardens
26	Bonham,Jas.+ 1 other	2 cottages
27	Primitive Methodists *	Chapel
28	Griffin, George	(a) house (b) bakery
29	Fleet, Chas + 7 others	8 cottages + gardens

30	Mortimer, M* + Fleet, E	Cottage + gardens
31	Kirby, James *	House + cottage
32	Fleet,Bignell,Dover,T'g	Cottages + gardens
33	Shackley, Sarah	Bell Inn
34	Gurney, Wm + 3 others	4 cottages + gardens
35	Rickard, Jos.* + others	Little Aston
36	Thorne, Jas + Fleet	Cottages + land
37	Seamons, Josiah	House + land
38	Mortimer, Thomas	Parish cottage + land
39	Newman, Thomas *	House, shop + gdn
40	Seamons, William *	Houses + garden
41	Reynolds, Thos.	Baldway Hse + land
42	Coleman, John	House + land
43	Brandon, Hannah	House+smith's shop
44	Fleet, Mary Ann	Hse+carpenter's shop
45	Gibbs, James *	House + 3 cottages
46	Wyatt, James	School +school house
47	Mortimer, Charles	Rose & Crown Inn
48	Dimmock, John *	House and Cottage
49	Orlebar, Ann	Cottage and garden
50	Biggs, Thomas E.	Baldway Farm
51	Eustace, William	Floyds Farm
52	Smith, Thos & son	Floyds Cottages
53	Seamons, Josiah	Maltby Farm
54	Humphrey, Joseph, etc.	2 cottages + gardens
55	Horwood, William, etc.	3 cottages + gardens
56	Seamons, Josiah	Waterloo Farm
57	French Mrs, etc	6 cottages + gardens

58	Roads, Alfred	Windmill Farm
59	The Infants' School *	
60	Gibbs, Mrs M.	The Anchor
62	Baker, Thomas	Mitchell Leys Fm
63	Griffin, Mrs J.W.*	Ox-hole Farm
64	Hedges, Dan + 1 other	Cottages + gardens
65	. . . ks, Henry + 1 other	Cottages + gdns $
66	. . . . ., John + 1 other	Cottages + gdns $
67	Griffin, Mrs J.W.*	Betty Butts Farm
68	Griffin, Mrs J.W.*	Straws Hadley Fm
69	Fleet, Josiah* +7 more	8 cottages + gdns
70	Goldney, Jas.+ 4 more	5 cottages + gdns
71	Congregat'l Chapel*	
72	White, John + 5 more	6 cottages + gdns
73	Higgins, Wm + Hart,F	2 cottages + gdns
74	Ludlow, Levi +4 more	5 cottages + gdns
75	Pike, Rev. J	The Manse
76	Paine, Wm + 4 others	5 cotts + gdns
A	Fleet, Joseph	Allen's Close: grs
B	Newman, Thos	Winshill: arable
C	Mead, Wm	Mollards Hill: arab
D	Stonhill, Wm	Nup End Close: grs
E	Kirby, Jas	Horn's Closes: grs
F	. . . ard, Jo	Twelve Leys: grs
G	Fleet, Sarah	Grassland
H	Fleet, Sarah	Grassland
I	Fleet, Sarah	Grassland
J	Fleet, Sarah	Grassland

Key: . . . . . letters missing - original map damaged.
$ location assumed by reference to 1871/81 censuses.

* owner-occupier
grs = grassland

arab = arable
T'p = Tapping

George Griffin's map is reproduced by courtesy
of Deryck Bell

APPENDIX IV: ROWSHAM

GEORGE GRIFFIN'S PLAN, 1876

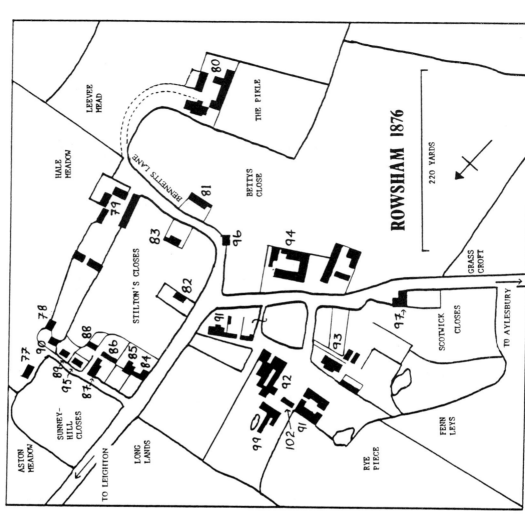

ROWSHAM 1876

220 YARDS

	Occupier	Property
77	Congregat'l Chapel*	
78	Bates, Chas. + 1 more	2 cottages + gdns
79	Roads, Alfred	Hale Farm
80	Lucas, Ed. M.Major-*	Seabrooks Farm
81	Jeffs, Wm + others	Cottages + gardens
82	Higgins, John + others	Cottages + gardens
83	Bateman, Ed. + others	Cottages + gardens
84	Gurney, Wm. K.*	House + brewery
85	Butler, Wm.	Cottage + garden
86	Ellis, Jas. + others	Cottages + gardens
87	Stilton, Wm.+George.J	2 cottages + gdns
88	Stilton, Joseph	Cottage + garden
89	Humphry, Reuben	Cottage + garden
90	Edwards,Wid+Higgs.S	2 cottages + gdns
91	Lucas, Ed. M. Major-*	Mercers Farm+yard
92	Lucas, Ed. M. Major-*	Old Brewery Yard
93	Lucas, Ed. M. Major-*	Home Farm
94	Lucas, Ed. M. Major-*	Baileys Farm
95	Church School*	
96	Brandon, Mrs	Blacksmith's shop
97	Malin, Edward*	The Old Red Lion
99	Lucas, Ed. M. Major-φ	Malthouse
102	Higgs, Jas. + 1 other	2 cottages + gdns
103	Keen, Sam. + 3 more $	4 cottages + gdns

Key:

* owner-occupier

φ ownership not established

$ location unknown – map damaged

George Griffin's map is reproduced by courtesy of
Deryck Bell

Appendix V: Wingrave's First 'Sale of the Century'

In April 1910 the thirty-five half-timbered cottages built at Wingrave for the late Countess of Rosebery (formerly Hannah de Rothschild) were sold by auction at the Rose and Crown. Details of three of the lots are reproduced below as they appeared in the original sale catalogue. The manuscript additions are the name of the purchaser and the price paid. Wingrave's second 'sale of the century' was in 1918, when Leopold de Rothschild's properties were auctioned.

LOT 12.

A Pair of Cottages and Shop,

Situated at the Corner of Nup End and the Main Road.

The construction and accommodation of the Property are similar to Lot 1, with the addition of the Shop (14ft. × 11ft. 3in.), which is built on to the Corner Cottage.

There is a Well of Water on the Premises, access to which is reserved to other Cottages on the same Estate, until provided with their own source of supply.

Fleet

The Tenants are Mr. W. FLEET and Mr. GEO. HIGGINS, who rents the Shop at a

Yearly Rental of £9 : 17 : 6.

The Partitions and Fittings in the Shop are the property of the Tenant.

£300

The necessary fencing to be erected and maintained by the Purchaser of this Lot.

LOT 15.

A BLOCK of THREE WELL=BUILT COTTAGES,

WITH GARDENS,

Pleasantly situated facing the Recreation Ground.

J. Fleet

£300

The Property is of brick, half-timber, and rough cast construction, with tiled roof. Each Cottage contains 3 Rooms upstairs, Sitting Room, Kitchen and Larder downstairs, with a Barn, E.C., and Ashpit.

There is a small Garden in front of each Cottage, separated from the Recreation Ground by Iron Railings, the latter to be the property of and maintained by the Purchaser.

The Tenants are Mrs. ALCOCK, Mrs. BONHAM, and Mr. UNDERWOOD.

There is a well of water on the Premises.

The Buildings on the Gardens are the Property of the Tenants.

A 4-foot right-of-way will be given to this Property along the North side of the Chapel from Chapel Street.

The Purchaser to erect and maintain a good and sufficient fence between this Lot and Lot 16.

LOT 19.

A Charming Detached Week=end Residence,

Of brick, half-timber, and part rough cast construction, with tiled roof, surrounded by a

BELT OF SHRUBS, AND HAVING A SMALL GARDEN.

£195

The House is artistically designed, and contains 3 Bed Rooms, 11ft. × 10ft., 11ft. 9in. × 11in., and 6ft. 9in. × 5ft. 6in.; Sitting Room, 11ft. 6in. × 10ft.; Kitchen, 11ft. × 10ft.; Small Larder, Barn, Ashpit, and E.C.

It is very pleasantly situated facing the Recreation Ground, and having a Moat in front and extensive Views over the Vale.

Spriggs

The Property is let to an excellent Tenant, Mrs. PAINE.

The fence between this and the previous Lot to be erected and maintained by the Purchaser of this Lot. The strip of Land between the footpath and the moat in front of this Lot will be sold with this Lot.

Chapter Notes and References

Abbreviations: B.R.O.   Buckinghamshire Record Office   PP   Parliamentary Papers
             O.R.O.   Oxfordshire Record Office   L.B.O   Leighton Buzzard Oberver
             B.L.(O)   Bodleian Library, Oxford   O.U.   Open University Library
             B.A.A.N   Bucks Advertiser and Aylesbury News
             B.H.   Bucks Herald
             B.A.S.L   Bucks Archaeological Society Library
             P.R.O.(C)   Public Record Office (Chancery Lane)
             P.R.O.(K)   Public Record Office (Kew)
             R. A. L   Rothschild Archive, London
             H.R.O.   Hertfordshire Record Office
             A.L.S.L   Aylesbury Local Studies Library

Chapter One: Fifty Years After Enclosure

1. Grey's Factory Act of 1847 was the first to limit women's hours in factories effectively.
2. To 'plash' a hedge was to 'lay' it.
3. 'Quicks' are young plants, especially white hawthorn, planted to grow into a hedge.
4. 1851 Census: parish population 813, less 163 for Rowsham.
5. 'South' represents all aspects between south-east and south-west.
6. Not Rowsham ale, though this could be obtained at the Bell and the Carpenters' Arms.
7. Hilda Roberts was writing of the 1880's, but this must have gone on for centuries.
8. The forge is now a private garage, but the spreading chestnut tree still survives.
9. The records suggest that Baldway House was once the farmhouse for Glebe Farm. If so, it must be distinguished from Baldway Farm (later called Old Manor Farm by the Freemans) in Mill Lane, opposite Floyds Farm. In recent times Old Manor Farmyard has been known as Essex Yard.
10. O.R.O: Oxford Diocesan Papers, Clergy Answers, mss..
11. BR0./PR235/8/1:Wingrave Vestry Minute Book.
12. Only live-in servants have been counted.
13. A holding with less than 10 acres was regarded as a smallholding.
14. 1851 Census: farmers in the parish claimed to employ 93 men, but 142 males (16-65 years) claimed to be agricultural labourers. Some may have worked outside the parish, but the most likely reason for the difference is unemployment.
15. Simpson, Bill: The Aylesbury Railway, Oxford Publishing Coy., 1989. Travel from Marston Gate was not possible for passengers until at least 1857. It was 1864 before plans were approved for a proper station.
16. BRO: Posse Comitatus, 1798.
17. Rose, Walter: Good Neighbours, O.U.P., 1942, pp. 41/42.
18. The Statute of Artificers, 1563.
19. BRO/D/A/WF/121/131: will of Thomas Fleet of Wingrave, 1846.
20. The Wingrave smithy produced a range of goods in the Twenties and Thirties including hinges and gate hooks. In addition hoes, horse chains and gates were repaired, and rivetting and forge welding were done.
21. The absence of sawyers in 1798 is puzzling. Accumulations of sawdust at sawing pit level were found when Wingrave Garage was re-built.
22. We have not found any documentary evidence, but experts claim to be able to distinguish between the two parts.
23. Mollards Cottage is Dept of the Environment listing SP8619/10/139
24. In the pre-1841 censuses figures for housing are not always reliable.
25. BRO/D/94/57: map and declaration of freehold in Nap End, 25.9.1841.
26. It was given this name by Miss Bim Pullen, who owned it from 1948 to 1988. The previous owner was Tom Payne, who kept a cow in the grounds, and sold the milk.
27. B.R.O./D/A/WF/121/131: Will of Thomas Fleet, 1846. It appears that Samuel and Caleb Fleet sold the property to Thos. Parsons, from whom Caleb rented it back. It later became the Carpenters Arms.

Chapter Two: Death and Life in the 19th Century

1. The infant and child mortality figures obtained by our calculations for figure 1 were much higher than the national figures for 1841 to 1910, but about the same for 1921 to 1990. Clearly, the parish wasn't a healthy place in which to rear children. Significantly, as polluted wells were closed down, the figures improved.
2. It was impossible to calculate the mortality rates for the parish in the usual way, as the registration dist-

ricts do not coincide with the parishes. Neither could baptisms be substituted for births, because baptism was not compulsory and was not carried out by some families. In any case, baptismal records for the Congregational Church were only available from 1920. To overcome these problems and the small numbers in a rural parish, burials were recorded over 35-year periods. This enabled the ratio 'death by age x / total deaths' to be calculated for 35 year periods.

3.   The phrase 'laissez-faire' summarises the principle of non-interference by government in the actions of individuals, especially in industry and trade. 'Laissez-mourir' indicates the same policy of non-interference, but in social matters.

4.   B.H: 26.1.1887.

5.   BRO/DRO/94/55: Sale of Chapel Row by Thomas and Ruth Reynolds to Hannah de Rothschild lists previous tenants at different periods.

6.   BL(O): Parliamentary Papers.

7.   BRO/DC2/39/1: Minutes of Rural Sanitary Authority, 1882-92.

8.   Gibbs, R: Bucks Local Occurrences, for 23. 6.1832.

9.   As 7 above.

10.   Roberts, Hilda: Remembrances of Old Wingrave, Ms., c.1930. The comment refers to the 1880's.

11.   As 7 above.

12.   As 7 above.

13.   BL(O): Parliamentary Papers 1864, vol. XXVIII. Dr Ord re Church Row, Church Street, Wing.

14.   Bucks Herald 26.1.1887.

15.   As 7 above, November 1887.

16.   Tannahill, Reay: Food in History, Paladin, 1973, quoting Florence Nightingale's 'Report on Sanitation'.

17.   The tubercule bacillus was not isolated until 1882, and it was a long time before cattle and milk were routinely tested: see also note 19. In the Chesham area in the 1930's only the local Cooperative Society was pasteurising its milk. The rest were selling milk straight off the farm. This was fairly typical.

18.   Smith, E.R: The People's Health 1830-1910, Croom Hill, 1979.

19.   Bucks Herald 1896.

20.   Evidence before the Select Committee on the Poor Law Amendment Act, reported in the Bucks Herald, August 18th and 25th, and September 1st, 1838.

21.   Until 1875 there seem to have been two rows of cottages called Chapel Row. One was designated 'South', presumably to distinguish it from the other.

22.   Roberts, Hilda: see 10 above.

23.   Bucks Herald 13.12.1834. The text of the letter is in chapter 3, 'Poverty'.

24.   Bosanquet, S.R: The Rights of the Poor and Christian Almsgiving Vindicated, 1841.

25.   BL(O): PP XVII Commission taking Evidence on the Employment of Children, Young Persons and Women in Agriculture, 1867. It was the largest first-hand enquiry since Sir Frederick Eden's researches of 1797.

26.   Smith, E: The Present State of the Dietary Question, 1864.

27.   BRO/PR235/8/2: Wingrave Vestry Minute Book, 13.7.1860.

28.   BRO/PR235/8/1: Wingrave Vestry Minute Book, 1835. The agreement was continued for 1836/37.

29.   Bucks Herald 25.2.1860.

30.   Roberts, Hilda: Many Happy Returns to Your Institute, m.s., c.1930.

31.   Ceeley, R: Account of a Contagious Epidemic of Puerperal Fever, Lancet 1834-5, Vol.1, pp 813-818.

Chapter Three: Poverty

1.   In "The Great Upheaval" the paupers were referred to as "the Miserable", following the terminology used by Sir Frederick Eden, The State of the Poor, 1797.

2.   The compulsory poor rate was a device first introduced in Elizabethan times when it was combined with harsh measures to punish the unemployed, who were regarded as Sturdy Beggars i.e. simply idle.

3.   In 1811 7/- per week was the rate in Wingrave with Rowsham for an able-bodied agricultural labourer with a family, on the roundsman system. By 1833 the Vestry Minutes indicate that the rate had risen to 8/-. A married man with no family got 7/- per week, while a single man of 24 and upwards received 5/-. These rates are roughly consistent with those for fully-employed labourers in the Vale quoted by Robert Ceeley, a surgeon at the Bucks Infirmary, Aylesbury. However, he is careful to point out that the wages of agricultural labourers "vary a good deal in different parishes: the average is 8/- to 9/- per week, though one individual pays his labourers 11/-, a very considerate man. In other parishes they are 9/-, and in one parish 10/-." [B.L.(O)/PP: Minutes of Evidence before the Select Committee on the Poor Law Amendment Act, in Reports, Committees 1837-8, vol. XVIII Pt 3, question 15302].

4.   BRO/PR235/12/2: Accounts of the Wingrave Overseers 1811-1816.

5.   BRO/PR235/11/1: Accounts of the Wingrave Overseers.

6.   Chambers, Jill: Buckinghamshire Machine Breakers, pub. Jill Chambers, 1991.

Hobsbawm, E.J. & Rude, J: Captain Swing, Lawrence and Wishart, 1969.

7. BRO/PR235/8/1: Wingrave Vestry Minute Book. It took time for the Aylesbury Union to provide the new centralised workhouse opposite Aylesbury Gaol, later to become Tindal Hospital. So it was June 1841 before the Wingrave workhouse was demolished. The parish house on the edge of the churchyard was retained, and the other three were sold by public auction.

8. Bucks Herald 12.6.1875. By this date the rule had been in operation for thirty years.

9. BRO/PR235/8/1: Wingrave Vestry Minute Book, August 1834.

10. BL(0)/PP: 3rd Report from the Select Committee appointed to enquire into the State of Agriculture, 1836. Minutes of Evidence taken before the Select Committee on Agricultural Distress.

11. PRO(K): MH12/406.

12. It may be that Gilbert and Cox assumed that a shortage of inmates at the workhouse meant a shortage of unemployed. In practice, most of the unemployed were succoured by their families.

13. In the same period the population of England & Wales increased by 44%.

14. BL(0)/PP Vol XIII: Select Committee on Railway Labourers, 1846.

15. PRO(K)/MH12/405: Letter to Poor Law Commissioners 8th Nov. 1834; reply 29th Nov. 1834.

16. Outdoor relief meant money from public funds paid to those who were not resident in the workhouse.

17. ALSL/L00034: 1st Annual Report of the Poor Law Commission for England and Wales.

18. PRO(K)/MH12/405: letters dated 13th and 26th July and 1st Aug 1837.

19. Bucks Herald 13.12.1834. See 'Death and Life in Wingrave' for the budget based on this letter.

Chapter Four: Straw Plaiting

1. BRO/PR235/12/2: Wingrave with Rowsham - Accounts of the Overseers of the Poor.

2. BRO/235/8/1: Wingrave Vestry Minute Book.

3. Roberts, Hilda: Remembrances, manuscript c. 1925. Jemima Mead was Hilda's mother, who was born in Wingrave in 1838.

4. Roberts, Hilda: op. cit..

5. PP 1864, XXII: Report on Straw Plaiting and Bonnet Manufactures.

6. As 5 above.

7. In Wingrave village in 1851, there was a direct relationship between socio-economic class and the number of children (3 to 9 years) employed:
73% of labourers' children were employed
60% of tradesmen's and artisans' children were employed
56% of professionals' and farmers' children were employed.
There is no evidence as to how the children with no stated occupation were occupied. They may have plaited at home; or have been taught other trades by their parents or relatives; or have carried out domestic duties in their own homes, especially where there were large families. A very few may have had private tutors.

8. The records used included the Census 1851 to 1891, George Griffin's map of Wingrave in 1876 (with index), and Hilda Roberts' Remembrances.

9. PP: Reports of Factory Inspectors, 30th April 1871, p.55.

10. PP XVII 1867-8: First Report of the Royal Commission on the Employment of Women and Children in Agriculture, Mr George Culley's Report quoting information from the Chief Constable of Buckinghamshire.

11. As 5 above: Page 202, Evidence of Mrs Turry of Edlesborough.

12. The number of plait schools admitting to 'candlelighting' in the 1867 Report is low judged by the widespread ad hoc reports from parishes. In practice the figure would vary over the year: some schools only worked in the evenings in winter, or when the trade was especially busy.

13. As 5 above: Mrs Honey of Toddington.

14. Roberts, Hilda: Grandmother's Tales, manuscript c. 1920's.

15. As 5 above.

16. Bucks Herald 3.10.1846: Aylesbury Plait Market, Toll Free.

17. Roberts, Hilda: Grandmother's Tales; and Preface to Becky Roddell's Business. Rebecca was the widow of Paul Radwell who died in 1797. They probably came to Wingrave in 1789. Their marriage is not recorded, in the Wingrave Parish registers, but the baptisms of three children are. Rebecca died on 22nd April 1828.

18. As 3 above.

19. As 3 above.

20. Luton and Dunstable Museum: 1/77/62.

21. As 3 above.

Chapter Five: Looking for a Better Life.

1. BRO/PR235/8/1: Wingrave Vestry Minute Book, January 1835.

2   B L (O)/PP: Third Report from the Select Committee on the State of Agriculture, 1836.
3.   Gibbs, Robert: Local Occurrences, 1880.
4.   As note 1, but November 1846.
5.   Tomlinson, G: Bring Plenty of Pickles, 1986, pp 16-17. Copies are available from the author at 7, Moor Drive, Littlemoor Drive, Pudsey, West Yorks..
6.   Beck, James, A: The Humphrey Pioneers from Wingrave.
7.   Tomlinson, G: op. cit. reproduces the original letters in full.
8.   Bourke, Carmel; and Holloway, Lucy: From Wingrave to Whitfield, Warrigal Press, 1990.
     Jarrott, J. Keith: The Jarrott Family – Aylesbury to Brisbane.
9.   Archer, Jean:Buckinghamshire Headlines, Countryside Books, 1992.
10. No-one is sure why the family went to Brisbane, if they really wanted to go to Victoria.
11. Wangaratta Chronicle: 2nd May, 1915.
12. Millburn, John, R; and Jarrott, Keith: The Aylesbury Agitator, 1988.
13. Labourers' Union Chronicle, 4th and 25th July 1874.
14. Bucks Herald, 6 June 1874, p.7.
15. BAAN: 14 Jan 1874 has the full text.
16. BAAN: 16 Nov 1872, p. 2, cols 2-3. The cleric was quoting from the Church of England Catechism.
17. BAAN: 18 July 1874, p. 4, col. 5.
18. Tomlinson, G: op. cit., p.39.
19. Shann: Economic History of Australia, 1938, p.343.
20. Tomlinson, G: op. cit., p.39.

Chapter Six: The Rothschilds to the Rescue

1.   BRO/D94/26: Deeds and correspondence relating to three farms sold to Baron Mayer de Rothschild,1842. A hunting box was simply a small country house used as a base for hunting.
2.   BRO: Return of Owners of Land, 1873, vol. 1, London, 1875.
3.   RAL/R. Fam C21: letter dated 4.2.1867 from Charlotte (Lionel de Rothschild's wife).
4.   RAL/ R. Fam C16/14: Letter from Juliana (Hannah's mother) to Charlotte. See also BH 7/3/1868.
5.   BH: 9.10.1875.
6.   Alterations to one of the Rothschild cottages revealed the slender bricks which tie together the two leaves of each wall.
7.   BRO/D/RO Add'l 6/58: an illustrated auction catalogue of the cottages to be sold on 28/4/1910 details the properties, rents, occupiers, etc..
8.   BH:25.3.1876.
9.   BH: 13.11.1875.
10. Fleet, William: This is the Story of my Life, ms., 1956.
11. RAL/T12/121: Letter dated 10.5.1877 from Hannah de Rothschild to Lionel de Rothschild, who would be well informed about the local property market. Only 5 years earlier he had purchased Tring Park and 4000 acres, a transaction which no estate agent would forget when further property became available.
12. BAAN: 10.1.1874.
13. Hart, Lloyd: Health in the Vale of Aylebury, HM&M, 1979.
14. RAL/XII/8/0: Lionel de Rothschild's Estate Books 1851-1879.
15. RAL/XII/25/1: Ascott Estate, list of holdings with descriptions.
16. Only seven houses were built, as two were on double plots.
17. Letter from Lord Rosebery to Mrs Duncan quoted by Cowles, 'The Rothschilds, a Family of Fortune' and reproduced with permission.
18. LBO: the 235 children attending school in Mentmore, Cheddington, Wingrave and Hoggeston were supplied with new clothing.
19. BH: 23/3/1878.
20. BH: 18/5/1878, page 8. For report of wedding see The Times 21/3/1878.
21. Attributed to Hannah's cousin, Mrs Flower, in 'Lady Rosebery' page 217.
22. Quoted by James, 'Rosebery', Phoenix, 1995, page 227.
23. BRO/D/RO/2/1-66.
24. BRO/D/RO/2/28.
25. BRO/D/RO/2/28: letter dated 2/6/1892 from Samuel Hedges, Secretary.
26. BRO/D/RO/2/8: letter dated 9/6/1892 from the Oddfellows Integrity Lodge, Wingrave.
27. BRO/D/RO/2/28:letter dated 17/2/1905 from Rev. Lockhart to Lord Rosebery.
28. BRO/D/RO/2/15. appeal for Queen Victoria's Diamond Jubilee, 1897. Rosebery sent £10.
29. BRO/D/RO/2/9: William Mead to Lord Rosebery.
30. BRO/D/RO/12 & 13: the 1901 census returns, to be released in 2002, may reveal more about this.
31. BRO/D/RO/2/32: Anon. to Lord Rosebery.
32. BRO/D/RO/2/ 44.

Chapter Seven: The Tide Begins To Turn

1. BRO/G2/31, 32, 33: Aylesbury Union – Mortality from Infectious Diseases.
2. Agricultural Committee of the Tariff Commission: Minutes of Evidence 6.2.1905.
3. 'Perquisites' included beer provided by the farmer, piece work and overtime especially at harvest time.
4. Board of Trade, Second Series of Memoranda, Statistical Tables and Charts, 1904.
5. Morley, Ken and Margaret: Grass Roots Democracy in Action, pp. 1 and 2, 1994. See also Recollections "Joey Versus the Vicar" in this volume, page 112.
6. Towards the end of the 19th century, Wingrave's sick clubs included: Wingrave Anchor Benefit Society (estab. 1838); Wingrave Labourers' Friendly Society; the Hearts of Oak Benefit Society (at the Bell); and the Manchester Unity of Oddfellows Integrity Lodge.
7. At the turn of the century, matters of public health in the Aylesbury area were dealt with by, inter alia, the Local Government Board, the Rural Sanitary Authority, the Aylesbury Union and the Bucks County Council.
8. It was called the 'English' cholera.
9. BRO/DC2/39/1: Minute Book of the Rural Sanitary Authority, 1882-1892.
10. BRO/G/2/5: Minute Book of the Aylesbury Union.
11. As note 1 above.
12. BH: 7.6.1889.
13. BH: 27.9.1890.
14. BH: 28.11.1891.
15. BH: 31.12.1892.
16. Parish Magazine: April 1909.
17. BH: 4.10.1893.
18. As note 10 above.
19. Thompson, Flora: Lark Rise, OUP, 1939.
20. Smockfrocks did not go out of fashion until the 1890's.
21. BH: 10.1.1874.
22. Wingbury is the farm on the Leighton Road, just outside the parish boundary and now named Upper Wingbury.

Chapter Eight: Wingrave Acquires Its Gentry

N.B: This chapter owes much to material prepared by the late John Camp. We are grateful to his widow, Rose Camp, for allowing us to use it.

1. BRO/D/RO/2/1: letter dated 6.3.1885 from W.R.S. Freeman to Lord Rosebery.
2. BRO/DX/476/3: Contract dated 1898 between the Earl of Rosebery and W.R.S. Freeman for the sale of the Manor House at Wingrave. Although only twenty years old, the Freemans' house became known as 'The Old Manor House', and the farm (formerly part of Baldways Farm) as 'Old Manor Farm'. It thus tended to be confused with Leopold de Rothschilds' "Manor Farm" just opposite the village pond, and in consequence the latter was often called Bell Leys Farm.
3. PRO (K): IR58/2041, Field Book of the 1910 Treasury Domesday of Wingrave.
4. PRO (C): Census 1891.

Chapter Nine: Worshipping in Wingrave

1. Morley, Margaret and Ken: The Great Upheaval, 1994, pp.22-23.
   Hamilton, Henry: History of the Homeland, Allen & Unwin, 1947, pp. 472-474.
2. Rebecca Radwell (d.1828) was the widow of Paul Radwell (d.1797). In 1800 she had three children, the eldest aged ten years. She was almost certainly the model for Becky Roddell in Hilda Roberts' playlet.
3. Later, as they gained in confidence, many Nonconformists made significant contributions to the wider community. See, for example, Phillips, G. and W: The First Hundred Years, Wingrave with Rowsham Parish Council, 1995.
4. Wingrave Church of SS Peter and Paul, parish magazines 1907-1919.
5. ORO/C376: Oxford Diocesan Papers, Clergy Answers, mss., 1914.

Chapter Ten: The Parish Church

1. The earliest peal of bells was probably four in number. In 1553 four great bells are listed. By 1618 the bell-frame had been modified to take two more, and in 1737/8 six are listed. In 1998 two more were added. BRO/PR235/3/1: Wingrave Vicarage Records Book. See p.95 for copy of the Roll of Church-yard Mounds (53 entries).
2. ORO: Mss Oxford Diocesan Papers d.550, comments by Bishop Wilberforce, c. 1845-50.
3. Griffin, Edward (great-great-grandson of William Griffin): Stories My Grandfather Told Me, ms. 1998.
4. ORO: as note 2 above, but d. 179 folio 818, and c. 331 folio 1.
5. Rickard, Minnie: Recollections of Preachers of Long Ago, ms., undated.

6. The Book of Common Prayer, c.1930: The Catechism.
7. May, Trevor: An Economic and Social History of Britain 1760-1970, Longman, 1987, p.136.
8. BH: 1.10.1887
9. BAAN 16.11.1872, p.4: The Rev. Butt addressing a meeting of the Wingrave, Aston Abbotts, Bierton, and Hulcott Agricultural Association.
10. Thompson, F.M.L: Social Control in Victorian Britain, Economic History Review, May 1981, p.196.
11. At that time the trustees of the Primitive Methodist Chapel did not include a single farmer. Although a majority of the Congregational trustees were farmers, corn dealers, and even 'a gentleman', only one of them lived in Wingrave.
12. BAAN: presentation of an address of thanks to Joseph Lucas for the gift of a church organ over two years earlier.
13. BH: 19.5. 1877.
14. BH: the school was built in 1847 and was first used only as a Sunday School. No scholars were mentioned in the 1851 census, so we assume that it only became a day school at some time after April 1851. Clergy Answers specifically mention a day school in 1854.
15. BH: 1.10.1887.
16. BH: 6.6.1885, 22.8.1885 and 7..9.1901.
17. BH: 4.5.1889.
18. Griffin, Frank, G: letter dated 7.1.1950 to Vic Rickard.
19. Morley, K.C., and M.I: Grass Roots Democracy in Action, 1994, pp. 1&2.
20. BH: 7.7.1906.
21. BRO/D/RO/2/32: letter dated 1.3.1906 from Rev. Francis to Lord Rosebery.
22. Includes some material from the Bucks Herald and the Parish Council minutes.
23. In past times most villages had one or two women who laid out the bodies of their dead friends and neighbours. It involved washing the body and dressing it in its Sunday best.
24. BRO/PR235/29/1 Wingrave and Rowsham Parish Council Minutes 18.3.1895.
25. Feast Day was the Sunday after St Peter's Day (June 29th). It was also called Festival Day, being the day of the Patronal Festival.
26. BH: 22.5.1897.
27. BRO/D/RO/2/46: letter dated 12.4.1910 from Rev. Francis to Lord Rosebery.
28. BRO/PR/235/3/2: letter dated 15.4.1910 from Charles Edmunds to Rev. Francis.
29. ORO: Oxford Diocesan Papers, C3361, Clergy Answers, mss., 1896.
30. BRO/D/RO/2/46: letter dated 17.4.1910 from Rev. Francis to Charles Edmunds.
31. BRO/D/RO/2/47: letter dated 9.5.1910 from Rev. Francis to Chas. Edmunds.
32. BRO/D/RO/2/46: letter dated 17.4.1910 from Rev. Francis to Chas. Edmunds.
33. ORO: Oxford Diocesan Papers, C376, Clergy Answers, mss., 1914.
34. Declaration of Trust dated 28.10.1918 between the Rev. Wm. Francis and the Oxford Diocesan Board.
35. The parish magazines (1907-1919) provide examples.
36. The parish magazines February 1913, and October 1919.
37. BH: 10.1.1874.
38. BH: 17.9.1897.
39. BH: 25.8.1890.

Chapter Eleven: The Independent Chapel

1. Broad, J (Ed): Buckinghamshire Dissent and Parish Life 1669-1712, Bucks Record Society no. 28.
2. During re-decoration in the mid- 20th century, workmen said that the rafters in the roof of the school-room looked like those of an old barn. This led to the conclusion that it was the barn that had been converted into the first meeting house. However, an indenture dated 10.10.1818 (BRO/D/94/55) recording a contract between Henry Newens of Rowsham and William Cox makes it clear that:
    (a) the land given to the congregation contained both a workshop (or malting!) and a barn.
    (b) The meeting house was "lately erected on the site of a workshop".
    (c) After the erection of the meeting house, the barn remained in use, and the users kept access to it.
3. The dates are from notes provided by the late Daphne Rickard. She did not indicate her source.
4. Information provided by Edward Griffin, the great-great-grandson of William Griffin. The rest of the story is told on page 106.
5. The Christian, 13.2.1908, p.16, 'Fifty Years Among Children'. And The Christian Herald, 14.10.1920.
6. Wingrave Congregational Church: minute book 1893-1909, Church Annual Meeting 1904.
7. BRO/DRO/2/41: letter dated 7.12.1908 from the Rev. J. Barton to Lord Rosebery.

Chapter Twelve: The Primitive Methodist Chapel

1. Dunker, D. S: Wingrave Methodist Church – Historical Notes, typescript, 1986.
2. Bates, E. Ralph: Rise of Methodism in the Vale of Aylesbury.

3. BRO/D/RO/2/23: letter dated January 1904 from John Stead (Minister), W. Rickard and T.Jones (Stewards) to Lord Rosebery.
4. Wingrave Methodist Church Centenary 1859 – 1959: Programme for 18th April 1959. This is the source of the quotation from the Circuit Report, and numerous other details.
5. Roberts, H: Recollections of Old Wingrave, ms., c. 1930.
6. Rickard, Minnie: Peculiarities of Preachers of Long Ago, ms., 1965.
7. BRO/D/RO/2/24: letter dated 25.2.1903 to Lord Rosebery from his agent.
8. The Rev. G.E.Butt must not be confused with the Anglican vicar of Wingrave. They were no relation.
9. Information supplied by Horace Bignell, Ron Bignell and Aylesbury Methodist Circuit Magazine (BRO/NM100/9/9/6)
10. BRO/Aylesbury Methodist Circuit Magazine, vol.XLII, May 1937, page 12.

Chapter Thirteen: Schooling

1. The British Society's full name was The British and Foreign Schools Society.
   The National Society's full name was The National Society for the Education of the Poor in the Principles of the Established Church.
2. Thompson, Flora: Lark Rise to Candleford, Chap XI. The School provides an example.
3. Robert Lowe outlining the Revised Code of 1862 to Parliament.
4. Charity Commissioners' Reports: (a) Buckinghamshire, 1833; (b) Public Enquiry into all charities of Wingrave with Rowsham.
5. These are the predecessors of the United Reformed Church (1972 to date), formerly the Congregational Church (1966-1972), and the Congregational Union (1831-1966).
6. Wingrave Parochial School Log Book: Report of HMI, June 1873.
7. Comment recalled by Mary Ann's daughter, Mrs Ethel Perkins (nee Higgs), during conversation 1997. In 1881 four Alcock children were attending Wingrave School at a cost of 5d per week.
8. Wingrave School Log Book 15.5.1878.
9. BL(O): PP1867 XVII Employment of Children, Young Persons and Women in Agriculture, pp. 527, 528, 531, 535.
10. At Rowsham, in 1871, only 3 boys and 5 girls were recorded as scholars. A further 12 girls, all under 13 years, were recorded as straw plaiters, and should have attended for 10 hours per week.
11. Only facts, not opinions, were allowed in the school log books. Presumably Mr Rees had broken the rule, maybe regarding the caning episode.

Chapter Fifteen: Farming

1. Morley, Margaret & Ken: The Great Upheaval describes and illustrates the process by reference to Wingrave.
2. The early land use figures are estimates. Sources include: 1797 Schedule to Enclosure Map (BRO); 1801 List and Index Society, vol. 189: 1801 Crop Returns; 1810 St John Priest, General View of the Agriculture of Bucks; 1876, George Griffin, Map of parish with schedule of owners and occupiers; 1905 Board of Agriculture. The figures for 1918 are for the following farms: Manor (Wingrave), Parsonage, Floyds, Straws Hadley, Windmill, Thistlebrook and a much reduced Home Farm.
3. In 1842 Mercers' farmhouse was vastly extended by the addition of what is now the main house. The name was changed to Manor Farm in the 20th century, when it was purchased by the Normans.
4. 'Partly enclosed' refers to the boundary fencing enclosing the overall area. This still had to be divided into fields.
5. A 'mound' is a hedge. To plash the hedges is to lay them.
6. Quoted by G. Eland: 'In Bucks', Fraine, Aylesbury, 1923.
7. Mitchell, B.R: British Historical Statistics 1750-1975, MacMillan, 1981, page 756.
8. Victoria County History: Buckinghamshire, Agriculture.
9. Most farms in the parish had a dairy. References to nine have so far been found.
10. 'Stores' were animals in course of being reared. 'Finishing' was fattening for the market.
11. Wheat straw was used to bed the cattle. Barley straw, when chopped, was used to feed them.
12. Drummond, J. C. and Wilbrahem, A: The Englishman's Food, London, 1964.
13. HRO/D/E/Bn P5 and B62: notebook, letters, etc..
14. OU: PP28 Evidence to the Royal Commission on Agriculture, 1895.
15. OU: PP29 Royal Commission on Agriculture, 1896.
16. May, T: An Economic and social History of Britain 1760-1970, Longmans, 1987.
17. OU: as note 15 above.
18. BH 1/12/1860.
19. Griffin, Geo: notebook recording farm income and expenditure,1864-1881.
20. Manor Farm was often called Bell Leys Farm to distinguish it from the Freemans' Old Manor Farm.
21. As note 19 above.

22. Fryer, D.W: Land Utilisation Survey, Buckinghamshire, p.184.
23. Much of the information for the interwar and postwar sections was supplied by, inter alia, Norman Brackley, Vic Clay, Gerald Evered, Edward Griffin, Michael Griffin, Michael Higgins, Frank King and Michael Page.
24. BRO/D/BML/24/16: Sales by Leopold de Rothschild, 1918.
    BH: 27/7/1918 'Sale of freehold farms at Aylesbury'.
25. BRO/D/X/476.
26. Griffin, Edward: Tales My Grandfather Told Me, typescript, 1998.
27. Mitchell, British Historical Statistics.
28. Compensation to tenant farmers for improvements funded by them did not become mandatory until the Agricultural Holdings Act of 1948.
29. BRO/D/BML: Brown and Merry papers include Straws Hadley.
30. Pitstone Local History Society: In Pitstone Green there is a Farm, 1979; The Countryman's Year, 1992.
31. Sewell, Clare: Report on Farming in Bucks, in Journal of the Royal Agricultural Society, Vol. 16, 1856.

Chapter Seventeen: Business Life in Wingrave
1. The numbers indicate the numbers of businesses, not the number of employees. Although in 1851 there were two wheelwrights, Henry Keen at 62 years was about to retire; Thos. Newman was just starting.
2. BRO/G2/31-33: printed reports of the Medical Officer of Health to the Aylesbury Union.
3. Because Josiah Dimmock lived there for so many years, villagers called the cottage 'Dimmocks'. Subsequently, it was named 'Dean Leys' and the name Dimmocks was used by the house next door.
4. The house between the graveyard and the pond is now one of several houses, for its outbuildings were converted into dwellings in the 1990's. The original house is on the corner of Winslow Rd. and Church Street.
5. Hilda Gibbs was referring to the shop which her grandmother, Caroline Higgins, established and bequeathed to Hilda's mother, Mary Ann Higgins, always known as Polly. Mary Ann married James Gibbs, son of John Gibbs of Home Farm in Cat Street. James continued to work on his father's farm, though he also kept ducks on the village pond. Just when Hilda took over the shop is uncertain, for her mother did not die until 1960 when she was 96.
6. The outbuildings have since been converted into a dwelling known as The Coach-house.
7. In the 19th century the Winslow Road was often known as Main Street, or Aylesbury Road.
8. Griffin, Edward: op. cit..
9. Roberts, Hilda: Memory Book 3, ms..
10. BRO/DRO/2/11: letter dated April 1895 from the Rev. Lockhart to Lord Rosebery, naming the unemployed labourers, and asking whether his lordship could help.
11. Figures for parishes will not be available until the enumeration papers for the 1901 Census are opened to the public in 2001.
12. Fleet and Roberts was masterminded from Wingrave, but its offices were in New Street, Aylesbury.
13. 1991 Census: 10% sample.
14. The criteria for listing firms as based outside Wingrave, but Wingrave orientated, were:
    (a) must be prepared to visit Wingrave.
    (b) must advertise in the parish, or be listed in the Wingrave/Rowsham Directory.
    (c) Must personally answer the telephone, or provide a message indicating availability.
15. The figures in square brackets indicate the number of enterprises in 1998.

Chapter Eighteen: Home Life in Days Gone By
1. Mill House is in Winslow Road, and the outhouses behind it were once the site of a steam corn mill. The cottage referred to has long since been demolished.
2. This is from a long poem written in 1930. The extract is not autobiographical, but is based on hearsay from old villagers.

Chapter Nineteen: Red Letter Days, Recreations and Other Relaxations
1. Roberts, Hilda: Remembrances, ms., c. 1930, pp.20-22.
2. BH: 11.7.1891 and 7.7.1892.
3. Whitfield, Joan: An Aspect of Wingrave in the 1940's, ms. 1992.
4. The 'tombstones' are the short concrete posts put in round the Green to prevent cars from parking on it.
5. As note 1 above: pp.24-28.
6. Buller Rickard's memory went back to the early 1900's. Mr Freeman died in 1907, though the May Day visits to the Old Manor House continued after that.
7. The first maypole that anyone remembers was used at the celebrations for George V's silver jubilee in 1935.
8. Whipps, Joyce: in correspondence with Margaret Morley.

9.   The school log for 1924 clearly states 'gramophone'.
10. BAAN: 5.8.1854.
11. BAAN: Saturday 8.6.1872.
12. BAAN: 15.6.1878.
13. BH: March 1878, Address from the inhabitants of Wingrave to Hannah de Rothschild on the occasion of her marriage.
14. Local press: 9.7.1892.
15. Griffin, Edward: op. cit..
16. BRO/DRO/2/24: letters dated 20.2.1904 and 5.4.1904 from F.R.Gibbs to Lord Rosebery.
17. BRO/DRO/2/25: letter dated 1904 from F.R.Gibbs to Lord Rosebery.
18. Griffin, Edward: op. cit.. There were two Trotts playing cricket for Australia in the 1890's: an H.Trott and an A.Trott. Both were bowlers!
19. BRO/DRO/2/6: letter dated 9.11.1891 from Wingrave Football Club to Lord Rosebery.
20. Griffin, Edward: op. cit..
21. Griffin, Frank: letter c. 1949/1950 to Vic Rickard.

Chapter Twenty: Everyday Stories of Country Folk

1.   The connection with the Paine family is deduced from the fact that at this time the names Elizabeth Paine and Susanna Paine only appeared in the family of Harley Paine. Also, the witnesses at William and Susanna's wedding included a J. Paine and a P. Paine. These could have been Susanna's uncles John or Joseph and her step-uncle Percival.
2.   George Rickard had a child, Elizabeth, baptised at Wingrave in 1824. Of course, he may have lived on in the village for some years, but no further trace of him has been found.
3.   As the 1861 Census shows there was a Mill House and a Mill Cottage. We assume that William occupied the former, and that it was slightly bigger than the Mill Cottage, which has survived as Rose Cottage, and was originally built on the two-up, two-down plan. We have not been able to identify the Mill House.
4.   It was April 1852 when the lease of the mill and bakehouse (to which a grocer's shop had been added) was next advertised.
5.   Ann's age at death was said to be 95, though she was actually 90.
6.   Cat Street is a name going back at least to the 14th century. However, after World War One the residents asked for it to be changed and it became Castle Street.
7.   The inscription definitely reads T. Rickard. The only T. Rickards in Wingrave at that time were under ten years of age. So who does the inscription commemorate?
8.   Earlier in the 19th century this field was called Short Nell.
9.   The information is in the first pier and relates to two local events. The London Butchers came down to Wingrave for a cricket match and they were dressed as clowns. William thought "it was wonderful". The other event was the wedding of Miss Daisy Fleet of Wingrave and Mr Richard Pritchard, a farmer of Kimble.
10. These invitations to Mentmore were almost certainly by, or on behalf of, Lord Dalmeny, the son of Lord Rosebery and Hannah. Lord Dalmeny was 'at age' i.e. 21 years old, in 1903, and many parties and receptions were given to celebrate the occasion.
11. During World War One, Will Roberts was employed by the Air Ministry as a building manager, in which capacity he supervised constructional work in various parts of the country.
12. The Fleets sold Sunny Bank to Tom and Minnie Rickard. Minnie was the daughter of Thomas and Ann Jones, so it was Minnie's childhood home. They re-named it 'Holmlea'. The price in 1935 was £450.

Chapter Twenty-one: The Great War 1914 – 1918

1.   Fred Rickard was nicknamed 'Buller' by his father, after General Buller CIC during the South African War, and he was known as 'Buller' throughout his life.
2.   Parish Magazine November 1917.
3.   Parish Magazine March 1917.
4.   Parish Magazine November 1917.
5.   Parish Magazine November 1918.
6.   Parish Magazine July 1918.

Chapter Twenty-two: Strangers and Villagers

1.   Marsden, T. and Murdoch, J: Reconstituting the Rural in an Urban Region – New Villages for Old, Countryside Change Working Paper 26, December 1991.
2.   Census 1991: Buckinghamshire Report, Small Area Statistics.

Subscribers

To 4th September 1999

Jean Adams
Sue Adams
Geoffrey & Hilary Aldridge
Lesley & John Alexander
Robin & Sue Anderson
Jennifer Armstrong
Peter & Janet Arnold
Andy Ashwell
Bob & Margaret Austin

A. Bailey
Ann & Paul Bailey
Arthur Frederick Bandy
Carole Bandy
Eric & Pam Bateman
Margaret R. Bateman
Mr and Mrs E.B. Beale
Mr & Mrs J. Beardmore
James A. Beck
Deryck & Renee Bell
Terry & Denise Benwell
Alec & Sue Bignell
Mrs A. Bignell
Bryan & Pat Bignell
Rhona & Humphrey Bignell
Ron & Doll Bignell
Anne & Kim Bircham
Daphne & Dennis Bissell
Ian & Nancy Blood & family
Emma Boddington
Gordon Bonham
Sidney & Ada Bonner
Michael & Vivien Borley
Sister Carmel Bourke
Kevin Bourke
Ann & Terry Bracey-Wright
Jean Bracey-Wright
Lee & Emma Bracey-Wright
Jayne Brackley
Norman & Sylvia Brackley
Paul Brackley
Ray Bradley
John & Jill Branham
Betty Brown
Alison, Philip & Anna Bruce
Buckinghamshire Records &
  Local Studies Service
Pheroze R. Bulsara
Edna & Gerry Burt
Jennie & Mike Butteriss
Mhairi Butteriss

Lee & Georgie Camfield

Gillian Campbell
Jill & Gary Campbell
Rose Camp
June Cannon
Betty Mary Carter
Caroline, Alan, Alexander &
  George Castle
Doris Charles
Paul Chennell
Carolyn & Dan Childs
Celia Childs
Carole & Paul Chinn
Richard, Hilary, Matthew &
  Amy Chipping
Isobel and David Clark
Richard & Jackie Clay
Vic Clay
Peter & Helen Cleasby
Colin & Sue Clifford
Ivor Collins
Gerard Connolly
Phil Connolly
Ann Cook
George Cook
Pete & Annie Cooper
Sheila & John Cotton
Michelle & Mark Croft
Avis Cousins & Pauline
  Hawkett
Michael Cornish & Lisa
  Harley
Fiona Crookes
Caroline Crossman
Mike & Ann Curry

Reg & Kathleen Darvill
Peter & Carol Davey
Gwynn Davies
Dan & Frances Dawson
Sheila & Pete Day
Julie Dent & Trevor Morgan
Tim Dimmock
George & Julie Djuric
Revd. Peter Dudeney
Douglas S. Dunker
Nina Dunn

Karen Earwicker
Guy Edmunds
Richard Edmunds
Susannah Edmunds
Jack Edwards
Lauren Edwards
Andrew R Ellis
Julia & Charlie Ellis
Fons & Jackie Elsenburg
Colin & Mavis Emerson

Gerald & Barbara Evered
Martin Evered

Michael, Nicola & Josie
  Featonby-Roberts
Derek & Violet Fleet
Mr & Mrs Jonathan Fletcher
Michael & Sally Foot
Ken & Sylvia Francis
Robert Nigel Burkly Freeman
Alan & Janet Frost
Sebastian Frost
Susan Vivien Fry

The Gardner Family
Barry & Jill Garland
David & Valerie Godfrey
Nick & Janice Godfrey
John, Joan & Dennis
  Goldney
Beatrice Goodwin
Derek & Prudence Goodwin
Ann Grant
Margaret Greene
Cyril Griffin
Doris Griffin
Edward Francis Griffin
James Griffin
Margaret Griffin
Peter & Diana Gulland
Bucks Archaeological Soc'y
Ivan Gurney
Ronald & Denise Gurney

Andy & Helen Hall
William & Louise Hammond
Joy Harries
Mark & Kathy Haslam
John Hawkes
Jeff Hawkins
Mrs Elsie Hazelgrove
Michael Heaton
David Hewitt & Tina
  Kempton
Kristian & Gareth Hewitt
Simon & Suzanne Hewitt
David Hill
David P. Hillier
Val & Richard Hockey
Lucy A. Holloway
Pat Holt
Doreen Honor
Tony & Brenda Horne
John & Rose Horton
Charlie Horwood
Gerard & Isabel Howe
Bron Hughes

Sarah & Julian Humphrey
Nick Jeffery
Dr Rosemary Jenkins
Richard & Pat Johnson
Christine Jones
Peter & Jean Jones
Sarah Jones
Shirley, Steve, Donna, Zoe &
  Bradley Jones
Simon Jones

Richard & Jean Keighley
Les & Sarah Kennedy
Nigel & Judy Kennedy
Brian & Trisha King
Frank & Grace King
Marie King
Pamela & Fred Kirby
The Kirkup family

Richard & Marie Lawton
Steve & Jo Lewington
David & Susan Lloyd
David & Marie Loades
John & Georgina Lowing
Pete & Val Lucas & family
Chris Lyddon
Pete & Viv Lynch

Macintyre School
Alan & Thelma Mallett
Peter & Judy Malpass
Steve & Linda Maltby
Adrian & Kate Mancha
Alisan Marchant & family
Roger & Pauline Marsh
Kim & Caroline Martin
Mr & Mrs Edward Masters
Rosemary Masters
David & Josephine Matthews
Trevor & Jennifer May
Eve McLaughlin
Derek & Wendy Mead
Professor W. R. Mead
Chris & Rosemary Meddows
Elisabeth Meddows
Tom Meddows
Fred & Carole Megram
Mrs J. Merricks
Mr & Mrs I. B. Meyer
John R. Millburn
Mr Ron H. Miller
Robin & Dominique Moat
Mr & Mrs C. W. Moorcroft
Per & Suzanna Moore-Friis
Liz & David Morgan
Mary Mountain

Jane & Andrew Muir
Terry, Ruth, Daniel, Michael
  & Eleanor Murphy
Rev. David Wingrave New-
  man
Paul & Vanessa O'Carroll
Muriel Page
Donald W. H. Paine
Charles R. Paine
Mrs Joan Partridge-King
Ethel Perkins
Ken & Val Perkins
Robin & Anne Perkins
Bill & Gladys Phillips
Fred and Joan Powell
John & Val Philpott
Simon & Cheryl Puddifoot
Bim Pullen
Doug & Sandra Purrett
Jennifer Purrett
Mark Purrett

Dr Kevin Quick
Maureen Quiller

Catherine & Nick Radclyffe
Dinah & Graydon Radford
Alan & Mary Rawlings
Mervyn William Rawlings
Andy Rees & Jo Measure
Beryl Reynolds
Desmond & Joan Rickard
Doug Rickard
Janet Rickard
Sybil Rickard
Jose & Ed Ricketts
Alan F. L. Ridgway
David & Clare Roberts
Paul & Diane Roberts
Jill Roberts
Mervyn Roberts
Pat Roberts
Mandy, Bob & Daniel
  Rodgers
The Earl of Rosebery
The Rothschild Archive
Sir Evelyn de Rothschild
Bryan & Joyce Round

Jeanette Rose May Schultz
Len J. Scutchings
Dorothy Simpson
Joyce Sinnott
Richard & Christine
  Skidmore
Betty Skinner

Celia Slater
Colin T. Smart
Geoff & Maggie Smith
Gerald & Rebecca Smith
Jonathan & Alison Smith
Peter & Roberta Smith
Barbara & David Snow
Richard, Alison & Hugo
  Sothcott
Mr & Mrs Southern
Michael & Katherine Spinks
Paul & Joanne Stevens
Virgina Stride

Mr & Mrs J. Talbot
Lee, Frazer & Kelly Tattam
David & Ross Thomson
Lesley & David Throup
George Charles Tighe
Bridgette Tilleray
Alan S. Timms
Pauline Laura Tremlett
Michael & Siv Tunnicliffe
Geoffrey & Irene Turner
Nick Turner

Alice Rose Vaughan
Paul & Julie Vaughan
Richard Caulfield Vaughan
William Mason Vaughan

Barbara Wallis
The Wallis family
Christine Ward
Conrad Watkins
Frank & Pip Watkins
Matthew Watkins
Frank & Joan Watson
Kenneth W. Watson
Roger & Kathy Westwood
Joyce Whipps
Adrian James White
Richard John White
Tony & Yvonne White
Steve, Carol & Alice
  Whitehead
Malcolm and Ann Whiter
Keith & Lesley Williams
Rev. Bob & Penny Willmott
Kirstie Wiltshire & Carol
  Edmonds
Wingrave C. of E. Combined
  School
L. Roy Woodruff
Robin A. Woodruff
The Woodward Family
Christa Wright

Books Published by
THE BOOK CASTLE

COUNTRYSIDE CYCLING IN BEDFORDSHIRE, BUCKINGHAMSHIRE AND HERTFORDSHIRE: Mick Payne. Twenty rides on- and off-road for all the family.

PUB WALKS FROM COUNTRY STATIONS: Bedfordshire and Hertfordshire: Clive Higgs.
Fourteen circular country rambles, each starting and finishing at a railway station and incorporating a pub-stop at a mid-way point.

PUB WALKS FROM COUNTRY STATIONS: Buckinghamshire and Oxfordshire: Clive Higgs.
Circular rambles incorporating pub-stops.

LOCAL WALKS: South Bedfordshire and North Chilterns: Vaughan Basham.
Twenty-seven thematic circular walks.

LOCAL WALKS: North and Mid Bedfordshire: Vaughan Basham.
Twenty-five thematic circular walks.

FAMILY WALKS: Chilterns South: Nick Moon. Thirty 3 to 5 mile circular walks.

FAMILY WALKS: Chilterns North: Nick Moon. Thirty shorter circular walks.

CHILTERN WALKS: Hertfordshire, Bedfordshire and North Buckinghamshire: Nick Moon.

CHILTERN WALKS: Buckinghamshire: Nick Moon.

CHILTERN WALKS: Oxfordshire and West Buckinghamshire: Nick Moon.
A trilogy of circular walks, in association with the Chiltern Society.
Each volume contains 30 circular walks.

OXFORDSHIRE WALKS: Oxford, the Cotswolds and the Cherwell Valley: Nick Moon.

OXFORDSHIRE WALKS: Oxford, the Downs and the Thames Valley: Nick Moon.
Two volumes that complement Chiltern Walks: Oxfordshire and complete coverage of the county, in association with the Oxford Fieldpaths Society. Thirty circular walks in each.

THE D'ARCY DALTON WAY: Nick Moon.
Long-distance footpath across the Oxfordshire Cotswolds and Thames Valley, with various circular walk suggestions.

JOURNEYS INTO BEDFORDSHIRE: Anthony Mackay.
Foreword by The Marquess of Tavistock, Woburn Abbey. A lavish book of over 150 evocative ink drawings.

JOURNEYS INTO BUCKINGHAMSHIRE: Anthony Mackay
Superb line drawings plus background text: large format landscape gift book.

BUCKINGHAMSHIRE MURDERS: Len Woodley.
Nearly two centuries of nasty crimes.

WINGRAVE: A Rothschild Village in the Vale: Margaret and Ken Morley.
Thoroughly researched and copiously illustrated survey of the last 200 years in this lovely village between Aylesbury and Leighton Buzzard.

HISTORIC FIGURES IN THE BUCKINGHAMSHIRE LANDSCAPE: John Houghton.
Major personalities and events that have shaped the county's past, including a special section on Bletchley Park.

TWICE UPON A TIME: John Houghton.
Short stories loosely based on fact, set in the North Bucks area.

MANORS and MAYHEM, PAUPERS and PARSONS:
Tales from Four Shires: Beds., Bucks., Herts., and Northants.: John Houghton
Little-known historical snippets and stories.

MYTHS and WITCHES, PEOPLE and POLITICS:
Tales from Four Shires: Bucks., Beds., Herts., and Northants.: John Houghton.
Anthology of strange, but true historical events.

FOLK: Characters and Events in the History of Bedfordshire and Northamptonshire:
Vivienne Evans. Anthology about people of yesteryear – arranged alphabetically by village or town.

JOHN BUNYAN: His Life and Times: Vivienne Evans.
Highly-praised and readable account.

THE RAILWAY AGE IN BEDFORDSHIRE: Fred Cockman.
Classic, illustrated account of early railway history.

A LASTING IMPRESSION: Michael Dundrow.
A boyhood evacuee recalls his years in the Chiltern village of Totternhoe near Dunstable.

GLEANINGS REVISITED: Nostalgic Thoughts of a Bedfordshire Farmer's Boy: E W O'Dell.
His own sketches and early photographs adorn this lively account of rural Bedfordshire in days gone by.

BEDFORDSHIRE'S YESTERYEARS Vol 2: The Rural Scene: Brenda Fraser-Newstead.
Vivid first-hand accounts of country life two or three generations ago.

BEDFORDSHIRE'S YESTERYEARS Vol 3: Craftsmen and Tradespeople:
Brenda Fraser-Newstead.
Fascinating recollections over several generations practising many vanishing crafts and trades.

BEDFORDSHIRE'S YESTERYEARS Vol 4: War Times and Civil Matters:
Brenda Fraser-Newstead.
Two World Wars, plus transport, law and order, etc.

PROUD HERITAGE: A Brief History of Dunstable, 1000–2000AD: Vivienne Evans.
Century by century account of the town's rich tradition and key events, many of national significance.

DUNSTABLE WITH THE PRIORY: 1100–1550: Vivienne Evans.
Dramatic growth of Henry I's important new town around a major crossroads.

DUNSTABLE IN TRANSITION: 1550–1700: Vivienne Evans.
Wealth of original material as the town evolves without the Priory.

DUNSTABLE DECADE: THE EIGHTIES: A Collection of Photographs: Pat Lovering.
A souvenir book of nearly 300 pictures of people and events in the 1980s.

STREETS AHEAD: An Illustrated Guide to the Origins of Dunstable's Street Names:
Richard Walden.
Fascinating text and captions to hundreds of photographs, past and present, throughout the town.

DUNSTABLE IN DETAIL: Nigel Benson.
A hundred of the town's buildings and features, plus town trail map.

OLD DUNSTABLE: Bill Twaddle.
A new edition of this collection of early photographs.

BOURNE and BRED: A Dunstable Boyhood Between the Wars: Colin Bourne.
An elegantly written, well-illustrated book capturing the spirit of the town over fifty years ago.

ROYAL HOUGHTON: Pat Lovering:
Illustrated history of Houghton Regis from the earliest times to the present.

THE STOPSLEY BOOK: James Dyer.
Definitive, detailed account of this historic area of Luton. 150 rare photographs.

THE STOPSLEY PICTURE BOOK: James Dyer.
New material and photographs make an ideal companion to The Stopsley Book.

PUBS and PINTS: The Story of Luton's Public Houses and Breweries: Stuart Smith.
The background to beer in the town, plus hundreds of photographs, old and new.

THE CHANGING FACE OF LUTON: An Illustrated History:
Stephen Bunker, Robin Holgate and Marian Nichols. Luton's development from earliest times to
the present busy industrial town. Illustrated in colour and mono.

WHERE THEY BURNT THE TOWN HALL DOWN:
Luton, The First World War and the Peace Day Riots, July 1919: Dave Craddock.
Detailed analysis of a notorious incident.

THE MEN WHO WORE STRAW HELMETS: Policing Luton, 1840–1974: Tom Madigan.
Meticulously chronicled history; dozens of rare photographs; author served in Luton Police for
fifty years.

BETWEEN THE HILLS: The Story of Lilley, a Chiltern Village: Roy Pinnock.
A priceless piece of our heritage – the rural beauty remains but the customs and way of life
described here have largely disappeared.

KENILWORTH SUNSET: A Luton Town Supporter's Journal: Tim Kingston.
Frank and funny account of football's ups and downs.

A HATTER GOES MAD!: Kristina Howells.
Luton Town footballers, officials and supporters talk to a female fan.